CHAR-GRILLER

GRILL & SMOKER

COOKBOOK

500 FRESH AND FOOLPROOF RECIPES TO EATING WELL, LOOKING AMAZING, AND FEELING GREAT

DONALD SMITH

Copyright © 2021 by Donald Smith All rights reserved worldwide.

No part of this book may be reproduced or transmitted in any form or by any means, electronic or mechanical, including photo- copying, recording or by any information storage and retrieval system, without written permission from the publisher, except for the inclusion of brief quotations in a review.

Warning-Disclaimer: The purpose of this book is to educate and entertain. The author or publisher does not guarantee that anyone following the techniques, suggestions, tips, ideas, or strategies will become successful. The author and publisher shall have neither liability or responsibility to anyone with respect to any loss or damage caused, or alleged to be caused, directly or indirectly by the information contained in this book.

CONTENTS

INTRODUCTION 10
How the Char-Griller Wood Pellet Grill Works 10
What Makes the Char-Griller Wood Pellet Grill Worthwhile? 10
Ten Tips for Using Your Char-Griller Wood Pellet Grill 11
Deep Clean Methods for the Char-Griller Wood Pellet Grill 13

PIZZA 14
Flat-iron Pizza Quesadillas 14
Gravity 980 Grilled Pizza 14
Meat Lovers Pizza 14
Grilled Caprese Pizza 15
Fire-grilled Pizza 15
Breakfast Pizza 15
Pepperoni Pizza 16
Grilled Fathead Pizza 16
Pesto Burrata Grilled Pizza 17
Flat Iron Cheesy Pizza Bagels 17

POULTRY 18
Turkey Tips 18
Roasted Spatchcock Turkey 18
Smoked Turkey Legs 18
Turkey Leg Lollipops 19
Chili Mesquite Lime Shredded Chicken Street Tacos . 19
Easy Chicken And Cheese Quesadillas 19
Creole Latin Spiced Rotisserie Chicken 20
Classic Smoked Spatchcocked Turkey 20
Fried Chicken And Corn 21
Chicken Teriyaki 21
Grilled Chicken And Vegetable Kebabs 21
Flat Iron East Meets West Chicken Fajitas 22
Honey Chipotle Chicken Wings 22
Creole Hush Puppy Fried Chicken Legs & Thighs 23
Smoked Spatchcock Turkey 23
Creole Latin Spatchcock Turkey 24
Beer Can Roasted Turkey Breast 24
Smoked Chicken Thighs 25
Grilled Duck Breast 25
Chicken Cordon Bleu 25
Cherry Chipotle Buffalo Wings 26
Pulled Chicken Crunch Wrap Style Burritos 26
Curried Chicken Skewers 26
2-burner Flat Iron Seasoned Chicken Breasts 27
Chicken Fajitas 27
Garlic Parmesan Chicken Wings 27
Buffalo Ranch Chicken 28
Garlic Lover's Chicken 28
Boneless Chicken Thighs Broccolini & Cheesy
Potatoes 28
Grilled Chicken And Broccoli Stir-fry 29
Bacon Wrapped Chicken Thighs 29
Grilled Nachos 29
Asian Chicken Salad 30
Izzy's Cowboy Grillers 30
Turkey-mushroom Burger 30
Spicy Honey Glazed Wings 31
Gravity 980 Smoked Chicken Wings 31
Smoked Carolina Turkey 31
Smoked Turkey Breast 31
Barbecued Turkey 32
Grilled Pizza Chicken Wings 32
Beer Soda Can Chicken 32
Picnic "fried" Chicken 33
Chicken Lollipops By Jeremy Souza 33
Creole Smokin' Fried Wings 33

SEAFOOD 34
Honey-bourbon Glazed Salmon 34
Buffalo Lemon Shrimp 34

Bacon Wrapped Seafood Stuffed Shrimp 34	Flavor Pro Cedar Plank Salmon 40
Gravity 980 Grilled Lobster Tails..................................35	Honey Sriracha Lime Salmon...................................... 40
Grilled Swordfish With Lemon-caper Sauce................35	Cedar Plank Salmon 40
Cedar Plank Smoked Salmon.......................................36	Fresh Garlic Parsley Butter Salmon............................ 41
Grilled Salmon 36	Spicy Crawfish Dip 41
Grilled Tilapia 36	Shrimp Po' Boy With Garlic Parsley Butter................ 42
Grilled Lobster Tails 36	Grilled Seafood Boil 42
Salmon Burger...37	Steamed Mussels With Pancetta 43
Creole Blackened Salmon 37	Shrimp 'n Grits 43
Lemon Pepper Shrimp..37	Fish Tacos... 43
Rosemary Shrimp Skewers...37	Lobster Mac 'n Cheese 44
Grilled Coconut Lime Foil Packets 38	2-burner Flat Iron Easy Shrimp Tacos 44
Shrimp Tacos 38	Seared Scallops With Pancetta 45
Blackened Catfish..39	Oysters "dougie-feller".. 45
Spicy Caribbean Shrimp..39	Fish And Chips... 45
Seared Sesame Ahi Tuna 39	Grilled Chilean Sea Bass 46
Lobster Roll..39	

BEEF 47

Biscuits, Briskets, And Gravy..47	Bacon And Pineapple Wrapped Meatballs................... 55
Certified Grilled Chicago Style Hot Dogs 47	Oklahoma Onion Burgers 55
Ultimate Stack Burger...47	Beef Brisket... 56
Smash Burgers...48	Picanha Crostini 56
Bbq Fiends Beef Fajitas...48	Certified Creole Ynot Beef N' Bacon Jerky 56
Bacon Garlic Burger With Chipotle Mayonnaise.........48	Mini Smash Burgers 57
Flat Iron Griddle Beef Shank Quesadilla Tacos With Consumé 49	Gravity 980 Brisket... 58
	Reverse Seared Tri-tip Pico De Gallo 58
Smoked Brisket 49	Korean Style Beef Short Ribs 58
Steak Night! Steak, Shrimp And Asparagus On The Akorn 50	Mac & Cheese Stuffed Meatballs On The Char-griller Akorn 59
Breakfast Burritos On The Flat Iron............................50	The All American Burger 59
Chili In A Bread Bowl 50	Smoked Beef Ribs... 59
Inch-thick Onion Char-burgers....................................51	Smoked Corned Beef.. 60
Brisket Hash On The Flat Iron Portable 52	Italian Burgers.. 60
Beef Tenderloin...52	Chi-lanta Pork Belly Burnt Ends 61
Smoked Bacon Wrapped Cheese Stuffed Avocado 52	Caprese Burger... 61
Flavor Pro™ Reverse Seared Steak 52	Cheesy Beef Burritos 61
Beer Brat Bites 53	Shrimp 'n Grits 62
Smoked Mexican Burgers...53	Corned Beef Brisket And Potatoes............................ 62
Steak And Shrimp On The Flat Iron............................54	Bacon Cheeseburger Pizza-dough Balls 63
Double Cheeseburger Kabobs 54	Arrachera Skirt Steak Tacos 63
Leftover Brisket Nachos 54	Smoked Beef Chili.. 63
Crab-stuffed Grilled Flank Steak With Asparagus.......55	Peppered Sirloin With Bacon-mushroom Sauce.......... 64

Homemade Grilled Meatballs 64	Beer Brined Grilled Costillas Beef Short Ribs 75
Spaghetti Stuffed Meatloaf 65	Bacon Burger With Shallots 75
Italian-style Meatballs 65	Beef Ribs 76
Burnt Ends And Tips 65	Chili Jalapeño Burger 76
London Broil N' Veggie Skewers 66	Spring Tomahawk Steak And Vegetables 77
Pastrami Swiss Burger 66	Flat Iron Sausage And Peppers Hash 77
Lou's Beef Brisket 67	Cheesy Chipotle Chili 77
Lou's Beef Plate Ribs 67	Chorizo Taquitos 78
Filet Mignon, Risotto, And Asparagus 67	Bacon Buster Burger 78
Smoked Jerky 68	Smoked Baked Spaghetti 79
Flavor Pro Italian Sausage Burgers 68	All American Blended Burger 79
The Flintstone Steak 69	Flat Iron Philly Cheesesteak 80
Weeknight Smokehouse Ribs 69	Grilled Ribeye Steak 80
Shrimp & Sausage Skewers 69	Akorn Dino Beef Plate Ribs 80
Bacon Ring Burger With Mushrooms 70	Flat Iron Steak Fajitas 81
Skirt Steak Gyros 70	Meat Loaf 81
Grilled Steak Caesar Salad 71	Coffee & Cocoa Tri-tip 82
Reverse Sear Ribeye 71	Over The Top Chili On The Grand Champ 82
Cold Weather Chili 71	Flat Iron Griddle Sizzler N' Veggies Sammies ... 83
Left Over Cheesy Mac N' Smoked Brisket Meat Pies Recipe 72	Saucy Brisket Burnt Ends 83
	Grilled Caesar Salad 84
Double Stack Cheeseburger 72	Smokin' Champ Smoked Beef Back Ribs 84
Dark Roast 72	Flat Iron Griddle Classic Steak Street Tacos 85
Smoked Chili 73	Bbq Crunch Wrap 85
Smoked Meatloaf 73	Smoked Prime Rib 85
Flavor Pro™ Flank Steak Tacos 73	Skirt Steak Pinwheels 86
Pork Brisket Burnt Ends 74	Foil Packet Short Ribs 86
Bbq Fiends Barbacoa Tacos 74	Dry Aged Rib Roast 87
Oktoberfest Beef Short Ribs 74	

DESSERTS 88

Salted Caramel Chocolate Tart 88	Crème Brûlée 92
Grilled S'mores 4 Ways 88	Low Carb Blueberry Cobbler 92
Bourbon Glaze For Candied Bacon Scones 88	Spooky Brain Cinnamon Buns 92
Grilled Stuffed Peaches 89	Strawberry And Rhubarb Crumble Pie 93
Chocolate Chip Skillet Cookie 89	Pineapple Upside-down Cake 93
Plum Galette 89	Akorn Cinnamon Streusel Coffee Cake 93
Glazed Oatmeal Raisin Cookies 90	Cheesecake Stuffed Apples 94
Candied Bacon Scones With Bourbon Glaze ... 90	Smoked Chocolate Chip Cookies 94
Grilled Pumpkin Pie With Smoked Gingersnap Crust 90	Puffy Pancake With Fruit Compote 95
	Lou's Peach Cobbler 95
Candy Jar Brownies 91	Deep Dish Apple Pie 96
Smoked Candied Pecans 92	Chocolate Lava Cake 96

Skillet Brownie On The Grill 96
Smoked Apple Crumb Pie 97
Smoked White Chocolate Christmas Candy 97
Smoked Blueberry Crisp 98
Faux Apple Pie 98
Guinness Cupcakes With Whiskey Salted Caramel Buttercream 98

PORK 100

Gravity 980 Smoked Pork Shoulder 100
Ultimate Pork Belly Sliders 100
Baby Back Ribs 100
Certified Grilled And Smoked Baby Back Ribs 101
Flavor Pro Pork Steaks 101
Grilled Pork And Sweet Potato Verde Chili 102
Smoked Pork Loin 102
Smoked Pork Shoulder 102
Hoppin' John 103
Quick And Easy Grilled Pork Tenderloin 103
Grilled Stuffed Pork Chops 103
Bbq Pork Spare Ribs 104
St. Louis-style Ribs 104
Apple Chipotle Glazed Smoked Ham 104
Bacon Wrapped Kielbasa Bites 105
Orange Pork Belly Burnt Ends 105
Pork Belly Street Tacos 106
Chipotle Orange Glazed Bacon Wrapped And Stuffed Pork Loin 106
Brown Sugar Glazed Smoked Ham 106
Father's Day Baby Back Ribs 107
Oktoberfest Schweinshaxe - Smoked Pork Shanks 107
Asian Pork Belly Skewers 107
Blueberry Pork Belly Burnt Ends 108
Certified Pork Butt 108
Smoked Meatballs With Sweet And Sour Sauce 109
Bacon Wrapped Kabob 110
How To: Easy Dry Rub Grilled Pork Tenderloin 110
Pork Tenderloin Sliders 110
Bacon Wrapped Kielbasa 110
Flavor Pro Smoked Pork Shoulder 111
Bone-in Pulled Ham 111
Grilled Pork Chops 112
Simple Smoked Bbq Pork Belly 112
Breakfast Bomb - Homemade Stuffed Breakfast Sausage 112
Smoked Chili Hotdogs 113
Easter Sunday Texas-style Pulled Pork 113
Flat Iron Griddle Breakfast Sandwich 114
Pork Belly Burnt Ends On The Akorn 114
Bacon Wrapped Pork Tenderloin Stuffed With Jalapeño Cream Cheese 114
Bacon Bourbon Compound Butter Recipe 114
Flavor Pro Quick And Easy Grilled Pork Tenderloin . 115
Raspberry Chipotle Glazed Pork Tenderloin 115
Memphis-style Dry Ribs 115
Bbq Burnt Ends 116
Oktoberfest Schweinebraten 116

OTHER FAVORITE RECIPES 117

Boneless Wings Made From Chicken Thighs On The Char-griller Akorn Kamado Grill! 117
Easter Sunday Coleslaw For Pulled Pork Sandwiches 117
Serrano Beer Cheese 117
Bbq Fiends Oktoberfest Beer Brats 117
Keto Grilled Brie 118
Smoked And Spiced Nuts 118
Smoked Rib Chili 118
Flavor Pro Smoked Eggs 119
Teriyaki Chicken And Mango Skewers 120
Flat Iron Candied Sweet Potatoes 120
Smoked Sweet Garlic Chili And Teriyaki Wings 120
Smoked Queso Dip 121
Beer Cheese Sauce 121
Grilled Eggs Benedict With Grilled Lemon Hollandaise 121
Fried Bacon And Cabbage 122
Cowboy Steak With Asparagus And Onion 122
Garlic Butter 123
Sausage Bbq Meat Balls 123
Garlic & Herb Seasoned Potatoes 123
Smoked & Spiced Pumpkin Seeds 123
Mediterranean Chicken & Mushroom Burger Bowls 124
Vegetarian Shepherd's Pie 124

Recipe	Page
Grilled Adobo Wings	125
Smoked Cedar Plank Salmon	125
Flavor Pro™ Smoked Turkey Breast	126
Ken's Famous Baked Beans	126
Jalapeño Popper Pizza	126
Smoked Lamb Shank	127
Grilled Pineapple	127
Fire Roasted Salsa And Homemade Tortilla Chips	127
Cheeseburger Chili With Burger Bun Croutons	128
Flat Iron French Toast	128
Flavor Pro Hot And Fast Ribs	129
Beer Brats With Marzen Beer Kraut	129
Brazilian Smoked N' Seared Picanha	129
Grilled Potatoes With Jalapeños	130
Smoked Bacon-brisket Bbq Beans	130
Grilled Flank Steak With Vegetables	131
Flavor Pro™ Smoked French Onion Dip	131
Bbq Glazed Bacon Wrapped Brussels Sprouts	132
Loaded Grilled Radish Bites	132
Buffalo Baby Back Ribs: Grilled N' Smoked	132
Skillet Corn Bread	133
Grilled Chicken Sandwiches	133
Jalapeño Bacon Blanket Poppers	134
Pretzel Ring Cheese Dip Recipe	134
Grilled Breakfast Sandwiches With Blueberry Chicken Sausage	134
Flat Iron™ Smash Burgers	135
Keto Cheesy Meatballs	135
Flat Iron Pineapple Coconut Pancakes	136
Cheesy Stuffed Mushrooms N' Veggies Recipe	136
Oktoberfest Chili	136
Mrs. Ccbbq Mac N' Cheese	137
Smoked Chicken Thighs And Veggies	138
Chimichurri Sauce	138
Grilled Mexican Street Corn	138
Flat Iron Bacon Egg & Cheese	139
Gravity 980 Smoked Mac & Cheese	139
Grilled Sausage	139
Sweet And Tangy Apple Coleslaw	139
Pancake Burgers On The Char-griller Flat Iron	140
Grilled Lemon Parmesan Asparagus	140
Maple-dijon Grilled Chicken Sandwich	140
Grilled Red Onion And Brussel Sprouts Skewers	141
Grilled Blue Cheese Wings	141
Butternut Squash Soup	141
Flat Iron 3-step Breakfast Sandwiches	142
Blueberry Bbq Sauce	142
Cheesy, Bacon Bbq Meatloaf	142
Bacon Buffalo Chicken Dip	143
Butternut Squash Risotto	143
Smoked Mac And Cheese	143
Gravity 980 Quick N' Fast Grilled Vegetables	144
Hickory Smoked Deviled Eggs	144
Grilled Cilantro Garlic Parmesan Chicken Wings	144
Fabulous Buttermilk Pancakes	145
Barbecue Chicken Foil Packets	145
Fried Kielbasa & Cabbage	146
Flavor Pro™ Smoked Chicken Breast	146
2-burner Flat Iron Grilled "bmp"	147
Fire Roasted Salsa Con Certi	147
Herb And Garlic Lamb Rack	147
Char Grilled Wings	148
Fresh Summer Corn Avocado Tomato Salad	148
5-minute Avocado Dip	148
Competition Ribs Recipe	149
Mediterranean Veggie Burgers With Vegan Feta Dip	149
Certified Competition Smoked Ribs Tips	149
Reverse Seared Pesto Lamb Racks	150
Smoked Bacon	150
Gravity 980 Reverse Seared Steak	151
Grilled Tomato Salsa	151
Flat Iron Artisan Garlic Bread Grilled Cheese	151
Red Pepper Eggs	152
Smoked Sausage Stuffing	152
Smoked Butternut Squash Soup	152
Flat Iron Hot Cakes	153
Fresh Chili Lime Watermelon Fries	153
Queso Fundido Stuffed Grilled Jalapeños	153
Grilled Pumpkin And Chayote Soup	153
Gravity 980 Smoked Baked Potatoes	154
Smoked Garlic Herb Chili Flake Grilled Cheese Sandwich	154
Grilled Mango Salsa	154
Chicken Breast Potatoes And Green Beans On The Char-griller Akorn	155
Chicken Fajita Quesadillas	155

Bbq Wang Thangs	155
Ratatouille	156
Lemon Pepper Wings	156
Ale Chicken Drumsticks	157
Ribeye Roast On The Char-griller Akorn Kamado	157
Flat Iron Homestyle Hash Brown Patties	157
Marinated Flat Iron Steak On The Flat Iron Portable Griddle	157
Mexican Street Corn	158
Supreme Grilled Portobello Pizza	158
Foil Packet Loaded Grilled Potatoes	158
Hasselback Potatoes	158
Smoked Irish-style Lamb And Potatoes	159
Flat Iron Portobello Bun Burgers	159
Easter Brunch French Toast	160
Flat Iron Lime Chicken And Mango Salsa Quesadillas	160
Grilled Stuffed Peppers	161
Smoked Mac 'n Cheese	161
Grilled Apple Strudel	161
2-burner Flat Iron Hot Dogs	162
Smoke Roasted Coffee	162
Grilled Summer Corn Salsa	162
Asian-inspired Sesame Soy Sauce	163
Flat Iron Fast Garlic & Balsamic Greens And Onions	163
Pork Tenderloin With Apple Chutney	163
Honey Mustard Chicken	164
Egg Roll Burgers	164
Dr. Pepper Bbq Chicken Wings	165
Bbq Bacon Cheeseburger Roll	165
Hassleback Potatoes	165
Satay Chicken Wings	166
Chicken Lollipops	166
Smoked Mashed Potatoes	167
Grilled Carrots	167
Smoked Buffalo Chicken Wing Dip	167
Smoked Sweet Potatoes With Cinnamon Maple Butter	168
Southwest Potato Skins	168
Bbq Fiends Chicken Lollipop Recipe	168
2-burner Flat Iron Seasoned Mushrooms	169
Flavor Pro Bacon Wrapped Jalapeño Poppers	170
Pumpkin Pie Burnt Ends	170
Caribbean Jerk Pork Pineapple Salsa	171
Dirty Bird Chicken Wings	171
Blueberry Jalbanero Smoked Wings	171
Smoked Classic Apple Pie	172
Grilled Juicy Skirt Steak With Cilantro Pesto	172
Smoked Mac & Cheese	173
Maple Bourbon Rubbed Stuffed Chicken Breasts	174
Caprese Grilled Chicken	174
Smoked Roasted Vegetables	174
Smoked Rack Of Lamb With Orange Marmalade Glaze	175
Grilled Romaine Salad With Creamy Jalapeno Ranch Dressing	175
Cheddar Jalapeño Chicken Burgers	176
Easy Grilled S'mores	177
Louisiana Hot Link Sausage & Smoked Cornbread Dressing	177
Bourbon Maple Grilled Wings	177
Flat Iron Lemon Pesto Vegetable Medley	178
Grilled Cauliflower	178
Irish Nachos	178
Smoked Sweet Potatoes	179
Classic Bbq Sauce	179
Gravity 980 Smoked Ribs	179
2-burner Flat Iron Eggplant Parmesan	180
Flavor Pro Smokey Grilled Chicken Wings	180
2-burner Flat Iron Omelet Rounds	180
Creole Smothered Chicken	181
Mushroom Bacon Swiss Blended Bison Burger	181
Raptor Claws	182
Smoked Bone-in Pork Shoulder Steak	182
Brown Sugar Maple Bacon	182
Jalapeño Poppers	183
Perfect Ribeye Steaks On The Akorn	183
Flat Iron Sundried Tomato Omelet	183
Smoked Jerk Chicken	184
Bacon Cinnamon Rolls	184
Sweet Potato Medallions	184
Grilled Lemon Pepper Potatoes	185
2-burner Flat Iron Asparagus	185
Grilled Garlic Bread	185
Bacon Egg And Cheesesteaks	185

Recipe	Page
Griddle Cheesesteaks	186
Grilled Arrachera Pita	186
Garlic And Herb Grilled Zucchini	186
Grilled Fire Veggies	187
Saucin' Bacon Wrapped Cheesy Meatballs	187
Good Morning Chili	187
Certified Competition Smoked Ribs	187
Creole Italiano Spaghetti And Smoked Meatballs	188
Simple Seasoned Dressed Greens	189
Smoked Beer Can Chicken Recipe	190
Flat Iron Southern Salmon Cakes	190
Smokin' Whole Bone-in Ham	190
Smoked Baked Beans	191
Spicy Thai Grilled Chicken Quarters	191
Smoked Potato Salad	191
Alabama White Sauce	192
Grilled Bacon And Blue Cheese Wedge Salad	192
Basic Thanksgiving Turkey Brine	192
Bacon Bourbon Compound Butter	192
Smoked Chex Mix	193
Super Pro Rotisserie Prime Rib	193
Aubrey's Og Grilled Chicken	193
Buttery Cinnamon Apples	194
Grilled Corn	194
Oktoberfest Skillet	194
Donut Monte Cristo	195
Cajun Sausage & Pepper Egg Muffins	195
Flat Iron Pancakes	196
Vinegar Based Sauce	196
Smoked Bacon Wrapped Water Chestnuts	196
Flat Iron Cereal French Toast	196
Spicy Vindaloo Chicken Thigh Skewers	197
Keto Burger Bites	197
Grilled Watermelon Salad	197
Smoked Pimento Cheese Spread	198
Perfect Smoked Crispy Chicken Wings On The Akorn	198
2-burner Flat Iron Spiced Sweet Potato Home Fries	199
Grilled Bruschetta Brie	199
Candied Bacon Recipe	199
Flat Iron Banana Pancakes	200
Flat Iron Spinach & Feta Omelette	200
Smoked And Stuffed Meatballs	200
Cheesy Potatoes	201
Fried Chicken On The Grill	201
Flat Iron Tomato Soup Grilled Cheese	201
Sweet N' Spicy Bbq Sauce	201
2-burner Flat Iron Simple Lo Mein	202
Rack Of Lamb With A Bourbon Glaze	202
Grilled Pumpkin Chili	202
Grilled Cheese With Apples	203
Smoked Jalapeño Mac & Cheese	203

RECIPE INDEX **204**

INTRODUCTION

How the Char-Griller Wood Pellet Grill Works

Pellet grills use all natural hardwood sawdust which is formed into little ¼ inch pieces as fuel. In the 1980s the popularity of using pellets in place of wood for household stoves was expanded to include grills. The burning pellets give your food a nice smoky flavor with consistent temperature.

Pellet grills work on the same principles as pellet stoves. Pellets are put into the hopper and the auger pushes the pellets from the hopper into the firepot to burn. On basic pellet grills the temperature cannot be adjusted, however on more sophisticated models, the temperature can be altered to suit the needs of the grill master. Pellet grills combine the best of both the grilling and smoking to produce the taste, texture, and appearance that you want when grilling meat, fish, vegetables or fruit. The infamous grill sear can also be achieved when using a cast iron grill grate or skillet preheated on the grill.

Pellet grills are much quicker to heat than traditional charcoal grills. While quick and easy, gas grills lack the taste and genuine flavor that pellet and charcoal grills provide and BBQ lovers insist upon.

What Makes the Char-Griller Wood Pellet Grill Worthwhile?

1. For Baking and More

Pellet grills are worth the price for those who want to bake and use other cooking methods beyond grilling. Grilling is fine when you want to cook a few steaks or burgers, but if you want to get the most out of a grill, consider a pellet model. You can reach a high temperature that is perfect for baking cakes and other desserts or broiling corn and other vegetables for side dishes. These grills can also handle barbecue and other cooking methods too.

2. Less Expensive

Not only do pellet grills cost less upfront, but they also cost less over the long term. You can get a good wood pellet grill for half of what it would cost to buy a gas grill of the same size and with the same features. With gas grills, you need to keep an eye on your propane tank too.

With pellet grills, you can get a bag of wood pellets for around the same amount as a new tank costs. That bag will last longer though, which helps you save money. Pellet grills are more affordable than charcoal models too because a bag of wood pellets costs so much less than a bag of charcoal briquettes.

3. **Other Reasons to Choose the Char-Griller Pellet Grill**
- Some of the other reasons why we think a pellet grill is worth the price include:
- You can better regulate and control the temperature of the grill
- Pellet grills give you the freedom to let your food cook as you do other tasks
- You don't need to deal with bulky and heavy propane tanks
- Most have a temperature setting that you can select, which will then maintain that temperature
- Pellet grills come in a range of prices for all budgets
- Many of the top pellet grills can last for a decade or longer
- You can easily experiment with different cooking methods and foods
- The grills are easy to clean after you finish cooking

Ten Tips for Using Your Char-Griller Wood Pellet Grill

1. **START EARLY:** Many of the flavor compounds in smoke are fat and water soluble, which means that whatever you are cooking will absorb smoky flavors best when it is raw. As the surface cooks and dries out, the smoke does not penetrate as well.

2. **GO LOW AND SLOW (MOST OF THE TIME):** Real barbecue is cooked slowly over low, indirect heat—with wood smoke—because that's a traditional way to make sinewy meats so moist and tender that you hardly need teeth. But don't miss easy opportunities for adding sweet wood aromas to foods that are grilled over a hot fire for just minutes, like steaks, shrimp, and even vegetables.

3. **REGULATE THE HEAT WITH A WATER PAN:** Big fluctuations in smoking temperatures can tighten and dry out foods. Whenever you cook for longer than an hour with charcoal, use a pan of water to help stabilize the heat and add some humidity. Obviously a water smoker already has one, but for a charcoal grill, use a large disposable foil pan, and don't forget to refill it.

4. **DON'T OVERDO IT.** The biggest mistake rookies make is adding too much wood, chunk after chunk, to the point where the food tastes bitter. In general, you should smoke food for no longer than half its cooking time. Also, the smoke should flow like a gentle stream, not like it is billowing out of a train engine.

5. WHITE SMOKE IS GOOD; BLACK SMOKE IS BAD: Clean streams of whitish smoke can layer your food with the intoxicating scents of smoldering wood. But if your fire lacks enough ventilation, or your food is directly over the fire and the juices are burning, blackish smoke can taint your food or lead to unpleasant surprises when you lift the lid.

6. KEEP THE AIR MOVING: Keep the vents on your charcoal grill open and position the vent on the lid on the side opposite the coals. The open vents will draw smoke from the charcoal and wood below so that it swirls over your food and out the top properly, giving you the best ventilation and the cleanest smoke. If the fire gets too hot, close the top vent almost all the way.

7. DON'T GO GOLFING: Smoking is a relatively low-maintenance way of cooking—but remain mindful and be safe. Never leave a lit fire unattended, and check the temperature every hour or so. You might need to adjust the vents or add more charcoal.

8. TRY NOT TO PEEK: Every time you open a grill, you lose heat and smoke—two of the most important elements for making a great meal. Open the lid only when you really need to tend to the fire, the water pan, or the food. Ideally take care of them all at once—and quickly. Otherwise, relax and keep a lid on it.

9. LET THE BARK GET DARK: Barbecued meat should glisten with a dark mahogany crust that borders on black. This "bark" is the delicious consequence of fat and spices sizzling with smoke on the surface of the meat and developing a caramelized crust over the luscious meat below. Before you take the meat off the grill or wrap it in foil, make sure the bark is dark enough that it tastes like heaven.

10. FEATURE THE STAR ATTRACTION: The main ingredient in any smoked recipe is like the lead singer in a rock-and-roll band. Every other flavor should play a supporting role. In other words, don't upstage something inherently delicious with a potent marinade, heavy-handed seasonings, or thick coats of sauce. Harmonizing flavors in ways that feature the main ingredient is what separates the masters from the masses.

Deep Clean Methods for the Char-Griller Wood Pellet Grill

1. Use an onion on a BBQ fork. The onion has acids that break down fat and the water inside the onion works like a steam cleaner. Rub-down the grates after cooking and scraping as usual and when the grates are still pretty warm. You can add some salt on the onion's scrubbing side to get better traction and scrubbing power. The onion can also be sliced thinner to reach between the grills.

Use the fork to angle under the grill edges to remove anything stuck underneath. You won't need to peel the onion, just slice it with the skin still on. After that, give a generous spray down with vinegar and water mix to wash away the onion build-up. This will further break down oils and fat that has dried onto the metal grill surfaces.

2. Caked on grills will need a strong cup of coffee. Brew up a batch of your favorite mud and put your grill into a washing tub. Pour the coffee over the grill until it's submerged. Let it sit until the natural acids in the coffee break down the fats and dried-on food. This can take 3 hours of soaking, so sit back and have a cup as well. Afterward, you can scrub off the grill with any scrubby sponge or pot cleaner.

This method is great for cleaning both sides of the grill and should be done at least once per season. It doesn't matter what kind of coffee you use, but the stronger you make it- the better. Arabica coffee is good to use, and it should be made from coffee grounds on a drip machine.

3. You can't beat the power of white vinegar and water at getting any grill sparkling clean. Put your grills in a plastic tub and fill it up with a 60/40 mix of vinegar and water. Let it sit for 5 minutes and then use a lemon to scrub-off the remaining caked-on grill grate. You could use nearly anything handy such an onion, lemon, or dried corn cobs. This method is especially strong to remove very gunked-up grates in a hurry.

Especially if you didn't have the time to clean your grill in a while! Not only is this method safe and chemical-free, but your metal also isn't getting scratched by using scraping tools. The left-over vinegar and water mix can simply be flushed without harm to the environment.

PIZZA

Flat-iron Pizza Quesadillas

Cooking Time: 10 Min

Ingredients:
- 8 Flour Tortillas
- 1 Pack Of Pepperoni And Or Salami
- 2 Cups Of Mozzarella Cheese
- 4 Tbsp Of Butter Or Margarine
- 2 Cups Of Spaghetti Sauce
- 4 Tbsp Of Dried Basil And Or Oregano

Directions:
1. Heat Flat Iron to medium heat. Add butter to flat top and spread across allowing it to melt. Once heated, place 4 tortillas flat on top. Immediately layer cheese, oregano/basil, meat and more cheese on the tortilla. Top with another tortilla. (Optionally, you can make each tortilla its own mini-quesadilla by only layering meat and cheese on one half then folding it in half.) Allow the cheese to fully melt on the inside before using a spatula to flip each over, adding more butter to the flat top, if necessary. Once cheese is melted and tortillas are browned and crisped to your liking, remove from Flat Iron. Serve each quesadilla with spaghetti sauce for dipping. Enjoy!

Gravity 980 Grilled Pizza

Cooking Time: 12 Min

Ingredients:
- 1 Lb. Fresh Pizza Dough
- 1/4 Cup of Extra Virgin Olive Oil
- All Purpose White Flour
- 1 Cup of Fresh Mozzarella Cheese
- Optional Toppings: Pepperoni, Vegetables, Sausage, Bacon, etc.

Directions:
1. Remove the fire shutter from your Gravity 980, load and light the hopper, then preheat to 500-600°F. Add flour to your counter or cutting board before prepping your dough into the desired pizza shape. Add pizza sauce, olive oil and cheese then add your pizza to the pizza stone. Add any toppings that must be cooked then add to the grill. Cook the pizza for 8-12 minutes or until desired brownness. Add any remaining fresh toppings and serve immediately. Enjoy!

Meat Lovers Pizza

Cooking Time: 9 To 12 Min

Ingredients:
- Pre-made Pizza Dough
- Pizza Sauce
- Garlic Powder - 2 tsp
- Shredded Mozzarella - 1 to 1.5 Cups
- 8 to 10 Slices of Pepperoni
- 1-2 Slices of Ham - Chopped
- 1/2 Cup Spicy Sausage - Browned
- 1/2 Cup Ground Beef - Browned
- Parmesan Cheese - Grated
- 1/2 Cup Arugula
- Olive Oil - 1 Tbs
- Salt and Pepper to Taste

Directions:
1. This Meat Lover's pizza packs on the flavor with ham, spicy sausage, ground beef, pepperoni, and two types of cheese. The optional arugula can take it over the top with its peppery bite. Cook this hot and fast on the AKORN for restaurant quality crust.
2. Allow pizza dough to come up to room temperature (about 8 hours). Tip: Place Pizza Dough in a large plastic bag that seals for the best results.
3. Brown ground beef and spicy sausage. Set aside.
4. Preheat AKORN to 500-600 degrees Fahrenheit. Insert Smokin' Stone. Place Pizza Stone on grates to heat.
5. Shape dough into pizza on a cutting board covered in semolina.
6. Add desired amount of pizza sauce and garlic powder.
7. Add ground beef and sausage to pizza. Add pepperoni and ham. Add mozzarella cheese.
8. Add parmesan cheese to taste.

9. Place pizza on pizza stone. Close lid and cook for 9 minutes or until crust is crisp and cheese melted.
10. Remove from pizza stone and allow to rest for 5 minutes.
11. Toss arugula with olive oil, salt and pepper.
12. Top pizza with arugula if desired.

Grilled Caprese Pizza

Cooking Time: 6 To 8 Min

Ingredients:
- 1 Ball of Pizza Dough, Rolled out Thinly
- 1/2 Cup Pesto
- 1 Small Ball Fresh Mozzarella, Torn to Shreds
- 1/2 Cup Cherry Tomatoes, Halved
- 4-5 Fresh Basil Leaves, Whole or Torn
- 1 Tbsp Fresh Parsley, Chopped
- 1 Tbsp Fresh Parmesan, Shredded or Grated
- 2 Tbsp Olive Oil
- Salt & Pepper to Taste

Directions:
1. Preheat Char-Griller to high heat. Scrape and oil your grates well so the dough does not stick.
2. Spread 1 T of oil to one side of the dough, and place oiled side down on heat first. Immediately turn burners to low and let dough cook for 2-3 minutes that side, until dough bubbles up.
3. Brush remaining oil on uncooked side, and then carefully use spatula to flip dough over. Turn heat off.
4. Spread the dough evenly with pesto, and scatter the torn mozzarella and halved tomatoes over the top. Close the lid, and allow residual heat from the grill to finish cooking the pizza for 5 minutes.
5. Remove pizza from heat and add fresh basil, parsley, and grated parmesan. Serve while warm. Enjoy!

Fire-grilled Pizza

Cooking Time: 10-15 Min

Ingredients:
- 3 C. bread flour
- 2 Tsp. salt
- 3 Tbsp. vegetable oil
- 1 Tsp. sugar
- 1 packet rapid-rising yeast
- 1 C. water
- Corn meal, for dusting
- Tomato sauce
- Garlic powder
- Cheese, if desired
- Toppings of choice

Directions:
1. In a stand mixer fitted with a dough hook, add water and yeast to the bowl and mix well. Then add sugar, salt and vegetable oil and mix.
2. Add bread flour, 1 C. at a time, and mix until a dough forms. Add water as needed to keep dough from sticking to the sides of the bowl. 3. Remove dough and knead for 1 minute by hand, forming it into a ball. Lightly spray a bowl with cooking spray, add dough ball and lightly spray the top. Cover with plastic wrap and allow dough to rise for 1 hour, until doubled in size.
3. Note: Dough is enough to make 2 medium pizzas. Cut dough in half, wrap unused portion and refrigerate or freeze for later use.
4. Pizza
5. Lightly flour counter. Stretch and work dough by hand, kneading until a 12" circle forms. Transfer dough to a wooden pizza peel lightly dusted with corn meal, to prevent sticking. 2. Pre-heat grill to 450°F. Sprinkle pizza dough with garlic powder. Spoon a layer of tomato sauce in the center and spread around to edges of dough. 3. Sprinkle a layer of cheese on top, if desired. Place other toppings on top of cheese layer. 4. Place pizza on pizza stone and allow pizza to cook for 10-15 minutes with lid closed. Rotate pizza after 5 minutes to ensure even cooking. Remove pizza from grill and allow to rest for 4-5 minutes. Slice and enjoy!

Breakfast Pizza

Cooking Time: 10 To 12 Min

Ingredients:
- Pre-made Pizza Dough
- Sun-dried Tomatoes - 1 Cup
- 1 Fresh Mozzarella Ball
- Deli Ham - 4 slices

- 1 Egg
- 1 (8 oz) Jar Tomato Sauce
- Baby Spinach - 2 Cups
- Dried Basil to Taste
- Salt and Pepper to Taste
- Semolina
- Garlic Powder to Taste

Directions:
1. Allow pre-made pizza dough to sit at room temperature covered with a clean dishcloth for at least 6 hours.
2. Preheat grill to medium high heat
3. Add pizza stone to grill and allow to preheat
4. Spread out pre-made pizza dough on a cutting board covered with semolina
5. Cut up ham and spinach.
6. Cut mozzarella into thin slices
7. Add tomato sauce to pizza. (As much as desired.)
8. Season with Garlic Salt and Basil
9. Add mozzarella slices
10. Add ham, spinach, and sun-dried tomatoes.
11. Add extra semolina to pizza stone and carefully slide pizza on grill.
12. Tip: Have a friend help with this step.
13. Allow to cook for 7 minutes with the lid closed.
14. Open grill and crack one egg onto the pizza.
15. Close the lid and allow to cook for 3 to 4 more minutes or until egg white is opaque.
16. Remove from grill and let rest for 5 minutes.
17. Serve and enjoy

Pepperoni Pizza

Cooking Time: 3-5 Min

Ingredients:
- Pizza Dough/Crust
- Pizza Sauce
- Mozzarella Cheese
- Pepperonis
- Other Toppings

Directions:
1. Add a layer of sauce
2. Spread your favorite toppings
3. Add an even layer of cheese
4. Add more toppings if desired
5. Heat grill to 550°F
6. Place pizza on stone
7. Cook for 3-5 minutes
8. Slice and serve!

Grilled Fathead Pizza

Ingredients:
- 10 oz Shredded Mozzarella Cheese
- 1 Egg
- 5 oz Balanced Almond Flour
- 1 tsp Pizza Seasoning
- 1/3 Cup Marinara Sauce
- 1/2 Pound Ground Italian Sausage, Ground
- 15 Pepperoni Slices
- 1 Green Bell Pepper, Chopped
- 1/2 Red Onion, Chopped
- 1 can sliced black olives
- 1 can sliced mushrooms
- 1.5 Cups Shredded Mozzarella Cheese (Topping)

Directions:
1. Preheat grill to a low temp of about 250°.
2. Melt 10 oz mozzarella cheese in microwave in 30 second increments until all melted, add 1 egg & mix. Once egg is mixed add the almond flour, baking powder & pizza seasoning.
3. Knead with hands until well incorporated (for about 3 minutes).
4. Spread dough out on a baking sheet with parchment paper.
5. Put on grill for about 5-6 minutes until crust is turning golden.
6. Then take crust off the grill, flip over & put back on parchment paper.
7. Add toppings & then put back in the grill for about 10 minutes or until desired doneness.

Pesto Burrata Grilled Pizza

Cooking Time: 3 Min

Ingredients:
- 1 Pizza Dough Ball (Store bought Dough or Homemade Dough)
- 1 Cup pesto
- 1 Cup Fresh Greens (Arugula or Spinach)
- 2 Burrata Balls
- 1/2 Cup Fresh Basil Leaves
- 4 T Olive Oil
- Salt And Pepper To Taste

Directions:
1. Fill chimney with charcoal. Place over side burner and turn flame to high, allowing charcoal to catch fire. If you do not have the side burner on your Texas Trio, you can light paper under the chimney so that it catches. We are cooking on the Akorn Jr today, so prep the base for charcoal, scrape the grates to make sure they're clean, and grab your stone or cast iron for the pizza.
2. Once coals have heated through, about 20 minutes, add them to the base of the Akorn Jr and place grates over the coals, add cast iron, and close lid to allow grill to heat up.
3. Let's prep the pizza. Cut dough ball into four equal pieces and roll each piece out to a thin circle.
4. I like to plate up all my toppings and take them out to the grill so I can make the pizzas quickly. When it's time- add a drizzle of the olive oil to the stone or cast iron and lay the dough out. Flip after about 60 seconds, once the sides start to golden and you see some bubbles forming. On the now cooked side that is up- spread ¼ cup of the pesto, add half a ball of burrata and close the lid for an additional 1-2 minutes, until the pie is cooked through. Remove from heat and top with arugula, fresh basil leaves, a drizzle of olive oil, and salt and pepper. Repeat three more times until all the pies are done. Serve hot, and enjoy!

Flat Iron Cheesy Pizza Bagels

Cooking Time: 15 Min

Ingredients:
- 3 Bagels Cut in Halves (Whatever type you prefer)
- 1 Can of Pizza Sauce
- 1 Cup of Pepperoni or Salami (Sliced)
- 2 Cups of Mozzarella Cheese
- 2 Tbsp of Butter

Directions:
1. Melt 1 Tbsp of butter on Flat Iron over Medium Heat.
2. Place bagels face down in butter and allow 2-3 minutes for them to lightly toast. Remove from heat.
3. On a separate section of the griddle, warm pepperoni/salami over medium heat for 3-4 minutes then set aside
4. On a tray or large plate, assemble bagel pizzas by spreading each with sauce, then adding desired amount of pepperoni/salami and cheese on top.
5. Place each bagel pizza back on the griddle on another Tbsp of melted butter over on medium-low heat until cheese has thoroughly melted and the bottom is toasted. (It might help to cover each bagel pizza with a basting/grill cover)
6. Serve hot.

POULTRY

Turkey Tips

Cooking Time: 3½ Hrs

Ingredients:
- 7-8 lb. turkey breast, cubed
- 1 medium onion, thinly sliced
- Chicken BBQ rub
- BBQ sauce
- 1-2 Tbsp. butter
- Salt and pepper, to taste

Directions:
1. Place turkey in a large roasting pan in an even layer, add BBQ sauce and turn to evenly coat. Allow to marinate for an hour.
2. Pre-heat grill to 230°F. Place pan with turkey on the grill and smoke for 30 minutes per pound or until internal temperature reaches 165°F.
3. While turkey is smoking, place a cast iron skillet on the grill and heat until very hot.
4. Remove turkey from roasting pan and add to skillet with onions, butter and more BBQ sauce. Allow to smoke for an additional 25 minutes, stirring occasionally.

Roasted Spatchcock Turkey

Cooking Time: 45 Min

Ingredients:
- 12-20 lb. Turkey
- 1½ Tsp. rosemary
- 3 Tbsp. Kosher salt
- ¾ Tsp. pepper
- ¾ Tsp. garlic powder

Directions:
1. Combine rosemary, Kosher salt, pepper and garlic powder in a bowl and mix well. Set aside.
2. Rinse the turkey and pat dry with paper towel. Place turkey breast-side down. Using sharp kitchen shears, cut along both sides of the backbone, beginning at the tail end.
3. Tip: Set aside the backbone and giblets for stock, if desired.
4. Open the turkey, remove any large pieces of fat and break the breastbone.
5. Tip: Place your hand on one side of the breast, close to the breastbone, and push down firmly until you hear a crack. Repeat on the other side.
6. Separate the legs and thighs and loosen the skin from the breast and season the meat with herb mixture from Step 1. Do this by slowly working your fingers between the breast and the skin.
7. Generously butter under the skin and on top of the turkey pieces.
8. Place an aluminum pan underneath the grates to catch drippings and juices. Place the breast on the grill first and allow to roast for 20 minutes at 325°F. Collect the juices from the pan and pour into a small bowl for basting.
9. After 20 minutes, add the legs and thighs. Baste the turkey every 25 minutes.
10. Cook until center of breast meat reaches 165°F and skin is golden brown. Remove from grill and let rest 5-10 minutes before slicing and serving.

Smoked Turkey Legs

Cooking Time: 3.5 Hrs

Ingredients:
- 1 Gallon of Water
- 1 cup of Kosher Salt
- 2 Tbsp of Garlic (Minced)
- 2 Tbsp of Ground Black Pepper
- 4 Tbsp of Garlic Powder
- 4 Tbsp of Onion Powder
- 1/3 Cup of Brown Sugar
- 2 Tbsp of Dried Basil
- 2 Tbsp of Dried Sage
- 2 Tbsp of Dried Thyme
- 1 Tsp of Paprika
- 1 Tsp of Cayenne Pepper
- 2-3 Bay Leaves

Directions:

1. Combine all the brine recipes in a large pot and bring to a boil. Let it cool. As it boils, rinse the turkey legs. Once the brine cools, submerge the turkey legs in it. Cover and refrigerate it overnight. Heat your smoker to 225-250°F. Remove the turkey legs from the refrigerator and pat dry with paper towels, allowing them to sit for 15-20 minutes. Transfer the turkey legs to the smoker and cook for 3-4 hours until the legs have a dark exterior and the juices run clear.
2. Allow them to rest for 10-15 minutes before serving as is, with barbecue sauce and with any desired sides

Turkey Leg Lollipops

Cooking Time: 1.5 Hrs

Ingredients:
- 4 Large Turkey Legs
- 1/2 Cup Char-Griller Original Rub
- 1 Tbsp Olive Oil
- 3/4 Cup BBQ Sauce of Choice
- 1/4 Cup Apple Juice
- 1 tsp Honey
- 1 tsp Char-Griller Original Rub (For Sauce)

Directions:
1. With your boning knife cut where the turkey meat starts to thin out going towards the joint. Cut all around the bone and use a paper towel to help with the removal of the skin and joint. Tip: You will notice tendons and a little bone that runs parallel to the leg after you have cut it. Make sure to remove these with your boning knife or kitchen shears.
2. Wrap the exposed bones in foil (this will help with presentation).
3. Next, rub the turkey legs down with olive oil and apply seasoning liberally to lollipops. Make sure to get as even as a coat as possible.
4. Get your grill between 325 F and 350 F. Add hickory chunks to give the meat an extra layer of flavor.
5. Once the grill is up to temp put the turkey legs on indirect heat.
6. Start preparing the glaze by combining BBQ sauce, apple juice, honey, and seasoning in a microwavable safe cup. Set aside till it is time to glaze. Tip: Warm your sauce up right before it is time to glaze so that it is smooth and doesn't tack on the meat too heavily.
7. Once your turkey has reached internal temp around 165 F it is time to glaze. Dip each turkey lollipop into the cup with your glaze mixture until you have obtained a nice shine.
8. Quickly put the turkey back on the grill and let the internal temp reach 170 F.
9. Pull the turkey and let rest for 10 minutes before you eat. Enjoy!

Chili Mesquite Lime Shredded Chicken Street Tacos

Cooking Time: 45 Min

Ingredients:
- 6 Tbsp Mesquite Lime Sea Salt
- 2 Tbsp Chili Powder
- 1 Lime (Squeezed)
- 4 Chicken Breasts (Skinless)
- Chili Lime Sauce
- 1 Package Provolone Cheese Slices

Directions:
1. Mix sea salt, powder and lime together Trim any excess fat off chicken breasts Season chicken with sauce and let sit for 10-15 mins Get your grill up to temp at about 400° - 450° Place chicken on grill until IT of 165° Pull chicken and place in the Instant Pot for 30 mins (add 1/2 cup water) Shred chicken and place on shells, top with pico de gallo and Sriracha Warm up a pan and throw cheese slice in pan When cheese begins to bubble flip over until brown

Easy Chicken And Cheese Quesadillas

Cooking Time: 10 Min

Ingredients:
- Pack Of Soft Tortillas
- 2 Lbs Chicken Tenderloin
- Your Choice of Cheese
- Your Choice Of Other Toppings

Directions:

1. Bring your griddle to high / medium-high heat, throw down some oil and cook up your chicken. Once they are cooked and chopped up, move them off to the side.
2. Throw down a little more oil because the griddle may be pretty dry by now, then a couple of tortillas to brown and soften up.
3. After flipping the tortillas once, add your toppings. Start with cheese all over the tortillas, then add your other toppings only on one half of the tortilla.
4. Fold the tortilla in half to create your quesadilla. Press firmly to activate the 'cheese glue'.
5. Flip once more to ensure everything is melty goodness inside.
6. Cut with a pizza cutter and serve with your choice of dips!

Creole Latin Spiced Rotisserie Chicken

Ingredients:
- Whole Chicken (Any Size)
- Olive Oil
- Creole Seasoning To Taste
- Sazon To Taste
- Adobo To Taste
- Fresh Parsley Flakes or Fresh Cilantro Flakes
- Kitchen Twine
- 1 Onion (Sliced)
- Char-Griller Grills Super Pro & Rotisserie Kit

Directions:
1. Rinse and pat dry chicken. Trim access fat and skin. Apply coating of olive oil to all sides of the chicken. Add Sazon, Creole and adobo seasonings. Add twine and knot the legs and also the wings over the breast. Add chicken to rotisserie rod and lock in using the rotisserie forks. Then Sprinkle fresh parsley or cilantro flakes on to the chicken. Slice onion and place on to a hook. Heat grill with lump charcoal: When coking over an open fire I don't cook at specific temperature. I begin with an equivalent of a ½ chimney full of lump charcoal and monitor the fire by feel. I place the charcoal in the middle of the grill in the back. As the charcoal burns I add pieces as the cook goes along. Place rotisserie chicken in the grill along with the onions. Roast chicken until internal 165°. Remove chicken and onions from the grill. Allow to rest for 15 minutes. Slice and enjoy!

Classic Smoked Spatchcocked Turkey

Ingredients:
- 14 Lb Turkey
- Char-Griller Chicken Rub
- Ghee or Butter

Directions:
1. Preheat offset smoker to between 225 and 250.
2. Tip: You can also do use the AKORN with a Smoking Stone.
3. Add mesquite or hickory chunks to Side Fire Box.
4. Place turkey on a cutting board breast-side down.
5. Using a pair of kitchen shears, cut the backbone out of the turkey.
6. Flip the turkey so the breast-side is up and using two hands, press down on the breastbone until you hear it break and the turkey lies flat on the cutting board.
7. Season the inside and the outside of the turkey with Char-Griller Chicken Rub making sure to rub it into the meat.
8. Place a drip pan under the grates where the turkey will sit.
9. Place the turkey on the grates in the middle of the main barrel of the smoker.
10. Baste turkey with melted ghee every 30 to 45 minutes.
11. Add additional lit charcoal if needed to maintain temperature.
12. The turkey is done when a thermometer reads 165 when interested into the thickest part of the breast.
13. Tip: Turkey will take about 30 to 40 minutes per pound to cook.
14. When turkey reaches 165 degrees, remove from grill and let rest for 20 minutes before carving.

Fried Chicken And Corn

Cooking Time: 10 Min

Ingredients:
- 2 C. flour
- 2 oz. corn starch
- 2 oz. paprika
- 1 Tbsp. cinnamon
- Salt & pepper to taste
- 4 ears of corn
- 4 oz. melted unsalted butter
- 1 Tbsp. paprika

Directions:
1. Soak chicken up to 24 hours in buttermilk and hot sauce
2. In a bowl mix corn starch, salt & pepper, cinnamon, and paprika
3. Mix ingredients well
4. Add chicken to mixture and coat thoroughly
5. Once coated, let sit for 30 minutes
6. Heat grill to 375°F
7. In a hot cast iron skillet, add chicken and oil
8. Cook chicken 3-5 minutes per side
9. Soak corn in saltwater for up to 24 hours
10. Boil them in butter water for 10 minutes before adding to grill
11. On a plate, mix paprika, salt, pepper, and melted butter
12. Mix and roll corn and cover with mixture
13. Add to grill and cook for 3-5 minutes

Chicken Teriyaki

Ingredients:
- 1 whole chicken
- 1 C. soy sauce
- ½ C. brown sugar
- ¼ C. mirin
- 2 Tbsp. honey
- 3 Tsp. fresh ginger, grated
- 2 Tsp. sesame oil
- 2 Tsp. minced garlic
- ½ C. water
- ¼ C. cornstarch

Directions:
1. In a blender combine soy sauce, brown sugar, mirin, honey, fresh ginger, sesame oil and minced garlic and blend until well combined to create marinade.
2. Rinse the chicken and pat dry with paper towel. Place chicken breast-side down. Using sharp kitchen shears, cut along both sides of the backbone, beginning at the back end. Set aside the backbone and giblets for stock, if desired.
3. Using a sharp knife, slice the keel bone at the back of the chicken and crack it open.
4. Tip: Remove the bone by placing your fingers under it and sliding it out. Doing this will allow the chicken to lay flat when turned over.
5. Place the chicken in a large resealable storage bag and pour in the marinade from Step 1. Seal the bag, making sure there is no excess air inside, and allow to marinate overnight in the refrigerator.
6. Pre-heat grill to 350°F. Place chicken on the grill, skin side up for the first 30 minutes. After 30 minutes, flip the chicken and grill for another 1½-2 hours. Chicken is done when internal temperature reaches 165°F-170°F.
7. Allow to rest before slicing and serving. Enjoy!

Grilled Chicken And Vegetable Kebabs

Cooking Time: 15 Min

Ingredients:
- 2 lbs. boneless, skinless chicken thighs
- 1 C. whole yogurt
- 2 Tbsp. unsalted butter, melted
- 1 Tbsp. salt
- ½ Tsp. ground coriander
- ¼ Tsp. ground turmeric
- Pinch red pepper flakes, optional
- 1 garlic clove, finely grated
- 3 bell peppers, stemmed and cored
- 1 red onion, cut into wedges
- 2 Tbsp. olive oil
- Flatbread, for serving
- Fresh mint and parsley leaves, chopped, for garnish
- Bamboo skewers

Directions:
1. Rinse chicken, pat dry with paper towel and cut into 2" thick pieces. Whisk together yogurt, butter, salt, coriander, turmeric, red pepper flakes and grated garlic in a medium bowl until smooth.
2. Add chicken and toss to evenly coat. Cover bowl with plastic wrap and let marinate at room temperature for 1 hour.
3. Rinse produce. Slice peppers into 2" thick pieces. Toss peppers and onion wedges in a medium bowl with the olive oil, and season with salt, to taste.
4. Soak bamboo skewers in water for 30 minutes. Divide chicken and vegetables evenly between the skewers, alternating between the two.
5. Pre-heat grill to 400°F. Grill kebabs, turning as needed, until the chicken has cooked through, about 15-20 minutes. Chicken is done when internal temperature reaches 165°F.
6. Let rest for 3-5 minutes, then garnish with chopped mint and parsley leaves, and serve with flatbread.
7. Enjoy!

Flat Iron East Meets West Chicken Fajitas

Cooking Time: Varies Min

Ingredients:
- 6 Chicken Breasts, Cut into Fajita Slices
- 4 Green Peppers, Cut into Slices
- 4 Yellow Peppers, Cut into Slices
- 2 Large Onions, Sliced
- 2 Packs Tortillas
- 2 Eggs
- 2 Tbsp Soy Sauce
- 1 Tbsp Brown Sugar
- 1 tsp Fresh Ginger, Minced
- 2 Cups Cooked Rice
- Sesame Oil
- Sesame Seeds
- 4 Scallions, Sliced
- Char-Griller Chicken Rub
- Salt and Pepper to Taste

Directions:
1. Taking traditional fajita flavors and adding and extra twist to it, you can cook this whole meal on the Flat Iron at one time! Fried rice, marinated chicken, veggies and toasted tortillas all come together to make this great dish.
2. Pre-heat griddle on Medium High
3. Slice chicken breasts into fajita slices
4. Slice peppers, onions, and scallions
5. Mix together soy sauce, brown sugar and ginger. Pour over chicken in bowl and toss to coat
6. Create 4 cooking zones, high, medium high, medium and low
7. Spread sesame oil on griddle
8. Place chicken on high cooking zone and peppers and onions on medium high cooking zone
9. Season peppers and onions with salt and pepper.
10. Place rice on medium cooking zone.
11. Make a circle of oil, crack two eggs into it. Add Char-Griller Chicken Rub to taste and scallions. Scramble eggs.
12. Add eggs to rice and mix well to incorporate. Add more soy sauce to rice if desired.
13. Check on chicken and vegetables. Flip if needed.
14. Place tortillas on low cooking zone to toast.
15. After chicken reaches 165, remove from grill and build fajitas with chicken, peppers, onions, and rice.
16. Garnish with extra scallions and sesame seeds.

Honey Chipotle Chicken Wings

Cooking Time: 15 Min

Ingredients:
- 2 lbs. chicken wings
- 2 oz. apple cider vinegar
- 4 oz. honey
- 2 Tbsp. chipotle pepper
- 2 oz. mustard
- 1-2 Tsp. red pepper flakes
- 4 oz. olive oil
- Salt and pepper to taste

Directions:
1. Mix mustard, red pepper flakes, honey, chipotle peppers, and apple cider vinegar to make chipotle sauce
2. Slowly infuse olive oil slowly while stirring

3. Season with salt and pepper and stir
4. Using only half the sauce, toss the chicken wings in the sauce and set aside the remaining half
5. Place wings on the grill at 350°F, cook for 7-8 minutes
6. Flip wings, and cook another 7-8 minutes
7. Remove wings and toss in the remaining sauce

Creole Hush Puppy Fried Chicken Legs & Thighs

Ingredients:
- 4 Chicken Legs & 4 Thighs
- 2 Cups of Milk
- Garlic Parsley Butter
- CharGriller Creole Seasoning
- Caribeque Lemon Garlic Seasoning
- 2 Tbs of Sazon
- Garlic Powder To Taste
- Black Pepper To Taste
- Crispy Creole Tony Chachere's Hush Puppy 9.5 Oz
- 1 Cup of All Purpose Flour
- 1/2 Cup of Panko Bread Crumbs
- Cayenne Pepper To Taste
- Lard For Frying
- Char-Griller Grills Hybrid Gas and Charcoal Grill With a Side Burner

Directions:
1. Garlic Parsley Buttermilk Prepping
2. In a large bowl add 2 cups Milk Add melted Garlic Parsley Butter: 4 oz. to the milk. -Full Garlic Parsley Recipe links: Written Recipe & Video Recipe Add Char-Griller Grills Lemon Pepper: to taste Add Caribeque Lemon Garlic: to taste Add Black Pepper to Taste Add Garlic powder to Taste Add Creole Seasoning to Taste Mix ingredients thoroughly. Rinse and clean the chicken legs and thighs with cold water and pat dry with a paper towel. Trim any fat or cartilage from the chicken. Place the chicken in the Garlic Parsley Butter Mixture and mix thoroughly. Place in the fridge for 6-24 hours.
3. Batter/Breading Prep
4. In a large pan add the hush puppy mix: 9.5 oz., All Purpose Flour: one cup and Panko Bread Crumbs: ½ cup Add Cayenne Pepper: to taste Add Creole Seasoning: to taste Add Sazon: 2 tbs Add Black Pepper: to taste Mix all the ingredients thoroughly. Remove the chicken from the fridge and bowl. Then place the chicken legs and thighs in the batter/breading. Tip: apply pressure onto the chicken so the batter/breading can be thickly applied to the chicken. Set aside while the cast iron skillet heats up.
5. Cooking Directions
6. Fire up your Char-Griller Grills Hybrid Gas and Charcoal Grill side burner using a large cast iron skillet with lard. Preheat the Cast Iron Skillet with the oil to 335°. Place the chicken into the cast iron skillet for 15 minutes or until internal temperature 175°. Tip: place the chicken thighs skin side down when placing into the cast iron skillet. Remove the chicken from the cast iron skillet and allow it to drain/cool for 7 minutes. Serve and Enjoy

Smoked Spatchcock Turkey

Cooking Time: 3-4 Hrs

Ingredients:
- 12-20 lb. turkey
- 3/4 C. olive oil
- 3 Tbsp. minced garlic
- 2 Tbsp. fresh rosemary, chopped
- 1 Tbsp. fresh basil, chopped
- 1 Tbsp. Italian seasoning
- 1 Tsp. ground black pepper

Directions:
1. In a small bowl, mix the olive oil, garlic, rosemary, basil, Italian seasoning, black pepper and salt. Set aside.
2. Rinse the turkey inside and out; pat dry. Loosen the skin from the breast. Work it loose to the end of the drumstick being careful not to tear the skin.
2. Tip: This is easily done by slowly working your fingers between the breast and the skin.
3. Using your hand, spread a generous amount of the rosemary mixture under the breast skin and down the thigh and leg. Rub the remainder of the rosemary

mixture over the outside of the breast and all over the turkey. 4. Place turkey in your smoker, and smoke at 250°F for 3 to 4 hours, or until the turkey internal temperature reaches a minimum of 165°F.

Creole Latin Spatchcock Turkey

Cooking Time: 1-2 Hrs

Ingredients:
- Whole turkey
- Kitchen Scissors & Pairing Knife
- Char-Griller Marinade Injector
- Creole Seasoning: Generous Coating
- Sazón Seasoning: Generous Coating
- Adobo Seasoning
- Garlic Powder
- Onion Powder
- Creole Butter Injectable Marinade (17 Oz)
- Fresh or Dry Cilantro
- Olive Oil
- Turkey Oven Bags
- Bucket Or Cooler
- Char-Griller Grill

Directions:
1. Chop up fresh cilantro and set aside.
2. Remove turkey from bag & remove everything inside the cavity area along with the plastic tie holding the legs. 3. Using kitchen scissors & pairing knife remove the backbone to Spatchcock the turkey. Also trim and remove any access fat & skin.
3. Flip Turkey breast side up & push down on the breast using both hands to help flatten the turkey.
4. Inject turkey with Creole Butter. Use any extra Creole & rub on breast under skin.
5. Generously add olive to the both sides of the turkey. Tip: continue to trim access fat & skin as you go along.
6. Generously season the turkey with Adobo, Sazón, Creole, onion powder & garlic powder. Then sprinkle cilantro 8. Place turkey in turkey/oven bag & place in bucket or cooler. Place in refrigerator & allow the turkey to rest for 12-24 hours. Cooking Directions 1. Remove turkey from bucket/cooler & allow to rest at room temperature for 1-2 hours. 2. Preheat your Char-griller Smoker to 240°. 3. Place turkey in smoker and smoke until the turkey reaches 165° internal temperature. Product tip: use the Char-griller remote thermometer or folding prob thermometer. 4. Check on turkey about every hour & baste turkey with butter & spritz with apple juice. Tip: rotate turkey in different directions to allow even cooking. 5. After turkey reaches 165° internal temperature allow the turkey to rest for a minimum of 25 minutes. Sprinkle additional cilantro. 7. Slice, serve & enjoy.

Beer Can Roasted Turkey Breast

Cooking Time: 4-5 Hrs

Ingredients:
- Turkey Breast
- Favorite Rub/Seasonings: Blues Hog Sweet & Savory and a 50/50 blend of Coarse Salt & Coarse Pepper.
- Olive Oil
- Char-Griller Grills Beer Can Chicken Rack with Beer Can
- Char-Griller Grills Ceramic Akorn Kamado Charcoal Grill, Smokin' Stone & Drip Pan
- Fuel: Fogo Eucalyptus Lump Charcoal
- Char-Griller Grills Folding Probe

Directions:
1. -pound turkey breast with bones: Trim all loose fat and skin. Place the turkey breast on the Beer Can Chicken Rack Apply olive oil to all the sides of the turkey. Season all sides of the meat with your favorite Char-Griller Rub/Seasonings. Preheat grill/smoker to 250°. Once the grill/smoker is preheated, add the Smokin' Stone & Char-Griller Drip Pan filled with water to the grill/smoker. Remember to use your Char-Griller Grills Probe to take the guess work out your cooking. Place turkey in grill/smoker and smoke until internal temperature 165° is met, roughly takes 4-5 Hours
2. Tip: while smoking, if a spot on the meat/skin gets too much char, place a small piece of foil

3. Over the spot to help prevent that spot from burning/drying out. Rotate in the smoker/grill every 45 minutes and rotate the turkey for even cooking. Remove from the smoker/grill and allow to rest for 15-30 minutes. Slice and enjoy.

Smoked Chicken Thighs

Cooking Time: 1 Hrs

Ingredients:
- 7 lbs bone in, skin on chicken quarters
- 1 C. apple cider vinegar
- 1/2 C. extra virgin olive oil
- 1/2 C. extra virgin olive oil
- 1/2 C. minced onion
- 1 1/2 Tsp. kosher salt
- 4 minced garlic cloves

Directions:
1. Mix apple cider vinegar, extra virgin olive oil, minced onion, kosher salt, and garlic cloves in a bowl 2. Pour mixture over chicken.
2. Set in fridge for at least an hour
3. Heat grill to 250°F
4. Add Smokin' Stone 6. Place chicken on grill 7. To crisp up the skin, take temp up to 350°-400°F when chicken has internal temp of 140°F for about 15 minuets 8. Remove chicken when internal temp reaches 165°-185°F
5. Let cool for 10 minutes, then serve.

Grilled Duck Breast

Cooking Time: 20 Min

Ingredients:
- 8 skinned, boned duck breast halves
- ½ Tsp. hot sauce
- 2 Tbsp. minced garlic
- ¼ C. Worcestershire sauce
- ¼ Tsp. black pepper

Directions:
1. Whisk together Worcestershire sauce, olive oil, hot sauce, garlic, and pepper in a large bowl.
2. Rinse duck breasts and pat dry with paper towel. Score the skin of the duck with a sharp knife in a ¼" diamond pattern to render out the fat for crispy skin.
3. Add the duck breasts to bowl and toss well to coat. Cover with plastic wrap and marinate in the refrigerator for 30 minutes or best overnight.
4. Pre-heat grill to 375°F and put an aluminum pan under the grates to catch drippings. Grill the duck, skin side down, for 4-5 minutes per side.
5. Duck is done when internal temperature reaches 135°F for medium-rare. Remove from the grill and allow to rest 5-10 minutes before slicing and serving.

Chicken Cordon Bleu

Cooking Time: 20 Min

Ingredients:
- 2-3 Chicken breasts
- 6 strips of bacon
- 2 slices deli ham
- 4 slices of cheese
- Jalapeños, seeded and sliced, optional
- Garlic powder
- Salt and pepper, to taste

Directions:
1. Rinse chicken breasts and pat dry with paper towel. Place inside a resealable plastic bag and flatten using a mallet, until about a ½" thick. 2. Remove chicken from bag and layer a slice of ham and 2 slices of cheese on each. Place jalapeño slices on each, if desired. 3. Tightly roll chicken breast, keeping ham and cheese inside. Wrap each breast with 3 slices of bacon and lightly season with garlic powder, salt and pepper on both sides, to taste. Refrigerate for 10-20 minutes. 4. Pre-heat grill to 400°F and place chicken directly on grates, for about 20 minutes, flipping halfway through for good sear marks. Chicken is done when internal temperature reaches 165°F.
2. Slice, serve and enjoy!

Cherry Chipotle Buffalo Wings

Cooking Time: 1 Hrs

Ingredients:
- 4 lbs. chicken wings
- 14 oz. bottle cherry Chipotle BBQ sauce
- 3 Tsp. dried minced onion
- 2 Tsp. Chipotle chili powder
- 1 ½ Tsp. garlic powder
- 1 ½ Tsp. chili powder
- ½ Tsp. smoked paprika
- 2 C. sour cream
- 1 C. blue cheese salad dressing
- 1 C. blue cheese, crumbled
- 1 C. green onions, thinly sliced
- Salt and pepper, to taste

Directions:
1. Combine 1 Tsp rub, sour cream, salad dressing, crumbled blue cheese and green onions together in a medium bowl and mix well. 2. Refrigerate at least 2 hours to blend flavors.
2. Buffalo wings
3. Rinse chicken wings and dry with paper towel. 2. Combine dried minced onion, Chipotle chili powder, garlic powder, chili powder, smoked paprika and salt and pepper, to taste, into a small bowl and mix well. Reserve 1 Tsp. to mix with dipping sauce. Season chicken wings generously with rub. Place wings on the grill, equally spaced in rows, to smoke for 30 minutes when grill temperature reaches 250°F. 4. After letting wings smoke, increase grill temperature to 350°F and cook wings until internal temperature reaches 165°F. 5. Brush on sauce during the last 15 minutes, flipping once and coating evenly every 5 minutes.

Pulled Chicken Crunch Wrap Style Burritos

Cooking Time: 10 Min

Ingredients:
- 1 Cup of Pulled Chicken Mixed with Taco Seasoning and Enchilada Sauce
- 2 Large Burrito Sized Tortillas
- 2 Corn Tostadas, Or Tortillas You Crisp In The Oven
- 2 Small flour tortilla
- 1 Cup Shredded Lettuce
- 1/2 Cup Pico De Gallo, Or Chopped Tomatoes
- 1/2 Cup Queso
- 1/2 Cup Shredded Cheese
- 1/2 Cup Sour Cream

Directions:
1. Place large tortilla on a flat surface, add half of the chicken mixture and half of the queso. Top with a tostada and half of the sour cream. Sprinkle on half the lettuce, pico, and shredded cheese, and top with the remaining small tortilla. Fold inward over the small tortilla to close and repeat the same process to finish the second crunch wrap.
2. Preheat Char-Griller Flat Iron Griddle over medium heat. Drizzle with 1 tsp oil, and spread evenly. Place Crunch Wraps seam side down on the griddle and cook for about 5 minutes until golden brown. Flip, and cook for another 5 minutes until the other side is golden brown. Serve while hot and enjoy!

Curried Chicken Skewers

Cooking Time: 10-12 Min

Ingredients:
- 3-4 lb. chicken tenders
- 2 Tbsp. vegetable oil
- 2 Tbsp. yellow mustard
- 2 Tbsp. honey
- 2 Tbsp. curry powder
- 1 Tsp. salt
- ½ Tsp. garlic powder
- ½ Tsp. pepper
- ½ Tsp. allspice

Directions:
1. Soak the bamboo skewers in water for 15 minutes, so they don't burn on the grill.
2. While skewers are soaking, rinse the chicken tenders and pat dry with paper towel.
3. Combine oil, mustard, honey, curry powder, garlic powder, allspice, salt and pepper in a medium bowl to

make curry seasoning and mix well. Add chicken, turning to coat evenly and skewer.

4. Place skewered chicken tenders on the grill at 375°F for 10 minutes, until internal temperature reaches 165°F.

2-burner Flat Iron Seasoned Chicken Breasts

Cooking Time: 20 Min

Ingredients:
- 4 Boneless Chicken Breasts
- 1/4 Cup of Extra Virgin Olive Oil
- 1 Lemon
- 1 Tbsp of Garlic Powder
- 1 Tbsp of Onion Powder
- 1 Tbsp of Italian Seasoning or choice of herbs
- 1 Tbsp of Char-Griller Lemon Pepper Rub
- 1 Tsp of Cayenne Pepper

Directions:
1. If you prefer to rinse your chicken breasts, do so in cold water. Pat completely dry with paper towels. In a resealable bag add olive oil, and all herbs and seasonings. Add chicken and seal the bag before mixing until all pieces are thoroughly coated. Place the bag(s) in the refrigerator for 1 hour-overnight. With Flat Iron preheated to medium heat, add chicken breast and generous squirt of water to the cooktop before covering with the Char-Griller Basting Dome. Keeping covered, allow it to cook for 9-10 minutes. Remove Basting Dome and generously squeeze juice from lemon over each chicken breast. Allow chicken to cook uncovered for 5-6 more minutes, letting water to evaporate and slight crusting to form on bottom before flipping once more. Cook chicken until the internal temperature reaches 165°F. Serve immediately. Enjoy!

Chicken Fajitas

Cooking Time: 20 Min

Ingredients:
- 1 lb. chicken breasts, filleted in half
- 1 ½ Tsp. seasoned salt
- 1 ½ Tsp. dried oregano
- 1 ½ Tsp. ground cumin
- 1 Tsp. garlic powder
- ½ Tsp. chili powder
- ½ Tsp. paprika
- 2 Tbsp. lemon juice
- 2 Tbsp. vegetable oil
- 1 onion, thinly sliced
- 1-2 bell peppers, cored, stemmed and thinly sliced
- Pico de Gallo, for serving
- Shredded cheese, for serving
- Tortillas

Directions:
1. Rinse chicken and pat dry with paper towel. Pour dry ingredients, lemon juice and vegetable oil into a large resealable plastic bag, add chicken and gently shake to evenly coat. Marinate for 2–3 hours in the refrigerator, or best overnight. 2. Pre-heat grill to 400°F. Place chicken directly on the grill and sear for 5-7 minutes on each side, flipping halfway through for good sear marks. Chicken is done when internal temperature reaches 165°F. Remove chicken from grill and wrap in foil to keep warm. 3. While chicken is searing, place 1-2 Tbsp. of oil on a heated cast iron fajita pan. Using a heat resistant grill glove, carefully pick up the pan and spread the oil around evenly. Place the onions and peppers on the pan and sauté for 5-7 minutes until softened. 4. Toast tortillas on warming rack for 5 minutes. Unwrap chicken from foil and slice into 1" thick strips.

2. To serve, spoon a layer of Pico de Gallo and cheese on tortilla. Top with a layer of peppers and onions and add chicken. Enjoy!

Garlic Parmesan Chicken Wings

Cooking Time: 45-60 Min

Ingredients:
- 4 lbs. Chicken Wings
- 16oz. bottle Italian dressing
- 1 C. shredded parmesan cheese
- 1/2 Tbsp. onion salt
- 1/2 Tbsp. black pepper
- 1 C. butter
- 1 Tbsp. oregano

- 2 Tbsp. garlic powder
- A pinch of rosemary

Directions:
1. Add charcoal to one side of grill for indirect grilling, or use Smokin' Stone and add flavored wood chips/chunks if desired
2. Let grill preheat to 275°F
3. Place wings on indirect heat side of grill
4. Smoke wings for 45-60 minutes, until internal temp reaches 170°F
5. While wings are smoking, make garlic Parmesan sauce by mixing Parmesan cheese, garlic powder, onion salt, black pepper, butter, oregano and rosemary
6. Remove wings from grill and toss in garlic Parmesan sauce

Buffalo Ranch Chicken

Ingredients:
- 24 Oz Greek Yogurt
- 1 Ranch Seasoning Packet
- 5 lbs Chicken Legs

Directions:
1. Combine Greek yogurt and ranch seasoning packet. Add Chicken to mixture and stir, making sure to coat chicken well. Cover and place in refrigerator for 2 hrs. Preheat grill to 350F. Grill chicken using direct heat until an internal temperature of 165F. Remove chicken and toss in your favorite buffalo sauce. Serve and enjoy!

Garlic Lover's Chicken

Cooking Time: 10 Min

Ingredients:
- 7 lb. whole chicken
- 16 oz. bottle Italian dressing
- 4-5 handfuls peeled garlic cloves, to taste
- 2 Tbsp. butter, melted
- 1 Tsp. olive oil
- 2 Tsp. dried thyme leaves
- 1 Tsp. seasoned salt
- 2 Tsp. white pepper
- 2 Tbsp. flour
- 1 C. low fat milk
- 2 C. dry white wine
- Garlic dry rub or Chicken BBQ rub, to taste

Directions:
1. Rinse chicken, dry with paper towel and cut in half. Marinate chicken halves in Italian dressing for four hours, or overnight. Season generously with garlic dry rub or use Chicken BBQ rub.
2. Roast chicken on the grill at 400°F for 45 minutes. Chicken is done when internal temperature reaches 170°F. Remove chicken from the grill and let rest 5-10 minutes.
3. Garlic sauce
4. Sauté garlic cloves in a medium sauce pan with butter and olive oil until lightly browned. Stir frequently and cook until garlic is soft, 5-7 minutes.
5. Whisk together flour, milk, white wine, thyme and white pepper in a small bowl. Add to garlic, stir to combine and simmer for 10 minutes.
6. To serve, pour garlic sauce over baked chicken halves and enjoy!

Boneless Chicken Thighs Broccolini & Cheesy Potatoes

Cooking Time: 25 Min

Ingredients:
- Boneless Skinless Chicken Thighs
- 4 Large Potatoes
- 1 Small White Onion
- 2 Bundles of Broccolini
- 1 Loaf Garlic Bread
- 1/2 Cup Cheddar Cheese
- Green Onion for Garnish
- Favorite BBQ Rub
- Favorite BBQ Sauce

Directions:
1. First, season chicken thighs on both sides with your favorite BBQ rub
2. Set in fridge while preparing the vegetables
3. Dice potatoes into equal sized pieces
4. Dice onion, combine with potatoes and season with same BBQ rub 5. Wash, clean, and season broccolini with same BBQ rub

5. Fire up the Char-Grillers Triple Play
6. Start cooking potatoes and onions first in a preheated cast iron skillet on the grill
7. Grill chicken thighs over direct heat (Charcoal Side)
8. Char Broccolini over direct heat (Propane Side)
9. Flip chicken once and begin basting with BBQ sauce
10. Once potatoes are fork tender, sprinkle cheddar cheese over top
11. Flip and sauce other side of chicken and remove once an internal temp of 165*F is reached
12. Garnish potatoes with green onion and serve

Grilled Chicken And Broccoli Stir-fry

Cooking Time: 10 Min

Ingredients:
- 1 lb. chicken breast
- 8 oz. bottle Italian dressing
- 1 Tbsp. extra-virgin olive oil
- 1 head broccoli, stemmed and cut into florets
- ½ red pepper, sliced
- ½ green pepper, sliced
- ½ yellow pepper, sliced
- ½ red onion, sliced
- 1 Tbsp. dried basil
- 1 Tbsp. dried oregano
- 1 Tbsp. garlic powder
- Olive oil, for brushing
- Salt and pepper, to taste

Directions:
1. Rinse chicken and pat dry with paper towel. Pour Italian dressing into a large resealable plastic bag, add chicken and gently shake to evenly coat. Marinate for 2–3 hours in the refrigerator, or best overnight.
2. Rinse produce and pat dry with paper towel. Preheat grill to 400°F and brush a grill wok with olive oil.
3. Remove chicken from marinade, cut into 1" thick strips and place in grill wok. Discard dressing.
4. Sear the chicken strips evenly on all sides, until golden brown, for about 3 minutes.
5. Add the broccoli, red pepper, green pepper, yellow pepper, and red onion to the wok and cook for about 5 minutes, stirring occasionally.
6. Mix together basil, oregano and garlic powder in a small bowl to make seasoning and add salt and pepper, to taste. Sprinkle over chicken and vegetables and stir to combine.
7. Serve over cooked rice and garnish with fresh basil and chopped cashews or peanuts, if desired.

Bacon Wrapped Chicken Thighs

Cooking Time: 2-3 Hrs

Ingredients:
- 1 Pack of small chicken thighs (remove any excess fat)
- 1 C. Tony Chachere's Creole Seasoning
- 1 lb. smoked bacon
- 1 bottle squeeze butter

Directions:
1. Squirt on a little squeeze butter and spread it over the chicken thigh and the underside of the skin.
2. Replace skin and wrap each thigh in a strip of bacon. Sprinkle lightly with Tony Chachere's Creole Seasoning. Go light as it is very salty.
3. Place on the grill's top rack of the gas grill for 2 hours at 300°F, depending on the size of the thighs it may take a little longer.

Grilled Nachos

Cooking Time: 25-30 Min

Ingredients:
- 3 boneless skinless chicken breasts
- 6 mini sweet peppers
- 1 bag of tortilla chips
- 1 8oz. bag of shredded fiesta cheese
- 1 jar of your favorite salsa
- Original All-Purpose BBQ rub, or your favorite rub

Directions:
1. Heat grill to 325°F.
2. While grill is heating, rub the chicken breasts liberally with your favorite rub or use Original All-Purpose BBQ rub, to taste.

3. Place chicken breasts on the grill and cook for 6 minutes per side until internal temperature reaches 165°F, flipping halfway through for good sear marks.
4. Remove chicken and chop into chunks. Chop up sweet peppers.
5. In a grill safe pan, layer chips, chicken, peppers and cheese for three layers.
6. Place pan on the grill and grill for 12-15 minutes.
7. Once cheese is melted, remove from the grill and top with your favorite salsa.
8. Enjoy!

Asian Chicken Salad

Cooking Time: 25 Min

Ingredients:
- 4 Cups Mixed Greens
- 2-3 Chicken Breasts
- 1/2 Cup Chopped Carrots
- 1/2 Cup Chopped Cucumber
- 1/2 Cup Chopped Radish
- 1/2 Cup Chopped Cilantro
- 1 Cup Cooked Quinoa
- 1/2 Cup Crispy Wonton Strips
- 1/2 Cup Soy Sauce (Marinade)
- 1/2 Cup Rice Wine Vinegar (Marinade)
- 1/4 Cup Sesame Oil
- 2 Tbsp Chili Garlic Paste or Sriracha
- 2 Tbsp Honey

Directions:
1. Whisk ingredients for marinade and reserve half.
2. Add 2-3 chicken breasts to the remaining marinade and let it sit for at least 30 mins.
3. While your chicken is marinating, preheat your Char-Griller to high heat, scraping your grates to keep your chicken from sticking! Grill chicken for 10-12 mins per side, until inside temp reaches 165. Let rest 10 mins before slicing.
4. Add chicken to a bed of mixed greens with an assortment of veggies the remaining veggies, and pro-tip: I always have a bag of crispy wonton strips in the pantry, so add those for a delicious crunch! Divide the dressing in half and store with the salad for a quick & easy week day lunch!"

Izzy's Cowboy Grillers

Cooking Time: 20 Min

Ingredients:
- 8 Chicken Breasts
- 1 Block Pepper Jack Cheese
- 1 Lb Bacon
- Jalapeño Slices
- All Purpose Seasoning (Pappys Blue Label Is What I Used)

Directions:
1. Slice a pocket in the middle of each chicken breast and place jalapeño slices and a slice of pepper jack cheese inside. Preheat grill to 325F. Wrap each prepared chicken breast in 2 pieces of bacon. Season using your favorite all purpose rub. Grill direct at 325F to an internal temp of 165F. Remove, serve and enjoy!

Turkey-mushroom Burger

Cooking Time: 20 Min

Ingredients:
- 1¼ lb. ground turkey
- 1 large Portobello mushroom cap
- 1 Tbsp. shallot, coarsely chopped
- 3 Tbsp. fresh parsley
- 2 Tbsp. olive oil
- 1 Tsp. Worcestershire sauce
- 8 thin slices white cheddar cheese
- 4 Hamburger buns
- Salt and pepper, to taste
- Avocado slices, for topping
- Condiments of choice

Directions:
1. Pre-heat grill to 375°F. Clean the mushroom cap, remove the gills and cut into 1" pieces. Transfer to a food processor and add the shallot and parsley; pulse until chopped. 2. Combine mushroom mixture, turkey, olive oil, Worcestershire sauce, 1 Tsp. salt, and pepper to taste in a large bowl. Mix by hand until just blended. Divide into 4 balls, and form 1" thick patties. Put on a large

plate, cover and refrigerate until firm, about 30 minutes.
3. Grill the patties for 4- 5 minutes on each side, with a quarter turn halfway through for good sear marks. Top each with 2 slices of cheese during the last 3 minutes of cooking and allow cheese to melt. Toast hamburger buns on the grill until lightly browned. Allow burgers to rest for 5 minutes before serving.
2. Serve the turkey burgers on hamburger buns and top with avocado slices and condiments of choice.

Spicy Honey Glazed Wings

Cooking Time: 25 Min

Ingredients:
- 3 Lbs Chicken Wings
- A.Vogel Spicy Herbed Sea Salt
- Mikes Hot honey

Directions:
1. Preheat grill to 350F. Season wings with spicy herbed sea salt. Grill wings direct to an internal temperature of 190F. Remove from heat and glaze with Mikes hot honey. Serve and enjoy!

Gravity 980 Smoked Chicken Wings

Cooking Time: 2.5 Hrs

Ingredients:
- 2 lb. of fresh, thawed Chicken Wings
- 2 Tbsp of Extra Virgin Olive Oil
- 1/4 Cup of Char-Griller Chicken Rub
- 1 Tsp of Cumin
- 1 Tsp of Cayenne Powder

Directions:
1. If you prefer to rinse your chicken wings, do so in cold water. Pat them completely dry with paper towels. In a resealable bag, combine olive oil, and all seasonings, then add chicken and seal bag. Thoroughly mix chicken and oil mixture within bag until all pieces are coated. Place in the refrigerator and allow to sit for 1 hour through overnight. Remove the fire shutter from the Gravity 980, load and light the hopper then set to 225-250°F. Place chicken wings in the grill in a single layer and smoke for 2 to 2 ½ hours or until the internal temperature reaches 165°F. Allow wings to rest for 10-20 minutes then serve. Enjoy!

Smoked Carolina Turkey

Ingredients:
- 10-12 lb. turkey
- 3 Tbsp. red pepper flakes
- ¼ C. paprika
- ¼ C. ground mustard
- ½ C. brown sugar
- 2 Tbsp. coarse black pepper
- 2 Tbsp. Kosher salt
- 2 Tbsp. melted butter

Directions:
1. Pour melted butter over turkey, or use marinade injector to inject butter into turkey
2. Mix red pepper flakes, paprika, ground mustard, brown sugar, black pepper and salt in small bowl to create seasoning mix
3. Rub turkey all over with seasoning mix
4. Place turkey on grill over indirect heat at 250°F or use Smokin' Stone
5. Inject turkey with its own juices every other hour
6. Cook time is 1 hour per pound or until turkey reaches internal temp of 165°F

Smoked Turkey Breast

Ingredients:
- 1 Turkey Breast (Thawed)
- 10-12 Cups of cold water
- 1/2 Cup of Kosher Salt
- 1/4 Cup of Brown Sugar
- 1/4 Cup of Extra Virgin Olive Oil
- 1 Tbsp of Chili Powder
- 1 Tbsp of Paprika
- 1 Tbsp of Garlic Powder
- 1 Tbsp of Ground Black pepper
- 1/2 Tbsp of Seasoning Salt

Directions:
1. Mix all the brine ingredients (2-4) in a large container. Submerge the turkey breast and allow it to marinate for 8 hours up to overnight. Remove from the

brine and pat dry with paper towels. You may refrigerate for an extra 2 hours to allow skin to completely dry. Preheat your smoker to 225°F. Coat the exterior of your turkey with the olive oil before massaging in the rest of the seasonings and spices ingredients (5-10). Add the turkey to the smoker, breast side up. Smoke until the internal temp reaches about 150°F. This should take about 2 hours. Increase the temperature to about 500-550°F for about 5 minutes to allow skin to crisp up until the internal temperature reaches 165°F. Allow the turkey to rest for 20-30 minutes before carving. Enjoy!

Barbecued Turkey

Cooking Time: 4 Hrs

Ingredients:
- 13 lb. turkey, cut into pieces
- 1/2 C. Chicken BBQ rub
- BBQ sauce for brushing

Directions:
1. Season both sides of turkey pieces generously with Chicken BBQ rub, or your favorite rub.
2. Smoke turkey pieces on the grill on direct heat at 225°F for 3 hours and then raise the temperature to 350°F for another hour to finish it off.
3. Brush one side of turkey pieces with BBQ sauce at the 30-minute mark.
4. Flip and brush the other side after 15 minutes. Remove turkey pieces when internal temperature reaches 165°F.
5. Note: The turkey's internal temperature will continue to increase by 5-10 degrees after you pull it off the grill.

Grilled Pizza Chicken Wings

Cooking Time: 20 Min

Ingredients:
- 1.5 Lbs Chicken Wings
- 1 Cup Marinara Sauce
- 2 Tsp Garlic Powder
- 1 Tsp Chili Flake
- 1 Tsp Dried Oregano
- 1 Tsp Salt & Pepper
- 1/3 Cup Grated Pecorino
- 2 T Fresh Parsley (Chopped)
- 2 T Olive Oil
- 1/3 cup Pepperoni, (Crispy)

Directions:
1. Preheat Grill to Medium heat, we want to keep heat moderately low so we give the wings a chance to crisp slowly without burning.
2. Toss wings in salt, pepper, and olive oil, transfer to grill and cook over medium-low heat for 10 minutes per side, moving around 1-2 times per side, allowing char marks to form.
3. After you've flipped the wings and they've finished cooking, toss in a large bowl with fresh parsley, grated cheese, and remaining spices.
4. Sprinkle rubbed wings with crispy pepperoni and serve with warm marinara for dunking. Enjoy!

Beer Soda Can Chicken

Cooking Time: 1.5 Hrs

Ingredients:
- Olive Oil
- Chicken BBQ rub
- Favorite beer/soda

Directions:
1. 4.5 lb whole chicken
2. Cover chicken in olive oil
3. Season the whole chicken on both sides with Chicken BBQ rub, or your favorite poultry rub
4. Open your favorite beer/soda can
5. Place inside the beer can chicken rack
6. Place chicken over the can on the rack
7. Pre-heat grill to 350°F
8. Add Smokin' Stone
9. Place drip pan on Smokin' Stone and add more beer/soda and lemons
10. Cook for about an hour and a half 11. Remove when internal temp reaches 165°F

Picnic "fried" Chicken

Cooking Time: 35 Min

Ingredients:
- 6 bone-in chicken thighs
- 3 Tbsp. Chicken BBQ rub
- 2 C. dried bread crumbs
- 2 eggs, beaten
- ½ C. buttermilk

Directions:
1. Rinse chicken thighs and pat dry with paper towel.
2. Prepare breading by mixing Chicken BBQ rub with bread crumbs in gallon sized storage bag.
3. Whisk eggs with buttermilk in large bowl until smooth. Dip chicken thighs in egg/buttermilk mixture and evenly coat all sides.
4. Place chicken thighs in bag with breading mixture, seal bag and shake gently to even coat thighs on all sides.
5. Place breaded chicken thighs on a cast iron griddle in the middle of the grill at 375°F for 35 minutes. Chicken thighs are done when internal temperature reaches 165°F.

Chicken Lollipops By Jeremy Souza

Ingredients:
- Chicken Drumsticks
- Favorite Seasoning
- Favorite Sauce or Glaze
- Charcoal
- Smoking Wood Chunks

Directions:
1. Transform the drumsticks into lollipops Using a sharp knife and kitchen shears cut around the chicken ankle to create the handle Remove the skin, meat, tendons, and cartilage to expose the bone. This will be your "lollipop stick" Remove any loose tendons with the kitchen shears To ensure that the chicken legs will stand up straight, flatten the bottoms with a sharp cleaver Cover the chicken leg handles with foil to protect from burning and discoloration Season the chicken liberally with your favorite seasoning. We decided to go with a habanero seasoning to pair with a sweet apricot glaze to come later Preheat your grill or smoker and set it up for 2 Zone Cooking (Direct and Add any smoking chunks or chips at this point if you wish Place the chicken on your grill away from the direct heat and allow to cook and smoke until an internal temperature of 165*F is reached At this point it's time to sauce! Use your favorite sauce and coat each drumstick Return to the smoker and cook for an additional 10 minutes Remove from the smoker and glaze one last time until they're nice and saucy Remove the foil, plate them nicely on a platter and enjoy. These are sure to impress!

Creole Smokin' Fried Wings

Cooking Time: 1 Hrs

Ingredients:
- 16-20 chicken wings
- 1/2 Tbsp Creole seasoning
- 1/2 Tbsp adobo seasoning
- 1 Tbsp sazón seasoning
- 12 oz. buffalo sauce
- Olive Oil
- All-vegetable shortening

Directions:
1. Coat wings in even layer with olive oil in a large bowl or plastic bag
2. Season with Creole, Adobo & Sazón
3. Place wings in fridge for at least on hour to allow the seasoning to absorb into the wings.
4. Heat grill to 340°F
5. Place wings in grill and smoke with apple wood chunks or your favorite
6. Smoke for 30 mins or until the wings reach internal temp of 140°F
7. Remove wing and place in pan. Set aside pan.
8. Add charcoal to grill and get extremely hot for frying the wings in the cast iron skillet
9. Add all-vegetable shortening to cast iron skillet and then place on grill allowing to heat up
10. Place small batch of wings into skillet and fry for 2-3 minutes or until crispy
11. Remove from skillet and place on baking rack in pan
12. Warm your favorite buffalo sauce
13. Toss wings in warmed buffalo sauce
14. Serve with ranch or blue cheese, carrots, and celery.

SEAFOOD

Honey-bourbon Glazed Salmon

Cooking Time: 45-60 Min

Ingredients:
- 1 Cedar Plank
- 1 Wild Salmon Filet
- 1 Lemon, sliced
- Lemon pepper seasoning (to taste)
- ½ C. Bourbon
- Water (enough to cover the cedar plank)
- 3 Tbsp. Honey
- 1 oz. Bourbon
- 1 Tsp. Lemon Zest

Directions:

1. Remove the pin bones from the salmon filet with fish bone tweezers. Pour water and bourbon into a large baking dish and soak cedar plank for a minimum of 1 hour.
2. Place salmon filet on cedar plank, sprinkle with lemon pepper seasoning, to taste, and cover with sliced lemons.
3. Prepare the grill for offset smoking by adding citrus wood chunks to the Side Fire Box. Place the salmon on the grill and smoke at 250° - 275°F for approximately 45 - 60 minutes.
4. Mix the honey, bourbon and lemon zest together in a bowl to make the glaze. After 30 minutes, intermittently brush the honey/bourbon glaze on the salmon.
5. Enjoy the deliciousness!

Buffalo Lemon Shrimp

Cooking Time: 12 Min

Ingredients:
- Raw Shrimp, Peeled and Deveined - 1 Pound
- Hot Sauce (I Use Buffalo Sauce for this Recipe) - 3 Tablespoons
- Minced Garlic - 1 Tablespoon
- Olive Oil - 2 Tablespoons
- Juiced Lemon - 1
- Lemon Cut Into Wedges for Serving - 1
- Salt to Taste

Directions:

1. Taking advantage of seasonal ingredients is the name of the game, so for the remainder of the summer, chicken wings are going to have to move aside. If you haven't been grilling shrimp this season, now is the time. She loves to use charcoal for this recipe, as shrimp cook quickly and charcoal flame provides so much flavor in such a short amount of time. Let's dig in!
2. Light your charcoal in your chimney and wait until the bricks are glowing red and ashy around the edges. Dump under the grates of your Char-Griller Grill, and close the lid, letting the grates heat for 5-10 minutes.
3. While grill is heating, toss shrimp with buffalo sauce, minced garlic, the juice of one lemon, olive oil, and plenty of salt. Let marinate on the counter for a few minutes.
4. Once the grill is heated, spray the grates with non-stick spray, and lay your shrimp and lemon wedges out to cook. Grill on each side for 2 minutes, until some deep char marks form, and they are curled up and a beautiful vibrant pink color.
5. Serve on a large tray with grilled lemon wedges and an extra sprinkle of salt! These are super delicious on a salad, in a taco, or as the main dish at your next barbecue! Happy Grilling.

Bacon Wrapped Seafood Stuffed Shrimp

Cooking Time: 20 Min

Ingredients:
- 2 lbs. jumbo shrimp, deveined and butterflied
- 1 lb. Applewood smoked bacon strips, cut in half
- 1lb. lobster tail meat and/or lump crab meat, cooked and chopped
- 2 Tbsp. butter, melted
- 1 medium yellow pepper, chopped
- 1 small green pepper, chopped
- 1 medium sweet onion, chopped
- 2 Tbsp. fresh garlic, minced

- ¼ C. mayonnaise
- 1 Tbsp. horseradish mustard
- 1 egg, beaten
- 2 Tbsp. seafood all-purpose sauce
- 1 Tsp. seasoned salt
- 1 Tsp. white pepper
- 1 Tsp. garlic powder
- 1 Tsp. onion powder
- 2 Tsp. Chipotle chili powder
- 1 C. cheese crackers, crushed

Directions:
1. Melt butter in a large cast iron skillet and sauté onion, peppers and garlic until tender, 5-7 minutes.
2. Allow to cool and then gradually fold in the remaining ingredients, except shrimp, to seafood mixture from Step 1.
3. Mound 1-2 Tbsp. of stuffing mixture onto shrimp, wrap with ½ strip of bacon and secure with toothpick.
4. Place bacon wrapped shrimp on a metal tray onto the indirect side of the grill at 375°F for 20 minutes.

Gravity 980 Grilled Lobster Tails

Cooking Time: 10 Min

Ingredients:
- 6 Lobster Tails
- 1/3 Cup of Melted Butter
- 1 Tbsp OF Extra Virgin Olive Oil
- 1 Lemon
- 1 Tbsp of Parsley
- 1 Tbsp of Chives
- 1 Tbsp of Minced Garlic
- 1 Tbsp of Char-Griller Creole Rub
- 1/2 Tsp of Salt
- 1/2 Tsp of Pepper

Directions:
1. To prep lobster tails, using kitchen shears, cut the top of the shell lengthwise down the middle. Using a sharp knife, cut through this slit, halfway through the flesh, excluding the very tip of the tail. Flatten each tail so the shell opens around the meat. Place a skewer through each tail to prevent it from curling during cooking. In a bowl, combine butter, parsley, ½ the chives, minced garlic and Creole rub. Line tails on a baking sheet and brush each lightly with oil, salt and pepper. Remove the fire shutter from your Gravity 980, load and light the hopper then set to 350°F. Place the lobster tails, flesh side down on the grill and allow to cook for 5 minutes. Flip each tail over and drizzle the tops generously with garlic butter mixture. Grill for additional 5 minutes or until lobster becomes fully cooked. Sprinkle finished lobster tails with remaining chives and serve with lemon wedges. Enjoy!

Grilled Swordfish With Lemon-caper Sauce

Ingredients:
- 8oz. swordfish steaks
- 4 oz. jar capers, drained
- ½ C. mayonnaise
- ½ C. sour cream
- 1½ fresh lemons, juiced
- ½ Tsp. seasoned salt
- ¾ Tsp. white pepper
- 1 Tsp. dried minced onion
- 5 Tbsp. green onion tops, minced (optional, for garnish)

Directions:
1. Blend all ingredients, except green onion tops.
2. Transfer to bowl, cover with plastic wrap and refrigerate for 1 hour.
3. Swordfish
4. Season swordfish steaks on both sides with seasoned salt, to taste.
5. Place on the grill at 400°F for 10 minutes per side. Swordfish is ready when the internal temperature reaches 140°F.
6. Remove the fish and let it rest for 5-10 minutes before serving.
7. Sauce swordfish steaks with lemon-caper sauce and garnish with green onion tops.

Cedar Plank Smoked Salmon

Cooking Time: 1-1.5 Hrs

Ingredients:
- Salmon fillets
- 1/3 C. olive oil
- 1/3 C. soy sauce
- 1/3 C. maple syrup
- ½ Tsp. cayenne pepper

Directions:
1. Rinse salmon and pat dry with paper towel. 2. Mix all ingredients together and pour evenly over salmon in an airtight container. Reserve some for basting and set aside. 3. Place in refrigerator and allow to marinate for 1 hour, or longer if desired. 4. Pre-heat grill to 275°F. Soak cedar planks in water for 3 minutes before placing on the grill to warm for 5-10 minutes. 5. Place salmon on cedar planks and smoke until the internal temperature of the fish reaches 145°F, basting with reserved marinade every 30 minutes.
2. Remove from grill and serve. Enjoy!

Grilled Salmon

Cooking Time: 20 Min

Ingredients:
- 4 Salmon Fillets
- 1/4 Cup of Olive Oil
- 2 Tbsp of Char-Griller Creole Seasoning
- 1/2 Tbsp of Garlic Powder
- 1 Tsp of Dried Parsley
- Kosher Salt
- Ground Black Pepper
- 4 Lemon Wedges

Directions:
1. Generously coat the salmon with olive oil and all seasonings. Heat your grill to medium-high heat. Add salmon fillets, flesh side down, cooking for 6-8 minutes with the grill closed. Once the meat is firm enough, flip it over, closing the lid, cooking for an additional 3-8 minutes depending on desired doneness. Remove from heat and allow the fillets to rest for 5 minutes before removing the skin and serving with lemon wedges along with any desired condiments and toppings.

Grilled Tilapia

Cooking Time: 15-20 Min

Ingredients:
- 3 whole Tilapia
- 2 oz. smoked paprika
- 2 oz. Old Bay seasoning
- Salt and pepper, to taste
- Chopped parsley
- Olive oil
- 4 garlic cloves thinly sliced

Directions:
1. Set up grill for indirect heat and preheat to 350°F.
2. While grill is heating, stuff the inside of each fish with chopped parsley and garlic, then season inside and out with smoked paprika and Old Bay seasoning. Drizzle with olive oil and top with more parsley, smoked paprika/seasoning mix and remaining garlic.
3. Place fish on the grill oiled side down and drizzle with more oil and season with remaining parsley, smoked paprika/seasoning mix. Allow fish to cook for 7-10 minutes on each side.
4. Enjoy!

Grilled Lobster Tails

Cooking Time: 10 Min

Ingredients:
- 8oz. lobster tails
- 2 sticks salted butter
- 1 Tbsp. garlic

Directions:
1. Butterfly the lobster. To do this, use a sharp knife or kitchen shears to split the lobster shell all the way to the tail. Slice the meat in half along the cut line on the shell, being careful not to slice through the lobster. Open the lobster shell-side down and lay it flat. 2. To make clarified butter, melt butter in a pan. Bring to a boil and reduce to a simmer. Skim the foam from the surface. Strain the butter to further remove residue, if desired. Add garlic and stir to combine. Pour into a small bowl

and set aside to keep warm. 3. Brush lobster tails with clarified garlic butter and place on the grill, shell-side up, at 400°F for 3-4 minutes. Flip and grill for another 5-6 minutes. Lobster is done when internal temperature reaches 135°F.

Salmon Burger

Cooking Time: 10 Min

Ingredients:

- 10 oz. ground salmon
- 1½ Tbsp. mayonnaise
- 1 Tbsp. Dijon mustard
- 1 Tbsp. horseradish
- 3 scallions, thinly sliced
- ⅛ oz. chives or tarragon, finely chopped
- Juice of 1 lemon
- ¼ C. panko breadcrumbs
- 1 Tbsp. capers, roughly chopped, optional
- Brioche or hamburger buns
- Olive oil
- Salt and pepper, to taste

Directions:

1. Pre-heat grill to 400°F. In a medium bowl, combine salmon, mustard, horseradish, bread crumbs, capers, if using, and scallions. Season with ½ Tsp. salt and pepper, to taste. Mix ingredients by hand until well blended. 2. Form 2 equal patties, about 1" thick. Transfer to a plate and chill in refrigerator until firm, 5-10 minutes. 3. While burgers chill, whisk together mayonnaise, chives (or tarragon, if substituting), lemon juice, salt and pepper to taste in a small bowl to make aioli. Cover with plastic wrap and refrigerate until ready to serve. 4. Grill salmon burgers for 4-5 minutes on each side, until cooked through and opaque. 5. Place buns cut-side down on grill and toast until lightly browned, 2-3 minutes.
2. To serve spread aioli on salmon burgers and top with condiments of choice. Enjoy!

Creole Blackened Salmon

Cooking Time: 10 Min

Ingredients:

- 1 Salmon Filet
- Avocado Oil
- Char-Griller Creole Seasoning

Directions:

1. Preheat grill to 400F
2. Slice salmon filet into approx 3" portions.
3. Lightly coat portions in avocado oil and season using Creole seasoning.
4. Place salmon on grill (I like to use copper grill mats for fish) grill approx 5-6 minutes, flip salmon and grill another 3-4 minutes.
5. Remove and enjoy!!

Lemon Pepper Shrimp

Cooking Time: 7 Min

Ingredients:

- 1.5 lbs Peel-n-Eat Shrimp
- 1 Tbsp Avocado Oil
- 1/2 Stick Butter, Melted
- 1/2 Tbsp Black Pepper
- 1 Tbsp Lemon Zest
- 1 Tbsp Minced Garlic
- 1 Tbsp Parsley, Chopped
- 1/2 Tbsp Salt

Directions:

1. Fill your chimney with charcoal, and light over side burner flame until coals are lit. Allow them to burn for 20-30 minutes, then release into grill and close lid, allowing grates to heat to high temp.
2. Toss shrimp in avocado oil, and scatter on grill. Close the lid and let shrimp cook 3-5 minutes, until pink and charred. Remove from heat
3. Mix butter with pepper, lemon juice & zest, garlic, salt, and parsley. Toss the hot grilled shrimp in sauce, and serve immediately with tons of napkins! Enjoy!

Rosemary Shrimp Skewers

Cooking Time: 5 Min

Ingredients:

- Shrimp Seasoned with Salt, Pepper, and Jerk Seasoning - 1 Pound

- Fresh Rosemary - Use full stalk and remove half of leaves to expose the stalk, this becomes your skewer

Directions:
1. Skewer two shrimp per skewer
2. Cook on grill at 350 degrees, 5 minutes per side till cooked thoroughly

Grilled Coconut Lime Foil Packets

Cooking Time: 12 To 15 Min

Ingredients:
- 1 Small, Yellow Onion - Chopped
- 3 Garlic Cloves
- Shredded Sweetened Coconut - 1 Cup
- Zest and Juice from 1 Lime
- Fresh Cilantro - 1 Cup
- Extra Virgin Olive Oil - 1/4 Cup
- Soy Sauce - 1/4 Cup
- Raw Shrimp, Peeled and Deveined - 1 Pound
- Corn Kernels - 2 Cups
- 1 Zucchini - Sliced into 1/4 inch rounds and halved
- Halved Cherry Tomatoes - 1 Cup
- Salt and Pepper to Taste
- Fajita Seasoning - 1 tsp

Directions:
1. Using a blender, combine onion, garlic, coconut, lime zest, lime juice, cilantro, olive oil, and soy sauce. Blend until smooth.
2. Place marinade and shrimp in a bowl and toss to coat.
3. Set aside for 5 minutes.
4. Preheat grill to medium high heat.
5. Tear off four large squares of foil.
6. Spray one side of foil with cooking spray.
7. Divide vegetables and shrimp evenly among each packet.
8. Season with salt, pepper and fajita seasoning.
9. Foil up packets and seal completely.
10. Put packets on grill, close the lid, and grill for 6 minutes. Turn packets over and grill for 7 minutes.
11. Open packets and stir.
12. Sprinkle with fresh cilantro and serve.

Shrimp Tacos

Cooking Time: 20 Min

Ingredients:
- 2 Lbs of Shrimp (Tail off, Peeled, and Deveined Shrimp)
- Jalapeno-Lime Seasoning
- Tequila Lime Marinade
- 1 Head Green Cabbage
- 3-4 Jalapenos
- 1 Bundle Cilantro
- White Onion
- Green Onion
- Lime (Zest and Juice)
- Coleslaw Dressing
- 2 Tbsp Sriracha Hot Sauce
- 16 Oz Sour Cream
- Corn Tortillas

Directions:
1. Prep shrimp by removing shell, tail, and devein if this is not already done
2. Season and marinate with Jalapeno-Lime Seasoning and Tequila-Lime Marinade Shred green cabbage and add to large mixing bowl
3. Remove seeds and Julianne jalapenos
4. Chop cilantro and green onions and add to the mixing bowl
5. Add zest and juice from 1 lime
6. Season coleslaw with Jalapeno-Lime seasoning
7. Add coleslaw dressing and mix all together
8. Dice white onion and set aside for taco topping
9. In a separate mixing bowl combine sour cream, Sriracha, Tequila-Lime Marinade, and Jalapeno-Lime seasoning
10. Preheat your grill and cast iron skillet
11. Cook shrimp hot and fast in a cast iron skillet
12. Char tortillas directly on the grill
13. Assemble tacos and enjoy!
14. Pitt Tips: Fresh shrimp is always best, but frozen shrimp works perfectly fine also! NEVER microwave your tortillas!

Blackened Catfish

Cooking Time: 15 Min

Ingredients:
- 4-6 Catfish Filets
- 3-4 Tbsp of Blackening Seasoning (Few Of My Favorites, Mis Rubins Fish Magic, Ashman Bayou Blackening, Pappys Lemon Pepper)
- 2 Tbsp Avocado Oil

Directions:
1. Preheat grill to 450F, I like to use a copper grill mat when grilling fish, works very well. Coat filets with oil and season. Place fish on grill mat, grill 6-8 minutes until you get desired blackened look, flip fish and cook another 3-4 minutes. Remove catfish from grill serve over rice and enjoy!

Spicy Caribbean Shrimp

Cooking Time: 6-8 Min

Ingredients:
- 2 lbs. large shrimp, peeled and deveined
- Pineapple cubes
- 2 C. pineapple juice
- ½ C. coconut milk
- ¼ C. dark rum
- 4 habanero peppers, cored and seeded
- 2 Tsp. lime juice
- Your favorite jerk seasoning, to taste

Directions:
1. Pre-heat grill to 400°F. Combine pineapple juice, coconut milk, dark rum, habanero peppers and lime juice in a blender and mix well. Place shrimp and pineapple cubes on to bamboo skewers and add marinade. Marinate in the refrigerator no longer than 30 minutes in a non-reactive pan, i.e. ceramic or glass. The acid from the lime juice and pineapple juice will cook the shrimp (like in a ceviche) if left in longer. Remove shrimp skewers from marinade and season to taste on both sides with jerk seasoning. Discard marinade. Cook 3-4 minutes per side at 400°F, until shrimp is pink and opaque.
2. Remove from grill and serve!

Seared Sesame Ahi Tuna

Cooking Time: 20 Min

Ingredients:
- 2 Ahi Tuna steaks
- 2 Tbsp. olive oil
- 1 Tsp. sesame oil
- 3 Tbsp. black sesame seeds
- 3 Tbsp. white sesame seeds
- Salt and pepper, to taste
- Wasabi, for serving
- Lemon wedges, for serving
- Soy sauce, for serving

Directions:
1. Pre-heat grill to 400°F. Rinse tuna steaks and pat dry with paper towel. Place steaks on a clean cutting board and coat with olive oil and 1 Tsp. of sesame oil. Season on both sides with salt and pepper, to taste. 2. Toss black and white sesame seeds together in a large bowl and season with salt and pepper, to taste. Press the tuna steaks into the sesame seeds, covering all sides of the steaks. 3. Place the steaks on the grill to sear for 2 minutes on each side, flipping halfway through. Watch the steaks closely so that the sesame seeds don't burn. Use tongs to lift and sear the edges of the steaks. 4. Remove steaks from the grill and allow to rest for 5-10 minutes. Slice the steaks against the grain into 1" thick strips. The steaks should have a rare, bright-red middle.
2. Serve with wasabi, soy sauce and lemon wedges, if desired.
3. Allergy notice: Recipe contains sesame seeds and sesame oil.

Lobster Roll

Cooking Time: 10 Min

Ingredients:
- 8 oz. lobster tails
- ½ C. mayonnaise
- 3 Tbsp. lemon juice
- 2 celery stalks, finely chopped
- 2 Tbsp. fresh parsley leaves, chopped
- 4 rolls, split and lightly toasted
- Melted butter, for brushing

- Salt and pepper, to taste

Directions:
1. Brush lobster with butter and place on the grill, shell-side up, at 400°F for 3-4 minutes. Flip and grill for another 5-6 minutes. Lobster is done when internal temperature reaches 135°F.
2. While lobster is grilling, stir together mayonnaise, lemon juice, celery, parsley in a large bowl and add salt and pepper, to taste.
3. When lobster has cooled, scoop meat from shells and roughly chop. Fold into mayonnaise mixture from Step
4. Butter both sides of rolls and fill with lobster mixture. Enjoy!

Flavor Pro Cedar Plank Salmon

Cooking Time: 25 Min

Ingredients:
- 2 Cedar Planks
- 2 Salmon Filets
- Olive Oil
- Rosemary
- Salt and Pepper to Taste

Directions:
1. Soak cedar planks in water for at least 8 hours. Set up the Flavor Pro for Indirect cooking Add 30 to 40 charcoal briquettes to one side of the flavor drawer Ignite charcoal with gas burners set to medium high Once charcoal is lit, turn off gas burners and allow to fully ash over Rub salmon on both sides with olive oil. Season with salt and pepper, rosemary sprigs and slices of lemon Place Salmon on the side of the grill away from the charcoal Cook salmon for 15 minutes or until flakey.

Honey Sriracha Lime Salmon

Cooking Time: 25 Min

Ingredients:
- 1 Lb Salmon
- 1 Tsp Kosher Salt
- 1/2 Tsp Coarse Black Pepper
- 1/2 Tsp Garlic Powder
- 1 Tsp Olive Oil
- 1/4 Cup Sriracha
- 1/4 Cup Honey
- 2 Garlic Cloves (Minced)
- 1 Lime

Directions:
1. Coat salmon with a light layer of olive oil on both sides. Lightly season with salt, pepper, and garlic powder.
2. Heat grill to 325 F. Place salmon skin side down indirectly from the heat once the grill has reached the targeted temp.
3. In a heat safe bowl combine sriracha, honey, minced garlic, and lime. Bring the mixture to a boil and reduce heat to let simmer. Once salmon has reached an internal temp between 140F - 142F apply a layer of the sauce mixture to the top of the salmon.
4. Once salmon has reached an internal temp of 145 F pull from grill. Garnish with an extra squeeze of lime and cilantro. Serve and enjoy!

Cedar Plank Salmon

Cooking Time: 20-25 Min

Ingredients:
- Whole Coho Salmon 2 Lbs
- Cedar Plank Boards
- Olive Oil
- Kary's Roux All Purpose Seasoning
- Caribeque Lemon Garlic Seasoning
- Lemons
- Dill
- Parsley
- Asparagus (Optional)
- Garlic Parsley Butter

Directions:
1. Soak the cedar plank boards in water for one hour prior to prepping the salmon. Slice the whole salmon into four fillets, it is fine to leave the skin on. Place the salmon fillets on the cedar plank boards with a few lemon slices and asparagus.Tip: Apply olive oil directly on the cedar plank side you place the salmon to keep it from sticking.
2. Apply even coat of olive oil to the top/sides of the salmon fillets. Apply Caribeque Lemon Garlic

Seasoning and Kary's Roux All Purpose Seasoning: use to taste. Add Garlic Parsley Butter to the top of each salmon: 1tsp per fillet. Add dill, parsley and additional lemons to the salmon fillets. Sprinkle parsley flakes when done to complete the prepping process.
3. Grilling directions: 20-25 minutes, internal temperature 145°
4. Preheat your grill to 400° Add cedar planks with the salmon to the grill directly over the lump Charcoal. No need to rotate, allow the grill, charcoal and cedar plank salmon to roast the salmon. Tip: It's also okay if your temperature drops: check out the recipe video on YouTube full for temperature control tips. Cook to internal temperature 145° and remove the cedar planks from the
5. Grill and it's ready for immediate eating.Tip: take the guesswork out and use the Char-Griller Grills folding probe to easily see what temperature the salon is at. Enjoy!

Fresh Garlic Parsley Butter Salmon

Cooking Time: 30 Min

Ingredients:
- Garlic Parsley Butter
- 2 (6 oz) Salmon Mignons
- Tajin to Taste
- Dry Parsley Flakes to Taste
- Olive Oil

Directions:
1. Make Garlic Parsley Butter
2. Add Tajin seasoning to butter to taste or use favorite seafood seasoning.
3. Add 1 tbsp. of Fresh Garlic Parsley to each salmon mignons patty.
4. Add dry parsley flakes to taste.
5. Preheat your Char-griller Premium Red Kettle 14822 to 350°.
6. Insert the Char-griller Chimney in the middle of the grill in the fire pit area and do not remove it and no need to release the coals.
7. The handle will not melt inside the Premium Kettles. This will give you a hot fire in the middle of the grill for easy cast iron cooking and also raises the charcoal. The middle small grill grate can be easily moved with a Char-griller grate lifter to add charcoal.
8. Add olive oil to your cast iron skillet: just enough to coat the bottom of the skillet and place over the fire to preheat.
9. Then place the salmon on the cast iron skillet.
10. Flip Salomon after 12 minutes and toss the melted fresh garlic parsley on all sides of the salmon using a spoon.
11. Add 2 additional tbsp. to the skillet for extra flavor.
12. Then move the cast iron skillet away from the middle of the grill for a quick offset cook for 15 minutes.Tip: Continuously add the melted fresh garlic parsley on all sides of the salmon using a spoon for extra flavor.
13. Enjoy!

Spicy Crawfish Dip

Cooking Time: 15 Min

Ingredients:
- ½ C. butter
- ½ C. chopped bell pepper
- ½ C. chopped onion (or green onion)
- 1 Tbsp. basil
- 2 cloves minced garlic
- 2 Tsp. Old bay or Cajun seasoning
- Salt and pepper, to taste
- 1 lb. pack frozen, cooked, peeled crawfish tails, thawed and undrained
- 8 oz. cream cheese, softened
- Sriracha, to taste

Directions:
1. Pre-heat grill to 350°F and add Smokin' Stone under the grates. Place a cast iron skillet on top of the grates and heat until very hot.
2. Add butter to skillet and allow to melt. Add bell pepper and onion. Sauté for 2 minutes, stirring occasionally.
3. Add basil, garlic, seasoning and salt and pepper to taste and stir. Add crawfish and stir to combine.

4. Stir in cream cheese until mixture is smooth. Stir in Sriracha sauce, to taste and allow to smoke for 10 minutes with lid closed at 350°F.
5. Remove from grill and serve with crackers or toasted French bread slices. Enjoy!

Shrimp Po' Boy With Garlic Parsley Butter

Cooking Time: 15 Min

Ingredients:
- 4 cloves chopped fresh garlic
- 1/3 C. chopped fresh parsley
- 1 Tsp. Kosher salt
- 1 stick butter
- 20-25 shrimp, peeled and deveined
- ½ Tbsp. Creole/Cajun seasoning
- 2 Tbsp. Sazón seasoning
- 1 lemon, sliced in half
- 1 Tbsp. chopped fresh parsley (can substitute dried)
- 2-4 cloves chopped fresh garlic
- 3 Tbsp. garlic-parsley butter
- Shredded lettuce
- Tomato slices
- Your favorite bread rolls, sliced lengthwise
- Olive oil for drizzling

Directions:
1. Combine 4 cloves chopped garlic, 1/3 C. chopped parsley, Kosher salt and butter in a medium bowl and mix thoroughly by hand with gloves to make garlic parsley butter.
2. Place bowl in refrigerator to chill and use when needed.
3. Shrimp Po' Boy
4. In a large bowl, season shrimp with Creole/Cajun and Sazón seasonings, or use Original All-Purpose BBQ rub, to taste, and mix well. Add in juice from half lemon, remaining chopped garlic and lightly drizzle with olive oil.
5. Place shrimp in refrigerator for 30 minutes to allow the seasonings to absorb. After 30 minutes, put shrimp on skewers or place in grill wok.
6. Pre-heat grill to 225° and prepare for offset smoking by placing cherry wood chunks or preferred wood chunks in the Side Fire Box. Smoke shrimp for 9 minutes or until the internal temperature reaches 130°F.
7. Char the shrimps over direct heat for 3 minutes on each side or until the internal temperature reaches 140°F. Toast bread rolls until golden brown. Melt garlic parsley butter and toss with shrimp in a bowl until evenly coated.
8. Add shrimp, lettuce and tomatoes to toasted bread rolls and enjoy!

Grilled Seafood Boil

Cooking Time: 20-25 Min

Ingredients:
- 2 Lb. Of Large Shrimp, Deveined and Peeled, Remove the tails during prep if you prefer
- 2 Andouille Sausages (Thinly Sliced)
- 2 Large Ears Of Corn, Shucked and Each Cut Into 4 Small Cobs
- 1 Lb. of Red Bliss potatoes (Cut Into Small Cubes)
- 1 Lemon (Sliced Into 4 Wedges)
- 4 Tbsp of Butter
- 4 Tsp of Char-Griller "Creole" Rub
- 4 Tsp Of Italian Seasoning
- 4 Tsp Of Minced Garlic
- Extra Virgin Olive Oil
- Salt and Pepper To Taste

Directions:
1. Preheat your grill to medium-high heat. Arrange 4 pieces of aluminum foil, about 1 foot long for each packet. Evenly divide shrimp, sausages, corn, potatoes and lemon amongst each "packet". Drizzle each packet with olive oil, 1 tsp of garlic, salt and pepper, and 1 tsp of Char-Griller's Creole seasoning. Use hands to mix to ensure all elements are coated evenly. Top each off packet with 1 tsp of Italian Seasoning, and 1 Tbsp of butter. Fold each packet, ensuring the entire mixture is covered and twist the edges seal it closed. Place the foil packets directly on the grill and cook for 20-25 minutes or until they are cooked to your liking. Serve warm, enjoy!

Steamed Mussels With Pancetta

Cooking Time: 30 Min

Ingredients:
- 2 lbs. fresh mussels, scrubbed and de-bearded
- 4 oz. pancetta, diced
- 3/4 C. dry white wine
- 2 Tbsp. olive oil
- 1/2 onion, diced
- 4 cloves garlic, peeled and minced
- 1 1/4 C. fish stock
- 2 Tbsp. lemon juice
- 2 Tbsp. chives, minced
- 8-10 grape tomatoes, sliced lengthwise
- Pinch of crushed red pepper flakes
- Salt and pepper to taste
- French bread, sliced and toasted for serving

Directions:
1. Add pancetta from Step 1 and mussels to pan and allow to steam with lid closed, until mussels have opened, about 5-10 minutes.
2. Open grill lid and stir in dry white wine, fish stock, lemon juice, chives, sliced tomatoes and crushed red pepper flakes, if desired, and season with salt and pepper, to taste. Simmer for 3-5 minutes until almost all of the liquid is evaporated.
3. Remove pan from the heat and discard any shells that do not open. Serve with toasted French bread. Enjoy!

Shrimp 'n Grits

Cooking Time: 20-25 Min

Ingredients:
- 1 lb. shrimp, peeled and deveined
- Original All-Purpose BBQ rub, to taste, or preferred rub
- ½ red bell pepper, chopped
- ½ onion, chopped
- Handful of cilantro, chopped
- 4 C. water
- 1 Tsp. salt
- 1 C. stone-ground grits
- 2-3 Tbsp. butter
- 4 oz. heavy cream
- 2 oz. Parmesan cheese
- Salt and pepper, to taste

Directions:
1. Pre-heat grill to 375°F. Bring water to a boil, add grits and cook until water is absorbed, about 20-25 minutes. Remove from heat, stir in butter, cheese and heavy cream. Add salt and pepper, to taste and stir. Set aside. 2. While grits are cooking, melt butter in skillet and sauté red pepper and onions until soft, about 5-7 minutes, stirring occasionally. 3. Add shrimp and season with Original All-Purpose BBQ Rub and cook for 3-5 minutes, until opaque and fully cooked. Add cilantro and salt and pepper, to taste and stir to combine.
2. To serve, spoon grits into bowls and top with shrimp and red pepper mixture. Garnish with more cilantro and enjoy!

Fish Tacos

Cooking Time: 10 Min

Ingredients:
- 1 lb. mahi mahi fillets
- 2 Tbsp. fresh cilantro, finely chopped
- 1 garlic clove, finely chopped
- 2 Tbsp. olive oil
- ¼ head cabbage, thinly sliced
- 2 avocados, peeled, pitted, thinly sliced
- 8 corn tortillas
- 1/3 C. sour cream, for serving
- 1/3 C. fresh cilantro leaves, chopped, for garnish
- Lime wedges, for serving
- Pico de Gallo, for serving
- Salt and pepper, to taste

Directions:
1. Rinse fish and pat dry with paper towel. Place on a platter and season with chopped cilantro, garlic, olive oil and salt and pepper, to taste.
2. Marinate for 30 minutes, or cover and refrigerate to marinate for up to 6 hours.
3. Pre-heat grill to 400°F. Grill fish for 3 minutes per side, until cooked through and opaque. Turn halfway through for good sear marks. Fish is done when internal

temperature reaches 135°F. Remove from grill and allow to rest for 2 minutes.
4. Warm tortillas on the grill until heated through. Remove tortillas from heat and cover to keep warm.
5. Slice the fish into 1" thick strips and divide among tortillas. Top with cabbage, avocado slices, Pico de Gallo, and sour cream. Garnish with cilantro and serve with lime wedges.

Lobster Mac 'n Cheese

Cooking Time: 30-35 Min

Ingredients:
- 8oz. lobster tails
- 1 lb. Cavatappi or elbow macaroni
- 1 qt. milk
- 1 stick unsalted butter, divided
- ½ C. all-purpose flour
- 12 oz. Gruyere cheese, grated
- 8 oz. extra-sharp Cheddar, grated
- 1½ C. breadcrumbs
- ½ Tsp. black pepper
- ½ Tsp. nutmeg
- Kosher salt, to taste

Directions:
1. Butterfly the lobster. To do this, use a sharp knife or kitchen shears to split the lobster shell all the way to the tail. Slice the meat in half along the cut line on the shell, being careful not to slice through the lobster. Open the lobster shell-side down, lay it flat and brush with butter.
2. Place lobster on the grill, meat side down at 375°F for 4-5 minutes. Flip and grill for another 6-7 minutes. 3. While lobster is grilling, make the Mac 'n cheese. Lobster is done when internal temperature reaches 135°F.
4. Remove lobster from grill and allow to cool. Scoop meat from shells and roughly chop.
2. Mac 'n cheese
3. Pour oil into a large pot of boiling salted water. Add pasta and cook according to package directions, 6-8 minutes. Drain well. 2. Meanwhile, heat the milk in a small saucepan until hot, being careful not to boil it. Whisk together 6 Tbsp. butter and flour in a large pot. Add hot milk and cook for 1-2 minutes, until thickened and smooth. Remove from heat and add cheese, 1 Tbsp. salt, pepper, and nutmeg. Add cooked macaroni and lobster and stir well. Spoon mixture into cast iron pan. 4. Melt the remaining butter, stir in breadcrumbs and sprinkle on top. Place pan on the grill at 375°F and bake for 30- 35 minutes, or until the sauce is bubbly and the macaroni is lightly browned on top.

2-burner Flat Iron Easy Shrimp Tacos

Cooking Time: 10 Min

Ingredients:
- 1 Lb. of medium-sized shrimp, deveined and peeled with tails removed
- 6-8 Flour or Corn Tortillas
- 1 Tbsp of Extra Virgin Olive Oil
- 1 Tbsp of Char-Griller Chili Lime or Taco & Fajita Rub
- 1/2 Tbsp of Garlic Powder
- 1/2 Tbsp of Onion Powder
- 1/2 Tbsp of Pepper
- A Dash of Salt
- Optional Toppings: Iceberg Lettuce, Sour Cream, Tomatoes, Cilantro, Salsa, Avocado

Directions:
1. Make these simple shrimp tacos as complex or as stuffed as you'd like. Our Rubs will take this dish to the next level, preparing it perfectly for whatever your taste buds have in mind.
2. Prep shrimp, by drying as much as possible with paper towels. In a bowl, combine shrimp with olive oil and all seasonings. With Flat Iron preheated to medium-high heat, add shrimp to cooktop and cook while occasionally stirring for about 5-6 minutes or until shrimp are no longer pink. Remove from Flat Iron. Add tortillas to the cooktop and warm up, cooking for 2-3 minutes per side. Assemble the tacos with desired toppings and serve immediately. Enjoy!

Seared Scallops With Pancetta

Cooking Time: 15 Min

Ingredients:
- 12 U-10 Scallops
- 4 oz. pancetta, chopped
- ½ red onion or 1 shallot, minced
- 2 C. green peas, drained and divided
- 4 oz. Parmesan cheese
- 1 Tbsp. olive oil
- Juice of 1 lemon
- 4 oz. mint, divided
- Salt and pepper, to taste

Directions:
1. Pre-heat grill to 375°F. Fry pancetta in a cast iron pan for about 5 minutes and drain grease. Add minced red onion (or shallot, if substituting) and 1 C. peas to pan and season with salt and pepper, then add ½ of mint and stir to incorporate. Cook until warmed through. 2. Combine 1 C. peas and lemon juice, remaining mint, olive oil and Parmesan cheese in a food processor. Season to taste with salt and pepper and blend until smooth. 3. Rinse scallops and pat dry with paper towel. Season scallops with salt and pepper to taste on all sides. Place on the grill and sear for 3-5 minutes per side.
2. To serve, spoon peas onto plate, add scallops and top with pancetta mixture. Enjoy!

Oysters "dougie-feller"

Cooking Time: 15 Min

Ingredients:
- 10-12 Large Oysters
- 2 oz. pancetta
- 2-3 Tbsp. shallot, chopped
- 2 Tbsp. unsalted butter
- 4 cloves minced garlic
- 3 Tbsp. hot pepper sauce
- 2 oz. panko crumbs
- Juice of ½ lemon
- 2 C. spinach, chopped
- Bed of rock salt

Directions:
1. Shuck oysters
2. Melt 2 Tbsp. unsalted butter in cast iron skillet
3. Sauté pancetta in skillet until crispy (5-7 minutes)
4. Add chopped shallot, and cook until fragrant, about 1 minute
5. Add 4 cloves minced garlic, cook until fragrant, about 1 minute
6. Add 3 Tbsp. hot pepper sauce, stir to incorporate
7. Mix in chopped spinach
8. Sauté until spinach begins to wilt
9. Add 2 oz of panko crumbs
10. Season with salt and pepper to taste
11. Stir in lemon juice
12. Remove from heat and set aside
13. Place 10-12 large oysters on grill at 350°F, shell side up, cooking for 5-7 minutes
14. Remove from grill and lay oysters on a bed of rock salt
15. Top oysters with pancetta and spinach mixture

Fish And Chips

Cooking Time: 12 Min

Ingredients:
- 4 cod filets
- 3-4 Idaho potatoes
- 1 C. flour
- 1 C. milk
- 1 egg
- 1 Tsp. Old Bay seasoning

Directions:
1. Heat grill to 350-400°F.
2. Let oil heat up in skillet until it sizzles when splashed with a few drops of water.
3. 3-4 Idaho potatoes with skin on, cut into french fries.
4. Let them soak in water for 20-30 minutes to remove excess starch.
5. Pat dry on paper towels before frying.
6. Fries are done when they begin to turn golden
7. Mix batter until only a few clumps of flour remain. Don't over mix.
8. Dredge fish in flour seasoned in Old Bay, if you prefer, before dipping in batter
9. Let fish filets fry on each side for 2-3 minutes, until golden crispy brown.
10. Serve with coleslaw and tartar sauce. Delicious!

Grilled Chilean Sea Bass

Cooking Time: 30 Min

Ingredients:
- Whole Chilean Sea bass
- 2 oz. parsley, chopped
- 1½ oz. Original All-Purpose BBQ Rub or your favorite seafood seasoning
- 2 lemons, sliced
- 2-3 sprigs of dill
- Salt and pepper, to taste
- 4 oz. olive oil

Directions:

1. Pre-heat grill to 350°F. Place the charcoal on one side for indirect heat.
2. Score fish diagonally on each side in the thickest part of the meat.
3. Stuff the inside cavity with dill sprigs and lemon slices.
4. Season both sides of the outside of the fish to taste with olive oil, salt and pepper and top with an even layer of Original All-Purpose BBQ Rub, or use your favorite seafood seasoning, and parsley.
5. Lay the fish on the grill for 5-7 minutes on direct heat, then move to the indirect heat side for 15-20 minutes.

BEEF

Biscuits, Briskets, And Gravy

Cooking Time: 30 Min

Ingredients:
- 1 Cup Chopped Brisket
- 1 Package Of Biscuits (6-8 Count)
- 3 1/2 Tbsp Unsalted Butter
- 3 Tbsp All-Purpose Flour
- 2 Cups Whole Milk
- 1 Tsp Kosher Salt
- 1 Tsp Coarse Black Pepper

Directions:

1. Preheat grill to 325 F. Place biscuits on a wire rack and cook indirectly from heat source.

2. Place a medium size pan over the heat source and add butter, stirring until melted. Add flour and stir until it is well mixed with the melted butter. Add the milk and continue to stir until the mixture is well blended and starting to bubble.

3. Once the gravy has a thick consistency add the brisket, salt, and pepper. Stir until well blended and bubbling.

4. Remove the gravy from the heat and pour onto the biscuits. Serve and enjoy!

Certified Grilled Chicago Style Hot Dogs

Cooking Time: 10 Min

Ingredients:
- Vienna Beef Franks or Jumbo Beef Franks
- Poppy Seed Buns
- Beef Frank
- Yellow Mustard
- Chicago Style Relish
- White Onions (Chopped)
- Tomatoes (Moon Sliced)
- Sport Peppers
- Pickles
- Celery Salt
- Akorn Kamado Charcoal Grill
- Fogo Premium & Eucalyptus Lump Charcoal

Directions:

1. Preheat AKORN Kamado & Smoke at temperature 350°: used Fogo Premium Lump Charcoal & Eucalyptus Lump Charcoal. Place Beef Franks in the AKORN Kamado, roll them a few times and grill until internal temperature 140° is met, roughly takes 10 minutes Place the poppy seed buns on the warming rack and warm for 3 minutes. • Remove the beef franks and poppy seed buns from the grill. Build your Certified Grilled Chicago Hot Dog by adding the beef frank to the poppy seed bun, add mustard, add Chicago Style Relish, add chopped onions, add moon shaped tomatoes, add the sport peppers, add a pickle and sprinkle with celery salt Enjoy!

Ultimate Stack Burger

Cooking Time: 16 Min

Ingredients:
- 2 lbs. ground beef
- ¼ lb. bacon
- 4 slices Extra Sharp Cheddar
- 4 slices Swiss cheese
- 1 red onion, sliced
- 1 tomato, sliced
- 4 lettuce leaves
- 1-2 Tsp. Worcestershire sauce
- 1-2 Tbsp. Steak BBQ rub
- Hamburger dill pickle slices, optional
- 4 hamburger buns
- Condiments of choice

Directions:

1. Place ground beef in large bowl and season with Steak BBQ rub, or your favorite rub and Worcestershire sauce. Mix all ingredients by hand until just blended. 2. Form 1" thick patties and place on a wax paper lined tray. Place tray with patties in refrigerator and allow to chill for 10-15 minutes. 3. Fry bacon in batches, if needed, in a pan to desired crispness according to package directions, drain grease and set aside. 4. Place burgers from tray directly on the grill at 400°F for 8 minutes per side, with a quarter turn halfway

through for good sear marks. 5. Flip burgers after 8 minutes, add bacon and top with cheese. 6. Allow cheese to melt. Burgers are done when internal temperature reaches 165°F. 7. Let burgers rest for 3-5 minutes before building the burger.

Smash Burgers

Cooking Time: 15 Min

Ingredients:
- 1 lb Ground Beef
- White Onion
- American Cheese
- Sesame Buns
- Burger Sauce: Mayo, Ketchup, Mustard, Dill Relish

Directions:
1. Make small meatballs roughly ¼ pound each
2. Finely slice your onions
3. Fire up the Char-Griller Flat Iron Griddle
4. While the grill heats, prep the burger sauce
5. In a bowl add 3 tbsp each of mayo, mustard, ketchup, and dill relish
6. Oil the griddle and add your meat balls and top with a generous handful of onions
7. Smash the patties until flat and allow a crust to develop
8. Flip and season each patty with salt and pepper
9. Top with American cheese and allow to melt
10. Toast your buns and begin assembling
11. Build your burgers as tall as you like and enjoy!
12. Pitt Tips: We recommend at least a double for best experience! Don't be shy with the burger sauce!

Bbq Fiends Beef Fajitas

Cooking Time: 8 Min

Ingredients:
- 1 Lb Skirt Steak
- 1 Tbsp Char-Griller Steak Seasoning
- 1/2 Cup Orange Juice (Marinade)
- 1/4 Cup White Onion (Marinade)
- 1 Jalapeno, Seeds Removed (Marinade)
- 1 Habanero, Seeds Removed (Marinade)
- 4 Garlic Cloves (Marinade)
- 1 Tbsp Olive Oil
- 1 Lime, Juiced (Marinade)
- Pinch of Salt & Pepper (Marinade)

Directions:
1. Combine all marinade ingredients in a blender and lightly pulse
2. Place skirt steak in a Ziploc bag with the marinade. Make sure the marinade is covering all sides of the fajitas. *Tip* leave the fajitas refrigerated in the marinade for 1-2 hours for increased flavor.
3. Remove the fajitas from the marinade and lightly season with Char-Griller steak seasoning on both sides. Get the grill up to 375 F and place the fajitas over the direct heat. Grill for 3-4 minutes on each side for medium rare.
4. Pull the fajitas and let rest for 5 minutes. Slice against the grain and serve with tortillas. Enjoy!

Bacon Garlic Burger With Chipotle Mayonnaise

Cooking Time: 40 Min

Ingredients:
- 2 lbs. ground beef sirloin
- 2 oz. bacon
- 1 Tsp. garlic powder
- 1 Tsp. Chipotle chili powder
- ½ C. mayonnaise
- 2 eggs, beaten
- ¼ C. crushed garlic
- ½ Tsp. ground white pepper
- 1 large sweet onion, chopped
- ½ Tsp. black pepper
- ½ Tsp. salt
- 1½ C. all-purpose beef sauce, or preferred (reserve ½ C.)
- Hamburger buns
- Condiments of choice

Directions:
1. Combine the mayonnaise, white pepper, garlic powder, Chipotle chili powder and ½ C. of reserved sauce in a small bowl. Mix thoroughly. 2. Cover

with plastic wrap and place it in the refrigerator for 30 minutes to chill.
2. Garlic skillet
3. Place ½ of crushed garlic in a cast iron skillet with bacon to smoke on the grill at 350°F for 30 minutes. 2. Add chopped onion to garlic and bacon in skillet and mix well. Allow to smoke for another 30 minutes at 350°F. Pull off the grill and set aside when done.
4. Ground beef
5. Place ground beef in large bowl and add eggs, remaining garlic, salt and pepper, and remaining sauce. Mix ingredients by hand until just blended. 2. Form 1" thick patties and place on a wax paper lined tray. Place tray with patties in refrigerator and allow to chill for 10-15 minutes. 3. Place patties on the indirect side of the grill at 350°F for 5 minutes per side, with a quarter turn halfway through for good sear marks. 4. Top burgers with cheese, if desired, during the last few minutes and allow to melt. Add garlic skillet mixture from earlier on top of cheese. Burgers are done when internal temperature reaches 165°F. Let burgers rest for 3-5 minutes before building the burger.
6. To serve, top burgers with bacon strips and the garlic and onion mixture.

Flat Iron Griddle Beef Shank Quesadilla Tacos With Consumé

Cooking Time: 5:10 Hrs

Ingredients:
- 1-2 Pounds of Beef Shank
- Small Bundle Of Cilantro (Chopped or Whole)
- 1 Onion (Diced)
- 3 Garlic Cloves
- 1 Cup Chihuahua Cheese
- Sazón, Adobo & Char Griller Grills Taco Fajita Seasonings (Use Seasonings To Taste.)
- Beef Stock 32 Oz
- 1 Pack Of Corn Tortillas
- 1-2 Limes (Cut Into Quarters)
- Char-Griller Flat Iron Griddle

Directions:
1. Instruction
2. Beef Shank Cooking Directions
3. Seasoned the beef shank meat with Sazón, Adobo & Char Griller Grills Taco Fajita seasonings to taste with ½ onion and three garlic cloves. On stove or Char-Griller Grills side burner on low boil the beef shank in the beef stock for roughly five hours or until it's soft and tender. Shred the beef. Strain the beef juice for the consomé that is used for dipping. Added a bit of water and additional Sazón, Adobo & Char Griller Grills Taco Fajita seasonings and simmered for few minutes. Now it's time to fire up the Flat Iron Griddle for the beef shank quesadilla tacos with consumé.
4. Flat Iron Griddle Beef Shank Quesadilla Tacos with consume Cooking Directions
5. Fire up your Flat Iron Griddle to medium heat. Have the beef shank meat and consume on top of the griddle off to the side. ☒ Add cheese and then the shredded beef shank to the hot griddle top and also the tortillas. Once the cheese melts, add one tortilla on top of the shredded beef and then flip. After flipping it, add another tortilla to the top of the melted cheese and then add a ladle full of the consumé and cook for an additional few minutes. Repeat this process until all your Beef Shank Quesadilla Tacos completed. Added fresh chopped onions, limes and cilantro to the consumé. Dip the Beef Shank Quesadilla Tacos in the consumé and enjoy!

Smoked Brisket

Cooking Time: 10 Hrs

Ingredients:
- 10 ½ lb. beef brisket
- ½ C. paprika
- ¼ C. packed light brown sugar
- 3 Tbsp. salt
- 3 Tbsp. coarse black pepper
- 3 Tbsp. Chili powder
- Apple juice
- Water

Directions:
1. Using a sharp knife, trim the fat from the brisket leaving an even, thin layer on the top. 2. In a medium

bowl, combine paprika, light brown sugar, Chili powder, salt and pepper and mix well to make rub seasoning. Using your hands, or a shaker, generously apply rub all over. 3. Wrap the brisket in plastic wrap and refrigerate for at least 12 hours. 4. When setting up the grill, add wood chips/chunks to charcoal and add Smokin' Stone with an aluminum pan on top. Pour apple juice and water into pan, about halfway full. Place a temperature probe at grate level and heat grill to 220°F. 5. Place brisket on grates, fat side up, and allow to smoke for 5 hours. After 5 hours, wrap brisket in butcher paper and return to grill at 220°F. Brisket is done when internal temperature reaches 195°F. Allow brisket to rest for 1 hour.

2. Slice, serve and enjoy!

Steak Night! Steak, Shrimp And Asparagus On The Akorn

Cooking Time: 20 Min

Ingredients:
- NY Strip Steaks
- Asparagus
- Raw shrimp
- Salt & Pepper
- 2 Lemons
- Minced Garlic
- Olive Oil
- Shrimp seasoning (we used Uncle Steve's Shake - gator shake)

Directions:
1. Pat your steak dry and cover with a thin coat of olive oil Cover all sides with some salt and pepper Let the steak sit on the counter while you get the shrimp and asparagus ready Peel the shrimp place on skewers and cover with your favorite seasoning Cut the woody portion off the bottom of the asparagus, coat with oil and season with salt, pepper, minced garlic. Squeeze some lemon juice over Bring your grill up to 500F and place your steaks on there no diffuser plate. After 2 minutes, twist 45 degrees After 2 minutes, flip After 2 minutes twist 45 degrees After 2 minutes temp probe and let cook until 130F internal for medium rare Pull steak and let it rest room temp while you cook your shrimp and asparagus With grill still at 500F, place shrimp skewers on grill Place asparagus directly on grill as well single file if possible Keep an eye on these flip the shrimp after about 3 minutes and move the asparagus around. Cook until desired doneness shrimp should be 145F if you would like to be safe. Enjoy!

Breakfast Burritos On The Flat Iron

Ingredients:
- Pack of 8 Breakfast Sausage Circles
- Pack of Shredded Cheese
- Burrito Tortillas (Large)
- Pack of Thick-Cut Bacon
- Dozen Eggs
- Package of Diced Frozen Hash Browns

Directions:
1. Perfect for taking on the go or preparing for the family to add some pizzazz into your mornings, these Breakfast Burritos are easy to assemble and allow you to choose toppings to make it your own.
2. Start with the hash browns on high-med/high heat with some oil. Keep an eye on them. Throw on the sausage and bacon. Cut up the sausage for the burritos. Once everything is cooked, move off to the side Warm-up a burrito to make easier to fold Ladle some eggs on to the griddle Add cheese and other toppings Remove burrito wrap Fold the egg into an omelet place on burrito wrap and fold Enjoy!

Chili In A Bread Bowl

Ingredients:
- 2 Lbs Ground Beef
- 8 Hot Link Sausages
- 8 Hot Italian Sausage
- 5 McCormick Mild Chili Seasoning Packets
- 2 Red Onions
- 1 Red Bell Pepper
- 1 Green Bell Pepper
- 2 Jalapenos
- 4 Garlic Cloves
- 4 10oz Cans of Diced Tomatoes and Green Chilies

- 2 Cans Pinto Beans
- 2 Cans Red Kidney Beans
- Shredded Cheese
- Bread Loaf (Bread Bowls)

Directions:

1. Chop your green pepper, red pepper, and red onion Using the Side Burner on our Triple Play, cook ground beef with diced garlic and jalapenos in a large pot Once the beef is cooked, add the 4 cans of diced tomatoes and green chilies Add the 4 cans of beans and mix to combine Add the 5 McCormick seasoning packets Now that your sausages are charred, slice them all and add to the pot Simmer for 30-45 minutes Hollow out your bread loaf with a paring knife to create the bowls Serve in the bread bowls and top with shredded cheese and raw red onions (or whatever else you like!)

2. Pitt Tips: Spice it up a little more by adding your favorite hot sauce, we like Tapatio! Add even more flavor by adding in your favorite beer!

Inch-thick Onion Char-burgers

Cooking Time: 15 Min

Ingredients:

- Angus Ground Beef 85% Lean - 1.5 lbs
- White Bread with Crust Removed - 2 slices
- Milk - 1/4 cup
- Kosher Salt - 1 tsp
- Coarse Ground Pepper - 1/2 tsp
- 1 Clove Garlic - Minced
- Half Large Sweet Onion - Chopped
- Paprika - 1/2 tsp
- Parsley - 1/2 tsp
- Garlic Powder - 1/2 tsp
- Cumin - 1 tsp
- Chili Powder - 1 tsp
- Melted and Cooled Bacon Grease - 3 to 4 Tbsp
- Vegetable Shortening - 1 tsp

Directions:

1. If you have bacon grease on hand, melt 3-4 tbsp in a skillet and set aside to let cool slightly. If you do not have bacon grease, fry 6-8 slices of bacon and spoon 3-4 tbsp aside to let cool slightly.

2. Next you'll want to prep your bread paste. Take the 2 slices of uncrusted white bread and break into small 1/2" pieces and place into small bowl. Add milk and let sit for 5 minutes. Mash down with fork until a paste forms. Set aside.

3. Place ground beef into large mixing bowl. Add salt, pepper, paprika, cumin, parsley, chili powder, garlic powder, minced garlic, chopped fresh onion, bread paste, and slightly cooled bacon grease.

4. Use gloved hands to mix all ingredients evenly into the ground beef. Divide into 4 even portions and form into balls. Flatten each ball to form inch-thick patties. Make center of patties thinner because it will rise as it cooks.

5. Add one fully lit chimney of coals to your favorite Char-Griller charcoal grill. This is a direct, high-heat cook.

6. Place 12" cast-iron skillet on grill grates and close lid. Allow 5-10 minutes to allow skillet to get nice and hot. Add vegetable shortening to ensure a non-stick sear.

7. Place patties in skillet. Sear 1 minute per side.

8. Remove skillet and carefully place patties on AKORN grates directly over coals. Grill 8-11 minutes flipping once.

9. For best results, monitor temp with instant thermometer. For medium-well, pull burgers off the grill at 150° F.

10. Let rest 5-10 minutes.

11. (Optional) While burgers rest, place 12" cast-iron skillet back on grill and fry your eggs with lid closed. Make sure not to over cook, you want a firm egg, but a "drippy" yolk on the inside. Sunny side up.

12. Add burger patty to your bun, top with egg, and your favorite toppings and get ready for one of the juciest, thickest, and most flavorful burgers you've ever had!

Brisket Hash On The Flat Iron Portable

Cooking Time: 30 Min

Ingredients:
- 1 Bag Of Frozen Shredded Hash Brown Potatoes (30 oz)
- 2 Cups Smoked Brisket (Cubed or Chopped)
- 4-6 Slices Bacon
- 1 Yellow Onion (Diced)
- 1 Red Bell Pepper (Seeded and Diced)
- 1 Green Pepper (Seeded and Diced)
- 1 Tbsp Minced Garlic
- 3 Tbsp Olive Oil
- 2 Tbsp Char-Griller Original AP Seasoning
- 2 Tsp Salt
- 1 Tsp Black Pepper
- 5-10 Large Eggs
- Optional: BBQ Sauce

Directions:
1. Heat some olive oil to grease Flat Iron Griddle Cook bacon over medium-high heat until fully cooked but not crispy, chop and set aside for later Heat more olive oil and cook onions over medium-high heat about 3 minutes, until translucent in color Add in peppers and garlic Cook for 1-2 more minutes Add in hash brown potatoes and cook for 15-20 minutes turning often to ensure all ingredients brown evenly (Add more olive oil if needed) Add in your brisket and chopped bacon, season all ingredients with the Char-Griller Original AP seasoning, salt, pepper Cook for 5-10 minutes until brisket is brown and potatoes are fully tender Remove from heat and keep warm Cook eggs as you like, sunny side up or even scrambled eggs go great with this recipe (Optional) Warm BBQ sauce in microwave for 30 seconds and stir To plate, scoop hash onto plate then top with cooked eggs and optional BBQ sauce!

Beef Tenderloin

Ingredients:
- Beef tenderloin
- Salt and pepper, to taste

Directions:
1. Pre-heat grill to 350°
2. Place meat directly over heat
3. Grill 10-12 minutes on each side
4. Mid-rare when internal temp reaches 135°
5. Remove, and let rest for 3-5 minutes

Smoked Bacon Wrapped Cheese Stuffed Avocado

Cooking Time: 1.5-2 Hrs

Ingredients:
- 2 avocados
- 1 lb. ground beef
- 1 lb. bacon
- 1 C. shredded cheese
- ¼ C. Original All-Purpose BBQ rub
- BBQ Sauce

Directions:
1. Split, peel and pit avocado
2. Make 2 cheese balls the size of removed avocado pit
3. Put cheese ball in seed hole
4. Add rub on each side of avocado, then close avocados
5. Use half of the ground beef for each avocado and wrap avocados until fully covered
6. Season ground beef generously with Original All-Purpose BBQ Rub, or your favorite rub, to taste.
7. Wrap bacon around the beef (4-5 strips per avocado)
8. Season bacon with rub
9. Cook for 1 1/2 - 2 hours at 250°F
10. Baste with BBQ sauce and cook for additional 15 minutes

Flavor Pro™ Reverse Seared Steak

Cooking Time: Varies Min

Ingredients:
- 4 Ribeyes
- Salt
- Char-Griller Steak Seasoning
- Compound Butter of Choice

Directions:
1. Set up the Flavor Pro for Indirect cooking

2. Add 20 to 25 charcoal briquettes to one side of the flavor drawer
3. Ignite charcoal with gas burners set to medium high
4. Once charcoal is lit, turn off gas burners and allow to fully ash over
5. Prepare the steak by salting and seasoning both sides with Char-Griller steak Rub
6. Add wood chips or chunks to charcoal
7. Show what has been soaked
8. Adjust smoke stacks until temperature is 250 degrees
9. Add steaks to side away from the coals
10. Cook steaks until they reach 115 degrees.
11. Remove steaks from grill and let rest for 5 minutes while you preheat the grill for direct high heat with the gas burners.
12. Sear steaks until internal temperature is 125. Remove from grill and let rest for 5 minutes.

Beer Brat Bites

Cooking Time: 15 Min

Ingredients:
- 6-8 bratwurst
- (1) 12 oz. bottle beer
- ½ C. brown sugar
- 1 Tbsp. Dijon mustard
- 1 Tbsp. chopped parsley
- 2 Tsp. cornstarch
- 1 onion, diced
- 2 garlic cloves, minced
- 1-2 C. sliced mushrooms
- 1 Tsp. salt
- 1 Tsp. pepper
- Cold water, as needed

Directions:
1. Place the bratwurst on the grill at 350°F and cook, flipping occasionally, until they reach an internal temperature of 170°F. Remove from grill and set aside.
2. While the bratwurst is cooking, make the sauce. Pour the beer and brown sugar into a pot over medium high heat; bring to a boil. Lower the heat and simmer for 10-15 minutes or until mixture is reduced and thickened. Whisk in the mustard until smooth.
3. Whisk the cornstarch with 1 Tbsp. cold water in a bowl and add to the beer mixture. Bring the beer to a boil and cook for 1 minute, stirring constantly, until sauce is thick. Add rest of the ingredients and stir to combine.
4. Slice the bratwurst into 1-inch pieces and add them to the pot with the sauce; toss to coat. Sprinkle with parsley and serve.

Smoked Mexican Burgers

Cooking Time: 40-45 Min

Ingredients:
- 2 lbs. ground beef
- ½ lb. Chorizo or spicy Italian sausage
- Jalapeños or Poblano peppers, halved, cored and seeded
- Sriracha or Chipotle aioli sauce
- Cheese slices
- Condiments of choice
- Hamburger buns
- Salt and pepper, to taste

Directions:
1. Pre-heat grill to 225°F and set up for indirect heat, with charcoal to one side.
2. Combine ground beef and Chorizo or spicy Italian sausage together in a large bowl and mix by hand until just blended. Season to taste with salt and pepper.
3. Form 1" thick patties and place on the indirect side of the grill, away from the heat source. Smoke until internal temperature reaches 130°F. Add peppers alongside the burgers and smoke for 40-45 minutes.
4. Increase heat to 400°F. Remove the peppers from the grill and set aside. When grill is at temperature, transfer burgers to the direct heat side. Sear for 6 minutes per side with a quarter turn halfway through.
5. Add cheese and allow to melt, 2-3 minutes. Burgers are done when internal temperature reaches 160°F.
6. Place cheese burger on bun, add peppers and sauce. Top with condiments of choice. Serve and enjoy!

Steak And Shrimp On The Flat Iron

Cooking Time: 10 Min

Ingredients:
- Strip Steak
- 1 Lb Raw Shrimp
- 1 Yellow Onion
- Handfull Of Mushrooms
- Char-Griller Steak Seasoning
- Char-Griller Creole Seasoning
- 1 Stick Of Butter
- Salt and Pepper
- Garlic Powder

Directions:
1. If frozen, thaw your shrimp in the sink under running cold water. While that's going, cut up your onion and mushrooms. Prepare your steak by patting dry, adding the steak seasoning, and finally coating with some olive oil. Next, heat up your griddle to high heat for the onions/mushrooms and medium for the shrimp. Toss on the onions and mushrooms on the high heat side and the shrimp on the medium heat side. Add some butter, salt, pepper, garlic to the onions/mushrooms and the creole seasoning on the shrimp. Move them around a bit so you don't end up burning them. Remove when done. Clear your griddle and throw the steaks on the high heat. You should hear a nice sizzle. Flip every couple minutes until done to your liking. Plate it up and enjoy!

Double Cheeseburger Kabobs

Cooking Time: 30 Min

Ingredients:
- Grass Fed Ground Beef- 1 Pound
- Sea Salt
- Fresh Ground Pepper
- American Cheese Slices
- Dill Pickle Chips
- Iceberg Lettuce
- Small Vine Cherry Tomatoes

Directions:
1. Gently form the ground beef into small slider size patties and generously sprinkle both sides with salt and pepper. Grill over medium high heat until desired doneness and then melt a quarter of a slice of American cheese on top of each.
2. Cut the iceberg lettuce into small squares. Slide a cooked slider patty, pickle chip, lettuce square, and tomato onto a skewer. Repeat twice on each skewer. 3. Serve with sugar free ketchup and yellow mustard to dip.
3. Other options to add: cooked bacon, red onion, grilled mushrooms—get creative!

Leftover Brisket Nachos

Cooking Time: 20 Min

Ingredients:
- Tortilla Chips
- Leftover Brisket
- Shredded Cheddar and Monterey Jack Cheese
- Heavy Cream
- Canned Diced Chilis
- Sour Cream
- Limes
- Pickled Jalapenos
- Black Beans
- Avocados
- Radish
- Pico De Gallo: Tomatoes, Onion, Jalapeno, Cilantro

Directions:
1. Prepare your pico de gallo and guacamole
2. Combine diced tomato, jalapeno, onion and cilantro in a bowl and mix with salt and pepper and lime juice
3. Mash 2 avocados together and combine with ½ cup of the pico for some easy guacamole
4. In a skillet prepare the cheese sauce by adding 3 cups shredded cheese and 2 cans of diced chilis. Slowly mix in ½ cup heavy cream and stir until smooth
5. Reheat your leftover brisket in another skillet
6. On a large cookie sheet begin layering your nachos
7. Chips, brisket, black beans, cheese sauce, more chips, brisket, beans cheese sauce.
8. ALWAYS double layer the nachos when possible
9. Top with pico de gallo, pickled jalapenos, sour cream, and guacamole!
10. Garnish with radish and lime wedges and enjoy!

Crab-stuffed Grilled Flank Steak With Asparagus

Cooking Time: 30 Min

Ingredients:

- 2 lb. flank steak
- 6-8 oz. crab meat
- 4 oz. cream cheese, softened
- 1 bunch asparagus, divided
- ¼ C. parsley, chopped
- 2 Tsp. garlic powder
- 2 Tbsp. olive oil
- 2 Tsp. salt, or to taste
- 2 Tsp. pepper, or to taste

Directions:

1. Flank Steak: Remove any excess fat and sinew from the flank steak. Rinse steak and pat dry with paper towel.
2. Butterfly the flank steak lengthwise, keeping the knife parallel and stopping approximately ½ inch from the other long edge, until the meat can open like a book. 3. Generously season flank steak with salt, pepper and garlic powder. 4. Spread an even layer of cream cheese on the steak. 5. Sprinkle parsley evenly on top of the cream cheese layer. 6. Spread crab meat evenly on top of cream cheese/parsley layer.. 7. Starting at one end, roll steak and fillings tightly, and tie securely in multiple spots with kitchen twine. Snip off any excess twine. 8. Brush steak roll with olive oil, salt and pepper, flipping over to evenly coat top and bottom. 9. Place steak on direct heat at 400°F and sear for 2 minutes on each side, rotating a quarter turn each time. 10. Transfer steak to indirect heat side of grill and cook 20-25 minutes until internal temperature reaches 140-145°F. 1 Remove from the grill, allow to rest for 8-10 minutes before slicing in 1"-1½" increments. 12. Cut and remove kitchen twine before serving.
2. Asparagus:
3. Rinse asparagus spears and cut off the ends.
4. Coat lightly with olive oil and season with salt and pepper, to taste.
5. Place asparagus on the grill at 400°F and cook for 4-5 minutes.

Bacon And Pineapple Wrapped Meatballs

Cooking Time: 30-45 Min

Ingredients:

- 1 lb. ground beef, chilled
- 1 lb. maple bacon
- 1 pineapple, cored and peeled
- 1 small yellow onion, finely chopped
- 2 Tbsp. dried parsley
- 1/2 C. bread crumbs
- 1 egg, beaten
- Applewood dry rub, to taste
- Salt and pepper, to taste

Directions:

1. Place chilled ground beef in a medium bowl and add 1 Tsp. dry rub, bread crumbs, egg, dried parsley, onion, and salt and pepper. Mix by hand until just blended.
2. Cut peeled pineapple into ¼" thick rings. Form meatballs and wrap each with 2 pineapple rings.
3. Wrap 2-3 strips of maple bacon around each pineapple-wrapped meatball and dust with Applewood dry rub, to taste.
4. Place on the indirect side of the grill at 225°F to smoke for 30-45 minutes, until bacon has caramelized on the outside.

Oklahoma Onion Burgers

Cooking Time: 20 Min

Ingredients:

- 1 Lb 80/20 Ground Beef
- 1 Large Sweet Onion
- 4 Slices American Cheese
- 4 Potato Rolls
- Yellow Mustard
- Salt & Pepper

Directions:

1. Slice the onions as thin as you can - translucent
2. Make 4 balls from your ground beef - approx. 3 oz. each
3. Over high heat, place ground beef balls on griddle
4. Put a healthy helping of sliced onions on each ball

5. Flatten them like you are making smash burgers - use parchment paper to keep from sticking
6. Once you see some browning on the edges flip over - onions and all
7. Smash those guys down again
8. Place 1 slice of American cheese on each patty
9. Place the lid of the bun on the cheese - this will let the rolls take in some of the meat/onion goodness. Lean the bottom rolls up against each patty.
10. Once the cheese is melted, remove from heat
11. Add 3-4 pickles on each burger and some yellow mustard.
12. Enjoy!

Beef Brisket

Cooking Time: 12 Hrs

Ingredients:
- 10 lb. beef brisket
- Rosemary salt, to taste
- Coarse ground pepper

Directions:
1. Place 1 C. packed fresh rosemary leaves and 1 C. coarse salt in a food processor and pulse until the texture resembles table salt. 2. Transfer to a large bowl and add 1 C. Kosher or sea salt and mix well. 3. Spread evenly on a baking sheet to dry for 1-2 hours, then pour into a jar with an airtight lid. Keeps indefinitely.
2. Beef brisket
3. Pre-heat grill to 275°F. Using a sharp knife, trim the fat from the brisket leaving an even, thin layer on the top.
2. Season brisket generously on both sides with rosemary salt, coarse black pepper and your favorite dry rub, or use Original All-Purpose BBQ rub, to taste. Place brisket on the grill fat side up, with a Smokin' Stone or heat deflector under the grates, and allow brisket to smoke at 275°F for 12 hours or until internal temperature reaches 190°F.
4. Let rest for 5-10 minutes before slicing and serving.

Picanha Crostini

Ingredients:
- 1 1/2 Green Bell Peppers (Diced)
- 4 Large Firm Tomatoes (Diced)
- 1 White Onion (Diced)
- 2 Garlic Cloves (Minced)
- 1/2 Cup Olive Oil
- 1/4 Cup White Vinegar
- 1/2 Lime Squeezed
- Salt and Black Pepper to taste
- 3 Lb Top Sirloin Cap (1" Cut Steaks)
- 3 Long Crusty Italian Bread

Directions:
1. Combine all ingredients in a large bowl and mix well
2. Season with salt and black pepper to taste. Top Sirloin Cap "Picanha"
3. About 20 minutes before grilling, remove the steaks from the refrigerator and let sit, covered, at room temperature.
4. Heat your grill to high. Brush the steaks on both sides with oil and season liberally with salt and pepper. Place the steaks on the grill and cook until golden brown and slightly charred, 4-5 mins. Flip them bad boys over and continue to grill 3-5 minutes. For medium rare internal temp 135F, medium 140F, medium-well 150F.
5. Transfer the steaks to a cutting board or platter, tent loosely with foil and let rest 5 minutes before slicing. Crostini
6. Slice the Italian bread and drizzle with olive oil
7. Toast preferably on the grill for that smoky char flavor
8. On a toast place two slices of steak , and top with vinaigrette
9. Enjoy

Certified Creole Y not Beef N' Bacon Jerky

Cooking Time: 4 Hrs

Ingredients:
- Bottom Flat Steak- 1 Pound
- Skirt Steak- 1 Pound
- Bacon- 12 ounces
- Kikkoman Teriyaki Baste and Glaze- 11.8 ounce bottle
- Char-Griller Grills Steak Rub

- Pepper Flakes
- Olive Oil
- Large Ziplock Bag
- Fogo Charcoal The Rub
- Fogo Charcoal Eucalyptus & Premium Blends
- Apple Wood Chunks

Directions:
1. Prepping: Slice the Bottom Flat Steak & Skirt Steak into small-medium personal pieces & set aside. Tip: cut small end pieces & excess fat.
2. Pour Kikkoman Teriyaki Baste & Glaze in Ziplock Bag.
3. Apply Olive Oil & Char-griller Grills Steak Rub to both sides of the meat & place in ziplock bag.
4. Mix the meat in the Ziplock bag & place in the refrigerator for 2-24 hours.
5. Remove from fridge and place on tray and allow the meat to get to room temperature.
6. Bacon: No need to marinade. When your ready to cook apply olive oil on both sides of the bacon & season both sides with Fogo Charcoal The Rub. Tip: placing the bacon to a baking rack allows easy handing/rotating of the bacon during the cooking process.
7. Cooking: Preheat smoker/grill with charcoal & apple wood chunks to 180°-200°. Tip: don't allow temperature to rise over 200°. Add charcoal/wood chunks as needed. Low smoke is needed to help dry out the meat. Check fire about 30-45 mins. Tip: do not use a spritz because the goal is to dry out the meat.
8. It will roughly take four hours to cook the jerky. dry out the meat.
9. Jerky will be dark in color, tender & a bit crispy when completed.
10. Dry out the meat.
11. When done, remove jerky from the smoker/grill and enjoy your Beef n' Bacon Jerky throughout the week with Family & Friends.
12. Store jerky in a ziplock bag. No need to place in refrigerator but can if you like.

Mini Smash Burgers
Cooking Time: 20 Min

Ingredients:
- 20 oz Fresh Ground Angus Beef
- Mini Buns
- 4 oz Butter
- Shredded Cheese of Choice
- Favorite Rub or Seasoning

Directions:
1. Loosely roll 2.5 oz of the fresh angus beef into a ball.
2. Melt butter in bowl
3. Place Shredded cheese in a bowl
4. Select favorite Rub/seasoning
5. Have all items available in your grilling area. This is a quick hands on cook.
6. Place cast iron hot plate/skillet over the grill grates on the gas side of the grill.
7. Turn all burners on high and allow a few minutes for the hot plate/skillet to get hot.
8. When hot, apply the melted butter using the basting brush to the hot plate/skillet.
9. Pick up the burger ball with the delicatessen paper and place on the hot plate/skillet.
10. Then using the burger press with delicatessen paper still over the burger ball, press and hold down for a few seconds. Then remove the burger press and delicatessen paper. You will now have perfect circle smash burger patty.
11. Now apply favorite Rub/seasoning to one side of the smash burger patty.
12. Flip smash burger patty after 3 minutes.
13. Then cook for another 3 minutes then flip one last time and add the shredded cheese
14. Allow the cheese to melt & warm buns at the same time.
15. Then remove and dress your mini smash burger with your favorite toppings.

Gravity 980 Brisket

Cooking Time: 8 Hrs

Ingredients:
- 1 Whole Brisket (Flat And Point) Trimmed
- 1/4 Cup of Extra Virgin Olive Oil
- Kosher Salt
- Freshly Ground Black Pepper
- Garlic Powder (Optional)

Directions:

1. Remove your brisket from the refrigerator, pat it dry and allow it to sit out for 30 minutes to an hour. In a small bowl, combine your seasonings then thoroughly coat the exterior of the brisket with olive oil. Remove fire shutter from the Gravity 980, load the hopper, then preheat it to 225-250°F. Season the exterior of your brisket thoroughly with the seasoning mixture. Close the lid and allow it to smoke for 7-8 hours without opening the lid. After this point, you may optionally remove it from the smoker and wrap it in butcher paper or aluminum foil before returning it to the smoker. Cook until the brisket's internal temperature has reached around 200-205°F and a nice dark bark has formed. Remove it from the smoker and allow it to rest 1 hour in the butcher paper or on a cutting board before slicing. Be sure to slice against the grain. Enjoy!

Reverse Seared Tri-tip Pico De Gallo

Cooking Time: 2 Hrs

Ingredients:
- Tri-Tip- 2 to 3 Pounds
- Kosher Salt- 1 Tablespoon
- Coarse Black Pepper- 1 Tablespoon
- Onion Powder- 1 Teaspoon
- Garlic Powder- 1 Teaspoon
- Hot Sauce- 2 Teaspoons
- Oak Splits
- Large Tomatoes (Chopped)- 2
- White Onion (Finely Chopped)- 1/2 Cup
- Cilantro (Finely Chopped)- 1/4 Cup
- Jalapeno (Seeds Removed to Preference, Finely Chopped)- 1/2 to 1 ounce
- Lime Juice- 2 Tablespoons

Directions:

1. Remove all excess fat and silver skin from the tri-tip. Mix together all the dry ingredients in a shaker until they are well blended. Use the hot sauce as a slather on both sides of the tri-tip to help get the rub to stick. Carefully season both sides and ensure that the tri-tip has a nice even coat of seasoning.
2. Start prepping your fire and working on getting your smoker up to 275 F. Once your smoker has reached 275 F it is time to put the tri-tip on and let the smoker do its job.
3. Once the tri-tip has reached an internal temperature of 125 F it is time to take it out of the smoker and prep for the sear. Place the tri-tip in a pan and cover with foil while you begin to get the grill up to 450-500 F.
4. Tip: you can get a good sear on either the grill or a cast iron skillet.
5. Once the grill has reached 450-500 F place the tri-tip directly on the grill and sear both sides till internal temp reaches 135 F. Pull the tri-tip off the grill and let rest for 15-20 minutes before slicing.
6. Tip: internal temp for beef varies by preference so feel free to pull it sooner for rare or later for well done.
7. Slice the tri-tip against the grain and top with Pico De Gallo. Enjoy!
8. Pico De Gallo Directions:
9. In a bowl combine the onion, jalapeno and lime juice. Salt to taste and let marinate for 3-5 minutes.
10. Add chopped tomatoes and cilantro into the bowl with the other ingredients. Stir well.
11. Let the mixture marinate so the flavors can meld. Serve and enjoy!
12. Tip: If you let the Pico De Gallo marinate for 1-3 hours the better the flavors will be when it is time to eat.

Korean Style Beef Short Ribs

Ingredients:
- 4-6 Lbs Beef Short Ribs
- 2 Tbsp Minced Garlic
- 1/2 Cup Brown Sugar
- 1 Cup Soy Sauce

Directions:

1. Mix soy sauce, brown sugar, and minced garlic. Add beef short ribs and marinate for at least 4 hrs. Preheat grill to 450F. Grill direct over coals for 3-4 minutes per side. Garnish with sliced green onions if desired, enjoy!

Mac & Cheese Stuffed Meatballs On The Char-griller Akorn

Cooking Time: 20 Min

Ingredients:
- 2-3 lbs 80/20 Ground Beef
- 1 Cup Shredded Cheddar Cheese
- 2/3 cup Panco Bread Crumbs
- Ground Black Pepper
- Your Favorite BBQ Sauce
- Velveta Mac & Cheese (Or Homemade)

Directions:
1. Cook up the Mac & Cheese Mix up ground beef, cheese, bread crumbs and pepper in a bowl Make little meat plates (3-4" in diameter) Place 4-5 noodles in each 'plate' Wrap the meat around the noodles so they're in the middle of a ball Heat up grill (indirect) to 350-375F Cook for 15 minutes Move around so everyone gets a turn Cook another 10-15 minutes, paint on some BBQ sauce Cook another 5 or so minutes to get tacky Enjoy!

The All American Burger

Cooking Time: 6 Min

Ingredients:
- 80/20 Ground Chuck- 1 Pound
- Steak- 8 ounces
- Salt
- Pepper
- Fire

Directions:
1. Cube your steak and grind together with coarse plate in the grinder.
2. Once fully ground, change the plate to a finer grind, and grind again. This will help the fat and meat combine well so that the burgers stay together.
3. Once ground, form the patties, about 4 inches.
4. Create a well in the center of the patties to help with even cooking.
5. Put the burgers in the fridge for up to 1 hour after forming the patties.
6. Fire up the grill and bring up to 400F
7. Season the patties with fresh ground black pepper and fresh ground sea salt.
8. Cook the burgers for about 4-6 minutes. Close the lid while doing this.
9. Flip once, and let cook.
10. Add cheese to the burgers and let the cheese melt over the patties.
11. Toast the bun on the grill to prevent a soggy bun when the juices of the burger comes out.
12. Once done, assemble your burger as you like and show your friends and family how you have become a true #grillionaire and that you are the KING of the cul de sac.

Smoked Beef Ribs

Cooking Time: 7-10 Hrs

Ingredients:
- 1 4-5 lb. Rack Of Beef Ribs
- Water and Apple Cider Vinegar in a spray bottle
- 2 Tbsp of Kosher Salt
- 2 Tbsp of Ground Black Pepper
- 1 Tsp of Brown Sugar
- 1 Tsp of Brown Sugar
- 1 Tsp of Brown Sugar
- 1 Tsp of Cayenne Pepper

Directions:
1. Alternatively, you can use your favorite pre-mixed rub/seasoning.
2. Preheat your smoker to 225-250°F. Thoroughly mix the rub ingredients together. Ensure your ribs are as dry as possible for the crispiest exterior. Pat dry with paper towels if necessary. Coat the exterior of your ribs in the rub mix, massaging it with hands to make sure it is thoroughly rubbed into the meat. Place the ribs into the smoker, fat side up with a water pan underneath close to the Side Fire Box. Close the lids and allow to smoke for 2-3 hours before beginning to spritz with water/vinegar

mixture every hour until internal temperature reaches 200-203°F. This process should be 7-10 hours depending on the rack. Remove the ribs from the smoker and wrap in butcher paper, allowing them to rest for an hour before slicing and serving.

Smoked Corned Beef

Ingredients:
- 3-5 Lb Corned Beef Brisket
- 1 Tbsp of Onion Powder
- 1 Tbsp of Garlic Powder
- 2 Tbsp of Paprika
- 2 Tbsp of Coriander Powder
- 2 Tbsp of Black Pepper
- 3 Tbsp of Brown Sugar

Directions:
1. Place corned beef brisket in a bowl covered with water. Refrigerate overnight, Preheat the smoker between 250-275 degrees by adding desired coals and/or wood to the Side Fire Box. If you do not own a Side Fire Box, no problem! To accomplish the same effect, simply arrange coals and/or wood opposite your cooking area. If you want to place your brisket on the right side of the grates, then arrange coals/wood on the left side, etc. Add desired wood chips to the smoker. Combine seasonings and spices in a bowl to create rub Remove the meat from the water and use paper towels to pat dry. Prepare meat by trimming excess fat if you desire. Coat the meat all over with the rub. Place meat in the smoker until the internal temperature reaches 160 degrees.(2-3 hours) Wrap the meat in butcher paper or aluminum foil and return to the smoker until the internal temperature reaches 195 degrees. (2-3 hours) Allow the meat the rest for a minimum of 30 minutes before slicing Serve warm, enjoy!

Italian Burgers

Cooking Time: 20 Min

Ingredients:
- Italian Sausage - 1/2 Pound
- Ground Beef - 1/2 Pound
- Portabella Mushroom Caps, Gills Removed - 5
- Ciabatta Rolls, Sliced Lengthwise - 4
- Shredded Parmesan - 1/3 Cup
- Diced Green Peppers - 1/2 Cup
- Crushed Red Pepper - 1/2 Teaspoon
- Bacon - 24 slices
- Prepared Marinara - 1/2 Cup
- Munster Cheese - 4 Slices
- Ball of Mozzarella Sliced into 1/4" Slices
- Italian Seasoning - 1/2 Teaspoon
- Whisked Egg - 1
- Oil for Frying

Directions:
1. Light charcoal and push to one side of the grill, leveling them out to one layer
2. Pour 1" of oil in pan and place directly over coals and heat to 350F
3. Place flour, salt, and Italian seasoning in a shallow bowl and dip each slice of cheese in the flour mixture, coating each side
4. Dip each slice into egg
5. Fully coat each slice in egg, then back again in the flour mixture. Allow to set, refrigerated for 15 minutes.
6. Meanwhile, dice one portabella cap 7. Mix both meats, diced mushrooms, bell pepper, red pepper, and parmesan together just until combined
7. Spoon meat mixture into each portabella cap
8. Wrap each burger patty with bacon. I found it easiest to weave 6 pieces of bacon, lay the patty in the middle and wrap the weaved bacon carefully around
9. Place patties on the side of the grill with no charcoal, flip patties half way through
10. While patties are cooking, fry the mozzarella until golden brown on each side and place on paper towel to drain
11. Cook burgers until bacon is crispy and internal temperature is 140F
12. Place cheese slices on top of each burger. Remove from grill when internal temperature reaches 145F
13. Add patties to bottom bun, top with fried mozzarella and marinara sauce

Chi-lanta Pork Belly Burnt Ends

Cooking Time: 4.45 Hrs

Ingredients:
- Pork Belly
- Sharp Knife
- Olive Oil
- Blues Hog Original BBQ Sauce
- Sweet Baby Rays Barbecue Sauce
- Char-Griller Grills Rib Rub
- Foil
- Butter (Not Margarine)
- Apple Juice (Non From Concentrate)
- Pan
- Drip Pan
- Baking Rack
- Golden Protective Services Nitrile Powder Free Gloves For Food Safety

Directions:
1. Prepping: Using a sharp knife slice and remove the skin and excess fat from the pork belly.
2. Slice into cubes
3. Coat with olive oil
4. Season with Char-Griller Rib Rub
5. Smoking
6. Fire up your Char-Griller Grill to 250°.
7. Place drip pan filled with water under the grill grates.
8. Place the pork belly on the baking rack.
9. Spritz every 30 minutes with Apple Juice and rotate the baking rack for even smoking.
10. After 3 hours of smoking, remove the pork belly from the baking rack and place directly in a pan with Apple Juice, Char-Griller Rib Rub, Butter & cover the pan with foil.
11. Place covered pan into the Smoker/Grill and cook for an additional 90 minutes.
12. Remove foil and discard the juices and then add BBQ sauce to the pork belly and mix.
13. Smoke uncovered for an additional 15 minutes and are done.
14. Enjoy.

Caprese Burger

Cooking Time: 40 Min

Ingredients:
- 1 lb. ground beef
- 2 thick slices Mozzarella cheese
- Sliced tomatoes
- Fresh basil, chopped, to taste
- Beef/steak all-purpose sauce
- Steak BBQ rub
- Salt and pepper, to taste

Directions:
1. Place ground beef in large bowl and season with Steak BBQ rub, or your favorite rub, to taste and sauce. Add salt and pepper if needed. Mix all ingredients by hand until just blended.
2. Form 1" thick patties and place on a wax paper lined tray. Place tray with patties in refrigerator and allow to chill for 10-15 minutes.
3. Place burgers on the grill at 375°F for 6 minutes per side, with a quarter turn halfway through for good sear marks.
4. Cover each burger with 3-4 basil leaves and top with a tomato slice. Add mozzarella cheese and allow to melt. Burgers are done when internal temperature reaches 165°F. To serve, top with condiments of choice and enjoy!

Cheesy Beef Burritos

Cooking Time: 40 Min

Ingredients:
- 2 lbs. ground beef
- 10 oz. can diced tomatoes with green chilies, drained
- 1 ½ C. hot fresh salsa, drained
- 2 C. sweet peppers, chopped
- 1 large red onion, chopped
- 3 Tbsp. fresh minced garlic
- 1 Tbsp. carne asada seasoning
- 6 C. shredded sharp cheddar cheese, divided
- 28 oz. can red enchilada sauce
- Burrito size tortillas

Directions:

1. Brown ground beef in a large cast iron skillet. Drain grease and set cooked beef aside in a large bowl. Do not wipe pan.
2. Sauté garlic, onions and peppers in the same pan until tender, about 5-7 minutes.
3. Combine green chilies, fresh salsa, sweet peppers, onion, garlic and seasoning mix in a large bowl and mix well.
4. Add mix from Step 3 to bowl with ground beef and mix in 3 C. of shredded cheese to make burrito filling. Mix all ingredients thoroughly.
5. Divide filling to fill six tortillas and wrap, placing seam side down in an oiled 9 x 13 baking dish.
6. Pour sauce over burritos and top with remaining cheese.
7. Place baking dish with burritos on the grill at 350°F for 40 minutes or until heated through.

Shrimp 'n Grits

Cooking Time: 20-25 Min

Ingredients:
- 1 lb. shrimp, peeled and deveined
- ½ lb. andouille sausage
- 1 C. stone-ground yellow grits
- 3 Tbsp. butter
- 4 C. water
- 2 C. shredded sharp Cheddar cheese
- 4 Tsp. lemon juice
- 2 Tbsp. parsley, chopped
- 1 C. scallions, thinly sliced
- 1 large garlic clove, minced
- Olive oil
- Salt and pepper, to taste

Directions:
1. Pre-heat grill to 375°F. Bring water to a boil and add salt and pepper, to taste. Add grits and cook until water is absorbed, about 20- 25 minutes. Remove from heat, stir in butter and cheese. 2. While grits are cooking, place sausages on the indirect side of the grill for 10-12 minutes, turning occasionally, until cooked. Sausage is done when internal temperature reaches 160°F. Remove from grill, allow to cool and roughly chop. 3. Rinse shrimp and pat dry with paper towel. Season with olive oil, salt and pepper, to taste. Grill shrimp for 2 minutes on each side, until opaque. 4. Remove shrimp from grill and toss with parsley, lemon juice, scallions and garlic.
2. To serve, spoon grits into bowls, top with chopped andouille sausage, and place shrimp on top of sausage. Garnish with more scallions and enjoy!

Corned Beef Brisket And Potatoes

Cooking Time: 5 Hrs

Ingredients:
- 18 lb. corned beef brisket
- 2 Tbsp. cinnamon
- 1 Tbsp. nutmeg
- 2 Tbsp. Allspice
- 3 Tbsp. salt
- 2 Tbsp. minced garlic
- 2 Idaho potatoes
- 6 oz. shredded cheese of your choice
- 6 oz. heavy cream
- 2 oz. chopped shallot
- Salt and pepper
- 2 oz. peppercorn

Directions:
1. Mix peppercorn, cinnamon, nutmeg, Allspice, salt and garlic.
2. Add vinegar based BBQ sauce to brisket.
3. Add spice mix all over the brisket on both sides.
4. Heat smoker to 225°F.
5. Smoke brisket until internal temp reaches 165°F.
6. Heat butter in a cast iron skillet
7. Add chopped shallot.
8. Chop and boil Idaho potatoes for 10 minutes in water.
9. Add salt and pepper to taste.
10. Add heavy cream to potatoes.
11. Close grill and bring to a boil.
12. Add your favorite shredded cheese
13. Mix well and cook for another 10-15 minutes.

Bacon Cheeseburger Pizza-dough Balls

Cooking Time: 30 Min

Ingredients:
- 22oz pizza dough
- 1.5 Lb Ground Beef
- 15 Slices Cheddar Cheese
- Half a Pack Of Bacon
- Seasonings
- 2 Eggs
- Sesame seeds

Directions:

1. Using your Flat Iron and your charcoal grill, accomplish the perfect game day appetizer or fun weeknight finger food with these bacon cheeseburger pizza dough balls. Rob Kennedy of Mr. Homeowner has got you covered with yet another fun and easy family friendly recipe!
2. Take your ground beef and make approx 15 little patties Cook your patties and bacon on your griddle about halfway cooked Wrap cheese, bacon and mini-patty in some pizza dough Cover with egg wash and some sesame seeds Set grill to 350F and 'bake' indirect heat for 25-30 minutes Enjoy!

Arrachera Skirt Steak Tacos

Cooking Time: 10-12 Min

Ingredients:
- 3 lb. Arrachera/Skirt Steak
- Sazón seasoning, three packets or to taste
- Adobo seasoning, to taste
- Meat seasoning, to taste
- 32 oz. bottle of Tecate or your favorite Mexican beer
- 8 limes (6 for the brine, 1 for the avocado dip, 1 for the tacos)
- 1 bunch green onions, ends removed
- 1 jalapeño, seeded, cored and sliced
- 1 onion, diced
- 1 bunch cilantro, chopped
- Corn or Flour tortillas
- Olive Oil

Directions:

1. Pour 32oz of Tecate or your favorite Mexican beer into a large resealable plastic bag and add the juice from 6 limes. Measure out and add the Sazón, Adobo and meat seasonings, to taste.
2. Tip: Add the squeezed lime peels to the bag for additional flavor and also to squeeze on the steak while it's cooking.
3. Mix brine thoroughly and add the steak, green onions and sliced jalapeño and gently shake to evenly coat. Marinate in the refrigerator for 2 hours or best overnight.
4. Arrachera/Skirt Steak
5. Pre-heat the grill to as hot as you can get it.
6. Tip: Spray grill grates with canned olive or vegetable oil.
7. Add green onions and jalapeño and grill until charred or to personal preference. Add steak to the grill for 5-6 minutes on each side or to personal preference.
8. Tip: Squeeze lime peels on to the steak while it's cooking. The limes become filled with the beer brine and the additional flavor and moisture it adds is amazing.
9. Tip: Also add additional meat seasoning to both sides of the steak while on the grill.
10. Remove the steak from the grill and allow it to rest for 5-10 minutes before slicing. Warm tortillas on the grill for about 1 minute.
11. Tip: Brush both sides of each tortilla lightly with olive oil.
12. Gather the onions, cilantro and avocado dip and create your tacos. Serve with salsa, limes, green onions, jalapeño and tortilla chips.
13. Enjoy!

Smoked Beef Chili

Cooking Time: 4 Hrs

Ingredients:
- Chuck Roast - 2 Lbs
- 1 Tbsp Kosher Salt (for beef)
- 1 Tbsp Coarse Black Pepper (for beef)
- 1 tsp Garlic Powder (for beef)
- 1 Tbsp Olive Oil (for beef)
- 3 Tbsp Vegetable Oil

- 1 Large Yellow Onion (Diced)
- 6 Garlic Cloves (Minced)
- 1/4 Cup Chili Powder
- 1 Tbsp Ground Cumin
- 1 (28 oz) Can Diced Tomatoes
- 1 (14 oz) Can Tomato Sauce
- 2 (15 oz) Cans Red Kidney Beans (Rinsed)
- Salt and Pepper to Taste
- Fritos, Cheddar Cheese, Cilantro (Toppings)

Directions:

1. Heat your Char-Griller to a temperature of 275 F. Rub the chuck roast with olive oil and season with the mixture of salt, pepper, and garlic powder. Place chuck roast in the Char-Griller away from the fire.
2. When the chuck roast has reached an internal temp of 165 F pull from the grill and let rest. After 10 minutes cut the chuck roast into cubes.
3. Heat the vegetable oil in a large pan and add onions, season with salt/pepper to taste. Cook until onions have softened.
4. Add minced garlic, chili powder, and cumin to the onions and stir until fragrant. Add the cubed chuck roast and stir until coated with the chili mixture.
5. Transfer the chili mixture into a Dutch oven and add the diced tomatoes, tomato sauce, and beans. Stir well to combine.
6. Place Dutch oven back on grill and continue to cook at a temperature of 275 F. Stir occasionally.
7. When chili has melded, and the beef is fork tender it is ready to serve. Serve with your favorite chili toppers and enjoy!

Peppered Sirloin With Bacon-mushroom Sauce

Cooking Time: 2 Hrs

Ingredients:
- 12 oz. sirloin steaks, 1-1½" thick
- ½ lb. baby Portabella mushrooms, sliced
- ½ lb. peppered bacon, chopped
- 2 C. beef stock
- 2 Tbsp. all-purpose flour
- 2 Tbsp. minced garlic
- 2 Tsp. Steak BBQ rub

Directions:

1. Fry bacon in batches, if needed, in a pan to desired crispness according to package directions, drain grease and chop when cool. Set aside in a medium bowl. Do not wipe pan. 2. Add mushrooms to the same pan and sauté until tender, 5-7 minutes. Add to bowl with bacon and mix well. Do not wipe pan. 3. Add flour to pan from bacon and mushrooms and whisk into bacon grease. Add garlic and sauté 30-45 seconds, until fragrant. Slowly pour in beef broth and stir continuously to thicken sauce. 4. Add in mushrooms and bacon and stir to incorporate. 5. Transfer all ingredients to cast iron skillet with beans and mix well. 6. Remove pan from heat and set aside.
2. Sirloin
3. Rinse sirloin and pat dry with paper towel. Season sirloin generously on both sides with Steak BBQ rub, or your favorite rub and let rest until meat reaches room temperature. 2. Place sirloin directly on the grill at 400°F for 12 minutes per side, rotating a quarter turn halfway through for good sear marks on each side. Meat is done when internal temperature reaches 140°F for medium-rare. Remove sirloin from grill and allow to rest for 8-10 minutes before slicing.
4. Serve with bacon-mushroom sauce and enjoy!

Homemade Grilled Meatballs

Cooking Time: 10 Min

Ingredients:
- 1 Pound of Ground Beef(Chicken or Turkey)
- 2 Large Eggs
- 1/2 Cup of Breadcrumbs
- 1/2 Cup of White Onion(Chopped)
- 1/2 Cup of Grated Romano or Parmesan Cheese
- 1 Tbsp of Minced Garlic
- 1 Tbsp of Dried or Fresh Finely Chopped Parsley
- 1 Tbsp of Dried or Fresh Finely Chopped Basil
- 1 Tsp of Crushed Red Pepper Flakes
- Salt and Pepper to Taste
- Extra Virgin Olive Oil

Directions:

1. In a bowl, combine ground meat, eggs, breadcrumbs, onion, cheese, garlic, parsley, basil, and red pepper flakes. Mix thoroughly then roll meat into meatballs (1-1 ½ inch diameter) Line meatballs on a tray in a single layer and season all over with salt and pepper. Heat grill to medium-high heat and be sure grates are oiled. Brush meatballs with olive oil and place on the grill. Cook until meatballs are browned and cooked throughout for about 10 minutes total, 5 minutes per side. Serve hot, with dipping sauce of choice. Enjoy!

Spaghetti Stuffed Meatloaf

Cooking Time: 3 Hrs

Ingredients:
- 3 lbs. ground beef
- 1 C. grated parmesan cheese
- 4 eggs lightly beaten
- 2 C. oatmeal or bread crumbs
- 3/4 C. milk
- 3 cloves of garlic minced
- 1 Tsp. pepper
- 2 Tsp. salt
- 2 C. colby jack cheese
- 1/2 to 1 lbs spaghetti
- 1 jar spaghetti sauce

Directions:
1. Mix meatloaf ingredients
2. Add to ground beef & mix well.
3. Cook spaghetti, drain, then add 2 Tbsp. butter. Let cool.
4. Form bottom part of meatloaf and create a bowl shape.
5. Add spaghetti, sauce and 1/3 of Colby cheese.
6. Place the top part of meatloaf on top and work until closed all around.
7. Place on smoker set at 250°F.
8. Cook for 1.25 - 1.5 hours. 9. Pour sauce on top of meatloaf. 10. Smoke for 20 minutes, then add rest of cheese and cook until melted.
9. Smoke for 2 hours or until internal temperature reaches 160°F.
10. Let cool, then slice and serve!

Italian-style Meatballs

Cooking Time: 10 Min

Ingredients:
- 1 lb. ground chuck
- ½ lb. ground pork
- ¾ C. breadcrumbs
- 2 eggs, lightly beaten
- 1/3 C. grated Parmesan
- 1/3 C. grated Pecorino Romano
- 2 cloves garlic, minced
- 2 Tbsp. finely chopped fresh parsley
- ¼ Tsp. red pepper flakes, optional
- Olive oil, for brushing
- Salt and pepper, to taste
- Marinara sauce, for serving
- Slider buns, for serving, optional

Directions:
1. Pre-heat grill to 400°F. Combine chuck, pork, breadcrumbs, eggs, Parmesan and Pecorino cheeses, garlic, parsley, and red pepper flakes in a large bowl and mix by hand until just blended. 2. Roll mixture into 1½" diameter meatballs. Season generously with salt and pepper, to taste. 3. Brush meatballs with olive oil and place on grill. Turn occasionally until well-browned on all sides and cooked through, 2-3 minutes per side. 4. Remove meatballs, serve with your favorite sauce and top with more cheese, if desired.
2. Alternately, transfer grilled meatballs and sauce to a pan on medium heat and turn to evenly coat. Serve on toasted slider buns, if desired.

Burnt Ends And Tips

Cooking Time: 1 Hrs

Ingredients:
- 15-18 lb. beef brisket, cooked
- Original All-Purpose BBQ rub or preferred rub, to taste
- 2 C. BBQ sauce
- 1 C. beef broth
- ½ C. garlic wine vinegar
- Extra beef broth for injection and misting

Directions:
1. Smoke brisket the day before.
2. Trim the fat from the brisket leaving an even, thin layer on the top.
3. Season the brisket generously with Original All-Purpose BBQ rub, or your favorite rub, on all sides to your taste.
4. Inject the brisket with the extra beef broth, reserving some for misting. Place brisket fat side up in the smoker for 3 hours at 250°F, with wood chips/chunks, if desired.
5. Open the smoker after 3 hours and inject the brisket with more beef broth, without turning it and mist the exposed surface generously. 6. Remove brisket when internal temperature reaches 160°F, wrap tightly in foil and return to grill.
5. Brisket is done when internal temperature reaches 204°F. Burnt ends and tips
6. Cut the cooked brisket into bite-sized chunks and place into an aluminum roasting pan.
7. Add BBQ sauce, 1 C. beef broth and vinegar to pan and mix well.
8. Place pan on the grill at 300°F for 1 hour or until meat is heated through and sauce has caramelized.

London Broil N' Veggie Skewers

Ingredients:
- 2 Pounds London Broil cut into cubes.
- 2 Ounces of Char-Griller Steak
- 1 Ounce Soy Sauce
- 2 Ounces of Honey Mustard.
- 2 Ounces of White Wine Vinegar.
- 2/3 Cup of Extra Virgin Olive Oil
- 1 Ounce Sazón
- 1 Ounce of Fresh Cilantro (Chopped)
- 1 White Onion (Cut into Squares)
- 1 Yellow Pepper (Cut Into Squares)
- 12-15 Baby Bella Mushrooms (Remove Stem)
- 1 Red Pepper (Cut Into Squares)

Directions:
1. Marinade prep.
2. Using a large bowl mix olive oil, cilantro, sazón, steak rub, white wine vinegar, honey mustard & soy sauce. Mix thoroughly.
3. Then add the London Broil meat to the mixture. Mix thoroughly.
4. Allow to rest for 2-24 hours.
5. Skewer prep
6. Add veggies and meat to long metal or bamboo skewers.
7. Tip: I used long metal skewers, the metal skewers helps cook the meat inside quicker due to the heat transferring from the metal. Bamboo skewers are always a good option but tend to burn on the tips and you also have to remember to soak them prior to prepping/cooking them.
8. Preheat your smoker/grill to 340°-350°: allow the grill/smoker to thoroughly warm.
9. Add skewers to the grill and cook for 15 minutes: turn skewers periodically.
10. baste with warmed mixture of olive oil, cilantro, sazón, steak rub, white wine vinegar, honey mustard & soy sauce.
11. Remove after 15 minutes or desired internal temperature and enjoy.

Pastrami Swiss Burger

Cooking Time: 40 Min

Ingredients:
- 2 lbs. ground beef
- ½ lb. Pastrami, sliced
- 2 eggs, beaten
- Steak BBQ rub
- 1 C. beef all-purpose sauce
- Swiss cheese, sliced
- Hamburger buns
- Condiments of choice

Directions:
1. Place ground beef in large bowl, add eggs and season with Steak BBQ rub, or your favorite rub, to taste and sauce. Mix ingredients by hand until just blended.

2. Form 1" thick patties and place on a wax paper lined tray. Place tray with patties in refrigerator and allow to chill for 10-15 minutes.
3. Place chilled patties on the grill at 350°F for 5 minutes per side, with a quarter turn halfway through for good sear marks.
4. Bush burgers with more sauce, if desired and top with sliced pastrami and cheese. Allow cheese to melt, about 1-2 minutes. Burgers are done when internal temperature reaches 165°F for medium-rare.

Lou's Beef Brisket

Cooking Time: 10-12 Hrs

Ingredients:
- 15-18 lb. beef brisket
- ½ C. coarse ground pepper
- ½ C. Kosher salt
- Beef broth for injection

Directions:
1. Use the rub ingredients to sprinkle the brisket on all sides to your taste
2. Inject the brisket with the combined ingredients of the injection
3. Use half the combined ingredients for injection and other half for misting
4. Add in your favorite wood chips/chunks (hickory, cherry, etc.)
5. Place brisket onto your smoker, fat side up
6. Cook for three hours in the smoker at 250°F, open it and inject again without turning the brisket 8. Use some of the inject to mist the exposed surface generously 9. Remove brisket when internal temperature reaches 160°F and wrap tightly in foil 10. Return brisket to grill and cook until the internal meat temperature reaches 204°F 11. Remove from heat and allow it to rest for an hour before slicing and serving

Lou's Beef Plate Ribs

Cooking Time: 7 Hrs

Ingredients:
- 1 rack, three bones, Beef Plate Ribs (approx. 6-9 pounds)
- ½ C. coarse ground black pepper
- ¼ C. Kosher salt
- 2 C. beef broth

Directions:
1. Sprinkle liberally with the salt and black pepper mixture, coating lightly over all sides
2. Pre-heat your grill to 275°F
3. Place the ribs on the top rack and smoke for 6 hours at 275°F
4. Mist about every 2 hours with some beef broth in a spray bottle
5. At the end of the 6 hours remove from the smoker and allow to rest for 30 minutes to an hour, then cut and serve

Filet Mignon, Risotto, And Asparagus

Cooking Time: 20 Min

Ingredients:
- 1 C. Arborio rice
- 2 C. chicken stock
- 1 C. water
- 4 oz. heavy cream
- 4 oz. shredded Parmesan cheese
- 1/2 shallot, minced
- 1 bunch asparagus
- 1 lemon, sliced in half
- 2 oz. olive oil
- 6oz. filets
- 2 garlic cloves, minced
- Salt and pepper to taste
- A pinch of saffron (optional)

Directions:
1. Butter cast iron skillet over grill heat
2. Add minced shallot and garlic, and sauté for 30-45 seconds until fragrant
3. Add rice and sauté for 1 minute
4. Add 1½ cups of chicken stock, setting aside remaining ½ cup
5. Add 1 cup of water
6. Cook for 10 minutes, stirring frequently
7. Add remaining ½ cup chicken stock, and cook for additional 10 minutes

8. Season to taste with salt and pepper
9. Add a pinch of saffron (optional)
10. Slowly add heavy cream
11. Remove from heat and stir in shredded Parmesan cheese
12. Filet Mignon
13. Season generously with salt and pepper 2. Place filets on grill at 400°F for 5-7 minutes on each side for medium-rare 3. Top filets with slice of butter until melted
14. Asparagus
15. Add raw asparagus and grill for 2-5 minutes 2. Squeeze lemon juice over asparagus 3. Drizzle with olive oil 4. Spread minced garlic 5. Add salt and pepper to taste 6. Mix garlic, salt, and pepper with tongs to evenly coat asparagus 7. Cook for 3-5 minutes, depending on thickness

Smoked Jerky

Ingredients:

- 1 3-4 lb. round steak, thinly sliced against the grain
- 1 Tbsp of Worcestershire sauce
- 2 Tbsp of Kosher Salt
- 1 Tbsp of Brown Sugar
- 1 Tsp of Garlic Powder
- 1 Tsp of Onion powder
- 1 Tsp of Soy Sauce
- 1 Bottle of Dark Beer or IPA
- Black Pepper to taste

Directions:

1. Combine all the ingredients in a saucepan and bring to a bowl to form a marinade. Cool completely. Transfer the sliced beef to a resealable bag with the marinade, massaging it into the meat. Refrigerate for 12 hours to overnight. Preheat your smoker to around 180°F. Remove the meat from the marinade, discard the marinade and lay strips flat, thoroughly drying each with paper towels. Add marinated meat slices to the smoker on the grates or on a cooling rack and smoke for 2-5 hours depending on how thick your slices are. You want your jerky to be dry, yet chewy, but pliable if you bend it. If you bend it and it snaps, then it is too dry. Place jerky in a resealable bag while it is still warm, but do not completely seal it closed. This will create the steaming effect to add some moisture. Allow to rest for at least an hour before serving. Enjoy! (Finished jerky will last for 2 weeks in the fridge and 3-5 days at room temperature.

Flavor Pro Italian Sausage Burgers

Cooking Time: 15 Min

Ingredients:

- 2 Tbsp Canola Oil
- 1 Large Green Bell Pepper, Sliced Thin
- 1 Large Red Bell Pepper, Sliced Thin
- 1 Large Yellow Bell Pepper, Sliced Thin
- 1/2 Large Sweet Onion, Sliced Thin
- 1 Pound Sweet Italian Sausage Meat
- 1/3 Cup Panko Bread Crumbs
- 1 Large Egg
- 2 Tbsp Italian Seasoning
- 1 Tbsp Chili Powder
- 2 Tbsp Hot Sauce (Optional)
- 1 tsp Salt
- 1 tsp Pepper
- 8 Slices Provolone Cheese
- 4 Italian Sandwich Rolls

Directions:

1. Prepare Flavor Pro for direct heat (medium-high, 350-400°F) For best results, fill all three zones of the Flavor Drawer with charcoal. Light coals using all four gas burners on high. Be sure grill lid is open before you ignite the burners. Keep both smoke stacks open.
2. Heat the oil in a large cast iron skillet on the grill.
3. Add peppers and onions to oil. Cook with grill lid on, for 6-10 minutes, flipping occasionally. Look for peppers to be tender and onions to be translucent and browning on edges. Pull off and set aside.
4. In a large mixing bowl, add sausage, bread crumbs, egg, and seasonings. Combine well with hands.
5. Form into 4 evenly sized patties.
6. Ensure grill is still hot and add more coals if necessary.

7. Cook sausage burger patties 4-5 minutes per side until cooked through. Look for an internal temperature of 150°-160°F.
8. Remove from heat. Add 2 slices of provolone cheese immediately to each burger. Place on the Italian sandwich rolls and top with peppers and onions. Add your favorite condiments. Yellow mustard and hot sauce makes for great additions!
9. Enjoy!

The Flintstone Steak

Cooking Time: 20 Min

Ingredients:
- 24 oz. Tomahawk steak
- 4 oz. Au Jus, or to taste
- Steak BBQ rub

Directions:
1. Season both sides of steak with Steak BBQ rub, or your favorite rub, to taste
2. Place steak in middle of grill at 350°F
3. Grill each side for 8-10 minutes, until internal temp reaches 135°F for medium-rare
4. Pour Au Jus over steak
5. Let rest and enjoy!

Weeknight Smokehouse Ribs

Cooking Time: 75 Min

Ingredients:
- 2.5 Lbs Baby Back Rib
- 1/2 Cup Char-Griller Ribs Rub
- 1 Cup BBQ Sauce

Directions:
1. Clean ribs and remove silver skin membrane from the back of the ribs. If you're unsure how, slide a butter knife in-between the thick membrane and the meat, and slide until a pocket forms, allowing you to grab and easily peel away. Generously coat the ribs in the rub, and rub in, letting the ribs absorb all of the seasoning.
2. In the instant pot, add 1 cup of water, and the steaming tray to the bottom of the pot. Arrange your ribs, in a coil type shape on their side, and close lid- setting to seal. Select "Pressure Cook", high pressure, for 28 minutes. Let the IP do its thing.
3. Next, in your Char-Griller Charcoal Chimney, all charcoal, and alternating layers of hickory chunks. Place over burner on the Texas Trio, and light- letting the flame stay burning for about 2-3 minutes, until charcoal lights and begins to burn on it's on. Kill the heat and allow the charcoal to heat up for 20 minutes.
4. Next, add charcoal and wood to the smoking box on the Trio, and add 1-2 more large pieces of wood. Secure your air vents for a slow, steady inflow of air, and prepare your grates.
5. Once the instant pot is done cooking, manual release the steam, and remove ribs. Transfer to the Trio, and close the lid for 20 minutes, allowing the smoke to wrap around the ribs. 20 minutes later, slather the ribs in sauce, and close lid again, until sauce changes from a bright color, to a more sticky, darker hue, about 15 more minutes. Ribs are ready to serve! Enjoy!

Shrimp & Sausage Skewers

Cooking Time: 5 Min

Ingredients:
- 4 Smoked Sausage Links or Hot links
- 20 Large Shrimp
- 2-3 Tbsp Blackening seasoning (I used Ashman Co Bayou Blackening)
- 1/4 Cup Teriyaki Sauce

Directions:
1. Preheat grill to 400F
2. Peel and de-vein shrimp, slice links into 5 pieces each.
3. Wrap shrimp around sausage link and put on skewer.
4. Once all shrimp and sausage are on skewers, sprinkle with blackening seasoning.
5. Place on grill for approximately 3-4 minutes per side, just enough to get a good char.
6. Once cooked baste both sides with teriyaki sauce, remove from grill and serve!

Bacon Ring Burger With Mushrooms

Cooking Time: 1 Hrs

Ingredients:
- ½ C. apple jelly
- ½ C. balsamic vinegar
- ¼ C. brown sugar
- 2 ½ Tsp. Original All-Purpose BBQ rub (reserve ½ Tsp.)
- 2½ lbs. ground beef
- 1 lb. bacon
- ¾ lb. baby bella mushrooms, sliced
- 3 Tbsp. shallots or green onions, sliced
- 5 large sweet onion slices
- 1 Tbsp. butter
- Provolone cheese, or preferred
- Condiments of choice
- Salt and pepper, to taste

Directions:
1. Combine balsamic vinegar, brown sugar, ½ Tsp. rub and apple jelly in a small sauce pan on the stove. 2. Bring to a boil, then reduce heat and simmer for 15 minutes, stirring occasionally. Allow to cool.
2. Bacon Ring Burgers
3. Coat the onion slices with apple chipotle sauce and season with 1 Tbsp. Original All-Purpose BBQ rub, or your favorite rub, to taste. Wrap each onion slice with 3 strips of bacon and secure with toothpicks. 2. Place bacon-wrapped onion rings on the grill to smoke at 225°F for 1 hour. Remove onion rings from the grill and increase temperature to 350°F for burgers. While onion rings are in the smoker, place ground beef in large bowl and season with pepper and 1 Tbsp. rub. Mix all ingredients by hand until just blended. 4. Form 1" thick patties and place on a wax paper lined tray. Place tray with patties in refrigerator and allow to chill for 10-15 minutes. 5. Sauté garlic, mushrooms and shallots in butter for 5-7 minutes, until just tender, and set aside. 6. Place burgers on the grill at 350°F for 6 minutes per side, with a quarter turn halfway through for good sear marks. Burgers are done when internal temperature reaches 165°F.
4. To serve, top burgers with cheese and bacon-wrapped onion ring. Fill with sautéed mushrooms and shallots, top with condiments of choice and enjoy!

Skirt Steak Gyros

Cooking Time: 25 Min

Ingredients:
- 1 lb. skirt steak
- 1/3 C. olive oil
- 3 cloves garlic, minced
- 1 Tsp. dried mint (optional)
- 1 Tsp. dried oregano
- ½ Tsp. paprika
- 1 Tsp. salt
- 1 Tsp. pepper
- ½ C. Greek yogurt
- 1 green bell pepper, seeded and sliced
- 1 onion, sliced
- 1 tomato, chopped
- 4 pc. Pita bread
- 1 bunch watercress, rinsed and roughly chopped

Directions:
1. Pre-heat grill to 375°F. Whisk the olive oil, garlic, mint (if using), oregano, paprika, salt, and pepper together in a large bowl to make marinade. 2. Transfer 1 Tbsp. of the marinade to a small bowl; mix in the yogurt and 2 Tbsp. water to make yogurt sauce. 3. Add bell pepper and onion to bowl with remaining marinade and toss; transfer to a plate with a slotted spoon. Add steak to bowl and toss. 4. Arrange bell pepper, onion and steak on the grill at 375°F. Grill vegetables for 4 minutes per side, turning once, until lightly charred. Sear steak for 4-8 minutes per side (depending on thickness). Set aside to rest for 5 minutes. 5. Grill the pitas until marked, about 1 minute per side.
2. To serve, slice the steak against the grain. Fill the pitas with the steak, grilled vegetables, tomato and watercress. Drizzle with the yogurt sauce.

Grilled Steak Caesar Salad

Cooking Time: 30 Min

Ingredients:

- Hanger or Flank Steak (12 oz)
- Large Head of Romaine Lettuce
- 1/2 Baguette, Cut into Large Cubes
- 1/3 Cup Shaved Parmesan
- 1 Tbsp Olive Oil
- Salt and Pepper to Taste
- Juice of One Lemon (Dressing)
- 1 Tbsp Worcestershire Sauce (Dressing)
- 1 Tbsp Anchovy Paste (Dressing)
- 2 Cloves Fresh Garlic (Dressing)
- 1/2 Cup Grated Parmesan (Dressing)
- 1 Egg Yolk (Dressing)
- 1 Tbsp Dijon (Dressing)
- Salt and Pepper to Taste (Dressing)

Directions:

1. Cut washed romaine in half, and toss cubed baguette with a drizzle of olive oil, salt and pepper.
2. Once grill is heated to 500+, lay steak on clean grates, and add romaine cut side down, and crouton cubes as well. Turn croutons every 1-2 minutes, until they're golden brown.
3. Pull romaine and croutons from grill, and allow steak to cook evenly on both sides. I like my steak medium-rare, so I cooked each piece for 4 minutes per side.
4. Pull the steak and allow to rest for 15 minutes.
5. While your steak is resting, blend all the dressing ingredients except for the olive oil until a paste forms.
6. Then, with the blender running on low, slowly drizzle in the oil until well combined and thick- you know what caesar dressing should look like!
7. Chop grilled romaine, slice steak, and assemble on your salad plate, sprinkling with the grilled croutons and shaved parmesan. Drizzle the dressing over the top, and you've got dinner ready to go! Enjoy, friends!

Reverse Sear Ribeye

Cooking Time: 1 Hrs

Ingredients:

- 1½" thick Ribeye steaks
- Steak BBQ rub, or preferred seasoning, to taste
- Salt and pepper, to taste

Directions:

1. Allow steaks to come to room temperature, then rinse and pat dry with paper towel. Season steaks generously with Steak BBQ rub or preferred seasoning on both sides. Add salt and pepper if needed.
2. Place on the grill to smoke at 170°F for an hour; pull steaks off and set aside to rest.
3. While steaks are resting, increase grill temperature to 400°F.
4. Place steaks back on the grill and sear at 400°F for 5 minutes per side, with a quarter turn at 2½ minutes for good sear marks. Steaks are done when the meat reaches an internal temperature of 140°-145°F for medium-rare.
5. Note: The steak's internal temperature will continue to increase by 5-10 degrees after you pull it off the grill.

Cold Weather Chili

Cooking Time: 30 Min

Ingredients:

- 2-3 Tbsp. butter
- 1 lb. ground beef
- 1 medium white onion, chopped
- ½ green pepper, chopped
- ½ red pepper, chopped
- 14.5 oz can pinto beans, drained
- Your favorite chili powder or pre-made chili seasoning
- One small can tomato paste
- 1 can of your favorite beer (optional) or 1½ C. beef broth
- Salt and pepper, to taste

Directions:

1. Preheat grill to 350°F. Melt butter in a large cast iron pot.
2. Add chopped onion, peppers, ground beef and pinto beans and cook for 5 minutes, covered.
3. After 5 minutes, uncover and add chili powder or seasoning. Mix well, cover and cook for 10 minutes until meat is browned.

4. Add chili paste and/or tomato paste and beer (optional, or use beef broth) and stir. Cook 15 minutes to reduce and heat through. Add salt and pepper to taste and add water if needed.

5. Serve with your favorite chili fixings! Enjoy!

Left Over Cheesy Mac N' Smoked Brisket Meat Pies Recipe

Cooking Time: 10 Min

Ingredients:
- Left over Brisket: You Can Also Use Ground Beef 1 Pound
- Left over Mac n' Cheeses: 20 oz.
- Dough Discs: 7 (You Can Also Use Refrigerated Biscuit Dough)
- Green Pepper: 1/2 diced
- Green Onions: One Bush Chopped.
- Olive Oil: 2 Tablespoons
- Self-Rising Flour: 1 Tablespoon
- Garlic Powder: to taste.
- Shredded Cheeses: 7 oz
- Char-Griller Grills Akorn Kamado Charcoal, Black
- Fogo Eucalyptus & Premium Lump Charcoal.
- Large Cast Iron Skillet
- Lard: for Frying Quarter Skillet.

Directions:
1. Take your left over smoked brisket, green onions, green peppers, Self-Rising flour and place in a medium heated cast iron skillet with olive oil. Mix ingredients thoroughly for 15 minutes. Then set aside to cool. Spread a few sprinkles of Self-Rising Flour so the dough discs don't stick to the surface. Fill the dough discs with the smoked brisket seasoned up mixture, Mac n' Cheese and shredded Cheese. Seal the ingredients in the dough discs using a fork on one side only. Tip: you can also make some with just smoked brisket seasoned up mixture Fire up your grill, then place the cast iron skillet filled with the lard to medium heat for meat pie frying. Place Meat Pies in the cast iron skillet. Flip after 3-4 mins and then fry for an additional 4-5 minutes. Dough will turn golden brown. Remove and enjoy! Tip: you can also freeze any uncooked meat pies and fry them up another time

Double Stack Cheeseburger

Cooking Time: 15 Min

Ingredients:
- 1 lb. ground beef
- Beef/steak all-purpose sauce
- Steak BBQ rub
- 1 sweet onion, sliced
- 1 tomato, sliced
- 2 slices cheddar or pepper jack cheese
- Hamburger buns
- Condiments of choice

Directions:
1. Place ground beef in large bowl and season to taste with Steak BBQ rub or your favorite rub, and sauce. Mix by hand until just blended. 2. Form 1" thick patties and place on a wax paper lined tray. Place tray with patties in refrigerator and allow to chill for 10-15 minutes. 3. Place the onion slices on the grill at 400°F for 5-7 minutes, flipping halfway through, until tender. 4. Place chilled patties on the grill at 400°F for 3 minutes per side, with a quarter turn halfway through for good sear marks. 5. Top burgers with grilled onions and cheese. Allow cheese to melt and stack one burger on top of the other. Burgers are done when internal temperature reaches 165°F.

2. To serve, add more grilled onions and cheese if desired, top with condiments of choice and enjoy!

Dark Roast

Cooking Time: 4.5 Hrs

Ingredients:
- Chuck Roast- 2.5 Pounds
- Dark Roast Coffee - 3 Ounces
- Spice Beast Big Buzz Coffee Rub - 2 Teaspoons
- Additional Spice Beast Big Buzz Coffee Rub - 3 Tablespoons
- Butter - 1/2 Stick

Directions:
1. Mix coffee & coffee rub.

2. Using a meat injector, inject coffee/rub mixture into center of roast.
3. Rub outside of roast with additional 3 tbsp coffee rub.
4. Let marinate for 2 hours in refrigerator.
5. Smoke uncovered at 225° for 1.5 hours. Then wrap in foil with 1/2 stick of butter & return to grill at 200° for 3 hrs. Let rest before enjoying.

Smoked Chili

Cooking Time: 2-3 Hrs

Ingredients:
- 2 lb. ground beef
- 30 oz. tomato sauce
- 30 oz. kidney beans
- 30 oz. pinto beans
- 1 C. diced onion
- ¼ C. diced green chilies
- 3 medium tomatoes chopped
- 1½ Tsp. cumin powder
- 3 Tbsp. chili powder
- 2 Tsp. black pepper
- 1 Tsp. salt
- 1 Tsp. celery salt
- 2-4 cloves garlic, minced
- ½ C. chopped cilantro
- 2 C. water

Directions:
1. Pre-heat grill to 250°F. Season ground beef with salt and pepper, to taste and brown in a cast iron pan.
2. Mix all ingredients together, add to browned ground beef and stir well to combine.
3. Smoke for 2-3 hours at 250°F, stirring every 15-20 minutes.

Smoked Meatloaf

Cooking Time: 2 Hrs

Ingredients:
- 2 Lbs. Ground Beef
- 1/2 Cup of Onion (Minced)
- 1/4 Cup of Garlic (Minced)
- 2 Eggs (Cracked)
- 1 Tsp of Salt
- 1 Tsp of Pepper
- 1 Tsp of Cayenne Pepper
- 3/4 Cup of Bread Crumbs
- 1 Tbsp of Worcestershire Sauce
- 1/2 Cup of Ketchup
- 1/4 Cup of Brown Sugar
- 1 Tbsp Yellow or Dijon Mustard
- 1 Tbsp of BBQ Sauce

Directions:
1. Preheat your smoker to 225-250°F. In a large mixing bowl, combine all of the ingredients(1-9) for the loaf, thoroughly kneading together. Form into desired load shape. Place the meatloaf into the smoker and smoke for 2 hours or until the internal temperature reaches 160°F. Allow to rest for 30 minutes before slicing. Combine the ingredients(10-13) for the sauce thoroughly and apply to the top of the meatloaf once it has begun to cool down. Serve warm. Enjoy!

Flavor Pro™ Flank Steak Tacos

Cooking Time: 25 Hrs

Ingredients:
- 1 1/2 Pound Flank Steak
- 3 Tbsp Olive Oil
- Juice of 2 Limes
- 1 Clove of Garlic (Minced)
- 1/2 Cup of Fresh Cilantro(Sliced)
- Salt and Pepper to Taste
- 1 Tsp Chili Powder
- 2 Onions(Sliced)
- Cojita Cheese
- Salsa Verde

Directions:
1. Place steak in a bag or shallow pan with olive oil, lime juice, garlic, cilantro, chili powder and salt and pepper. Let marinate for at least half an hour. Prepare the Flavor Pro for direct grilling – Light the gas burners and reduce to medium high heat and allow to preheat. Chop peppers and onions. Place steak on the grill and allow to cook for 7 minutes on each side or until internal temperature is 150 degrees. Remove steak from grill and

let rest 10 minutes. Saute onions and peppers with more olive oil, salt and pepper in a cast iron pan on the grill until tender. Heat tortillas on the warming rack. Slice steak into thin slices. Build a taco with the steak, peppers, onions, cheese, and salsa.

Pork Brisket Burnt Ends

Ingredients:
- 2 Lbs Pork Brisket
- 4 Tbsp Blues Hog Original Rub
- 1/4 C Blues Hog Pork Marinade
- 1 Cup of Water
- 1/2 Cup Blues Hog Smokey Mountain Sauce

Directions:
1. Preheat grill to 300F and setup for indirect cooking. Trim silver skin and fat from top of pork brisket. Mix water and pork marinade in bowl and place trimmed brisket in marinade, marinate for 1 hr. Remove pork brisket from marinade and season using Blues Hog Original rub. Smoke pork brisket until internal temp reaches 190F, remove from heat, cut brisket into cubes and place in foil pan, sprinkle more Rub on top and add sauce. Place back on grill for 30 minutes, remove, serve and enjoy!

Bbq Fiends Barbacoa Tacos

Cooking Time: 5 Hrs

Ingredients:
- Beef Cheeks - 2 to 3 lbs
- Kosher Salt - 1 Tbsp
- Coarse Black Pepper - 1 Tbsp
- Olive Oil - 1 tsp
- Beef Broth (Low Sodium) - 2 Cups
- 1 White Onion
- Tortillas - 12
- Cilantro (optional)

Directions:
1. Combine salt and pepper in a shaker for easy application. Unwrap beef cheeks and trim excess fat and silver skin off the meat.
2. Rub down the meat with olive oil for a binder and season evenly with your salt/pepper mixture.
3. Start working on getting the fire going and your smoker up to 275 F. Once your smoker is at 275 F you can add a water pan to the side of your grill that is closest to the fire. This will help with keeping your beef cheeks moist. Center the beef cheeks on the middle of the grill and let the smoker do the work.
4. Once the beef cheeks have reached around 165 F internal temp it is time to braise (this should be around the 3-hour mark).
5. Apply a layer of onion slices to the bottom of an aluminum pan. Set your beef cheeks on top of the layer of onions.
6. Carefully pour the beef broth into the pan and make sure to cover the pan completely with aluminum foil.
7. Put the pan back into the smoker and continue to maintain a temperature of 275 F.
8. Once the beef cheeks have reached an internal temp between 203-205 F it is time to take them off the smoker and let rest for 10 minutes. The beef cheeks should be very tender and falling apart when probed.
9. After the beef cheeks have rested for 10 minutes inside of the pan it is time to remove them from the pan and shred them on a cutting board.
10. Once your barbacoa is all shredded go ahead and fill your tortillas with the delicious meat and serve with diced onions and cilantro!
11. Enjoy your barbacoa tacos with your family and friends!

Oktoberfest Beef Short Ribs

Cooking Time: 3.5 Hrs

Ingredients:
- 6 Lbs Beef Short Ribs
- 1 Package Brown Gravy Mix
- 1 Cup Beef Broth
- 1/8 Cup Beef Seasoning of Choice
- 3 Tbs Brown Sugar
- 3 Tbs Worcestershire Sauce
- 1 Package Egg Noodles

Directions:
1. While these short ribs are definitely going to get their time in the smoke, they aren't exactly your

traditional take on beef BBQ, but on cooler days this is going to hit the spot.

2. Serving these ribs up with a gravy over noodles much like beef stroganoff is a really fun way to take what you've learned about smoking meats, applying that knowledge to another dish, and really pushing it over the top with it. Char-Griller Ambassador Steve Dotson of Cookout Coach had a lot of fun making these and he hopes you will too.

3. Load Char-Griller AKORN with charcoal and light ¾ chimney full of charcoal. Once the chimney is completely lit add it to the AKORN along with one chunk of hickory wood.

4. Place the Cooking Stone in place along with the grate and allow the AKORN to come up to 300 degrees with no or light visible smoke.

5. Trim the fat cap off of 6 pounds of beef short ribs and cut into individual ribs..

6. Season with your preferred beef seasonings and rubs.

7. Place ribs on the smoker and let them smoke for two hours.

8. At the two hour mark combine all sauce ingredients into a half sized foil pan and place ribs in the sauce, cover ribs with thinly sliced half of a sweet onion and cover with foil.

9. Place covered pan back on the cooker for another hour and a half.

10. Check for probe tenderness and an internal temp of roughly 210 degrees. If the ribs are tender let them rest for a minimum of half an hour.

11. Prepare egg noodles according to package directions.

12. Remove short ribs from the bone and serve over noodles with sauce ladled over the top.

Beer Brined Grilled Costillas Beef Short Ribs

Ingredients:
- 2 lbs of Costillas/Beef Short Ribs
- Chef Merito Carne/Meat Seasoning: to taste.
- 32 oz Tecate Beer or favorite Mexican beer.
- 6 Limes.
- One Jalapeño (Sliced)
- One Serrano (Sliced)
- Four Cebollitas
- Olive Oil: Light Drizzle
- Char-Griller Grills Akorn Kamado, Blue
- Fogo Quebracho Lump Charcoal.

Directions:

1. Use a large plastic zip bag or bowl. Slice & squeeze limes. Add beer. Tip: add the squeezed lime peels to the zip baggie or bowl for additional flavor and also to squeeze on the Costillas/Beef Short Ribs when grilling. Add Chef Merito Carne/Meat Seasoning to taste Slice & Add Jalapeno Slice & Add Serrano Mix beer brine thoroughly. Add Cebollitas Once the brine is mixed, add it to the Costillas/Beef Short Ribs & sliced Jalapeño. Then rest for a minimum of two hours. Best if it rests for 24 hours.

2. Grilling/Cooking

3. Pre-heat grill to 370°-400° Tip: spray grill grates with canned Olive, canola or Vegetable oil. Add cebollitas, limes & jalapeño to the grill. Add the Costillas/Beef Short Ribs to the grill. Grill for 8-10 minutes on each side or to personal preference. Tip: squeeze lime peels on to the meat while it's cooking. The limes become filled with the beer brine and the additional flavor and moisture it adds is amazing. Tip: also add additional Chef Merito Carne/Meat Seasoning to both sides of the meat while on the grill. When the meat is removed. Allow it to rest for 5-10 minutes before slicing/dicing. After resting slice and dice the meat Warm tortillas on grill for roughly one minute. Tip: lightly and olive oil to both sides of the tortillas. Serve with fresh salsa, limes, jalapeño & tortilla chips. Enjoy

Bacon Burger With Shallots

Cooking Time: 10 Min

Ingredients:
- 4 lbs ground beef
- Salt and pepper to taste
- 2 oz chopped fresh parsley
- 6 strips of bacon, cooked and crumbled
- 1 Tbsp. burger seasoning
- 1 Tsp. cayenne pepper

- 2 shallots

Directions:
1. Add 4 lbs. of ground beef to mixing bowl
2. Add in bacon, fresh parsley, salt & pepper, burger seasoning, and cayenne pepper.
3. Mix ingredients into meat
4. Place on grill at 350°F
5. Cook burgers 7-10 minutes per side
6. Add 2 shallots, thinly sliced into hot cast iron pan with oil
7. Cook until golden, crispy brown
8. Add melted butter to buns and place on grill to warm
9. Add your favorite cheese to the burgers

Beef Ribs

Cooking Time: 5-9 Hrs

Ingredients:
- 5 lb Rack of Beef Plate Short Ribs
- Water & Apple Cider Vinegar Mixture in A Spray Bottle
- 1/2 Cup of Sea Salt
- 1/2 Cup of Black Pepper
- 1/3 Cup of Brown Sugar
- 1/4 Cup of Chili Powder
- 2 Tbsp of Paprika
- 1 Tbsp of Garlic Powder
- 1 Tbsp of Onion Powder
- 1 Tsp of Cayenne Pepper

Directions:
1. Combine all seasonings and spices together to prepare BBQ rub. Preheat the smoker between 225-275 degrees, adding desired wood chips, pellets, and/or chunks into the smokebox. If you do not own a smokebox, you can still accomplish the smoking experience! Simply arrange your coals/wood opposite the cooking area of your ribs. If you plan to place your ribs on the middle of the grates, then arrange coals everywhere EXCEPT under the middle of the grates, etc. While the smoker is preheating, sprinkle a decent amount of rub onto ribs and use hands to spread evenly. Store the remainder of the rub in an airtight container for a future cook. Place ribs in smoker, fat side up, Place a drip pan of water below the ribs. While smoking ribs, be sure to maintain the heat of the smoker, adding wood as needed Occasionally spritz the ribs with the water and vinegar mixture until ribs a dark brown with a developed bark on the exterior. Be sure they've reached an internal temperature of 165 degrees. This could take between 3-6 hours. Remove ribs from the smoker and wrap in butcher's paper or aluminum foil. Place ribs back in the smoker until they reach an internal temperature of 200 degrees. This may require 2 hours or more. Once you remove the ribs, keep them wrapped and allow them to rest for at least an hour. Serve warm, enjoy!

Chili Jalapeño Burger

Cooking Time: 10 Min

Ingredients:
- ½ C. mayonnaise
- ½ Tsp. ground white pepper
- 1 Tsp. garlic powder
- 1 Tsp. Chipotle chili powder
- 2 lbs. ground beef
- 2 eggs, beaten
- 1 ½ C. all-purpose beef sauce (reserve ½ C.)
- 1 Tbsp. Steak BBQ rub
- 15 oz. can chili, preferred (without beans)
- 2-3 jalapeños, sliced
- Hamburger buns
- Cheddar cheese slices
- Condiments of choice

Directions:
1. Combine the mayonnaise, white pepper, garlic powder, Chipotle chili powder and ½ C. of reserved sauce in a small bowl. Mix thoroughly. 2. Cover with plastic wrap and place it in the refrigerator for 30 minutes to chill.
2. Ground beef
3. Place ground beef in large bowl, add eggs and season with 1 Tbsp. Steak BBQ rub, or your favorite rub, to taste and remaining sauce. Mix ingredients by hand until just blended. 2. Form 1" thick patties and place on a wax paper lined tray. Place tray with patties in refrigerator

and allow to chill for 10-15 minutes. Prepare chili according to package directions. Set aside. 4. Place chilled patties on the grill at 350°F for 5 minutes per side, with a quarter turn halfway through for good sear marks. 5. Top burgers with cheese and allow to melt. Burgers are done when internal temperature reaches 165°F.
4. To serve, place a spoonful of chili on each burger and top with jalapeño slices. For another layer of flavor, spread Chipotle mayonnaise on top of the hamburger bun.

Spring Tomahawk Steak And Vegetables

Cooking Time: 20 Min

Ingredients:
- 20 oz. Tomahawk steak
- Mixed variety radishes, carrots, turnips, roughly chopped
- ¼ C. melted butter
- 2 oz. basil
- 2 oz. parsley, chopped
- 2 oz. salt
- 2 oz. pepper
- 2 oz. garlic
- 2 oz. smoked paprika
- 2 oz. ground rosemary
- 2 oz. Black and Bleu seasoning (optional)
- Salt and pepper, to taste

Directions:
1. Set grill temp to 350°F.
2. Add mixed variety of chopped radishes, carrots, and turnips to hot cast iron skillet or wok with butter.
3. Add salt and pepper to taste on vegetables.
4. Mix salt, pepper, garlic, smoked paprika, and ground rosemary in a bowl (or use Black & Bleu seasoning).
5. Rub seasoning mix onto both sides of the steak.
6. Add steak to grill and cook 5-8 minutes per side.
7. Add fresh basil and chopped parsley to vegetables.
8. Remove steak when internal temp reaches 145°F for medium rare.

Flat Iron Sausage And Peppers Hash

Cooking Time: 10 Min

Ingredients:
- 1 Pound Of Ground Sausage
- 1 Red Pepper (Chopped)
- 1 Green Pepper (Chopped)
- 1 White Onion (Chopped)
- 1-2 Large Potatoes Chopped Into Small Cubes
- Eggs (Optional)

Directions:
1. Heat the Flat Iron to medium heat. Add oil to the flat top. Cook ground sausage until well browned and move to the side. Add potatoes to allow them time to begin cooking first. Cook potatoes until they begin to brown/ ¾ of the way done. Use spatulas to push them to the side. Add more oil if necessary then add onions and peppers. Cook them until they begin to soften. Push those to the side with the potatoes. Mix all dish components together on the Flat Iron together and cook to your liking. Serve hot. Optionally add eggs to the dish at the end, especially if serving as a breakfast dish. Enjoy!

Cheesy Chipotle Chili

Cooking Time: 5 Hrs

Ingredients:
- 3 lb. roast beef or sirloin
- 2 large sweet onions, roughly chopped, divided evenly
- 2 cloves minced garlic, or to taste
- 7-8 dried Chipotle peppers, roughly chopped
- 12 oz. can tomato sauce
- 1 Qt. beef broth
- 1 C. flour
- 1-2 Tsp. Chipotle chili powder
- 2 Tbsp. cumin
- 2 Tbsp. coarse black pepper
- 3 Tbsp. bacon grease or oil
- ½-1 C. water
- ½ C. sharp cheddar cheese, shredded
- 1 sourdough or French bread bowl per person
- Seasoned salt, to taste

Directions:
1. Cube meat and brown in Dutch oven with bacon grease or cooking oil. Do not drain juices from pan. 2.

Sift flour into gallon sized storage bag and add Chipotle chili powder and pepper to taste. Add browned cubed meat, seal bag and shake to coat meat evenly with seasoned flour. 3. Return meat to pan and add garlic, ½ of chopped onion, cumin, chipotle peppers, tomato sauce and beef broth. 4. Season to taste with salt and pepper and add enough water to cover all ingredients and stir to combine. 5. Place covered Dutch oven in the middle of the grill at 225°F for 5 hours. 6. During the last hour of cooking, add the remaining onion and stir to combine. The meat should be fork-tender.

2. To serve, slice the top off the bread bowls and hollow them out. Fill with chili, top with cheese and put the top back on. Arrange the bread bowls on a baking sheet and place on the grill at 350°F for 3-5 minutes, enough to toast the bread slightly and melt the cheese, then serve.

Chorizo Taquitos

Cooking Time: 30 Min

Ingredients:
- 12 Corn Tortillas
- 8 oz. Fresh Chorizo
- 1/4 Cup Onion, Finely Chopped
- 1 Tbsp Butter
- 1 Tbsp Vegetable Oil
- 1 Potato, Cubed
- 1 Tbsp Char-Griller Original Seasoning
- 1 Tbsp Paprika
- 1/2 tsp Cumin
- 1 tsp Salt
- 1/4 Cup Cilantro, Chopped
- 1 Cup Shredded Colby Jack Cheese
- Oil for Heating Up Tortillas
- Queso Fresco and Cilantro for Garnish
- 1/2 Cup Sour Cream (Cilantro Lime Sour Cream)
- Juice of Half a Lime (Cilantro Lime Sour Cream)

Directions:
1. Light grill for indirect heat and heat grill to 350F
2. In a medium sized skillet, heat chorizo up thoroughly
3. Place on a paper towel lined plate, to drain access fat
4. Place butter and vegetable oil in the skillet
5. Add onions, potatoes, seasonings, and cilantro into the hot oil, stirring frequently until potatoes are crispy
6. Add chorizo and shredded cheese and stir until combined and melted, remove from heat
7. Brush both sides tortillas with oil (to make it easier, you can spray each side lightly with an olive oil cooking spray) and place in a dry clean pan or directly on the grill grates from a few seconds on each side
8. Place a spoonful of chorizo mixture into each tortilla and roll up tightly without breaking the tortillas.
9. When all tortillas are rolled up with filling, place them on a small greased cookie sheet
10. Place pan on grill for 30 minutes, flipping the taquitos half way through
11. While taquitos are cooling, mix together all the dip ingredients in a small bowl
12. Serve taquitos drizzled with sour cream mixture, topped with queso fresco and cilantro

Bacon Buster Burger

Ingredients:
- ¾ lb. thick-cut bacon, chopped
- 1 sweet onion, chopped
- 3 cloves garlic, minced
- 1/3 C. maple syrup
- 1/3 C. apple cider vinegar
- ¼ C. packed brown sugar
- 2 Tbsp. unsalted butter
- 2 lbs. ground beef
- 2 eggs, beaten
- 1 C. beef all-purpose sauce
- Steak BBQ rub
- Swiss cheese, sliced, or preferred
- Hamburger buns
- Condiments of choice

Directions:
1. Melt butter in a large cast iron skillet over medium-high heat. Add onion and garlic and cook until just tender and fragrant, 2- 3 minutes. 2. Add chopped bacon and cook 3- 5 minutes, until the fat begins to render and the bacon begins to brown. 3. Add maple syrup, brown

sugar and apple cider vinegar. Bring to a boil, reduce heat to low and simmer, stirring frequently, until the mixture is very dark and syrupy, for 15-20 minutes. 4. Allow bacon mixture to cool completely. Transfer to a food processor and pulse until well chopped. Store in an airtight container in the fridge for up to 3 weeks.

2. Ground beef
3. Place ground beef in large bowl, add eggs and season with Steak BBQ rub, or your favorite rub, to taste and sauce. Mix ingredients by hand until just blended. 2. Form 1" thick patties and place on a wax paper lined tray. Spread a thick layer of bacon jam on top of every other patty, then press two patties together. Press firmly around the seams to ensure the bacon jam doesn't run when cooking. Place tray with patties in refrigerator and allow to chill for 10-15 minutes. 4. Place chilled patties on the grill at 350°F for 5 minutes per side, with a quarter turn halfway through for good sear marks.
4. To serve, add more bacon and cheese if desired, top with condiments of choice and enjoy!

Smoked Baked Spaghetti

Cooking Time: 1 Hrs

Ingredients:
- 1 lb. ground beef
- 1 lb. spaghetti
- 2 Tbsp. melted butter
- 1 C. onion, diced
- 1-2 cloves garlic, minced
- 1 chopped green pepper, cored and seeded
- 1½ C. spaghetti sauce
- 2 C. grated or shredded cheese (Colby jack, Mozzarella or Parmesan)
- 2 C. mushrooms, sliced (optional)
- 2.25 oz. can of black olives, drained (optional)
- 1 Tsp. salt
- 1 Tsp. pepper

Directions:
1. Fill stockpot with water and salt and bring to a boil.
2. Cook spaghetti until al dente, following directions on package. Drain and set aside in a large bowl. 3. Sauté onion, green pepper and mushrooms in a large skillet until tender, about 5-7 minutes. Set aside in a small bowl. Do not wipe pan. 4. Brown ground beef in the same pan and add minced garlic, salt and pepper and stir. 5. Drain grease from ground beef and add green pepper, onion, mushrooms and spaghetti sauce. Mix well. 6. Add 2 Tbsp. melted butter and ½ cup of grated cheese to cooked spaghetti and stir. 7. Place 1/3 of meat sauce in the bottom of a well-greased 9 x 13 baking pan. 8. Layer 1/3 of cheese on top of meat sauce. 9. Add all of the spaghetti and spread evenly. 10. Pour the rest of the meat sauce on top of spaghetti in an even layer. 1 Bake for 45 minutes at 350°F. 12. Spread the remaining cheese and add black olives in an even layer across the top. 13. Bake at 350°F for an additional 10-15 minutes until cheese is melted.

2. Let cool for 10 minutes, then serve!
3. Note: The mushrooms and black olives in this recipe can be swapped out with toppings of your choice.

All American Blended Burger

Cooking Time: 15 Min

Ingredients:
- 80/20 Ground Chuck - 3 Ounces
- Baby Portabella Mushrooms - 1 Ounce
- Tomato - 1
- Green Leaf Lettuce - 1 Head
- Ketchup - 1 Tablespoon
- Mayonnaise - 1 Tablespoon
- Char-Griller Steak Rub - 2 Tablespoons
- Brioche Bun

Directions:
1. Chop mushrooms into pieces roughly the size of the grind of the beef.
2. Mix mushrooms and beef together and form a patty.
3. Bring your AKORN up to roughly 600 degrees.
4. Place the burger patty on the grill and season top side with 1 Tbsp of Char-Griller steak rub and let cook for four minutes.
5. Flip the burger, season the now top side with 1 Tbsp of Char-Griller steak rub, continue cooking until an internal temp of 140 degrees is reached.

6. Remove the burger from the grill to let rest. While resting place your bun on the grill to toast. After toasting apply mayo to the bottom bun and ketchup to the top.
7. Add cheese to the burger if desired and build burger from the bottom up as bun, burger, tomato slice, green leaf lettuce top bun and enjoy.

Flat Iron Philly Cheesesteak

Cooking Time: 25 Min

Ingredients:
- 2 Lbs Thinly Sliced Beef
- 1 Onion, Sliced
- 2 Green Peppers, Sliced
- 1 tsp Garlic Powder
- 2 Tbsp Butter
- Salt and Pepper to Taste
- 3 Tbsp Apple Cider Vinegar
- 12 to 16 Slices of Provolone Cheese
- 1 Can of Cheeze Whiz
- 6 Hoagie Rolls

Directions:
1. Preheat grilled to medium high heat
2. Add tablespoon of butter and some oil to griddle
3. Add onions and peppers to griddle.
4. Season with salt, pepper, vinegar and ½ tsp garlic powder. Toss to combine.
5. Add another tablespoon of butter and some oil to the griddle.
6. Add beef to the griddle and chop it up more with your metal spatulas to ensure it cooks evenly.
7. Season beef with salt, pepper and ½ tsp of garlic powder.
8. When meat is cooked, divide it up on the griddle top into 6 piles.
9. Turn griddle heat to medium and add a few tablespoons of Cheese Whiz to each pile of meat.
10. Divide veggies up evenly among the six piles of meat.
11. Add 2 to 3 slices of provolone cheese to each pile.
12. Split the hoagie rolls and toast them on the griddle.
13. Once the cheese is melted, put each pile of meat on hoagie roll and serve hot.

Grilled Ribeye Steak

Cooking Time: 8-10 Min

Ingredients:
- 1½" thick ribeye steaks
- Salt and pepper, to taste

Directions:
1. Allow the steaks to come to room temperature.
2. Pre-heat the grill to 450°F.
3. Generously season steaks on all sides with salt and pepper, or use Steak BBQ rub, to taste.
4. Place steaks on the grill and sear for 4-5 minutes on both sides. The steaks are done when internal temperature reaches 130°F for medium-rare.
5. Allow to rest for 5 minutes before slicing and serving. Enjoy!

Akorn Dino Beef Plate Ribs

Cooking Time: 5 Hours Min

Ingredients:
- Beef Plate Ribs
- Mustard
- Loot N' Booty What's Your Beef Rub
- 50/50 Coarse Salt & Coarse Pepper
- Akorn Kamado Charcoal Grill
- Smokin' Stone & Drip Pan
- Fogo Premium Lump Charcoal & Mesquite Wood Chunks
- Char-Griller Grills Remote Thermometer
- Butcher Paper
- Apple Juice With Spritzer

Directions:
1. Smoked Beef Ribs are full of flavor and are easy to make.
2. pounds beef plate bone ribs (3 bones): Trim fat and silver skin from the top and bottom. Apply mustard to all the sides. Season all sides of the meat with Loot N' Booty What's Your Beef Rub and 50/50 Coarse Salt & Coarse Pepper. Tip: Allow ribs to get to room temperature prior to smoking. This allows the seasonings to sweat and absorb into the meat and meat to start smoking faster. Prep Akorn Kamado Charcoal Grill,

Smokin' Stone & drip pan filled with water. Preheat Akorn Kamado & Smoke at temperature 250°: used Fogo Premium Lump Charcoal & Mesquite Wood Chunks. Tip: remember to use your Char-Griller Grills Remote Thermometer to take the guess work out your cooking. Spritz with apple juice every 45 minutes during the smoking process and rotate the ribs each time. Place ribs in Akorn Kamado and smoke until internal temperature 170° is met, roughly takes 4-5 hours. Tip: while smoking if a spot on the meat is getting too much char, place a small piece of foil covering the spot to help prevent that spot from burning/drying out. Wrap with peach/butcher paper and apple juice once internal temperature 170° is met. Place back in the Akorn Kamado and cook until internal temperature 199° is met, roughly takes one-two hours. Remove from the smoker and allow to rest in a cooler covered with a towel/blanket for 1-2 hours. Remove, slice and enjoy!

Flat Iron Steak Fajitas

Cooking Time: 20 Min

Ingredients:
- 2 lb. flat iron steaks
- 1 C. soy sauce
- 1½ C. pineapple juice
- 1 Tbsp. ground cumin
- 1½ Tsp. fresh garlic, minced
- 3 Tbsp. fresh squeezed lime juice
- 1 Tsp. Original All-Purpose BBQ rub
- 1 Tsp. olive oil
- 1 yellow onion, sliced lengthwise
- 1-2 bell peppers, seeded and sliced lengthwise
- 6" flour tortillas
- Cilantro, chopped, for garnish
- Shredded cheese (optional)
- Pico de Gallo and/or guacamole, for serving

Directions:
1. Whisk soy sauce, pineapple juice, cumin, garlic and lime juice together in a large bowl to make marinade. Transfer to a large resealable plastic bag with flat iron steaks and gently shake to evenly coat. Marinate in refrigerator for 4 hours or best overnight. 2. Pre-heat grill to 400°F. Heat olive oil in a large sauté pan over high heat. Add onions to pan and cook for 2-3 minutes, stirring constantly. Add peppers to pan and sauté for 3-4 minutes. Season with 1 Tsp. of Original All-Purpose BBQ rub or your favorite rub. Remove pan from heat. 3. Place steaks on grill for 5-7 minutes per side for medium rare. Steak is done when internal temperature reaches 140°F.
2. Slice steak across the grain. Place vegetables on a heated cast iron fajita platter. Place sliced Flat Iron steaks on top of the vegetables. Serve with tortillas, Pico de Gallo, cilantro and guacamole. Top with shredded cheese, if desired.

Meat Loaf

Ingredients:
- 2 Lbs KC Cattle Company Wagyu (Ground Beef)
- 1 Chopped Green Pepper
- 3/4 Cup Chopped Onion
- 1 Can Diced Green Chili's
- 2 Eggs
- 1/3 Cup G Hughes Sugar Free Hickory BBQ Sauce
- 1 Tsp Liquid Smoke
- 1/8 Cup Ketchup
- 1 Tbsp Char-Griller All Purpose Seasoning
- 1 1/2 tbsp Frying Pig Seasoning Beef Beef Baby Seasoning
- 1 Tbsp Jack Stack Seasoning
- 1 Tsp Salt
- 1 Tsp Pepper
- 1.5-2 Cups of Pork Rinds Crumbled (Any Flavor)

Directions:
1. Mix together with hands. Form into a loaf. Drizzle with ketchup or BBQ sauce Smoke for 2 hours at 300° Pull off grill & finish off in the oven on broil for 10 mins

Coffee & Cocoa Tri-tip

Cooking Time: 2 Hrs

Ingredients:
- 2-3 Lb Tri-Tip
- 4 Tbsp Coffee Rub
- 1 Tbsp Unsweetened Cocoa Powder
- Salt to Taste
- 1 tsp Olive Oil

Directions:
1. Remove all excess fat and silver skin from the tri-tip.
2. Mix together all the dry ingredients in a shaker until they are well blended.
3. Use the olive oil as a slather on both sides of the tri-tip to help get the rub to stick. Carefully season both sides and ensure that the tri-tip has a nice even coat of seasoning.
4. Start prepping your fire and working on getting your smoker up to 275 F. Once your smoker has reached 275 F it is time to put the tri-tip on.
5. Once the tri-tip has reached an internal temperature of 125 F it is time to take it out of the smoker and prep for the sear.
6. Place the tri-tip in a pan and cover with foil while you begin to get the grill up to 450-500 F.
7. Tip: You can get a good sear on either the grill or a cast iron skillet.
8. Once the grill has reached 450-500 F place the tri-tip directly on the grill and sear both sides till internal temp reaches 135 F.
9. Pull the tri-tip off the grill and let rest for 15-20 minutes before slicing.
10. Tip: Internal temp for beef varies by preference so feel free to pull it sooner for rare or later for well done.
11. Slice the tri-tip against the grain. Enjoy!

Over The Top Chili On The Grand Champ

Ingredients:
- 1 Pound of 80/20 Ground Beef
- 1 Pound of Hot (or your favorite) Italian Sausage
- 1 Pound of your favorite Bacon
- 1 Large Yellow Onion (Diced)
- 1 Green Bell Pepper (Diced)
- 1 Yellow Bell Pepper (Diced)
- 3 Cloves of Garlic (Minced)
- 15 oz Can of Red Kidney Beans- Drained (Not rinsed)
- 15 oz Can of Black Beans- Drained (Not rinsed)
- 29 oz Can of Yellow Sweet Corn Kernels- Drained (Not rinsed)
- 14.5 oz Can of Diced Tomatoes with Green Chiles (Kind of like a can of Rotel)
- 3 oz of Tomato Paste
- 1 Tbsp of Chili Powder
- 1 Tbsp of Paprika
- 2 Tsp of Onion Powder
- 1 Tsp of Black Pepper
- 3/4 Tsp of Salt
- 1 Tsp of Cayenne Pepper
- 2 Cups of Beef Broth

Directions:
1. In a large bowl, mix the ground beef and Italian sausage together well. Mix in the Paprika, Salt, Pepper, Cayenne, Cumin, Chili Powder and Onion Powder to the meat. Mix well with your hands or use a mixer! Place seran wrap or foil over the bowl with the meat and place in fridge to relax... In a medium/large skillet (I prefer cast iron skillets) lightly oil the skillet and set heat to medium high. Add in your onion and bell peppers and cook until the onions become translucent and just start to develop some color. Add in your 3 cloves of minced garlic. Cook until fragrant. Remove skillet from heat and put aside (I dumped the veggies into the chili pot at this point). Cook your bacon in the same skillet to your liking... I suggest you don't over cook your bacon. You don't want it crispy for the chili. It will continue to cook once on the smoker/in the cooker. When bacon is to your liking, add it to the pot with the onion and bell peppers. Add the remaining ingredients to your pot. The cans of beans/tomatoes, corn, beef broth, Worcestershire sauce, etc.... Time to fire up the smoker/cooker!
2. Tip: Make the meat into a ball by using seran wrap!! So much easier!

3. Place the pot on the bottom rack or ash pan grates of your cooker/smoker. Place the "meatball" on the grate directly above the pot of chili. Cook at 275 degrees F (135 Celsius) until the meatball reaches an internal temperature of 165 degrees F (74 Celsius). Remove both the pot and the meat. Cover the meat loosely in foil to allow to rest and reabsorb all those juices. Once rested, break apart and crumble (to the size of your liking) the meat ball into the pot of chili. Mix well and serve with some shredded cheese and sour cream, perhaps even some oyster crackers!!

Flat Iron Griddle Sizzler N' Veggies Sammies

Cooking Time: 10 Min

Ingredients:
- Thinly Sliced Steak or Beef Sizzlers
- 1/2 Onions
- 1 Jalapeño (Sliced)
- Favorite Beef Rub or Seasoning
- Italian Bread
- Olive Oil In Squeeze Bottle
- Beef Bouillon Juice Mixture In A Squeeze Bottle
- Cheddar Cheese (Shredded)

Directions:
1. Slice the green pepper, onions and Jalapeño and place in bowl. Apply olive oil to both sides of the meat as a binder for the seasonings. Apply favorite beef rub/seasoning to both sides of the meat. Heat up your Char-Griller Flat Iron Griddle to medium heat with good portion of olive oil. Add all the veggies and cook for 5 mins before adding the meat. Add meat to the griddle and cook on each side for 3 mins then chop the meat on the griddle into small pieces. Combine the meat and veggies, add some beef bouillon juice mixture to it and cook for 5 minutes. Add cheddar cheese and cook until melted, roughly 2 mins. Toast Italian Bread, then add the cheesy veggie meat to the bread and enjoy!

Saucy Brisket Burnt Ends

Cooking Time: 6-7 Hrs

Ingredients:
- 6 Pound Brisket Flat or Point.
- Original Sin Mustard for Binder
- Beef Rub
- 50/50 Salt & Pepper Blend

Directions:
1. Prepping
2. Trim brisket with sharp knife on a cutting board then place on a tray to apply binder and seasonings.
3. Apply mustard to all sides of the brisket as a binder for the seasonings.
4. Apply seasonings to all sides of the brisket.
5. Smoking
6. Add Char-Griller Drip Pan with water underneath the grill grate of your smoker/grill. This will add moisture to the brisket during the long smoke and also the meat drippings and juice from the spritz will fall in there for less of a mess.
7. Preheat your smoker/grill to 240°-250°: going low n' slow at this temperature is key for brisket. 1 Hour Per Pound.
8. Add Brisket to smoker/grill on to a cardboard with butcher paper. Using the Cardboard with butcher paper in the shape of the brisket is a great method that keeps the bottom of the brisket from drying out & allows you to easily move the brisket around in the smoker/grill from side to side. It will keep the brisket juicy and moist.
9. Tip: Place the brisket fat side up.
10. Spritz every hour with apple juice and rotate brisket from left to right for even smoking. Remember the brisket is on the cardboard and it's really easy to rotate without having to touch the meat. Spritzing with Apple juice helps keep the brisket moist during the long smoke, adds flavor and helps create the black bark we are looking for.
11. Maintaining your fire is key, check on your fire roughly every hour and add charcoal/wood as needed. Try to avoid your smoker from exceeding 250° and getting under 240°. Brisket is meant for low n' slow at about 240°-250° and keeping your fire steady throughout the cook is important.
12. Remove brisket from the smoker when it reaches 160°, discard the cardboard & butcher paper. Place the

brisket in a pan with apple juice, water & beef rub then cover with foil.

13. Tip: Take the guesswork out and use the Char-griller Grills Remote Thermometer & Folding Probe Thermometer to easily see what temperature the meat is at.

14. Add brisket back to the smoker until temperature 199°-200° has been reached. Tip: no need to waste your smoking wood when the brisket is wrapped. Use only the charcoal as your fuel at temperature 240°-250° until the brisket is done.

15. Remove brisket onto a cutting board and slice into cubes. Then add the the brisket cubes back to the pan with the brisket juices with Blues Hog Raspberry Chipotle Sauce. Get them sauced up and place back in the smoker/grill uncovered for an additional 30 minutes.

16. When you remove from the smoker/grill allow to rest for 5-10 minutes and enjoy!

Grilled Caesar Salad

Cooking Time: 20 Min

Ingredients:
- 2 Beef Strip Loin Steaks
- Olive oil
- Salt and pepper to taste
- 2-3 romaine hearts
- 1.5 C. parmesan cheese
- Lemon, halved
- Your favorite caesar dressing

Directions:
1. Rub steaks front and back with olive oil
2. Add salt and pepper to both sides and set aside
3. Cut the ends off 2-3 romaine hearts
4. Then slice in half longways to allow for easy grilling
5. In a cast iron pan add 1½ C. parmesan cheese
6. Preheat grill to 350°F
7. Grill steak for 5-7 per side
8. Cook the cheese in the pan for 8-10 minutes or until golden brown
9. Once ready, remove and flip onto ceramic bowl and let cool
10. Grill the 2-3 romaine hearts for 2-4 minutes
11. Spritz lemon over the romaine hearts
12. Once done, chop up the romaine hearts and place in the cooled parmesan cheese bowl
13. Add your favorite Caesar dressing

Smokin' Champ Smoked Beef Back Ribs

Cooking Time: 5-6 Hrs

Ingredients:
- 2 Beef Back Ribs
- Mustard
- Fogo Charcoal The Rub
- Foil
- Apple Juice For Spritzer and Wrap With.
- Char-Griller Grills Smokin' Champ 1624 & Drip Pan
- Fogo Quebracho Lump Charcoal

Directions:
1. Trim any fat and silver skin from the top and bottom of the Beef Back Ribs. Apply even coating of mustard to the top and bottom. Season the top and bottom of the meat with Fogo Charcoal The Rub. Tip: Allow ribs to get to room temperature prior to smoking. This allows the seasonings to sweat and absorb into the meat and the meat will begin to smoke faster. Prep your Char-Griller Grill Smokin' Champ 1624 with drip pan filled with water. Fire up your Char-Griller Grill Smokin' Champ 1624 to temperature 250°: used Fogo Quebracho Lump Charcoal & Mesquite Mini Wood Logs. Spritz with apple juice every hour minutes during the smoking process and rotate the ribs each time. Place ribs in your Char-Griller Grill Smokin' Champ 1624 and smoke until internal temperature 170° is met, roughly takes 3-4 hours. Tip: remember to use your Char-Griller Grills folding probe to take the guess work out your cooking. Wrap with foil and apple juice once internal temperature 170° is met. Place back in the Char-Griller Grill Smokin' Champ 1624 and cook until internal temperature 199° is met, roughly takes 1 hour 30 minutes to get from internal temperature 170° to internal temperature 199° Remove from the smoker and allow to rest in a cooler covered with a towel/blanket for 1-2hours. Remove, slice and enjoy!

Flat Iron Griddle Classic Steak Street Tacos

Cooking Time: 25 Min

Ingredients:
- Steak Taco Meat (diced chuck roast or any kind of steak): 1-2 pounds
- Small bundle of cilantro: chopped or whole
- 1 Onion: diced
- 1 - 7 oz bag of Chihuahua Cheese
- Sazón, Chef Merito Meat Seasoning & Char Griller Grills Taco Fajita seasonings to taste
- 1 bunch Cebollitas/Green Onions: Sliced
- 1-2 Jalapenos: Sliced
- 1-2 packs of corn tortillas
- 4 Limes: cut into quarters
- Favorite Salsa
- Sour Cream to Taste (As a garnish)

Directions:
1. Season the diced steak with Sazón, Chef Merito Meat Seasoning & Char-Griller Grills Taco Fajita seasonings to taste.
2. Squeeze lime juice from two limes.
3. Mix the ingredients thoroughly and it's ready.
4. Fire up your Flat Iron Griddle to medium heat using three burners.
5. Add the cebollitas/green onions, jalapenos and steak to the griddle and allow to cook.
6. Move the meat and veggies around every few minutes. Meat and veggies will be done when they are brown and charred. Takes about 20-25 minutes.
7. Tip: Remove any meat juices in the grease drawer to allow the meat to sear.
8. Add tortillas and cheese to the hot griddle top.
9. Once the tortillas warm and the cheese melts/golden brown, add the tortilla on top of the cheese and then flip the cheesy tortilla.
10. After flipping it, remove it from the griddle.
11. Repeat this process until all your tortillas are completed.
12. Add steak, fresh chopped onions, cilantro and salsa onto the cheesy tortilla.
13. Eat the cebollitas/green onions and jalapenos on the side.
14. Enjoy!

Bbq Crunch Wrap

Cooking Time: 20 Min

Ingredients:
- 1 Burrito Size Tortilla (10-12")
- 3/4 Cup Macaroni And Cheese
- 1/2 Cup Pulled Pork Or Chopped Brisket
- 4 Slices Of Thick Cut Bacon
- BBQ Sauce
- Cilantro Or Green Onions

Directions:
1. Heat 2 middle burners on the Flat Iron to medium
2. Cut bacon slices in half and weave the pieces together to form a square
3. Place bacon weave on Flat Iron and cook until crispy, flipping once during cooking. Place on paper towel to drain grease
4. Warm tortilla up on the Flat Iron, just into pliable and remove from heat
5. Add macaroni to center of tortilla and smooth out to about a 3" circle. Top with bacon weave, then pulled pork/brisket. Drizzle BBQ sauce over the meat and sprinkle with cilantro or green onions
6. Work your way around the tortilla, bringing the edges to the center forming pleats. Place crunch wrap pleat side down on the Flat Iron where the bacon was cooked.
7. Allow 4-5 minutes for the crunch wrap to get toasted and flip to toast other side
8. Carefully remove the crunch wrap and enjoy!

Smoked Prime Rib

Cooking Time: 8 Hrs

Ingredients:
- 15 lb. Prime Rib
- 2 oz. ground pepper
- 4 oz. coarse salt
- 2 oz. smoked paprika

Directions:
1. Mix salt, pepper, and paprika.
2. Cover rib side of prime rib in seasoning.
3. Flip and season the fat cap side of the prime rib.
4. Pre-heat smoker to 225°F.
5. Add prime rib directly to grates, fat cap up.
6. Smoke prime rib at 40 minutes per pound (About 8 hrs for a 15 lb. prime rib). Remove when internal temp reaches 135°F.
7. Let rest for 30 minutes, then slice, serve and enjoy!

Skirt Steak Pinwheels

Cooking Time: 10 Min

Ingredients:
- Skirt Steak- 1 Pound
- Chopped Chives- 1/4 Cup
- Diced Fresh Tomato- 1/4 Cup
- Minced Garlic- 1 Tablespoon
- Salted Butter- 1 Stick
- J Christopher Co. The Rub- 1 Tablespoon
- Vegetable Oil- 1 Teaspoon
- Wooden Skewers- 2

Directions:
1. 30 minutes before prep: Soak wooden skewers in water to avoid burning.
2. Prepare your Akorn or your favorite Char-Griller grill for direct high heat.
3. Lay out skirt steak and slice long way down the middle to make two evenly wide pieces. Each piece should be about 2 inches wide. Lay pieces out flat.
4. Prepare butter. In small mixing bowl add butter, vegetable oil, minced garlic, and The Rub. With spoon, mash butter until your able to whip smooth.
5. Spread butter mixture on the two skirt steak pieces. Sprinkle on chives and tomatoes.
6. Start at end closest to you and roll steak up and away from you, pulling in as you go to keep pinwheel tight. Once rolled, slide wooden skewer through the steak as if you were making a beef lollipop.
7. Sprinkle both sides of the pinwheels with The Rub and place directly on the grill over direct high heat. Shut lid and let cook 5 minutes, turn, and cook another 3-5 minutes with lid closed. Both sides should be seared and brown. I find cooking these to a medium warm pink center rather than medium rare allows for a more tender bite with this cut.
8. Let rest 5-10 minutes and enjoy!

Foil Packet Short Ribs

Cooking Time: 1.5 To 2.5 Hrs

Ingredients:
- Packed Brown Sugar - 1 Tbs
- Paprika - 1 Tbs
- Chili Powder - 1 Tbs
- Salt - 1 tsp
- Garlic Powder - 1 tsp
- 4 Pounds of Beef Short Ribs
- Barbecue Sauce of Choice - 1/2 Cup
- Ice Cubes

Directions:
1. Mix together sugar, chili powder, salt and garlic powder
2. Rub the meat with the mixture generously
3. Place ribs in a dish, cover and put in fridge for 30 minutes
4. Preheat grill to medium indirect heat.
5. Center ¼ of the ribs and two ice cubes on a sheet of foil, seal the packet allowing room for air to circulate.
6. Repeat for three more packets
7. Grill packets over medium, 375 to 400, indirect heat for 1 and a half to two hours or until tender.
8. Open packets and brush ribs with barbecue sauce, cover and grill over indirect heat for 5 minutes. Turning the ribs once.
9. Serve with additional sauce as desired.

Dry Aged Rib Roast

Cooking Time: 1.5 Hrs

Ingredients:
- 6-8 lb. dry aged rib roast
- ½ C. melted butter
- 4 sprigs of parsley
- 4 sprigs of basil
- 4 sprigs of rosemary
- Kosher salt
- Black pepper
- Paprika
- Garlic

Directions:

1. Finely chop parsley, basil, and rosemary, and mix with melted butter
2. Place rib roast on grill at 350°F over indirect heat and grill for approximately 45 minutes
3. Brush roast with buttered herbs
4. Continue to cook over indirect heat for additional 45 minutes or until internal temp reaches 145°F

DESSERTS

Salted Caramel Chocolate Tart

Cooking Time: 20 Min

Ingredients:
- 1- 8 oz Bag of Sea Salt Kettle Potato Chips, Crushed (Crust)
- 1/4 Cup Flour (Crust)
- 5 Tbsp Unsalted Butter, Melted (Crust)
- 1 Cup Sugar (Caramel)
- 1/2 Cup Heavy Cream (Caramel)
- 6 Tbsp Unsalted Butter (Caramel)
- 1 tsp Sea Salt (Caramel)
- 10 Oz Semisweet Chocolate Chips (Chocolate Layer)
- 1/4 Cup Heavy Cream (Chocolate Layer)
- 1/4 Cup Sugar (Chocolate Layer)
- 2 tsp Vanilla Extract (Chocolate Layer)
- 2 Large Eggs (Chocolate Layer)

Directions:
1. Light grill for indirect heat and heat to 350.
2. In a large bowl, combine crushed chips, melted butter, and flour. Mix until combined.
3. Press into tart pan and place on grill. Bake for 15 minutes.
4. Remove from grill and allow to cool.
5. In a sauce pan over medium heat, add sugar and allow to melt completely, stirring frequently.
6. Add cream and butter, stir until combined.
7. Add sea salt and allow to boil for 5 minutes.
8. Remove from heat and allow to cool for 15 minutes.
9. Pour caramel onto crust.
10. In a saucepan over medium heat, add cream and allow to heat up.
11. Add chocolate chips and sugar, stir until melted and smooth.
12. Add eggs one at a time stirring until combined.
13. Add vanilla and stir.
14. Pour chocolate until crust.
15. Place tart on grill and allow to bake for 20 minutes.
16. Remove from grill and let cool.

Grilled S'mores 4 Ways

Servings: 4
Cooking Time: 5 Min

Ingredients:
- Graham Crackers - 4 Full Crackers
- Large Marshmallows - 4
- Milk Chocolate Bar
- Dark Chocolate Bar
- Cookie Butter
- Peanut and Caramel Candy Bar
- Chili Powder
- Peanut Butter

Directions:
1. Heat grill to 350 degrees
2. Break four graham crackers in half and lay out.
3. Top the first graham cracker with milk chocolate bar and peanut butter.
4. Top the second graham cracker with milk chocolate and cookie butter
5. Top third graham cracker with dark chocolate and a sprinkle of chili powder.
6. Top fourth graham cracker with Snickers Bar cut in half longways.
7. Top each graham cracker with a marshmallow and the other half of the graham cracker.
8. Wrap each s'mores in its own foil packet.
9. Place on warming rack of the grill for 4 to 5 minutes.
10. Enjoy.

Bourbon Glaze For Candied Bacon Scones

Cooking Time: 15 Min

Ingredients:
- Bourbon - 3 Tbsp
- Vanilla - 1 tsp
- Powdered Sugar - 2 cups
- Milk - 4 Tbsp

Directions:

1. Place all ingredients in a small pan and stir to combine. Place pan on grill and allow to heat through for 15 minutes. Stir half way through. Remove from grill and cool. Open grill vents and increase temperature to 400 to cook the scones. Make the scone dough.

Grilled Stuffed Peaches

Cooking Time: 20 Min

Ingredients:
- 1- 2 peaches per person
- 2 Tbsp. honey, divided
- 4 oz. blue cheese, or to taste
- Coarse black pepper, to taste
- 2-3 slices of bacon, for garnish

Directions:
1. Rinse peaches and dry with paper towel. Slice in half, remove stone and cut the pit hole slightly larger.
2. Fry bacon in a pan to desired crispness according to package directions, drain grease and crumble when cool. Set aside in a small bowl.
3. Place peaches cut side down directly on the grill at 350°F for 5-7 minutes, depending on the size.
4. Turn peaches over and fill holes with blue cheese and crumbled bacon and bake for 5-7 minutes, until peaches are softened and cheese is melted.
5. Remove peaches from grill, drizzle with honey and sprinkle with coarse black pepper to serve.

Chocolate Chip Skillet Cookie

Cooking Time: 25-30 Min

Ingredients:
- 2 C. all-purpose flour
- 1 C. butter, melted
- 1 C. brown sugar
- ½ C. sugar
- 2 eggs, beaten
- 1 Tsp. vanilla extract
- 1 Tsp. baking soda
- ½ Tsp. salt
- ¾ C. milk chocolate chunks
- ¾ C. semi-sweet chocolate chips

Directions:

1. Pre-heat grill to 325°F. In a large bowl, combine melted butter and add sugars, stirring until dissolved. 2. Add eggs and vanilla and mix well. 3. Stir in flour, baking soda, and salt. Add in chocolate and stir to combine. 4. Transfer dough into heated cast iron skillet and spread evenly. 5. Bake at 325°F for 25-30 minutes or until the edges are golden brown. The inside will still be slightly gooey.
2. To serve, top with ice cream and eat warm.

Plum Galette

Cooking Time: 45-50 Min

Ingredients:
- 1½ C. and 3 Tbsp. all-purpose flour
- 1 ½ sticks unsalted butter, cut into ½" pieces
- ¼ Tsp. salt
- 1/3 C. ice water
- ¼ C. plus 1/3 C. sugar, reserve 1 Tsp.
- 3 Tbsp. ground almonds
- 2½ lbs. large plums, halved, pitted and cut into ½" wedges
- ½ C. good-quality plum preserves, strained if chunky or seedy
- Corn meal, for dusting

Directions:
1. Put 1½ C. flour, butter and salt into a food processor and mix for 5 seconds. 2. Add ice water and mix for 5 seconds longer, just until the dough holds together. Small pieces of butter should still be visible. 3. Remove the dough and gather it into a ball. On a lightly floured surface, roll out the dough into a large circle, 1/8" thick. 4. Drape the dough over the rolling pin and transfer to a large baking sheet. Refrigerate the dough until firm, 10-20 minutes. 5. While dough is chilling, pre-heat grill to 400°. In a small bowl, combine ¼ C. of the sugar with the ground almonds and 3 Tbsp. flour and mix well. Spread evenly over the dough to within 2" of the edge. 6. Arrange plum wedges on top and dot with butter. Sprinkle 1/3 C. sugar over the fruit. Fold the edge of the dough up over the plums to create a 2" border.

2. Tip: If the dough feels cold and firm when folding up the edges, wait a few minutes until it softens to prevent cracking.

3. Sprinkle the border with the remaining 1 Tsp. sugar.

7. Transfer the galette to a pre-heated pizza stone dusted with corn meal to prevent sticking, and bake at 400°F for 45-50 minutes, until the fruit is very soft and the crust is golden brown. 8. Remove from the grill and evenly brush the preserves over the hot fruit.

4. Allow the galette to cool before slicing and serving. Enjoy!

Glazed Oatmeal Raisin Cookies

Cooking Time: 15 Min

Ingredients:
- 2 C. oats
- 2 C. all-purpose flour
- 1 Tbsp. baking powder
- 2 Tsp. cinnamon
- ½ Tsp. nutmeg
- 1 Tsp. salt
- 2 sticks unsalted butter, softened
- 1 C. sugar
- ½ C. brown sugar
- 2 eggs
- ½ C. raisins
- 1 C. powdered sugar
- 1 Tbsp. vanilla extract
- 2-3 Tbsp. milk

Directions:

1. Pre-heat grill to 350°F. 2. In a medium bowl combine the oats, flour, baking powder, cinnamon, nutmeg, and salt. Mix well and set aside. 3. In a large bowl whisk the butter, sugar, and brown sugar together until sugar is dissolved. Add in the eggs one at a time, stirring well until combined. 4. Add the oat mixture to the butter mixture and stir until combined. Fold in the raisins. 5. Drop 1 Tbsp. of cookie batter onto cookie sheets, 2" apart. Bake 15 minutes or until the edges are golden brown. Remove from grill and transfer to a wire rack to cool. 6. While cookies are cooling, prepare icing by combining the powdered sugar and vanilla in a bowl.

Gradually add in milk until mixture is thick but spreadable.

2. Dunk the top of each cookie into the icing and let the excess drip off. Serve warm.

Candied Bacon Scones With Bourbon Glaze

Cooking Time: 15 Min

Ingredients:
- All Purpose Flour - 3 Cups
- Salt - 3/4 tsp
- Baking Powder - 1 Tbsp
- Sugar - 1/3 cup
- Cinnamon - 1/2 tsp
- Vanilla Extract - 1.5 tsp
- Heavy Cream - 1.5 Cups
- Chopped Bacon - 1/3 cup
- Heavy Cream - 1/4 cup

Directions:

1. Look here for the Candied Bacon Recipe and here for the Bourbon Glaze Recipe.

2. Have the Candied Bacon and Bourbon Glaze Ready nearby. Whisk together flour, salt, baking powder, sugar, and cinnamon. Add 1 1/2 c. cream, vanilla, candied bacon, and stir to combine. Divide dough in half. Flour a cutting board and pat each half into a 6" circle. Brush each circle of dough with the remaining cream. Place dough on parchment paper and cut into 6 triangles. Pull each wedge apart slightly and place in the freezer for 10 minutes. Transfer scones on the parchment paper to the grill grates. Bake for 15 minutes or until golden brown. Remove from grill and allow to cool. Using a 1/4 measuring cup, pour glaze over each scone and top with remaining chopped bacon.

Grilled Pumpkin Pie With Smoked Gingersnap Crust

Cooking Time: 45 To 60 Min

Ingredients:
- 15 Gingersnaps
- 5 Whole Graham Crackers, Broken Apart

- 2 Tbsp Light Brown Sugar
- 4 Tbsp Unsalted Butter, Melted
- 1 - 15 oz Can Pumpkin Puree
- 1 - 14 oz Can of Sweetened Condensed Milk
- 1 Tsp Cinnamon
- 1/2 tsp Ground Ginger
- 1/2 tsp Nutmeg
- 1/2 tsp Ground Cloves
- 2 Eggs, Lightly Beaten

Directions:

1. Add charcoal and a handful of mesquite wood chips to AKORN. Add the Smokin' Stone and preheat to 350 degrees F.
2. Place metal tin of gingersnaps and graham crackers on the grill.
3. Allow the cookies to smoke for 15 minutes.
4. Combine gingersnaps, brown sugar and butter into a food processor and process to moist crumbs.
5. Spoon crumbs into a greased pie pan and press into pan to form crust.
6. Return pie pan to grill and cook for 10 minutes.
7. Remove and allow to cool for 10 minutes.
8. While crust is cooling, whisk together pumpkin, sweetened condensed milk, eggs, and spices until combined.
9. Pour mixture into crust.
10. If desired, place foil around edges of crust to protect it from burning.
11. Return pie to grill and cook for an hour or until a toothpick inserted in the center comes out clean.
12. Cool and serve with whipped cream.

Candy Jar Brownies

Cooking Time: 25 Min

Ingredients:

- 20 Tablespoons Butter (Unsalted)
- 2 Cups White Sugar
- 1 Teaspoon Vanilla
- Four Large Eggs
- 1.5 Cups Unsweetened Cocoa Powder
- 1 Cup All Purpose Flour
- 2 Tablespoons Espresso Powder
- One Tablespoon Salt
- Variety of Candy (About 3 Cups)

Directions:

1. We didn't stop there. We also decided to cook it on the Char-Griller AKORN Kamado Grill because it is so versatile. The chocolate smell plus charcoal...we were in heaven. Before you start, check out our Guide to Baking on the AKORN.
2. Preheat AKORN to 350°F.
3. Cut up a variety of candy bars. Place in individual bowls.
4. Unwrap candy pieces that have foil and add those to individual bowls.
5. In a large bowl, cream together butter and sugar with hand mixer. Mix for 3 minutes.
6. To creamed butter and sugar, add vanilla and eggs. Mix together.
7. Sift four and cocoa into the bowl with the wet ingredients.
8. Add espresso powder and salt. Mix everything together.
9. Note: This mixture will be extremely thick. This is okay. The chocolate from the candy will melt, adding extra moisture to the brownie.
10. Butter baking pan. We used a foil pan so it wouldn't get smoke stains, but any 11 by 9 pan will do.
11. Add 1/3 of the brownie mixture to the bottom of the pan. Spread evenly.
12. Add 1/3 of the candy. (We used the Lava Cake Hersey Kisses and Heath Bar Pieces).
13. Add the second third of the brownie batter. Spread as evenly as you can.
14. Add the second third of the candy. (We used Hersey Cookie Bar and Butterfinger pieces)
15. Add the final layer of brownie batter. Spread evenly.
16. Add the final pieces if candy to decorate the top. (We used Reeses Hearts and M&Ms).
17. Bake on the AKORN for 20 to 25 minutes. Use a toothpick to test if it is done.
18. Cool, cut into pieces and enjoy!
19. Note: Use both the vents to adjust the temperature on the AKRON. More closed vents will help it cool down, open vents will help it heat up. Airflow is key.

Smoked Candied Pecans

Cooking Time: 1 Hrs

Ingredients:
- 1 Lb Pecan Halves
- 3/4 Cup White Sugar
- 1 tsp Ground Cinnamon
- Pinch of Salt
- Pinch of Nutmeg
- 1 Egg White
- 1 Tbsp Water

Directions:

1. Pre-heat Char-Griller smoker to 250 F.
2. In a large bowl whisk together egg white and water until frothy. In a separate bowl combine sugar, ground cinnamon, salt, and nutmeg. Stir until well mixed.
3. Add pecan halves to bowl with the egg white mixture and toss until well coated. Add sugar mixture to the pecans and toss until evenly coated.
4. Place pecans evenly on a baking sheet and smoke at 250 F for one hour or until pecans are evenly browned. Enjoy!

Crème Brûlée

Cooking Time: 30-40 Min

Ingredients:
- 2 C. heavy cream
- 1 Tsp. vanilla extract
- ⅛ Tsp. salt
- 5 egg yolks
- ½ C. sugar, plus more for topping

Directions:

1. Pre-heat grill to 325°F. In a saucepan, combine cream, vanilla extract and salt and cook over low heat just until hot, stirring continuously. Remove from heat and set aside.
2. In a bowl, beat yolks and sugar together until well combined. Add a ¼ C. of the vanilla-cream mixture from Step 1 and stir to incorporate.
3. Pour sugar-egg mixture into remaining cream in saucepan and stir. Pour into four 6 oz. ramekins and place into a baking dish.
4. Fill dish with boiling water halfway up the sides of the ramekins. Bake at 325°F for 30-40 minutes, until centers are just set.
5. Remove from grill and sprinkle a thin layer of sugar on top of each custard.
6. Tip: Use a butane torch to gradually melt sugar until caramelized and golden brown on top.

Low Carb Blueberry Cobbler

Cooking Time: 45 Min

Ingredients:
- Fresh or Frozen Blueberries - 2 Cups
- Water - 1/4 Cup
- Lemon Juice - 1 Tablespoon
- Monkfruit Sweetener - 2 Tablespoons
- Stevia - 10 Drops
- Xanthan Gum - 1/8 Teaspoon
- Softened Butter Chopped into Pieces - 1/4 Cup
- Coconut Flour - 1/3 Cup
- Additional Monkfruit Sweetener - 1/3 Cup
- Ground Cinnamon - 1 Tablespoon

Directions:

1. In sauce pan add blueberries, water, lemon juice & sweetener. Bring to a light boil and add xanthan gum. Stir occasionally as it thickens. Then remove from heat.
2. For crumble topping, mix coconut flour, monkfruit & cinnamon. Combine well, then add butter. Mix with fingers until well incorporated & crumbly.
3. Pour blueberry sauce into cast iron skillet & top with cinnamon crumb topping. Bake on grill heated to 350° for about 30 mins or until it bubbles & topping browns.

Spooky Brain Cinnamon Buns

Cooking Time: 30 Min

Ingredients:
- One Can Cinnamon Rolls
- Strawberry Jam
- Cinnamon Roll Frosting

Directions:

1. Layer the dough in a pan up against each other in and shaped it to look like a brain.
2. Heat oven or grill to 350°

3. Bake the cinnamon rolls for 30 minutes
4. While the cinnamon buns are baking, add the strawberry fruit spread to the icing and mixed it.
5. Then add the icing on to the cinnamon buns when they are done baking.

Strawberry And Rhubarb Crumble Pie

Cooking Time: 35-40 Min

Ingredients:
- 1¼ C. and ¾ C. all-purpose flour, plus 2 Tbsp. for filling
- 1 C. unsalted butter, diced and divided
- 1 C. sugar
- ½ C. light brown sugar
- 1 large egg
- 2 C. fresh rhubarb, cut into ½" dice
- 2 C. fresh strawberries, stemmed and sliced
- ¼ Tsp. orange zest, finely grated, optional
- 2 Tbsp. cold water, or more as needed
- 1 Tsp. vanilla extract
- Cold water, as needed

Directions:
1. Add 1¼ C. flour and salt to a large bowl and cut in ½ C. of butter with a pastry blender until the mixture resembles coarse crumbs. 2. Gradually add cold water to crumb mixture, until dough holds together when pressed. 3. Shape into a ball and wrap in plastic. Refrigerate 30 minutes. 4. Turn dough onto a floured surface and roll into a circle large enough to cover a buttered pie dish. Place dough into pie dish, trim the edges and prick the bottom with a fork.
2. Crumble Topping
3. In a medium bowl, combine ¾ C. flour, light brown sugar, and remaining ½ C. of butter Mix using a pastry blender or electric mixer until it resembles coarse crumbs.
4. Filling:Pre-heat grill to 400°F. In a large bowl, whisk 2 Tbsp. flour, egg, 1 C. sugar and vanilla together, until sugar is dissolved. 2. Add strawberries and rhubarb and mix until just blended. Let stand for 30 minutes at room temperature. 3. After 30 minutes, pour filling into pie crust. Sprinkle crumble topping evenly over pie and cover loosely with foil. Bake at 400°F for 35-40 minutes or until filling is bubbly and crumble topping is golden brown. Remove foil during the last 10 minutes.
5. Cool on wire rack before slicing and serving.

Pineapple Upside-down Cake

Cooking Time: 45 Min

Ingredients:
- 20 oz. can pineapple slices in juice, drained, with juice reserved
- 6 oz. jar maraschino cherries without stems, drained
- 1 box yellow cake mix
- ¼ C. unsalted butter
- 1 C. brown sugar
- Vegetable oil, according to box directions
- Eggs, according to box directions

Directions:
1. Pre-heat grill to 350°F. Melt butter in a cast iron pan and sprinkle brown sugar evenly over butter.
2. Place pineapple slices in pan on top of brown sugar and place a cherry in the center of each pineapple slice. Add remaining cherries around slices.
3. Add enough water to reserved pineapple juice to measure 1 C. Make cake batter according to package directions, substituting pineapple juice mixture for water. Slowly pour batter over pineapple and cherries in an even layer.
4. Bake at 350°F for 45 minutes or until a toothpick inserted into the center comes out clean. Run a knife around the side of the pan to loosen cake. Place a serving plate upside down onto the pan and turn plate and pan over.
5. Allow topping to drizzle over cake, then remove pan and allow cake to cool before slicing. Store covered in refrigerator.

Akorn Cinnamon Streusel Coffee Cake

Cooking Time: 2 Hrs

Ingredients:
- 1 ½ cups all-purpose flour (Topping)
- 1 ¼ cups packed light-brown sugar (Topping)
- 1 ½ tsp ground cinnamon (Topping)
- 1 ½ sticks cold salted butter, cut into fifths (Topping)

- 1 ½ cups chopped toasted pecans (Topping)
- 1 tsp kosher salt (Topping)
- 1 ¼ tsp baking powder (Cake)
- ½ tsp baking soda (Cake)
- 1 stick salted butter (room temperature) (Cake)
- 2 cups all-purpose flour (Cake)
- 1 ¼ cup granulated sugar (Cake)
- ½ tsp kosher salt (Cake)
- 2 large eggs (Cake)
- 1 ½ tsp vanilla extract (Cake)
- 1 cup plain greek yogurt (Cake)
- 1 cup powdered sugar (Glaze)
- 2 tbsp milk (Cake)

Directions:

1. Oktoberfest doesn't have to be just brats and sauerkraut. Bryan Head, @thebbqhead, made a classic Cinnamon Streusel Coffee Cake recipe and used his AKORN to bake it!
2. Toast pecans. Preheat oven to 275°F. In a bowl, melt a half stick of salted butter and toss pecans in the butter. Lay out pecans evenly on a baking sheet and toast for one hour flipping every 15 minutes. Let cool. Chop coarsely and set aside. Make the streusel topping. Mix together flour, ¾ cup brown sugar, 1 tsp cinnamon, and 1 tsp of salt. Cut in butter with sturdy fork or rub in with your fingers until pea-sized clumps remain. Mix in ½ cup chopped pecans. Refrigerate until ready to use. Make the streusel center. Mix together remaining ½ cup brown sugar, ½ tsp cinnamon, and 1 cup pecans. Prepare AKORN for indirect heat at 325°F. Make your cake: Butter the pan. Use a 9-inch tube pan with a removable bottom for best results. Sift in flour, baking powder, baking soda, and ½ tsp salt into a mixing bowl. Beat butter and granulated sugar with a mixer on medium speed for 2 minutes. Beat in eggs, one at a time, then vanilla. Beat in flour mixture in 3 stages alternating with greek yogurt, beginning and ending with the flour. Continue to beat at medium speed until well combined. Add half the batter into the pan. Sprinkle on the streusel center mixture evenly. Add the rest of the batter and spread evenly using a spatula. Sprinkle on the streusel topping evenly over batter. Bake until cake shows golden brown and a toothpick inserted into the center comes out clean, about 1 hour. Transfer pan to a wire rack to cool. Remove cake from pan. Make the glaze: Mix together powdered sugar and milk until you get your desired consistency. Drizzle over cake and down the sides and middle. Slice and enjoy!

Cheesecake Stuffed Apples

Cooking Time: 60 Min

Ingredients:

- Medium Baking Apples (I used Pink Lady) - 4
- Softened Cream Cheese - 8 Ounces
- Egg - 1
- Sugar - 1/3 Cup
- Cinnamon - 1/4 Teaspoon
- Crushed Graham Crackers - 1/4 Cup
- Prepared Caramel Sauce for Garnish

Directions:

1. Light AKORN and heat to 325
2. Cut bottoms of apples just enough to make them stand up straight
3. Hollow out apples with an apple corer or melon baller. Leave a ¼ inch of flesh around sides and bottom
4. Mix cream cheese, egg, sugar, vanilla, and cinnamon together until smooth
5. Spoon cream cheese mixture into each apple, leaving 1/2 inch space at the top
6. Sprinkle tops with graham crackers
7. Place apples in a small aluminum pan and place on grill
8. Allow to bake for 50-60 minutes. Filling should look semi set and apples should be soft
9. Allow to cool at room temperature then place in refrigerator until cold
10. Before serving, drizzle with caramel sauce

Smoked Chocolate Chip Cookies

Cooking Time: 15 To 20 Min

Ingredients:

- 2.25 Cups All Purpose Flour
- 2 Sticks of Butter
- 1 tsp Salt
- 1/2 Cup Sugar

- 1 Cup Light Brown Sugar
- 3 tsp Baking Powder
- 2 Eggs
- 1 tsp Vanilla Extract
- 2 Tbsp Milk
- Chocolate Chips (Your Choice with How Much)
- Chopped Pecans (Your Choice How Much)

Directions:
1. Melt the butter in a small pan.
2. Sift the flour, salt, & baking powder into a bowl.
3. Pour the butter in a mixing bowl & cream with the white & brown sugars.
4. Add the eggs, milk, and vanilla to the creamed sugar & mix.
5. Slowly add the flour mixture to the wet ingredients, beating constantly.
6. Mix in the chocolate chips & pecans.
7. Place the cookie dough in the fridge for a minimum of 30 minutes.
8. Heat your Char-griller Smoker/Grill to 350° or you can bake them in an oven at the same temperature.
9. Using a spoon make the cookies into a ball shape and place on pizza stone or cookie sheet using parchment paper or peach butcher paper.
10. Place in smoker/grill and smoke for 15-20 minutes or until golden brown.
11. Remove the cookies from the smoker/grill and allow them to cool for 10 minutes.
12. Enjoy.

Puffy Pancake With Fruit Compote

Cooking Time: 15 Min

Ingredients:
- 4 large eggs
- 1 C. all-purpose flour
- 1 C. milk
- 2 Tbsp. granulated sugar
- ¼ Tsp. salt
- 2 Tbsp. butter
- 2 ripe bananas, peeled and sliced
- 1 pint blueberries
- 1 Tbsp. granulated sugar
- 1 Tbsp. lemon juice
- Confectioners' sugar

Directions:
1. Pre-heat grill to 425°F, place a 10" cast iron skillet on grill and heat until very hot.
2. In a blender at medium speed, blend eggs, milk, flour, sugar, and salt together until smooth.
3. Remove skillet from the grill, add butter and swirl until melted. Pour batter into hot skillet and bake for 15 minutes until puffy and golden brown on the edges.
4. In a large bowl, toss bananas and blueberries with sugar and lemon juice to make compote.
5. Spoon compote onto pancake and sprinkle with confectioner's sugar. To serve, cut into wedges.

Lou's Peach Cobbler

Cooking Time: 50 Min

Ingredients:
- 5 large peaches, peeled, pitted and sliced
- 1 C. and 3 Tbsp. all-purpose flour
- ¼ C. brown sugar
- 1 C. sugar
- 1 Tsp. baking powder
- 1 Tsp. lemon juice
- ½ Tsp. grated lemon peel
- ½ Tsp. ground cinnamon
- ¼ Tsp. salt
- ¼ Tsp. ground nutmeg
- 1 large egg, lightly beaten
- ½ C. butter, melted

Directions:
1. Pre-heat grill to 375°F. Combine brown sugar, 3 Tbsp. flour, lemon juice, grated lemon peel and cinnamon in a bowl and mix well. 2. Place sliced peaches in a large cast iron pot with a lid and sprinkle sugar mixture over top. Do not stir. 3. Transfer to grill and allow to cook at 375°F for 10 minutes. 4. While peaches are cooking, make the dough. Add 1 C. flour, sugar, baking powder, salt, nutmeg, egg and melted butter to a food processor, pulse to combine and mix well until a dough forms. 5. Remove peaches from grill, tear dough into medium to large pieces and place over top of peaches until covered. Replace lid and return to grill. 6. Bake at 375°F for 40 minutes.
2. To serve, scoop onto a plate and top with whipped cream or vanilla ice cream. Enjoy!

Deep Dish Apple Pie

Cooking Time: 40 Min

Ingredients:
- 8 medium tart apples, cored, peeled and sliced (makes 10 C.)
- 2 C. and 3 Tbsp. all-purpose flour
- ½ C. shortening
- 2 large eggs
- ¼ C. cold water
- 2 Tbsp. apple cider vinegar
- 1 Tsp. lemon juice
- ¼ C. sugar
- ¼ C. brown sugar
- 1 Tsp. ground cinnamon
- ½ Tsp. ground nutmeg
- 1 Tbsp. milk
- Unsalted butter, softened

Directions:
1. Pre-heat grill to 350°. Add 2 C. flour to a large bowl and cut in shortening. Mix until crumbly.
2. In a small bowl, whisk 1 egg, water and apple cider vinegar together and gradually add to crumb mixture, tossing with a fork until dough holds together when pressed.
3. Shape into a ball and wrap in plastic. Refrigerate 30 minutes or overnight, if desired.
4. Filling: In a large bowl, toss apples with lemon juice, sugars, remaining flour, cinnamon and nutmeg until evenly coated. Arrange in a single layer on a baking sheet.
2. Place pan onto grill and bake at 350°F with lid closed for 10-15 minutes, until apples release their juices. 3. While apples are baking, turn dough out onto a floured surface and roll into 2 circles large enough to cover a buttered pie dish with an overhang of at least 1". Place 1 dough into pie dish and prick the bottom with a fork. 5. Remove apples from grill and place evenly into prepared pie dish. Place the other pie dough on top of the apples and crimp the edges. 6. In a small bowl, whisk 1 egg together with milk to make egg wash and brush over pie. Cut slits in top. 7. Bake at 350°F for 40 minutes or until crust is golden brown. Remove from grill and run a knife around the side of the pan to loosen pie.
5. Cool on a wire rack and serve with ice cream, if desired. Enjoy!

Chocolate Lava Cake

Cooking Time: 15 Min

Ingredients:
- ½ C. all-purpose flour
- 1 stick unsalted butter
- 2 oz. bittersweet chocolate
- 2 oz. semisweet chocolate
- 1¼ C. powdered sugar
- 2 eggs and 3 egg yolks
- 1 Tsp. vanilla extract

Directions:
1. Pre-heat grill to 425°F. Spray four 6 oz. ramekins with baking spray and place on a baking sheet.
2. Melt the butter, bittersweet chocolate and semisweet chocolate together in a pan on medium heat, stirring constantly. Stir in the sugar until dissolved.
3. Whisk in the eggs and egg yolks, then add vanilla. Gradually stir in flour. Divide the mixture among the ramekins.
4. Bake until the sides are firm and the centers are soft, about 15 minutes. Let stand 1 minute.
5. To serve, plate each cake while warm and serve with vanilla ice cream.

Skillet Brownie On The Grill

Ingredients:
- Softened Butter- 2 Tablespoons
- Heavy Whipping Cream- 1 Tablespoon
- Large Egg- 1
- Erythritol Blend (or Sweeter of Your Choice)- 3 Tablespoons
- Cocoa Powder- 2.5 Tablespoons
- Almond Flour- 2.5 Tablespoons
- Pinch of Sea Salt

Directions:
1. Preheat the grill to 350°.
2. Mix together all of the ingredients until smooth and spread the batter in a greased mini cast iron skillet.

3. Place the skillet directly on the preheated grill grate, close the grill, and bake for 6 to 8 minutes—or just until set. Do not over bake in the grill, as the hot skillet will continue to bake the brownie as it sits.
4. Top with sugar free vanilla ice cream, sugar free chocolate syrup, and a sliced strawberry. Serve warm.
5. This serves one to two, but can be doubled or tripled for more servings. Bake each batch in its own mini skillet.

Smoked Apple Crumb Pie

Cooking Time: 75 Min

Ingredients:
- Frozen Pie Crust
- 1 Cup Flour
- 1/3 Cup White Sugar
- Lemon Juice - 1/2 Tbs
- Lemon Zest - 1/3 tsp
- Cinnamon - 1 tsp
- Nutmeg - 1/8 tsp
- Flour - 3 Tbs (Topping)
- 1/3 Cup White Sugar
- 1/2 Cup Packed Brown Sugar
- 1/2 Cup Oats
- Stick of Butter

Directions:
1. Add Smokin' Stone to AKORN, add chunks of Applewood, and preheat grill to 350 degrees.
2. Combine flour, sugar, brown sugar, oats and butter. Mix with fork to make topping.
3. Peel, core and slice apples into thin slices.
4. Toss apples with sugar, lemon juice and zest, cinnamon, nutmeg, and flour.
5. Layer apples in pie shell and pour juice over apples.
6. Put crumb topping on top of apples.
7. Bake for 1 hour and 15 minutes.
8. Serve warm with ice cream or whipped cream.

Smoked White Chocolate Christmas Candy

Cooking Time: 1 Hrs

Ingredients:
- 3 Cups Cheerios
- 3 Cups Corn Chex
- 3 Cups Peanut Butter Chex
- 1 Cup Butter Snaps Pretzels
- 1.5 Cups M&Ms
- 32 oz white Chocolate Chips

Directions:
1. Smoke white chocolate chips using your Char-Griller Offset charcoal smoker.
2. Add 6 lit charcoals to the far side of firebox along with a mild smoking wood chunk. Maple wood goes well with this recipe. Feel free to leave vents fully open.
3. You will need 2 foil baking pans. Fill pan number one with a layer of ice cubes. About ¼ of the way full. Add white chocolate chips to the second pan. Place pan with white chocolate on top of the pan with the ice.
4. Place stacked pans in cooking chamber of your smoker. Keep as far away from fire box side as possible.
5. Smoke for 30-45 minutes. For a milder smoke flavor try 30 minutes. To impart a stronger smoke flavor, try 45 minutes.
6. Melt white chocolate over heat source.
7. Add white chocolate to a large saucepan or keep in foil pan.
8. Over medium heat or lit coals, melt until white chocolate is a smooth consistency able to be drizzled. Be sure to stir often and do not over melt.
9. In a large mixing bowl or 2 foil pans, combine dry ingredients (cheerios, corn chex, peanut butter chex, pretzels, and m&m's) making sure to evenly distribute the ingredients.
10. Drizzle white chocolate on the dry mixture. Stir in making sure to coat all the mixture in the white chocolate.
11. Lay out on parchment paper or leave in foil pans as a nice thin layer to dry/cool for 1 hour.
12. Break into small to medium pieces and enjoy!
13. This stores well in the fridge and the freezer!

Smoked Blueberry Crisp

Cooking Time: 45 Min

Ingredients:
- Blueberries - 5 Cups
- Sugar - 2 Tablespoons
- Ground Ginger - 1/2 Teaspoon
- Brown Sugar - 1/2 Cup
- Flour - 1/2 Cup
- Rolled Oats - 3/4 Cup
- Cinnamon - 1 Tablespoon
- Melted Butter - 1/2 Cup

Directions:
1. To begin, put your blueberries into a half size foil pan and spread them out evenly.
2. Mix your sugar and ground ginger and evenly coat all the blueberries.
3. Mix the remaining ingredients together and distribute evenly over the top of the blueberries.
4. Bring your AKORN Kamado up to 375 degrees with a chunk of cherry wood for smoke and the Smokin' Stone in place to set up for indirect cooking.
5. Once the smoke is a clean smoke, that is thin and blue, place your half steamer pan on the AKORN for forty minutes. After forty minutes remove from AKORN, let cool and enjoy.

Faux Apple Pie

Ingredients:
- 3 Cups Almond Flour (Crust)
- Baking Powder - 3 Tbsp (Crust)
- 1/3 Cup Xanthan Gum (Crust)
- 1/2 Cup and 1 Tbsp Coconut Flour (Crust)
- Apple Cider Vinegar - 2 Tbsp
- 3 Eggs, Whisked (Crust)
- Water - 3 Tbsp (Crust)
- 6 Chayote Squash, peeled, cored, sliced thin (Filling)
- 1 Cup Lakanto Golden Sweetener (Filling)
- Cinnamon - 2 Tbsp (Filling)
- Nutmeg - 1 tsp (Filling)
- Vanilla - 2 Tbsp (Filling)
- Lemon Juice - 3 Tbsp (Filling)
- 1/4 Cup Lankanto Classic Granulated Sweetener (Filling)
- Butter - 3 Tbsp (Filling)
- 1 Bag Cinnamon Pecan Lollis Cookie Clusters (Topping)

Directions:
1. Mix all wet ingredients in one bowl, set aside.
2. Mix all dry ingredients in large bowl, once dry ingredients are combined, slowly add were ingredients.
3. Mix with a spoon as good as you can, then knead with hands.
4. Shape into a ball, wrap in saran wrap and refrigerate for 2 hours.
5. Combine in a sauce pan, cook over medium heat for 20 minutes.
6. Add more sweetener if desired.
7. Remove from heat to cool.
8. Roll out dough between 2 sheets of parchment paper until 1/4 inch thin, place in aluminum pie pan - trim edges.
9. Poke holes in crust with fork.
10. Preheat grill to 325-350°.
11. Place pie crust on grill over indirect heat.
12. Cook about 5-8 minutes until crust starts to turn golden.
13. Remove from grill, add pie filling and even spread the crumbled Lollis Cookie Clusters over the top until filling is covered.
14. Place pie back on grill over indirect heat for about 25-30 minutes until nicely browned.
15. Let pie cool completely before serving.
16. Pairs well with vanilla Rebel Creamery ice cream.

Guinness Cupcakes With Whiskey Salted Caramel Buttercream

Cooking Time: 25 Min

Ingredients:
- 1 Devils food Cake Mix
- 1 3.9 Oz Instant Chocolate Pudding
- 1 Cup Sour Cream
- 1/2 Cup Guinness
- 1/2 Cup of Oil

- 4 Eggs
- 3/4 Cup Mini Chocolate Chips
- 1 Cup of Light Brown Sugar
- 1/4 Cup of Butter
- 1/4 Cup of Milk
- 1/4 Cup of Whiskey
- 1/4 Tbsp Sea Salt
- 4 Sticks of Unsalted Butter
- 6 Cup of Powdered Sugar
- 1/4 Cup of Salted Caramel

Directions:

1. Heat Akorn to 325 for indirect heat and add liners to a cupcake pan Add cake mix, pudding, sour cream, oil, Guinness, eggs, and ½ c. of the chocolate chips in a large bowl and mix together until combined Divide batter evenly into 24 cupcakes Bake for 20 minutes or until middle of the cake springs back when gently pushed down or until a toothpick inserted into the center comes out clean While cupcakes are cooling, add brown sugar, 1/4 c. butter, milk, and sea salt to a medium sauce pan On medium heat, melt caramel mixture stirring frequently until mixture starts to simmer Allow to simmer without stirring for 5-7 minutes until thickened. Remove from heat and allow to cool To make the frosting, add butter to mixer and beat until smooth and creamy. Slowly add the powdered sugar and beat until light and fluffy. Add caramel to frosting and beat until combined Top cooled cupcakes with a spoonful of buttercream and spread across the cupcake I like to add a drizzle of the leftover caramel on top of the frosted cupcakes with a little sprinkle of the leftover chocolate chips

2. If caramel starts to thicken too much to drizzle, you can microwave it for 10 seconds

PORK

Gravity 980 Smoked Pork Shoulder

Cooking Time: 3-4 Hrs

Ingredients:
- 1 7-9 Lb. Pork Shoulder, trimmed
- 3 Tbsp of Yellow Mustard
- 2 Tbsp Kosher Salt
- 2 Tbsp Black Pepper
- 2 Tbsp Garlic Powder
- 2 Tbsp Onion Powder
- 1 Tbsp Paprika
- 1 Tbsp Cumin
- 1 Cup of Apple Juice or Apple Cider Vinegar
- 1/2 Cup of Water

Directions:
1. No more babysitting your pork shoulder with the Gravity 980. Easily prepare an awesome pork shoulder for stellar dishes like sandwiches, mac and cheese or even nachos.
2. In a small bowl, combine seasonings, and in a spray, bottle combine apple cider/juice and water. Thoroughly rub mustard all over the surface of your pork shoulder then coat with all the seasonings. Remove the fire shutter from your Gravity 980 then light and load the hopper. Set the temperature to 225-250°F. Place your pork shoulder on the grill, close the lid and smoke it for 3 hours without opening the lid. Spray the shoulder generously with spray bottle mixture then continue to do so every hour for the next 3-4 hours until the shoulder reaches 200-205°F. Optionally, once the fat on top splits open, you may wrap the shoulder in butcher paper or aluminum foil for the duration of the cook. Remove from the smoker and allow it to rest for 1 hour before removing the bone and shredding. Enjoy!

Ultimate Pork Belly Sliders

Cooking Time: 2:15 Hrs

Ingredients:
- 4 lb. pork belly
- Yellow mustard
- Original All-Purpose BBQ rub, to taste
- Your favorite sweet BBQ rub, to taste
- Hawaiian sweet rolls or your favorite roll for sliders
- Your favorite toppings
- Your favorite BBQ sauce

Directions:
1. Remove the skin from the pork belly and season the top generously with a layer of yellow mustard, followed by Original All-Purpose BBQ rub and your favorite sweet BBQ sauce, to taste.
2. Pre-heat grill to 275°F for indirect heat with a Smokin' Stone. Allow the belly to smoke for 2 hours or until internal temperature reaches 175°F. Remove the belly from the grill and allow to rest.
3. After removing the pork belly and Smokin' Stone, stir the charcoal and open up both vents to allow the grill to reach maximum temperature for searing.
4. While the grill is heating up, slice the pork belly into ¼" thick strips and arrange on the grill. Work in batches if needed. Fry the belly for 3 minutes on each side, to allow the fat to render. Season the belly with BBQ rub again, if desired.
5. Slice the pack of Hawaiian sweet rolls in half and arrange the pork belly on the bottom half. Cover with the top half and brush with melted butter and garlic, if desired. Place the rolls in a large pan and back onto the grill to crisp up for 10 minutes.
6. Remove the pan from the grill and allow the rolls to cool slightly before slicing into individual sliders. Add your favorite toppings and sauce and enjoy!

Baby Back Ribs

Cooking Time: 3 Hrs

Ingredients:
- Salt
- Pepper
- Brown Sugar
- Garlic Salt
- Onion Salt
- Paprika

Directions:
1. Mix everything together and rub on ribs
2. Cover the ribs with foil and refrigerate overnight
3. Grill on 250° for 3 hours and take off
4. Throw your favorite BBQ sauce on and refold and grill till the BBQ sauce caramelizes. Take off and enjoy!

Certified Grilled And Smoked Baby Back Ribs

Cooking Time: 2 1/2 Hrs

Ingredients:
- Full Slabs of Spare Ribs.
- Hot Sauce
- Favorite BBQ Rub
- Favorite BBQ Sauce
- Apple Juice (Non Concentrate)

Directions:
1. Trimming
2. Using a sharp knife slice remove any meat loose on the ends of the ribs. Also remove any access fat from top/meat side of the ribs. Tip: If you can pull any fat, you should remove it.
3. Flip the ribs over so the bones are facing up. Remove the membrane and discard. Remove any access fat.
4. Seasoning
5. Begin by leaving the the ribs bone side up. Apply coating of hot sauce for a binder. Tip: don't apply hot sauce or rubs on the sides of the ribs. This helps the exposed bones from getting burnt during the smoking process.
6. Apply even coating of BBQ rubs on the ribs.
7. Flip ribs to the top/meat side of the ribs. Apply coating of hot sauce for a binder. Tip: seasoning the bottom of the ribs first will help prevent the top/meat side seasonings from being messy.
8. Apply an even coating of BBQ rub on the top of the ribs.
9. Ribs are ready to be Smoked.
10. Grilling & Smoking
11. Grill the ribs for 2 minutes on the meat side down on the grill grill grate. Reverse them after one minute.
12. Flip the ribs so they meat side is facing up and grill for an additional 1-2 minutes.
13. Using your Char-Griller Grill glove and grill grate lifter, lift the grill grate and move off to the side of the grill. Quickly insert the Char-Griller Akorn Smokin' stone, insert Char-Griller grill drip pan filled with water, place grill grate with meat back in the pit.
14. Shut the top smoke stack to a low setting and dodge same to the bottom of the vent. This will allow you to quickly lower your fire. Lock in the temperature when it hits temperature 325°-350° by adjusting the smoke stack and bottom vent.
15. Spritz with apple juice every 30 minutes and rotate ribs.
16. After smoking for 2 1/2 hours coat ribs with BBQ sauce and smoke for an additional 20 minutes.
17. Remove Ribs and allow to rest for 15 minutes. Slice and enjoy.

Flavor Pro Pork Steaks

Cooking Time: 12 Min

Ingredients:
- 4 Large Pork Steaks
- 1 Cup Stout Beer
- 2 Tbsp Canola Oil
- 3 Tbsp Minced Garlic
- 1/4 Cup Soy Sauce
- 2 Tbsp Worcestershire Sauce
- 1/3 Cup Packed Brown Sugar
- 2 tsp Hot Sauce
- 1 Tbsp Dijon Mustard
- 1 tsp Onion Powder
- 2 tsp Salt
- 2 tsp Pepper

Directions:
1. Add all ingredients to your favorite food-safe marinade container or ziplock bag along with the pork steaks.
2. Massage marinade into the steaks to ensure an even coating.
3. Store the container in the refrigerator for at least 2 hours but storing overnight is optimal.

4. Prepare the Flavor Pro for direct heat grilling (High, 400°F+) For best results, fill all three zones of the Flavor Drawer with charcoal and add a few wood chunks for added smoke flavor. Turn all four gas burners on high to ignite the coals, once the coals are fully lit, turn off the gas completely. Leave both smoke stacks fully open.

5. Remove pork steaks from the marinade and place them on the grill directly over the coals.

6. Cook for 4-6 minutes per side.

Grilled Pork And Sweet Potato Verde Chili

Cooking Time: 3.5 Hrs

Ingredients:
- 2 Lbs Pork
- 2 Large Sweet Potatoes - Diced
- 3 Ears of Corn on the Cob
- 1 Bunch Cilantro - Stems Cut from Leaves and Set Aside
- 2 Cloves of Garlic
- 3 Tbsp Ground Cumin
- 1/2 Cup olive Oil or Avocado Oil
- 2 Cups Salsa Verde
- 6 Cups Chicken Stock
- 1 Can White Beans
- Salt and Pepper to taste
- Garnish: Cilantro, Radish, Red Onion, and/or Sour Cream

Directions:

1. Remove stems from fresh cilantro, and add to blender with garlic cloves, oil, cumin, and a pinch of s&p. Pulse until smooth and combined.

2. Preheat Char-Griller to high heat, I recommend charcoal for this recipe as it will add even more flavor.

3. In a large bowl, transfer corn, pork, and sweet potato pieces. Pour blended marinade over the ingredients and toss to combine. Once grill is heated, add all to grill, and cook until charred on each side, 6-8 mins per side. Remove and set aside.

4. Once the grilled items are cool to the touch, dice sweet potatoes and pork into similar sized pieces, and cut corn off the cob. Transfer these items to a soup pot, adding salsa verde, & chicken stock. Bring to a simmer over low.

5. Add ½ cup chopped cilantro leaves, the white beans, and S&P to taste. Simmer on low partially covered for 3 hours, until pork is fall apart tender, and chili has thickened. Serve with garnishes of choice and enjoy! Leftover Chili can stay in the fridge for up to 7 days, and frozen for 6 months.

Smoked Pork Loin

Cooking Time: 2 Hrs

Ingredients:
- Pork Loin
- 2 Tbsp Of Your Favorite Rub Of Any Kind

Directions:

1. Remove loin from packaging and remove any silverskin if necessary. Cover the loin in the 2 Tbsp of rub Bring your cooker up to 300 degrees, set it up for indirect cooking and add 1 small piece of hickory wood. Place the pork loin on the grate and place a leave in thermometer in it and set it for 4 degrees. Once the loin hits 145 degrees internal temperature remove it from the cooker, cut it into 1 inch chops and serve

Smoked Pork Shoulder

Ingredients:
- 5 to 7 Pound Pork Shoulder or Boston Butt
- Char-Griller Rib Rub
- Spray Bottle Full of 2/3 Apple Juice and 1/3 Vegetable Oil

Directions:

1. Trim excess fat from the pork shoulder. (Skip this step if it is Boston Butt.) Score the remaining fat with a sharp knife.

2. Rub a liberal amount of Rib Spice Rub on the pork. Make sure each side is evenly coated.

3. Place pork in the fridge for at least 12 hours.

4. Remove pork from fridge one hour before placing on the grill.

5. Preheat offset smoker to 225 to 250 degrees Fahrenheit. Add Apple or Cherry wood chunks to coals.

6. Place drip pan filled with water under the grates. Place pork on the grates over the drip pan.
7. Baste pork with Apple juice every 30 to 60 minutes.
8. Make sure to keep an eye on the pit temperature. Add more pre-lit charcoal to the Side Fire Box if needed.
9. Smoke until internal temperature is 195 to 210 degrees Fahrenheit and remove from grill.

Hoppin' John

Cooking Time: 15 Min

Ingredients:
- 2 Tbsp. Olive oil
- ½ C. onion, diced
- ¾ C. bell pepper, diced
- 15 oz. can black-eyed peas
- Salt and pepper, to taste
- ¼ lb. smoked pulled pork
- Chipotle peppers
- 2 C. cooked white rice
- Andouille sausage

Directions:
1. Pre-heat grill to 350°F and place a 10" cast iron skillet on grill and heat until very hot. 2. Place sausages on the grill and allow to cook for 8-10 minutes, turning once or twice, until cooked through. 3. Pour 2 Tbsp. olive oil into hot skillet and add onion, bell pepper and black-eyed peas. 4. Season with salt and pepper and allow to cook for 1-2 minutes, stirring occasionally. 5. Add smoked pulled pork and Chipotle peppers and stir. 6. Add cooked rice to mixture. Close lid and allow to cook for 3-4 minutes. 7. Add grilled andouille sausage from Step
2. Remove from grill and serve. Enjoy!

Quick And Easy Grilled Pork Tenderloin

Cooking Time: 25 Min

Ingredients:
- 1 Pork Tenderloin
- 1 Tsp Paprika
- 1/2 Tsp Garlic Powder
- 1/2 Tsp Cilantro
- 1/2 Tsp Oregano
- Salt and Pepper to Taste
- Olive Oil

Directions:
1. Blend spices together in a bowl. Rub pork with olive oil and then season liberally on both sides with spice blend. Set up the Flavor Pro™ for direct cooking. Ignite burners and turn to medium high. Place pork on the grill and cook for 8 to 10 minutes per side or until the internal temperature reads 165 degrees. Remove from grill and let rest for 10 minutes.

Grilled Stuffed Pork Chops

Cooking Time: 15 Min

Ingredients:
- 1" thick bone-in pork chops
- 1 Tbsp. unsalted butter
- 2 Tbsp. chopped almonds
- 4 C. baby spinach, finely chopped
- 4 oz. cream cheese
- ¼ Tsp. cayenne pepper
- ¼ Tsp. salt
- Original All-Purpose BBQ Rub, to taste

Directions:
1. Pre-heat grill to 375°F. Rinse the pork chops and pat dry with paper towel. Cut a deep pocket in the side of each chop with a small sharp knife, cutting toward the bone but not all the way through. 2. In a medium bowl, combine butter, chopped almonds, baby spinach, cream cheese, cayenne pepper and salt and mix well to make stuffing. 3. Transfer mixture to a piping bag without a tip, fill pork chops with mixture and secure with toothpicks. 4. Generously season both sides of each chop with Original All-Purpose BBQ rub, or your favorite rub, to taste. 5. Place stuffed pork chops on the grill over direct heat at 375°F for 6 minutes per side, turning halfway through for good sear marks. Move to indirect side of grill to finish cooking if needed.
2. Pork chops are done when internal temperature reaches 145°F. Remove from grill and set aside to rest for 5 minutes and remove toothpicks before serving. Enjoy!

Bbq Pork Spare Ribs

Ingredients:
- Slab of Ribs- 1
- Mustard- 1/4 Cup
- Char Griller Rib Rub- 4 Tablespoon
- Butter- 1 Stick
- Apple Cider Vinegar- 1/2 Cup
- Jack Stack BBQ Seasoning- 6 Tablespoons
- G Hughes Sweet & Spicy BBQ Sauce (or Preferred BBQ Sauce)- 2/3 Cup

Directions:
1. Pat the ribs dry with a paper towel & tear off the membrane.
2. Rub a layer of mustard over the ribs.
3. Rub the ribs down with Char-Griller Rib Rub (to taste).
4. Rub the ribs down with Jack Stack BBQ seasoning (to taste).
5. Marinate for an hour.
6. Smoke ribs around 225° for 3 hours, bone side down uncovered.
7. Wrap in foil with butter & apple cider vinegar, smoke for 2 more hours.
8. Remove foil & brush with BBQ sauce & place on grill grate bone side down for 1 more hour basting occasionally.

St. Louis-style Ribs

Cooking Time: 5 Hrs

Ingredients:
- 3 racks of ribs
- Ribs BBQ rub, to taste
- 1 can Coca-Cola
- 1 C. molasses
- ½ C. agave nectar
- ½ C. Jack Daniels Tennessee whiskey (or a good bourbon whiskey)
- ½ C. apple cider vinegar
- ¼ C. honey, and more as needed for wrapping ribs
- 1 Tbsp. cayenne pepper
- Apple juice
- Brown sugar
- 12 oz. bottle of squeeze butter

Directions:
1. Rinse rib racks and pat dry with paper towel. Remove membrane from each rack by carefully prying back using the back of a sharp knife. Discard membrane. Flip racks and trim loose ends and excess fat. Tip: Use a paper towel to help hold the membrane, as it's slippery.
2. Season ribs generously with Ribs BBQ Rub, or your favorite rub.
3. When setting up the grill, use a full chimney of unlit charcoal in the attached Side Fire Box and pour another ½ chimney of hot coals on top to ensure good smoke and a temperature of 275°F. Add Applewood chunks on top.
4. Adjust the charcoal grate to the highest setting in the main compartment. Place an aluminum pan on the grate and fill halfway with apple juice. Smoke ribs for 1 hour and mist with apple juice. Close lid and smoke for another 3 hours. 5. After 3 hours, remove ribs from grill and wrap. Before wrapping, spread a layer of brown sugar, butter and honey onto aluminum foil. Place ribs meat side down and wrap securely. 6. Transfer wrapped ribs to the grill and smoke at 275°F for another hour. 7. During the last 10-20 minutes of smoking the ribs, make the glaze. Combine 1 can of Coca-Cola, molasses, agave nectar, whiskey, apple cider vinegar, honey and cayenne pepper in a saucepan and bring to a boil, stirring occasionally. Reduce heat to a simmer until glaze is thickened.
5. Remove ribs from the grill and carefully drain juices before brushing with glaze, slicing and serving.

Apple Chipotle Glazed Smoked Ham

Cooking Time: 90 Min

Ingredients:
- 5 ½ lbs. boneless Applewood smoked ham
- 1 C. apple jelly
- 1 Tsp. Chipotle chili powder
- 2/3 C. balsamic vinegar
- ½ C. brown sugar

Directions:
1. Place ham in an aluminum roasting pan onto the grill to smoke at 300°F for 90 minutes.

2. While ham is smoking, combine balsamic vinegar, brown sugar, Chipotle chili powder and apple jelly in a small sauce pan on the stove. Bring to a boil, then reduce heat and simmer for 15 minutes, stirring occasionally.
3. After ham has cooked for 1 hour, baste with glaze every 10 minutes, being careful not to burn the sauce. Ham is done when internal temperature reaches 140°F.
4. Remove ham from grill and let rest for 10 minutes before slicing and serving.

Bacon Wrapped Kielbasa Bites

Cooking Time: 50 Min

Ingredients:
- 14 oz Kielbasa
- 12 oz bacon
- 8 oz BBQ sauce
- Fresh or dry parsley
- Your Favorite Rub

Directions:
1. Pre-heat grill to 350°
2. Slice kielbasa into 1" pieces or same size as the bacon strip.
3. Wrap bacon around the kielbasa.
4. Lightly coat the kielbasa bacon wrapped bites with Char-Griller Original Rub or your favorite rub.
5. Place the kielbasa bacon wrapped bites on your baking rack. Tip: spray rack with olive or vegetable spray to avoid sticking.
6. Next, put the baking rack with the kielbasa bacon bites in your grill at 350°F.
7. After 30 minutes or when bacon becomes golden brown begin to glaze the kielbasa bacon wrapped bites with bbq sauce to your liking.
8. Stick the kielbasa bacon wrapped bites with toothpicks for easy removal and easy handling to eat. Remove them from the grill.
9. Place in a serving tray or if tailgating, eat them right off the grill. Tip: serve with BBQ sauce on the side for dipping.
10. Enjoy!

Orange Pork Belly Burnt Ends

Cooking Time: 4 Hrs

Ingredients:
- Pork Belly (2-3 Lbs)
- 1 Tsp Kosher Salt
- 1/2 Tsp Coarse Black Pepper
- 1/2 Tsp Garlic Powder
- 1 Disposable Aluminum Pan
- 1/2 Cup Orange Juice (For Spritzing)
- Hickory Wood (Splits or Chunks)
- 1/2 Cup White Sugar
- 1 Tbsp Soy Sauce
- 2 Tbsp Rice Vinegar
- 1 Tsp Sesame Oil
- 1/4 Tsp Ginger Powder
- 1/4 Tsp Garlic Powder
- 1/2 Tsp Red Chili Flakes

Directions:
1. Cut the pork belly into 1-1 ½ inch cubes. Combine salt, pepper, and garlic powder in a small bowl and season the pork belly cubes on all sides. Whisk together all the orange sauce ingredients in a medium size bowl and place in the refrigerator for later use.
2. Heat your smoker to a temperature of 275 F. Place the pork belly cubes into the side of the smoker that is furthest away from the fire. Spritz every 40-45 minutes until the pork belly starts to read an internal temp between 190 F – 200 F. *Tip* Place a water pan inside the smoker next to the fire box to help with added moisture.
3. Place the pork belly cubes in an aluminum pan and add the orange sauce mixture. Return the pan into the smoker maintaining 275 F.
4. Once the orange sauce has reduced and the cubes look caramelized it is time to pull from the smoker (This should take approximately 25-35 minutes). Top with sesame seeds and green onions. Enjoy!

Pork Belly Street Tacos

Cooking Time: 4 Hrs

Ingredients:
- Pork Belly - 2 to 3 lbs
- 1 Tbsp Salt
- 2 Tbsp Coarse Black Pepper
- 1 Tbsp Yellow Mustard
- 1/2 Cup Apple Cider Vinegar
- 1/2 Cup Water
- Tortillas, Onion, Cilantro

Directions:

1. Prep your Char-Griller offset smoker to a temp of 275 F. Unwrap the pork belly and trim any excess fat or meat that is not needed. *Tip* to achieve that true Central Texas Style flavor try to use oak chunks or splits throughout your cook.
2. Combine all dry ingredients in shaker for easy application. Rub the pork belly down with mustard or a binder of your choice. Season the pork belly liberally.
3. Put the pork belly on the smoker once it is seasoned and the smoker temperature is at 275 F.
4. At the hour mark spritz the pork belly with a mixture of apple cider vinegar and water. Continue to spritz every 45 minutes until the pork belly has reached an internal temp of 165 F.
5. Wrap the pork belly in butcher paper once it has reached an internal temp of 165 F.
6. Tip: This will help with rendering the fat and preserving the bark on the pork belly.
7. Once the pork belly has reached an internal temp of around 203 F it is time to take off the pit and let rest so the juices can redistribute. Rest for 30-45 minutes.
8. Chop up the pork belly and serve in a tortilla with cilantro and onions and enjoy!

Chipotle Orange Glazed Bacon Wrapped And Stuffed Pork Loin

Cooking Time: 2 Hrs

Ingredients:
- 1-1½ lb. pork tenderloins
- 1 lb. bacon
- 1 C. spicy honey BBQ sauce
- 1 C. sweet orange marmalade
- 1 Tbsp. crushed fresh garlic, to taste
- 1 Tbsp. Chipotle chili powder, to taste
- 3 Tbsp. pork rub or preferred seasoning

Directions:

1. Combine BBQ sauce, marmalade, garlic and Chipotle chili powder in a saucepan on the stove until heated through, 3-5 minutes or until all ingredients are well blended. 2. Mix well and turn heat to low until ready to use. 3. Stir occasionally and refrigerate leftovers.
2. Pork tenderloin
3. Generously season pork tenderloins with rub and layer 2-3 strips of bacon on top. 2. Evenly spread a ¼ of the Chipotle orange glaze over the bacon layer. Tie securely in multiple spots with kitchen twine. Snip off any excess twine. 4. Lay out remaining bacon in a basket weave pattern on a cutting board. 5. Wrap the pork tenderloin, tucking ends under and season with rub. 6. Place bacon wrapped tenderloin to smoke on the indirect side of the grill at 225°F for 2 hours. 7. Brush the remaining Chipotle orange glaze onto the pork tenderloin during the last ½ hour of smoking. Pork is ready when the internal temperature reaches 165°F. Note: The tenderloin's internal temperature will continue to increase by 5-10 degrees after you pull it off the grill.

Brown Sugar Glazed Smoked Ham

Cooking Time: 2 Hrs

Ingredients:
- 11 lb. ham
- 1 C. brown sugar
- 1 C. brown mustard, or preferred

Directions:

1. Combine brown sugar and mustard together in a small bowl to make glaze. Mix well.
2. Score ham in a diamond pattern and generously brush on glaze.
3. Place glazed ham in large baking dish or cast-iron skillet onto the grill to smoke at 325°F for 2 hours. Ham is done when internal temperature reaches 140°F.
4. Remove ham from grill and let rest for 10 minutes before slicing and serving.

Father's Day Baby Back Ribs

Cooking Time: 6 Hrs

Ingredients:
- 1 C. warmed honey
- 1/2 C. yellow or Dijon mustard
- 2 oz. brown sugar
- 1 oz smoked paprika
- 1 Tbsp. black pepper
- 1 Tsp. crushed red pepper flakes
- 2 C. water
- 2 oz chipotle peppers

Directions:
1. Mix mustard and honey in small bowl
2. Pour over ribs and coat evenly
3. Mix together brown sugar, black pepper, red pepper flakes, and paprika in a bowl
4. Coat ribs generously with the rub mix
5. Wrap in aluminum foil and leave in the refrigerator for 24 hours
6. Pre heat grill to 275° F
7. Mix 2 C. of water and 2 oz. of chipotle peppers in a cast iron skillet
8. Baste with liquid in skillet every hour
9. Smoke for about 6 hours or until internal temperature reaches 175° F

Oktoberfest Schweinshaxe - Smoked Pork Shanks

Cooking Time: 10 Min

Ingredients:
- Pork Shanks
- 2 Tbsp White Peppercorns
- 2 Tsps Caraway Seeds
- 2 Tsp Kosher Salt
- 1 Tsp Garlic Powder
- 1 Tsp Baking Powder
- 1 Tsp Dried Thyme

Directions:
1. In a skillet, lightly toast the white peppercorns and carways just until they become fragrant (toast separately) Put toasted peppercorns and caraway seeds into a spice grind and coarsely grind In a separate bowl, mix peppercorns and caraway seeds and remaining dry ingredients Rinse and pat the pork shanks dry with a paper towel Score the skin about every 2 inches all the way around they shank. Make sure to cross hatch the skin. Lightly oil the shanks and season w/ the seasoning mix be careful to get some spices underneath the skin at the score marks Heat smoker to an ambient temperature of 250 degrees. If using wood as fuel, I recommend hickory as it works well with the flavor profile of the shanks Insert an internal meat probe into the thickest part of the shank Smoke until internal temperature is approximately 190 to 200 degrees Remove shanks and lightly tent with foil Heat grill to searing temperature - anywhere from 500 to 600 degrees Sear pork shank skin rotating every 3 to 5 minutes until skin is crispy Remove from grill and server immediately. Skin should be crispy and meat should be fork tender.

Asian Pork Belly Skewers

Cooking Time: 2 Hrs

Ingredients:
- Pork Belly Cut into 1 1/2" Cubes - 2 Pounds
- Pineapple Cut into 1 1/2" Cubes - 1
- Char-Griller Rib Rub
- Skewers Soaked in Water
- Chopped Green Onions and Sesame Seeds - For Garnish
- Chili Garlic Sauce - 1 Tablespoon
- Rice Wine Vinegar - 1 Teaspoon
- Chopped Garlic - 1 Teaspoon
- Orange Zest - 1 Teaspoon
- Soy Sauce - 2 Teaspoons

Directions:
1. Light grill for indirect heat
2. In a large bowl, toss pork belly with rub until generously coated
3. Skewer pineapple and pork belly, alternating between the two
4. Please skewers on the grill
5. Rotate skewers after an hour

6. Meanwhile, place all sauce ingredients in a small sauce pan
7. Chili Garlic Sauce Rice Wine Vinegar Chopped Garlic Range Zest Soy Sauce Honey Ground Ginger
8. Bring the sauce to a simmer and allow to cook until thickened. Approximately 15 minutes
9. Allow to cool
10. After two hours, brush the skewers with sauce. Allow the sauce to set for approximately 30 minutes
11. When ready to serve, sprinkle with sesame seeds and green onions

Blueberry Pork Belly Burnt Ends

Cooking Time: 3.5 Hrs

Ingredients:
- Pork Belly - 2 lbs
- Char-Griller Rib Rub
- Butter - 1/2 stick
- Fresh Blueberries - 2 Cups
- Apple Juice - 1/4 Cup
- Sugar - 1/4 Cup
- Cornstarch - 1 Tbs
- Lemon Juice - 1 Tbs
- Cayenne - 1 tsp (optional)

Directions:
1. Cut the pork belly into 1-1 ½ inch cubes.
2. Season the cubes liberally on all sides.
3. Prepare the fire to get the smoker up to 275 F.
4. Tip: Put the pork belly into the freezer 20-30 minutes before you cube. This will help with the cutting process.
5. Once the smoker has reached 275 F put the pork belly onto the grill with the fat side facing down.
6. Spritz every 40-45 minutes until the pork belly starts to read an internal temp of 190 F.
7. Place the cubes in an aluminum pan and add one cup of the blueberry sauce and the butter. Toss the cubes to make sure the sauce adheres to all sides of the cubes. Return the pan into the smoker.
8. Once the sauce has reduced and the cubes look caramelized it is time to pull from the smoker. Put the burnt ends onto a plate and top with the remaining cup of blueberry sauce. Enjoy!
9. In a saucepan combine the blueberries and apple juice. Bring to a boil. Pour the cornstarch, sugar, and cayenne (optional) into the saucepan while stirring continuously. Let the sauce thicken and reduce heat. Add the lemon juice and stir. Set aside till it is time to use on the burnt ends.
10. Serving Suggestion: Over Homemade Waffles

Certified Pork Butt

Cooking Time: 12-20 Hrs

Ingredients:
- 2 Pork butts (6-10 lbs. each)
- Apple juice
- Your favorite rub/seasoning
- Mustard

Directions:
1. Remove the pork butt from the plastic wrap & pat dry using a paper towel.
2. Tip: Choose a pork butt with a full fat cap. This helps the meat while it's smoking for a long period of time.
3. Trim the excess fat that is loose and pulls up easily. Score the fat cap 1/8 to 1/4-inch-deep diagonally, spaced out 1/2 to 1 inch apart.
4. Tip: Scoring the meat allows the seasoning and smoke to penetrate into the pork butt.
5. Fill the marinade injector with apple juice and inject into the top and sides of the meat.
6. Spread a coating of mustard using a basting brush all over the pork butt.
7. Tip: This allows the rub to stick to the pork butt.
8. Generously season the pork butt on all sides with your favorite rub.
9. Tip: After seasoning, wrap in Saran Wrap and store in refrigerator overnight or 8-10 hours. This allows the rubs to penetrate and apple juice to tenderizer the pork butt.
10. Chef's Note: I used a combination of the Char-Griller Original All-Purpose BBQ Rub, Char-Griller Ribs BBQ Rub, TexJoy Butt & Rib Tickler Pork Rub,

Barker BBQ All Purpose House Blend Rub and Southside Market Barbecue Oak Smoked Black Pepper, Coarse Ground

11. Cooking Directions
12. Ignite charcoal and preheat smoker to 225°F.
13. Add boiling water to the drip pan and place under grill grate.
14. Tip: This will add moisture for the cook and collect the drippings .
15. Smoke the pork butts for 2 hours per pound at 225°F, until the meat reaches an internal temperature of 160°F.
16. Tip: Maintain a 225°F temperature, check fire hourly or when needed. Also spritz with apple juice every time you add fuel to your fire. Spritzing adds moisture and flavor. It prevents the pork butt from drying out and helps to create the bark. Monitor the temperature using a folding probe thermometer and/or remote thermometer.
17. Chef's Note: I used Fogo Eucalyptus Lump Charcoal for the heat and Mesquite mini logs for the smoke. Always keep the smoke stack vent open to allow the smoke to flow over the meat. Maintain the heat of smoker by adjusting the side vent on the fire box. Slightly close it if your fire gets too hot.
18. Remove the pork butts from the smoker and double wrap in foil. Before closing the wrap, add 1 C. apple juice and 1 stick of butter for each pork butt, more seasoning and BBQ sauce, to taste.
19. Place back in smoker and cook until the pork butt reaches an internal temperature of 199°F, then remove from the smoker.
20. Tip: Wrap pork butt in a large towel and place in a cooler or just set to the side for a minimum of 1-2 hours for resting. This allows the meat to cook down and stop cooking and is a major key in the process.
21. After resting, remove the towel and foil. Pull apart the pork using two forks or meat claws.
22. Make pulled pork sandwiches and endless pulled pork dishes. Enjoy!

Smoked Meatballs With Sweet And Sour Sauce

Cooking Time: 30 Min

Ingredients:
- 3/4 Cup Panko Breadcrumbs (Meatballs)
- 1/2 Yellow Onion, Minced (Meatballs)
- 1/2 Pounds 80/20 Ground Beef (Meatballs)
- 1 Egg (Meatballs)
- 2 Garlic Cloves, Minced (Meatballs)
- 1.5 tsp Worcestershire Sauce (Meatballs)
- 1 Tbsp Bacon Fat (Melted, Cooled) (Meatballs)
- 1/2 tsp Kosher Salt (Meatballs)
- 3/4 tsp Black Pepper
- 1 Tbsp Cornstarch (Sauce)
- 1/4 Cup Water (Sauce)
- 1/4 Cup Apple Cider Vinegar (Sauce)
- 1/2 Cup Brown Sugar (Sauce)
- 1/4 Cup Ketchup (Sauce)
- 1 Tbsp Soy Sauce (Sauce)

Directions:
1. Prepare smoker grill for 375°F add mild smoking wood for smoke flavor.
2. In a large mixing bowl, add ground beef, ground pork, melted bacon fat, onion, and breadcrumbs. Mix together with hands to coat. Let sit for a few minutes.
3. Add remaining meatball ingredients and mix with hands to combine.
4. Scoop out level tablespoons of the meat mixture and set on work surface. Roll each in hands to form a smooth meatball.
5. Spray down a racked baking tray with oil. Place meatballs on rack.
6. Bake/smoke for 30 minutes or until browned. Cook to at least 165°F internal temperature. Remove from heat and transfer meatballs to a large bowl immediately to avoid sticking.
7. Combine all ingredients in a small saucepan over medium heat. Whisk to combine.
8. Bring to simmer, stirring frequently. Then simmer until sauce thickens like maple syrup. (3-5 minutes)

9. Cover meatballs with sweet and sour sauce sauce. Transfer to a serving dish with toothpicks and remaining dipping sauce.
10. Keep warm and stir occasionally prior to serving.
11. Enjoy!

Bacon Wrapped Kabob

Cooking Time: 10 Min

Ingredients:
- 1 Lb KC Cattle Company (Wagyu Stew or Kabob Meat)
- 10 Strips of Bacon (Cut In Half)
- 1 Tsp Redmond Real Salt
- 1 Tsp Redmond Organic Garlic Pepper

Directions:
1. Season beef with salt & pepper, wrap each piece with bacon & skewer them. Cook on flat iron griddle (or grill) turning every 2 minutes, for 10 minutes. I finished mine off in the air fryer to crisp the bacon up a little more without over cooking the beef.

How To: Easy Dry Rub Grilled Pork Tenderloin

Ingredients:
- 1.5 Lbs Pork Tenderloin (Trimmed and Pat Dry)
- 1 Tbsp Brown Sugar
- 1 Tbsp Garlic Powder
- 1 Tbsp Chili Powder
- 1 Tbsp Salt
- 1 Tbsp Black Pepper
- 1 Tsp Smoked Paprika
- 1 Tsp Red Chili Flake

Directions:
1. Preheat Char-Griller Grill to high heat. For an easy weeknight dinner, I use the gas side of my Texas Trio for quick cooking, but of course, charcoal flavor would only add to this recipe! While grill is heating, mix spices together, sprinkle heavily over the meat, and rub well. Allow the meat to sit at room temperature for about 20 minutes, letting the spices marry. When grill has reached high heat, add pork loin and close lid. In 5 minutes, rotate meat clockwise to make diamond marks, and allow to cook another 5 minutes with the lid closed. After 10 minutes on one side has passed, flip your pork, and repeat- 5 minutes in one position with the lid closed, and rotate again, 5 minutes with the lid closed. I like to pull my pork off the grill at 145 degrees. While it rests, it will come up about 5-8 more degrees, allowing the meat to stay perfectly moist. Remove meat from the grill, cover loosely with foil, and let rest for 15 minutes before slicing. Serve with your favorite grilled vegetable or a large tossed salad. Enjoy!

Pork Tenderloin Sliders

Cooking Time: 8-10 Min

Ingredients:
- (2) 1 lb. pork tenderloins
- Salt and pepper, to taste
- Olive oil, for brushing
- Slider buns

Directions:
1. Pre-heat grill to 400°F. Rinse tenderloins and pat dry with paper towel. 2. Generously season with salt and pepper or use Original All-Purpose BBQ rub, to taste. 3. Place pork tenderloins on the grill at 400°F for 4 minutes per side, brushing with olive oil occasionally, and turning to ensure good sear marks on each side. Pork is done when internal temperature reaches 140°F. 4. Toast slider buns for 1-2 minutes before serving.
2. Brush with a layer of BBQ sauce and allow pork to rest for 10 minutes before slicing and serving on toasted slider buns.

Bacon Wrapped Kielbasa

Cooking Time: 1 Hrs

Ingredients:
- Smoked sausage or kielbasa
- 2-3 jalapeños, cored and sliced
- Block of Colby jack or pepper jack cheese, cut into thick slices
- Package of bacon
- Original All-Purpose BBQ Rub, to taste
- Favorite BBQ sauce for dipping

Directions:
1. Cut sausage into ½ inch thick slices. Place a slice of cheese on top, then a slice of jalapeño.
2. Wrap with 2 slices of bacon on opposite sides.
3. Season with Original All-Purpose BBQ rub, or your favorite rub, to taste.
4. Heat grill to 300°F. Place bacon-wrapped kielbasa on the grill and smoke for around 1 hour.
5. Let cool, then serve with your favorite BBQ sauce for dipping!

Flavor Pro Smoked Pork Shoulder

Cooking Time: 90 Minutes Per Pound And Then 1 Hour Rest Hrs

Ingredients:
- 5 to 6 Pound Bone-In Pork Shoulder or Boston Butt
- Char-Griller Rib Rub
- Spray Bottle Full of Apple Juice and Oil

Directions:
1. Trim excess fat from the pork shoulder. (Skip this step if it is Boston Butt.) Score the remaining fat with a sharp knife.
2. Rub a liberal amount of Rib Spice Rub on the pork. Make sure each side is evenly coated.
3. Place pork in the fridge for at least 12 hours.
4. Remove pork from fridge one hour before placing on the grill.
5. Cover the left-most and center Wood Product Zones of the Flavor Drawer with foil to catch the grease.
6. Place 15 to 20 charcoal briquettes in the far right side of the Flavor Drawer.
7. Turn the burners on high and ignite. Allow the briquettes to fully ash over.
8. Once the briquettes have ashed over, add two to three wood chunks to the charcoal.
9. To Use a Log: Place a log of no more than 3 inches in diameter and 7 inches long the right-most wood product zone. Light using the right most burner.
10. The log should take about 5 to 6 minutes to ignite.
11. After the log has ignited, turn off the gas burner and allow the grill to preheat.
12. Using a Grilling Glove, adjust the smokestacks until the internal temperature of the pit holds steady at 225.
13. Place the pork over the foil and close the grill.
14. Baste pork with Apple juice every 30 to 60 minutes.
15. Make sure to keep an eye on the pit temperature. Add another log every hour or so.
16. Smoke until internal temperature is 195 to 210 degrees Fahrenheit and remove from grill.
17. Tip: If your pork shoulder hits the dreaded "stall" (won't get above 165 degrees Fahrenheit or starts dropping, wrap it in foil, add some apple juice and place back on the grill. This will get it going again.
18. Allow pork to rest for 30 minutes to an hour for best results.

Bone-in Pulled Ham

Cooking Time: 8 Hrs

Ingredients:
- 12-15 lb. bone-in ham
- 2-20 oz. cans of crushed pineapple
- 4 C. brown sugar
- 6 Tbsp. mustard

Directions:
1. Get smoker ready and set at 250°F.
2. Place ham in an aluminum pan or cast-iron Dutch oven
3. Divide marinade in half, and pour one half marinade over top of ham
4. Place ham in smoker and baste hourly
5. Cook for around 8 1/2 hours, until ham reaches internal temp of 160°F
6. Remove ham from smoker and cover with foil for 1-2 hours
7. Shred ham and place in slow cooker or stock pot, adding juice and drippings from pan
8. Add additional marinade and pour over top of ham, mixing well
9. Cook for 1 hour until marinade is fully incorporated into shredded ham
10. All done! Makes good sandwiches or great to eat alone!

Grilled Pork Chops

Ingredients:
- 4 Bone-In or Boneless Pork Chops
- 1/4 Cup of Olive Oil
- 2 Tbsp of Soy Sauce
- 1 Tbsp of Worcestershire Sauce
- 1 Tsp of Crushed Red Pepper Flakes
- 1/2 Tsp of Cumin
- 1 Tbsp of Honey
- 1 Tsp of Chopped Parsley
- Kosher Salt
- Ground Black Pepper

Directions:
1. In a bowl, mix the olive oil, soy sauce, Worcestershire sauce, red pepper flakes, cumin, honey and desired amount of salt and pepper. Add the marinade and pork chops to a resealable bag and allow to marinate for 1 hour up to overnight. Heat the grill to medium heat and place each pork chop on the grill, cooking for 6-8 minutes per side or until the internal temperature of the thickest part reaches 145°F. Remove the chops from the grill and allow them to rest for 5-10 minutes before garnishing with parsley and serving with desired sides. Enjoy!

Simple Smoked Bbq Pork Belly

Cooking Time: 2.5 Hrs

Ingredients:
- Redmond's Pink Himalayan Salt- 1 Teaspoon
- Redmond's Organic Garlic Pepper- 1 Teaspoon
- Butter- 1 stick
- G Hughes Sweet & Spicy BBQ Sauce-1/4-1/2 Cup

Directions:
1. Pat pork belly dry with paper towel
2. Season to taste with Pink salt & garlic pepper
3. Baste with bbq sauce
4. Smoke at 250° in aluminum pan with butter for 2.5 hours. Then place directly over the coals for 5 minutes
5. Add more BBQ glaze if desired.

Breakfast Bomb - Homemade Stuffed Breakfast Sausage

Ingredients:
- Pork Sausage - 1 Lb
- 5 Eggs
- Bacon - 2 Strips
- Hash Browns - 1/4 Cup
- Shredded Cheese
- Salt & Pepper to Taste

Directions:
1. BBQ Fiends created what we think sounds like one of the best breakfasts ever. Instead of the standard, sausage with your breakfast, he filled the sausage with all of the other breakfast ingredients.
2. These sausages are stuffed with hash browns, eggs and cheese so you'll definitely stay full all day!
3. Begin by pre-heat the grill to 325 F.
4. As the grill is getting up to temp start to create the filling for the sausage. Scramble your eggs and add salt and pepper to taste.
5. Cook bacon and hash-browns to preference. Combine all ingredients together to use for the filling. Tip: Remove the eggs from the heat before they are completely finished, as they will finish once they are on the grill.
6. Lay the pork sausage out flat in a rectangle shape making sure it is evenly spread out. Place your filling in the middle and add cheese on top if desired. Tip: Remember that the sausage has to close around the filling so if needed remove some of the filling to help with closing and shaping the sausage into a log shape.
7. Bring all edges of the sausage to the top to enclose the filling. Ensure that the filling can no longer be seen and the sausage has completely enclosed it in a log shape.
8. Place on the grill at 325 F cooking on indirect heat.
9. Once the sausage is cooked and the internal temp reads 165 F it is time to pull. (This will be around the hour mark)
10. Cut the log into slices and serve with your favorite syrup!

Smoked Chili Hotdogs

Cooking Time: 20-30 Min

Ingredients:
- 8 hotdogs
- 8 hotdog buns
- 8 slices of cheese
- 1 cup of shredded cheese
- 1 can chili sauce
- 4 Tbsp. butter
- 1/2 Tsp. granulated garlic

Directions:
1. Place hotdog buns (whole) in a greased 9x13 pan
2. Cut hotdog sized slots with a knife
3. With finger, pack cut part of bun down
4. Melt butter and garlic
5. Baste buns with the butter and garlic mixture
6. Place a slice of cheese into each bun
7. Add some chili
8. Place the hotdog on top of the chili
9. Add more chili
10. Top with shredded cheese
11. Sprinkle with parsley flakes
12. Place on smoker at 250°F
13. Smoke for 20-30 minutes or until cheese is melted

Easter Sunday Texas-style Pulled Pork

Cooking Time: 8 Hrs

Ingredients:
- 6 to 7 Lb. Pork Shoulder
- 1/4 C. Kosher Salt
- 1/4 C. Coarse Black Pepper
- 2 Tbsp. Garlic Powder
- 2 Tbsp. Onion Powder
- 2 Tbsp. Paprika
- Hamburger Buns
- 1/2 C. Apple Juice (For Spritz)
- 1/2 C. Water (For Spritz)

Directions:
1. Easter Sunday is a time where we get together with family and friends. And what better way to feed all these people than with some Texas-style pulled pork sandwiches. Pulled pork really isn't a staple in Central-Texas BBQ but we love making it, and it feeds a lot of people. Your guests will be thanking you as they dive into some savory pork action!
2. Unwrap the pork shoulder and trim any excess fat or meat that may be hanging off.
3. You want to make it aerodynamic so the smoke flows evenly and does not create any burnt pieces.
4. Combine all dry ingredients in shaker for easy application.
5. Rub the pork shoulder down with olive oil or a binder of your choice. Season the pork shoulder liberally.
6. Get your grill up to 275°F and add a water pan to the side closest to the Side Fire Box.
7. This will allow for extra moisture inside the pit.
8. Once your grill is at 275°F you can go ahead and put the pork shoulder on. Let the pit do the work and tend to the fire as needed.
9. Tip: When preparing a fire, I usually use one large chimney of charcoal and add oak splits throughout the cook to maintain temp. The oak gives it that extra flavor you find in Central-Texas BBQ.
10. During the cook time is when I put my coleslaw together. Get the recipe here.
11. At around the 3-hour mark of the cook it is time to take-a-peek at the pork shoulder and spritz with the apple juice/water mixture to get some moisture on it.
12. Also, make sure that your water pan still has plenty of water left in it. Close the lid and keep on cooking.
13. Tip: Try to limit the amount of times you open the pit in order to limit fluctuations in temperature.
14. At around the 5-hour mark it is time to wrap the pork shoulder. Put it in an aluminum pan with some extra apple juice/water mixture to help with moisture.
15. Cover the pan with a layer of foil and put it back in the pit at 275°F.
16. Once the pork shoulder has reached 203°F (about 2-3 hours wrapped) it is time to take off the pit and let rest so the juices can redistribute.
17. Rest for 30-45 minutes.
18. Now is the moment of truth. Try to pull out the bone and if it gives little to no resistance then your pork shoulder is cooked to perfection!
19. Shred it and serve between a bun with a little coleslaw on top. Enjoy!

Flat Iron Griddle Breakfast Sandwich

Cooking Time: 5 Min

Ingredients:
- 2 Cups Of Kodiak Cakes Pancake And Waffle Mix
- 2 Cups Of Water
- 6 Eggs
- Egg Rings
- Syrup
- 1 Pack Of Bacon

Directions:
1. Mix pancake and waffle mix with water until the mix is no longer lumpy. Place egg rings on griddle and pour pancake batter into the egg rings, add a little swirl of syrup while batter is cooking. Once the batter has a nice bubble to it remove the egg ring and flip the griddle cake. Scramble or fry your eggs and cook the bacon, construct sandwich and enjoy

Pork Belly Burnt Ends On The Akorn

Cooking Time: 2 Hrs

Ingredients:
- Slab of Pork Belly
- BBQ Rub
- 1 Stick Butter
- 1/2 Cup Brown Sugar
- Honey
- BBQ sauce
- 8 oz Apple Juice

Directions:
1. Remove skin from pork belly Cut up pork belly in 5" squares Set smoker to 250-275F - indirect - add cherry wood Place cubed pork belly pieces on smoker - cook for 1.5-2 hours Place pork belly in aluminum pan - pour in brown sugar, honey and pads of your butter Cover, and place in smoker for another 1.5-2hrs (until about 205F) Grab a new pan.. drizzle with glaze(4 oz apple juice 1 cup of bbq sauce) and shake up so they're covered Return pieces to smoker, uncovered for approx 5-10 mins until tacky Enjoy!

Bacon Wrapped Pork Tenderloin Stuffed With Jalapeño Cream Cheese

Cooking Time: 3 Hrs

Ingredients:
- 2 Pork Tenderloin
- 5 Jalapeno Peppers (Seeded and Minced)
- 8 Oz Softened Cream Cheese
- 1 Cup Shredded Cheddar Cheese
- 1 Tbsp Salt
- 1 Tbsp Pepper
- 1 Tsp Garlic Powder
- 12 Bacon Slices

Directions:
1. Preheat your smoker to 275 degrees. Set up with a rack and pan to collect the bacon fat drippings and cheese that may seep out. While preheating, mix together the pepper, cream cheese and cheddar cheese in a bowl. Cut a pocket into your pork tenderloins making sure not to cut all the way through. Stuff the pork tenderloins with the mixture. Season the tenderloins with the salt, pepper and garlic. Lay your bacon out flat, slightly overlapping on a piece of cling wrap and place the tenderloin on the edge closest to you. Roll up the tenderloin in the bacon Place in smoker, pocket opening side up and smoke for 3 hrs.

Bacon Bourbon Compound Butter Recipe

Cooking Time: 30 Min

Ingredients:
- Softened Butter - 1 Stick
- Crispy Bacon Crumbled - 1 to 2 Slices
- Bacon Grease - 1 Tablespoon
- Bourbon - 1 Tablespoon

Directions:
1. Thoroughly mix and scoop onto a square of parchment paper, rolling up into a log, and twisting the ends closed.
2. Wrap in plastic wrap and refrigerate until firm.

Flavor Pro Quick And Easy Grilled Pork Tenderloin

Ingredients:
- 2 Pork Tenderloin
- 2 tsp Paprika
- 1 tsp Garlic Powder
- 1 tsp Cilantro
- 1 tsp Oregano
- Salt and Pepper to Taste
- Olive Oil

Directions:
1. Blend spices together in a bowl. Rub pork with olive oil and then season liberally on both sides with spice blend.
2. Set up the Flavor Pro for direct cooking. Ignite burners and turn to medium high.
3. Place pork on the grill and cook for 8 to 10 minutes per side or until the internal temperature reads 165 degrees.
4. Remove from grill and let rest for 10 minutes.

Raspberry Chipotle Glazed Pork Tenderloin

Cooking Time: 35 Min

Ingredients:
- 2 Lb Pork Tenderloin
- 1 tsp Mustard
- 1 Tbsp Char-Griller Rib Rub
- 3/4 Cup Raspberry Chipotle BBQ Sauce

Directions:
1. Pre-heat the grill to 325 F and set up for cooking with indirect heat
2. Trim excess fat off the pork tenderloin.
3. Rub down with a light coating of mustard to help the rub stick.
4. Season all sides of the pork tenderloin with Char-Griller Rib Rub
5. Once the grill has reached 325 F place the pork tenderloin on the grill in indirect heat.
6. Once the pork tenderloin has reached an internal temp of 140 F it is time to apply the glaze.
7. Heat up the raspberry chipotle sauce and use a brush to apply the glaze on the pork tenderloin.
8. Once the glaze has set and the internal temp of the pork tenderloin has reached 145 F it is time to pull off the grill and let rest for 10 minutes.
9. Slice and serve with extra raspberry chipotle sauce for dipping. Enjoy!

Memphis-style Dry Ribs

Cooking Time: 5 Hrs

Ingredients:
- 3 racks of ribs
- Ribs BBQ rub, to taste
- Apple juice
- Brown sugar
- Honey
- 12 oz. bottle of squeeze butter

Directions:
1. Rinse rib racks and pat dry with paper towel. Remove membrane from each rack by carefully prying back using the back of a sharp knife. Discard membrane. Flip racks and trim loose ends and excess fat.
2. Tip: Use a paper towel to help hold the membrane, as it's slippery.
3. Season ribs generously with Ribs BBQ Rub, or your favorite rub.
4. When setting up the grill, use a full chimney of unlit charcoal in the attached Side Fire Box and pour another ½ chimney of hot coals on top to ensure good smoke and a temperature of 275°F. Add Applewood chunks on top.
5. Adjust the charcoal grate to the highest setting in the main compartment. Place an aluminum pan on the grate and fill halfway with apple juice. Smoke ribs for 1 hour and mist with apple juice. Close lid and smoke for another 3 hours.
6. After 3 hours, remove ribs from grill and wrap. Before wrapping, spread a generous layer of brown sugar, butter and honey onto aluminum foil. Place ribs meat side down and wrap securely.
7. Transfer wrapped ribs to the grill and smoke at 275°F for another hour. Carefully drain juices before slicing and serving.

Bbq Burnt Ends

Cooking Time: 4.5 Hrs

Ingredients:
- 5-8lbs pork belly
- 1 - 1.5 C. BBQ sauce
- Favorite pork rub
- 1 stick of butter
- 1/3 C. of rum
- 1/3 C. brown sugar

Directions:
1. Trim top layer of fat
2. Cut into 2" wide vertical strips
3. Rotate and cut again to create 2" squares
4. Place in aluminum pan and season well with your favorite pork rub
5. Mix squares to thoroughly cover with rub
6. Heat grill to 250°F
7. Space out cubes evenly within grill
8. Let smoke for 3 hours at 250°F
9. Remove from grill and place in pan
10. Add 1.5 C. of your favorite BBQ sauce
11. Add 1/3 C. rum, 1/3 C. brown sugar, and 1 stick of butter
12. Mix well to evenly cover cubes
13. Smoke for another 1.5 - 1.75 hours

Oktoberfest Schweinebraten

Cooking Time: 30-40 Min

Ingredients:
- Boneless Pork Shoulder With Fat Cap and Skin
- 4-6 Cups Of Vegetable Broth
- 4 Carrots
- 4 Leeks
- 4 Celery Stalks
- 4 Medium Sized Onions
- 2 Bottles Of German Beer
- Salt & Pepper To Taste
- 3 Tbsp Butter

Directions:
1. Lay shoulder fat side down in a roasting pan Pour in enough vegetable broth to keep the fat cap covered Place on the grill at 300F for 30-40 minutes. This will help soften the skin. Cut up your vegetables into 1-2" lengths. Cut the onions into chunks Remove the meat from grill and set aside for next step Butter up your roasting pan and fill with your cut up vegetables. Brown the vegetables slightly Cut 1/2" or 1cm cubes into the fat cap being careful not to cut into the meat. Season with salt and pepper and get it down into the cube crevices. Pour the vegetable broth on top of your browned vegetables not too much, just enough to cover them. Place your seasoned shoulder on top of the vegetable bed Pour 2 bottles of your favorite dark german beer over shoulder and vegetables Raise grill heat to 340-350F and cook until internal temp of 160-165F checking throughout. Cut up and enjoy!

OTHER FAVORITE RECIPES

Boneless Wings Made From Chicken Thighs On The Char-griller Akorn Kamado Grill!

Cooking Time: 20 Min

Ingredients:
- 5-6 Boneless Chicken Thighs
- 1 Cup Flour
- Cup Bread Crumbs
- 4 Eggs
- Char-Griller Chicken Seasoning Rub

Directions:
1. Prepare chicken by trimming fat and cutting into bite size pieces Mix your favorite seasoning with the bread crumbs in a bowl Dip chicken pieces one at a time in flour, then egg wash, then breadcrumb mix Bring grill temperature to 300-350 degrees F Place chicken pieces single layer on grill Check temperatures after 20 minutes, then every 5 minutes Remove after the largest pieces are at least 165 degrees F

Easter Sunday Coleslaw For Pulled Pork Sandwiches

Cooking Time: 5 Min

Ingredients:
- Shredded Cabbage Mix - 2 Cups
- Kosher Salt - 1 1/2 tsp
- Sour Cream - 1/4 Cup
- Mayonnaise - 2 Tbs
- Apple Cider Vinegar - 1 Tbs
- Coarse Black Pepper - 2 tsp
- Dry Mustard Powder - 1 1/2 tsp

Directions:
1. During the cook time of the pork is when I put my coleslaw together.
2. Pour your cabbage into a large bowl and make sure that you try to dab away any extra water it may have on it.
3. In a small bowl combine all your coleslaw ingredients and stir thoroughly.
4. Transfer the mixture into the bowl with the cabbage and stir until it is well coated.
5. Store in refrigerator until it is time to serve.
6. Put slaw on top of pulled pork, top with a bun, and enjoy!

Serrano Beer Cheese

Cooking Time: 20 Min

Ingredients:
- Beer (your favorite) - 1.75 Cups
- Serrano Peppers - 5
- Shredded White Cheddar Cheese - 3 Cups
- Cream Cheese - 8 oz.
- Char-Griller Steak Seasoning - 1 Tbsp
- Cilantro - For Garnish

Directions:
1. Pre-heat grill to at least 350 degrees Fahrenheit
2. Roast serrano peppers over direct heat until skin blisters
3. Remove peppers and place in sandwich bag
4. Remove skins from peppers and de seed all but one
5. Chop peppers into small pieces
6. Add beer and peppers to cast iron skillet
7. Allow to simmer for 5 minutes
8. Add cream cheese and whisk until smooth
9. Add shredded cheese and whisk until melted completely
10. Sprinkle seasoning over the cheese and stir to combine
11. Garnish with cilantro
12. Enjoy with chips, soft pretzels or spoon it over a burger

Bbq Fiends Oktoberfest Beer Brats

Cooking Time: 25 Min

Ingredients:
- 5 Bratwurst
- 1 - 12 oz Can or Bottle of Oktoberfest Beer
- 1/2 Large White Onion - Sliced
- 5 Bratwurst Buns

- 1/2 Can or Jar of Sauerkraut
- Whole Grain Brown Mustard
- Kosher Salt
- Coarse Black Pepper

Directions:

1. Pre-heat the grill to 375 F and place a lightly oiled large skillet on the grill
2. Sauté the sliced onions in the oil and add salt and pepper to taste. Once the onions are tender add the can of beer into the skillet.
3. Bring the beer to a boil and add the bratwurst to the skillet.
4. Remove the bratwurst once the beer as almost reduced completely and set the bratwurst directly on the grill. Rotate on both sides for 2-3 minutes or until internal temp is at 160 F.
5. Serve the bratwurst in a bun with the beer onions, sauerkraut, and mustard as toppings. Enjoy!

Keto Grilled Brie

Cooking Time: 10 Min

Ingredients:
- Wheel of Brie- 1
- Chopped Pecans
- Chopped Strawberries
- Minced Fresh Basil
- Sugar Free Honey
- Balsamic Vinegar

Directions:

1. Grill a wheel of brie over medium high heat for 5 minutes per side, or until nice and soft with grill marks.
2. Meanwhile, toast chopped pecans in a mini cast iron over the same medium high grill heat.
3. Top with chopped strawberries, minced fresh basil, the warm pecans, and a glaze made from: one part sugar free honey, one part balsamic vinegar

Smoked And Spiced Nuts

Cooking Time: 40 Min

Ingredients:
- 3 Cups Mixed Nuts
- Dried Thyme - 1.5 tsp
- Light Brown Sugar - 1.5 tsp
- Ground Cayenne Pepper - 1/2 tsp
- Powdered Mustard - 1/2 tsp
- Chipotle Powder - 1/2 tsp
- Olive Oil - 3 Tsp

Directions:

1. Prepare AKORN for smoking. Preheat to 250 degrees Fahrenheit and add Smokin' Stone.
2. Whisk together spices and brown sugar.
3. Toss nuts in oil and spice mixture.
4. Lay nuts out onto baking sheet.
5. Place baking sheet on grill, close the lid and smoke for 30 to 40 minutes.
6. Serve warm or at room temperature.

Smoked Rib Chili

Cooking Time: 7 Hrs

Ingredients:
- 2 Racks of Baby Back Ribs
- 1 Tbsp Dark Chili Powder
- 1 Tbsp of Black Pepper
- 1 Tsp of Kosher Salt
- 1/2 Tsp of Onion Powder
- 1/2 Tsp of Garlic Powder
- 1/2 Tsp of Paprika
- 1-12 oz can of Pepsi (or coke)
- 1 Large Yellow Onion (Diced)
- 1 Red Bell Pepper (Diced)
- 1 Large Jalapeno (Diced)(Optional Heat)
- 1 Tbsp of Chili Powder
- 1/2 Tbsp pf Dark Chili Powder
- 1/2 Tsp of Cayenne Pepper (Optional)
- 1/2 Tsp of Garlic Powder
- 1/2 Tsp of Kosher Salt
- 1/2 Tsp of Crushed Red Pepper flakes
- 3 15 Oz cans of Black Beans (juices drained, do not rinse)

Directions:

1. Remove the membranes from the racks of ribs and discard. Cut the 2 racks in half, making a total of 4 half racks of ribs. In a gallon freezer ziploc bag, combine all of your marinade ingredients. Put the racks of ribs in the

freezer bag and seal the bag. Move the ribs around with the marinade to mix the ingredients all together and cover all surfaces of your ribs. Put the bag in the fridge and let marinade for at least 4 hours (overnight is prefered for this recipe). The next day (or after 4 hours) remove the bag and get your Char-Griller Offset smoker up to a temperature of 250 degrees F. Place the racks of ribs on the grates of the smoker and smoke with the indirect heat until you get the bark/color you desire (approx 2 hours, give or take a half an hour). While your ribs are cooking, put together your pot. Start with a cast iron skillet (or a medium/large sauce pan) and spray with your cooking oil. Add the 2 pads of butter and start to melt. To that, add your diced Onion, Bell Pepper and Jalapeno. Cook the veggies until fragrant and the onion becomes translucent (Season with salt and black pepper to taste). Remove from heat and put into a bowl, set aside. Next, in a large stock pot, add all of your powdered ingredients, sauteed veggies, black beans, tomato paste, crushed tomatoes, diced tomatoes with green chiles, and the guiness beer. Stir to combine and place the pot in the smoker with the ribs. After you get your ribs to the color/bark that you want, wrap your ribs in aluminum foil tightly and place back on the smoker. This is when you will cook for tenderness. Bring the smoker temps up to around 275-280 degrees F and cook until ribs are probe/fork tender (approx 2-3 more hours). Pro Tip: You can test doneness with the ribs by pulling on one of the bones. If it starts to slide out of the meat easily, they are done. Once the ribs are probe/fork tender, remove from smoker and allow to rest for approximately 30 mins to 1 hour. Remove the bones (they should pull right out) and shred/cut/dice the rib meat and add to your pot. Stir everything together to combine. You're DONE!! :) Nothing left to do but garnish with some sour cream, finely diced green onions and some shredded cheese!! Enjoy!!

Flavor Pro Smoked Eggs

Cooking Time: 1.5 Hrs

Ingredients:
- Dozen Large Eggs
- Char-Griller AP Seasoning
- Salt to Taste

Directions:

1. Prepare the Flavor Pro for indirect heat at 350°F. For best results, fill the far right zone of the Flavor Drawer with your favorite lump charcoal and a couple of small sized wood chunks. Ignite the far right burner to allow charcoal to light. Once fully lit, turn burner to off position and adjust your two smoke stacks to maintain temp at 350°F. Now you're ready for the eggs.
2. Place eggs directly on the grate but the opposite side, away from the heat. This will allow the eggs to "bake" on the grill.
3. Bake for 30 minutes then place the eggs in ice cold water to stop them from cooking any further. Over cooking the eggs can make them rubbery.
4. Once cooled, peel the shell off each of the eggs.
5. Note: This can sometimes be a bit difficult but I find that gently tapping and rolling them across a hard surface helps make this process a little easier. Your eggs may not peel clean every single time, and that's okay. They will still be just as delicious.
6. Next, set your Flavor Pro up for smoking. Add 6 pieces of charcoal to the far right side of the Flavor Drawer and light them using the far right gas burner. Add a few of your favorite wood chunks.
7. Note: Be sure not to let the pit temperature get above 185°F for smoking the eggs. 150°F is where I like to be for this recipe. For temperature adjustments, you can turn the far right burner to low or add more coals to get the temp to climb if it happens to dip. Make sure your wood chunks are always lit and are giving off smoke during the entire smoking process. For the smoke stacks, I kept the stack closest to the heat (right) closed and the far stack (left) 25% of the way open. Adjust as needed.
8. Season all sides of the eggs with the Char-Griller AP seasoning.
9. Place eggs back on the grill, directly on the grate. Again on the opposite side, away from the fire.
10. Smoke your eggs for 30-90 minutes.
11. Note: The longer they smoke, the more smoke flavor they will have. I find that 45 minutes of smoke is a great balance of flavor. You will notice your eggs will

change color. The longer you smoke them the browner they get.
12. Once smoked, you can refrigerate to chill them if needed.
13. Serve and enjoy! I like to serve mine chilled, sliced in half, and salted!

Teriyaki Chicken And Mango Skewers

Cooking Time: 10 To 12 Min

Ingredients:
- Teriyaki Sauce - 1 Bottle
- Boneless, Skinless Chicken Thighs - 4 Pounds
- 3 Mangos
- 1 Large Red Onion
- Sesame Seeds - For Garnish
- Salt and Pepper - To Taste
- Chopped Scallions - For Garnish

Directions:
1. Cut chicken thighs into 1-inch cubes and place in a bag with the teriyaki sauce.
2. Refrigerate overnight.
3. Peel and cut the mango into 1-inch cubes.
4. Preheat the grill to medium high heat.
5. Add the mango and chicken to the skewers.
6. Grill the skewers covered for 10 to 12 minutes, turning occasionally.
7. Remove from the grill and rest.
8. Sprinkle with sesame seeds and scallions.

Flat Iron Candied Sweet Potatoes

Cooking Time: 25 Min

Ingredients:
- 4 Large Sweet Potatoes
- 2 Tbsp of Butter
- 1 1/2 Cups of Honey
- 1/4 Cup Maple Syrup
- 2 Tbsp of Ground Cinnamon
- 1/2 Tsp of Cayenne Pepper

Directions:
1. Rinse and peel sweet potatoes. Cut them into small slices OR cubes.
2. Heat Flat Iron to medium heat and melt butter.
3. Add sweet potatoes and stir occasionally until all are softened, remove from heat and set aside.
4. In a large bowl, mix together honey, maple syrup, cinnamon, and cayenne pepper. Add cooked sweet potatoes and mix until all potatoes are coated.
5. Return griddle to medium heat and pour on the honey coated sweet potatoes. Stir around for about 3-4 minutes then reduce heat to low. Be sure to keep all the potatoes close together in a small pile (rather than spread out) and stir once or twice. Allow (about 10 minutes) for the honey mixture to become a nice glaze on the potatoes.
6. Serve hot.

Smoked Sweet Garlic Chili And Teriyaki Wings

Cooking Time: 30 Min

Ingredients:
- 1 Bag Of Party Wings
- Favorite Wing Rub
- G. Hughes Sugar Free Teriyaki Marinade
- Garlic Chili Paste
- Monk fruit sweetener
- Apple Cider Vinegar

Directions:
1. WINGS
2. Pat wings dry with paper towel and season with favorite wing rub (I like a maple bourbon base rub for chicken). Heat your grill up to 350*, coating the grates with oil while they warm up (for nonstick) Place wings on grill and cook for about 15 mins, flip wings over and cook for about another 15 mins. Chicken is technically done at 165* IT but I like to take my wings to about 175*-180*ish; this gives them a more fall off the bone texture while crisping the skin. Toss wings in Teriyaki or Sweet Garlic Chili sauce
3. SWEET GARLIC CHILI SAUCE
4. Mix ½ bottle of Garlic Chili sauce with ¼ cup of apple cider vinegar and monk fruit sweetener (to taste) in a pan over medium heat. Stir ingredients until everything has combined Pour directly over wings and toss

Smoked Queso Dip

Cooking Time: 30 Min

Ingredients:
- 1 Block of Velveeta Cheese (Cubed)
- 1 Small Bag of Mexican-style shredded cheese
- 2 Roma Tomatoes, diced
- 1 Cup of Diced Jalapenos (Seeded)
- 2 Tbsp of Cream Cheese
- 1/2 Red Onion (Diced)
- 1 Packet Of Taco Seasoning

Directions:
1. Preheat your smoker to 225-250°F. In an aluminum pan, arrange all the ingredients side-by-side and place in the smoker, cooking for 30 minutes before mixing all ingredients together. Cook for an additional hour or until all cheese is melted and smooth. Serve immediately with desired choice of chips. Enjoy!

Beer Cheese Sauce

Cooking Time: 10 Min

Ingredients:
- Butter - 3 Tbs
- Flour - 3 Tbs
- Lager Beer - 1/2 Cup
- Heavy Cream - 1 Cup
- Dijon Mustard - 1 tsp
- Garlic Powder - 1/2 tsp
- Salt - 1/2 tsp
- Pepper - 1/4 tsp
- Cheddar Cheese - 1.5 Cups
- Gruyere Cheese - 1.5 Cups

Directions:
1. We whipped up this beer cheese on the side burner of the Char-Griller DUO 5050 while we were grilling brats and peppers. It took just 10 minutes start to finish! Check out the whole recipe below.
2. In a saucepan on the side burner, melt butter.
3. Add flour and whisk until combined.
4. Cook for 30 seconds.
5. Add beer slowly, while continuously whisking.
6. Slowly add in cream while continuing to whisk.
7. Cook over medium heat until the mixture has thickened.
8. Stir in mustard, salt, pepper, and garlic powder.
9. Add cheese half a cup at a time and whisk until melted.
10. Serve warm and pour over brats, burgers, and more.

Grilled Eggs Benedict With Grilled Lemon Hollandaise

Cooking Time: 20 Min

Ingredients:
- 10 Eggs
- 4 English Muffins
- 8 Slices of Canadian Bacon
- 2 Lemons, Halved
- 1 Stick Unsalted Butter, Melted
- 1 Tbsp Dijon Mustard
- 1 Tbsp Salt

Directions:
1. From Aubrey:
2. "It's the week of Christmas and I couldn't be more thrilled to be spending my first 'warm' Christmas right here in my new home- the sunshine state. Usually the holidays are filled with blustery winds and snow, but this year, I'm thinking beach, and a grilled brunch. Who is with me!? Let's do a fun spin on everyone's favorite- Eggs Benedict. The star to the show is the lemon in the hollandaise sauce, so lets grill it. The best part about the grill?? Not having to clean up 7 different pans in one meal. This eggs benny is on your plate in less than 10. Plus- my hollandaise sauce is made in the blender, it's so easy! Let's do it! Happy Hollindaze! Ha!"
3. Preheat your Char-Griller Grill to high, and scrape those grates, we don't want any muffins sticking.
4. While our grill heats up, slice English muffins in half, and prepare the eggs for the hollandaise.
5. Separate 4 eggs, placing the yolks in a blender, and saving the whites for another day! (think omelet vibes).
6. Head out to the grill and grill your Canadian bacon, English muffins, and halved lemons, until crispy and golden brown. Pull from heat.

7. Cook remaining eggs to your liking, I love mine poached, but you can do sunny side up, or even scrambled.

8. In the blender with the yolks, squeeze the juice of 2 of the grilled lemon halves, and blend on high for 60 seconds, until light and fluffy. Add Dijon, salt, and pulse till combined. Then, while the motor is running slow, slowly drizzle in your melted butter until a thick and creamy hollandaise sauce has formed. It's really that easy!

9. Assemble the plates with English muffin, a slice of grilled bacon, an egg, and a dollop of your hollandaise. Garnish with fresh herbs and remaining grilled lemon pieces. Repeat until a Christmas nap appears, that's my gift to you! Enjoy!

Fried Bacon And Cabbage

Cooking Time: 30 Min

Ingredients:
- 1 Cup Chopped Bacon
- 1 Head Cabbage, Cored & Chopped
- Salt & Pepper to Taste
- Parsley for Garnish

Directions:
1. Preheat grill to medium high heat.
2. Place cast iron skillet on grill over direct heat, allow to heat up.
3. Place chopped bacon on skillet & stir occasionally until cooked through but don't let the bacon get over cooked.
4. Add chopped cabbage and stir, coating it in bacon grease & mixing it in with the bacon.
5. Add salt & pepper to taste.
6. Allow cabbage to fry up until wilted and slightly browned. Remove from grill.
7. Add parsley to garnish. Serve warm.
8. Tip: Add dried cranberries for a kick of sweetness!

Cowboy Steak With Asparagus And Onion

Cooking Time: 1½ Hrs

Ingredients:
- Cowboy Steak
- 1 bunch asparagus, ends trimmed
- 1 onion, sliced
- Steak BBQ Rub, to taste
- Original All-Purpose BBQ Rub, to taste
- Garlic butter
- Sea salt, to taste
- Olive oil

Directions:
1. #TeamCharGriller Ambassador James Llorens took innovation to the next level with this Cowboy Steak recipe. He decided to use the Char-Griller Rotisserie Kit as an innovative way to reverse sear the steak. After letting it reach 130°F, he took it off the Rotisserie and seared it off on the Char-Griller AKORN.
2. Asparagus and onions round out this impressive meal and Lloren's Garlic Butter recipe adds that final finishing touch to make the steak shine.
3. Using a sharp knife, make a small hole at the end of the bone so it can fit in the rotisserie fork.
4. Apply olive oil, sea salt and Steak BBQ Rub to both sides of the Cowboy Steak.
5. Tip: Do not add sea salt or rub/seasoning to the bone to avoid it from burning while roasting.
6. Place the Cowboy Steak in the rotisserie forks and set aside. Place two forks in the meat and one fork in the bone hole.
7. Season asparagus and onions with Original All-Purpose BBQ Rub and set aside.
8. Pre-heat the Char-Griller Super Pro™ 2121 to 300°F. Place the rotisserie with the Cowboy Steak and onions in the grill/rotisserie motor.
9. Tip: Make sure the charcoal is more on the meat side of the rotisserie versus the bone side.
10. Tip: Prop up the grill lid halfway using the grate lifter.
11. While your Cowboy Steak is roasting pre-heat the Akorn Kamado 6719 and cook your asparagus. Once the asparagus is done allow the grill to get extremely hot to sear Cowboy Steak.
12. Tip: Place a chimney starter in the center of the Kamado for extreme direct heat in the middle of the grill.

13. Roast the Cowboy Steak to 130°F or your desired temperature using the folding probe thermometer. Remove from the steak from the grill and remove the steak completely off of the rotisserie forks. Let rest for 5-10 minutes then apply the melted garlic butter to both sides.
14. Tip: Spray canned olive oil/vegetable oil on the grates to avoid the steak sticking to the grates.
15. Transfer the steak to the Kamado for 1-2 minutes on each side. Remove the steak from the grill and allow to rest for 10-15 minutes. Slice the steak and sprinkle on sea salt.
16. Plate the onions, asparagus and Cowboy Steak and serve with A1 Steak sauce for additional flavor, if desired. Enjoy!

Garlic Butter

Cooking Time: 10 Min

Ingredients:
- Fresh or jarred garlic, minced
- Butter (do not use margarine)
- Olive oil
- Sea salt, to taste

Directions:
1. Use this butter on steak, shrimp, and more for a powerful flavor boost.
2. Combine all the ingredients in a cast iron skillet without mixing and set aside until needed.
3. When needed, melt and stir the garlic butter.

Sausage Bbq Meat Balls

Ingredients:
- Two Pounds Ground Sausage
- 1 Tbsp Chipotle Mustard
- Favorite BBQ Rub to Taste
- Garlic Powder to Taste
- 2 Tbsp Fresh Cilantro, Chopped
- Favorite BBQ Sauce

Directions:
1. Pre-heat your grill to 300 degrees.
2. Make the meatballs.
3. After 20 minutes smoking, sauce the meatballs with desired BBQ sauce.
4. Remove meatballs from smoker after internal temperature is 165 degrees
5. Place meatballs in crockpot with additional BBQ sauce and sprinkle with dried parsley.
6. Serve with white bread and enjoy!

Garlic & Herb Seasoned Potatoes

Cooking Time: 10 Min

Ingredients:
- 3-4 Large Russet Pot
- 1/3 Cup Olive Oil
- 1 Tsp White Whine Vinegar
- 1 Tbs. Spicy Mustard
- 2 Tsp. Chargriller Garlic & Herb Seasoning
- 3 Garlic Cloves (Minced)
- 4 Tbs Melted Butter
- Parsley To Garnish

Directions:
1. Put your Char-Griller Garlic & Herb seasoning to delicious use beyond just meat with these Garlic & Herb seasoned potatoes.
2. Steam potatoes in pressure cooker for 5 minutes.
3. While that's cooking combine all the other ingredients listed above.
4. Once finished, drain in colander and place in bowl.
5. Pour mixture over potatoes while they are still warm and give them a good toss. Add salt and pepper to taste.
6. Top with parsley and enjoy with your next meal.

Smoked & Spiced Pumpkin Seeds

Ingredients:
- 3 - 4 Cups Fresh Pumpkin Seeds
- 3 Tbsp Salt
- 12 oz Water
- Olive Oil

Directions:
1. Cut open the top of the pumpkin and remove all the fibrous strands (pumpkin brains) inside and set aside.
2. Begin to separate the seeds from the fibrous strands and discard all the fibrous strands and set seeds aside.

3. Rinse pumpkin seeds in running water in the sink and continue to discard any remaining fibrous strands.
4. In a bowl add 12 oz. water with 2 tsp salt and mix thoroughly.
5. Add the pumpkin seeds to the mixture and place in the refrigerator for 2-24 hours.
6. Preheat your Char-griller Smokin' Champ 1624 to 300°
7. Tip: Ignite charcoal first, then add your favorite smoking wood.
8. Add small amount of water to your Char-griller drip pan for moisture.
9. Remove pumpkin seeds from the refrigerator and strain water
10. Add a drip of olive oil to the seeds and stir.
11. Add 1 tsp salt with a few sprinkles of Tajin to taste and stir thoroughly.
12. Then place the seeds on a large aluminum tray with a sheet of parchment paper and spread them evenly
13. Then place the large tray with the seeds to the smoker.
14. Maintain your fire at 300°
15. Rotate the tray periodically.
16. Remove seeds from the smoker after 1 hour of smoking or until golden brown.
17. Add a few fresh sprinkles of Tajin and enjoy!

Mediterranean Chicken & Mushroom Burger Bowls

Cooking Time: Ten Min

Ingredients:

- Ground Chicken Breast - 1 Lb
- Portobello Mushrooms - 1 Lb
- Fresh Basil & Parsley - 1/2 Cup
- 1 Egg
- Crumbled Feta - 1/3 Cup
- 1 Tbs Salt - For Burgers
- Cucumber - 2 Cups
- Grape Tomatoes - 2 Cups
- Crumbled Feta - 1/2 Cup for Salad
- Fresh Basil & Parsley - 1/2 Cup for Salad
- Olive Oil - 1/4 Cup
- Salt and Pepper to Taste for Salad

Directions:

1. Ambassador Aubrey Johanson of @thatswhatsheeats came up with a blended burger, ditched the bun and added some fresh veggies. A lighter burger option for people who want to eat a little healthier or are following keto, Aubrey runs through how she created these Mediterranean Chicken & Mushroom Burger Bowls.
2. Not only is adding mushrooms to your burger blend delicious, it provides a ton of moisture to what could be a drier protein, like ground chicken breast. Adding mushrooms is a great way to cut back on meat consumption for the summer, and still having that delicious cook out meal. I love to add mushrooms and herbs to burger blends for a bowl. Pair these burgers with my favorite summer cucumber salad and you'll have a new cook-out favorite.
3. In a blender, add mushrooms, egg, herbs, and salt. Pulse until mushrooms are broken down. Add mixture to ground chicken, and crumble feta. Combine, and form into 6 burger patties.
4. Preheat grill to high, and spray some cooking spray on the grates. Grill each burger for 4 minutes per side, until cooked through.
5. While burgers are cooking, make the cucumber salad. Cut cucumbers and tomatoes, chop the herbs, and mix with feta, vinegar, olive oil, salt and pepper.
6. Build your burger bowl! Fill a bowl with greens, a big serving of cucumber salad, and a chicken mushroom burger on top. Enjoy!

Vegetarian Shepherd's Pie

Cooking Time: 25 Min

Ingredients:

- 2 lbs. Russet potatoes, peeled and quartered
- 3 shallots, minced
- 16 oz. Cremini or baby bella mushrooms, diced
- 6 medium carrots, peeled and finely chopped
- 2 Tbsp. tomato paste
- 2 Tbsp. all-purpose flour
- ½ C. red wine, optional

- 1-2 C. vegetable broth
- 2 Tbsp. olive oil
- 2 C. frozen peas
- ½ C. full fat Greek yogurt
- ¼ C. butter or margarine
- Fresh whole herbs, to taste
- Salt and pepper, to taste

Directions:
1. Boil potatoes in salted water until fork tender. Drain, mash, and mix in yogurt and butter. Season to taste. 2. In a large pan, heat the oil over medium heat. Add shallots and sauté until fragrant. Add mushrooms, carrots, and whole herbs. Sauté until carrots are softened, about 10 minutes. 3. Add tomato paste and flour to the pan and stir. Pour in the red wine, if using, and deglaze the pan. Stir occasionally for 1-2 minutes. 4. Slowly add the broth, stirring until a gravy starts to form. Season with salt and pepper, to taste then simmer over low heat until thickened. 5. Remove the herbs and stir in the peas. Transfer mixture to a cast iron pan and spread the mashed potatoes on top. 6. Place on the grill at 350°F to bake for 15 minutes.
2. Allow to cool slightly before serving. Enjoy!
3. Note: Substitute ½ C. vegetable broth or water for red wine.

Grilled Adobo Wings

Ingredients:
- 3-4 Lbs of Chicken Wings
- 5 Dried Chipotle Chilis
- 10 Dried Ancho Chilis
- 8 Garlic Cloves
- 1 tsp Salt
- 1/4 Cup White Vinegar
- 1/4 Cup of the Chili Soaking Liquid
- 1/2 tsp Cumin
- 1 tsp Black Pepper
- 1 tsp Oregano

Directions:
1. Destem and deseed the chiles, and place in a bowl with very hot tap water and allow to soak for 20 minutes.
2. Add the chiles and the remaining ingredients into a blender and blend until smooth. Add a splash of the water if too thick or lumpy. Marinade wings for 2 hours, up to overnight.
3. Grill over medium high heat on an oiled grill until done, about 20 minutes flipping every 5 minutes.

Smoked Cedar Plank Salmon

Cooking Time: 45 Min

Ingredients:
- Salmon
- Lemons
- Green Onion
- Sesame Seeds
- Marinade/Glaze (Soy Sauce,Sriracha,Honey,Garlic,Ginger)
- Veggie Skewers (Zucchini, Yellow Zucchini, Whole Mushrooms,Mini Sweet Peppers)

Directions:
1. Season salmon fillets with salt, pepper, garlic and place in a dish or large zip lock bag Prepare marinade of ¾ cup soy sauce, 1 tbsp Sriracha hot sauce, 2 tbsp honey, tbsp minced ginger and 2-3 garlic cloves Reserve some marinade for basting Marinate salmon for 30 mins -1 hour Slice lemons into rings Cut salmon into 4 inch wide fillets Place salmon fillets on cedar planks and top each fillet with 2 lemon rings Fire up your Char-Grillers Triple Play Grill and keep temperatures between 225-250*F Smoke low and slow and baste every 5-10 minutes Chop green and yellow zucchini and begin skewering vegetables Grill the veggie skewers on the propane side of the Triple Play Baste the skewers with the marinade as well Remove salmon from smoker when an internal temperature of 145*F is reached Serve with cilantro-lime rice, garlic bread, and enjoy!
2. Pitts Tips
3. Soak the cedar planks in water ahead of time at least 1 hour to prevent burning Baste the salmon every 5-10 minutes to a allow for the sugars to caramelize Don't forget to grill the lemon halves also!

Flavor Pro™ Smoked Turkey Breast

Cooking Time: 2 Hrs

Ingredients:
- 3 Lb All Natural Turkey Breast Roast
- 2 Tbsp Onion Powder
- 2 Tbsp Garlic Powder
- 1 Tbsp Paprika
- 1 Tbsp Chili Powder
- 1 Tbsp Parsley
- 1 1/2 Tsp Black Pepper
- 1 Tbsp Paprika

Directions:

1. Rinse off your turkey breast roast and pat dry with a paper towel. (Leave the netting on, you will cut that off at the end of the cook) Spray on a coat of olive oil cooking spray. Generously apply all the ingredients or salt-free seasoning to all sides of the turkey breast roast. Place the seasoned turkey in the refrigerator for 15 minutes while your grill heats up. Prepare your Flavor Pro for indirect heat at 275°f by filling the far left slot and the middle slot of the Flavor Drawer with charcoal. Add a few chunks of smoking wood to the coals as well. I used hickory for this recipe but feel free to use whatever smoking wood you like. Use both burners on the left to light the charcoal. Once charcoal is lit, you may turn your burners off. Keep both smoke stacks open. Use a water pan for this recipe. Feel free to use water, apple juice, or a mixture. Place pan on the far right slot of the Flavor Drawer underneath the grate. Once your Flavor Pro is up to temperature, add your turkey breast roast to the far right side of the grill grate, away from the heat source and directly above your water pan. Add more coals or wood as needed to maintain your temperature. Smoke for approximately 2 hours or until your turkey reaches an internal temperature of 165°f. Start temperature probing your turkey around an hour of cooking time. Be sure to keep a close eye on the internal temperature, going over 165°f can cause your turkey to dry out. Let rest for 15 minutes. Cut of netting with scissors then slice. Enjoy!

Ken's Famous Baked Beans

Cooking Time: 2 Hrs

Ingredients:
- ½ lb. bacon
- 1 large sweet onion, chopped
- 1 lb. cans of baked beans
- 1 Tbsp. minced garlic, or to taste
- ½ Tbsp. smoked paprika
- 1 C. brown sugar
- 3 Tbsp. Worcestershire sauce
- 2 Tbsp. prepared mustard

Directions:

1. Drain liquid from baked beans and pour into a large cast iron skillet.
2. Fry bacon in batches, if needed, in a pan to desired crispness according to package directions, drain grease (reserving 2 Tbsp.) and crumble when cool. Set aside in a medium bowl. Do not wipe pan.
3. Sauté onion and garlic in the same pan with reserved bacon grease until tender, about 5-7 minutes.
4. Add crumbled bacon and stir in minced garlic, brown sugar, Worcestershire sauce and mustard.
5. Transfer all ingredients to cast iron skillet with beans and mix well.
6. Place on the grill at 325°F and smoke uncovered for 2 hours.

Jalapeño Popper Pizza

Cooking Time: 7 To 9 Min

Ingredients:
- 6 Slices of Diced Bacon
- 2 Tbs Olive Oil
- 4 Jalapeno Peppers, Sliced
- 1 Thai Red Chili, Sliced
- 1 Shallot Sliced
- 1/4 Cup Semolina
- 1 Package Premade Pizza Dough
- 2 Cups Monterey Jack Cheese, Shredded

Directions:

1. Add Smokin' Stone to AKORN, add Pizza Stone to grates, preheat grill to 600 degrees.

2. Slice peppers and shallots.
3. Cook bacon to crispy and dice.
4. Add peppers, shallots and olive oil in bow. Mix and set aside.
5. Shape pizza dough on a semolina covered cutting board.
6. Spread cream cheese on pizza dough. Top with bacon, pepper mixture, and Monterey jack cheese.
7. Place pizza on Pizza Stone and cook for 7 to 9 minutes or until cheese is melted and crust is golden brown.

Smoked Lamb Shank

Cooking Time: 40 Min

Ingredients:
- Two Lamb Shanks
- 2 oz. Olive Oil
- 2 oz. Paprika
- 1 oz. Granulated Garlic
- 1 oz. Brown Sugar

Directions:
1. Mix together Paprika, Granulated Garlic, and Brown Sugar. Set aside.
2. Rub lamb shanks with olive oil.
3. Dry season each lamb shank by rubbing in spice mixture.
4. Heat Smoker to 225 degrees Fahrenheit.
5. Smoke until internal temperature of lamb shanks are 165 degrees.
6. Rest for 10 minutes and enjoy!

Grilled Pineapple

Cooking Time: 4 Min

Ingredients:
- 1 Fresh Pineapple, cored and sliced
- 3 Tbsp of Melted Butter
- 1/2 Tsp of Hot Sauce
- Kosher salt to taste
- 1 Tsp of Honey

Directions:
1. In a large bowl or bag, combine pineapple slices with honey, butter, hot sauce and salt. Allow to marinate for an hour through overnight. Heat grill to high, direct heat. Grill pineapple slices for 3-4 minutes per side, allowing grill marks to form. Serve with the desired dish. Enjoy!

Fire Roasted Salsa And Homemade Tortilla Chips

Cooking Time: 60 Min

Ingredients:
- 8 tomatillos/1 pound: Remove Flaky Shell
- 3 Garlic Cloves: 2 Smoked
- 2 Jalapenos
- 2 Serrano Peppers
- 1 Lime
- 1 Tbsp Salt
- 1/2 White Onion (Yellow if you want sweet)
- Olive Oil
- One Pack Tortillas, Sliced into Quarters

Directions:
1. Preheat grill/ smoker to 400°.
2. Place the tomatillos (sprinkle with a little salt), jalapeños, serrano pepper, garlic cloves, onion and lime in the grill/smoker.
3. Tip: offset the veggies & lime. You don't want the tomatillos to burst.
4. Smoke for 35 minutes or the veggies are tender. The tomatillos will turn a light brown color.
5. Remove the veggies & lime from the grill.
6. Creating Salsa
7. Time: 15 minutes
8. Using the molcajete (or mortar and pestle), first mix 1 tbsp salt and one raw garlic and mix. Then add grilled/smoked garlic to the mixture with the jalapeño & serrano peppers(remember to remove the stems). Mix in the molcajete until it turn into a chunky paste.
9. This will be a three step process.
10. Step 1: Using a food processor, drizzle olive oil, add onion, add some ingredients from the molcajete, some of the tomatillos(remember to remove the stems), half lime juice. Mix until it's turn into a purée and set aside.
11. Step 2: Using the food processor add the remaining tomatillos (remember to remove the stems), remaining

ingredients in the molcajete, cilantro and squeeze half lime juice. Mix until chunky.

12. Step 3: Combine both mixtures from step 1 & 2 together and stir throughly. Your salsa is all done.
13. Fresh Tortilla Chips
14. Total Time: 15 minutes per pack
15. Frying instructions
16. minute per side: 2 minutes total
17. Add generous amount of olive oil to the cast iron skillet.
18. Turn the side burner heat on high and allow a few minutes to warm.
19. Add tortillas to the hot olive oil in the cast iron skillet and flip after one minute or until golden brow. Allow to cook for an additional minute then remove and sprinkle with salt to taste. Repeat the this process a few times until done.
20. Dip in the the salsa and enjoy.

Cheeseburger Chili With Burger Bun Croutons

Cooking Time: 1.5 Hrs

Ingredients:
- Finely Diced Char Grilled Burgers - 4
- Diced White Onion - 1/2 an Onion
- Diced Tomato - 1/2 a Tomato
- Chili Powder - 1/3 Cup
- Ground Cumin - 2 Tablespoons
- Garlic Powder - 2 Tablespoons
- Tomato Puree - 16 Ounces
- Chili Beans - 16 Ounces
- Water - 1 Cup
- Salt - 1 Tablespoon
- Shredded Cheddar - 1/2 Cup
- Melted Butter - 2 Tablespoons

Directions:
1. What to do? The least favorite option in Personal Chef and Char-Griller Ambassador Aubrey Johansen's mind is to reheat a burger in the microwave- too many opportunities to end up with a dry hockey puck.
2. Let's repurpose these goods. Leftover cheeseburgers from the grill make an incredibly flavorful meat base for chili. Let's dice up those buns and toss them with some cheese for a delicious crouton topping. You can make both of these recipes directly on the grill in a cast iron skillet, or on the stove, baked in the oven. Up to you! Let's dig in!
3. 1. In a large cast iron skillet, combine oil, onion, and dry spices, and toast for 3-4 minutes over a grill flame, or medium heat on the stove top.
4. After the onions and spices become toasted, add the remainder of the ingredients, and simmer on low for 30-60 minutes, stirring occasionally.
5. While the chili simmers, combine the diced buns with melted butter and garlic salt. Sprinkle with grated cheese and bake at 350 for 10-12 minutes, until golden brown and toasted.
6. Serve your chili with additional shredded cheese, diced onion, croutons, and cilantro. Enjoy!

Flat Iron French Toast

Cooking Time: 7 To 9 Min

Ingredients:
- 8 Slices Low-Carb Brioche Bread
- 6 Eggs
- 2 Tbsp Heavy Whipping Cream
- 1 tsp Cinnamon
- 1 tsp Sweetener

Directions:
1. Preheat Flat Iron to medium high.
2. Combine eggs, whipping cream, cinnamon, and sweetener (Shenna uses Monkfruit) and whisk thoroughly.
3. Dip bread slices into mixture and ensure they are fully coated.
4. Places slices on griddle and flip after about 3 to 4 minutes.
5. Flip and add butter on top while the other side cooks.
6. Remove from griddle and serve with fruit, syrup, whipped cream and more!

Flavor Pro Hot And Fast Ribs

Cooking Time: 3 To 4 Hrs

Ingredients:
- 2 Racks of Ribs
- Char-Griller Rib Rub
- 1 Cup Apple Juice
- 1/4 Cup Brown Sugar
- 8 Tbsp Butter
- BBQ Sauce of Choice
- Wood Chips of Choice

Directions:
1. Remove membrane from ribs and season liberally on both sides with Char-Griller Rib Rub.
2. Set up the Flavor Pro for Indirect cooking
3. Add 15 to 20 charcoal briquettes to one side of the flavor drawer
4. Ignite charcoal with gas burners set to medium high
5. Once charcoal is lit, turn off gas burners and allow to fully ash over.
6. Add a handful of soaked wood chips to charcoal.
7. Using a grilling glove, adjust smokestacks until grill is 300 degrees.
8. Place ribs bone side down on the opposite side of the grill as the charcoal and wood and allow to cook for 2 and a half hours at 300 degrees.
9. Remove ribs from grill and place bone side up on a large sheet of tin foil. Fold up the foil to create a well and add ½ apple juice to the ribs.
10. Add 1/8 cup of brown sugar and 4 tablespoons of butter to the top of the ribs.
11. Close foil tightly around ribs and place back on the 300 degree grill for 1 hour and 15 minutes.
12. Add more charcoal if needed.
13. Remove ribs from foil and place back on grill. Brush with your favorite BBQ sauce and cook for an additional 15 minutes.

Beer Brats With Marzen Beer Kraut

Cooking Time: 25 Min

Ingredients:
- 1 Package of Beer Brats
- Sauerkraut - 2 Lbs Bag
- 1/2 Yellow Onion, Minced
- 1 Clove Garlic, Minced
- Butter - 2 Tbsp
- 1/2 tsp Coarse Ground Black Pepper
- ½ cup Marzen-Style Oktoberfest beer
- 6 oz water
- Stone Ground Brown Mustard

Directions:
1. Prepare grill for medium-low heat around 300-350°F
2. In a medium sized saucepan, melt butter
3. Add onion and garlic, cook 3-4 minutes until softened
4. Add beer and cook for 2 minute
5. Add sauerkraut, water, and pepper
6. Cook until warm and simmering
7. Prepare grill for medium-low heat around 300-350° F
8. Place bratwursts in grill over direct heat source
9. Cook low and slow, be sure to turn frequently for even cooking
10. Try not to overcook or use high heat. Pull when outside is browned/caramelized and internal temperature is between 160-165° F
11. Butter inside of sausage rolls and toast over heat source until desired texture is achieved
12. Serve bratwurst on roll topped with sauerkraut and stone ground mustard

Brazilian Smoked N' Seared Picanha

Ingredients:
- Picanha (3-4 Pounds)
- 1 Whole Pineapple (Cut Into Squares Only Half Is Needed.)
- Brazilian Salt To Taste For The Picanha
- Habanero Sea Salt To Taste For The Pineapples
- Trompo King Meat Stacker Or Skewers
- Fogo Eucalyptus Lump Charcoal
- Char-Griller Grills Ceramic Akorn
- Char-Griller Grills Smokin' & Pizza Stones
- Char-Griller Grill Gloves

Directions:

1. Prepping Directions
2. Cut Pineapples into small squares. Only ½ of the pineapple will be needed. Rinse the Picanha using cold water and pat dry with a paper towel. Remove any loose fat from the top and bottom of the meat but don't remove off to much fat. The fat on Picanha tastes great and provides tremendous flavor to the meat during the cooking process. Slice the Picanha into two inch thick strips. Use Slice the meat diagonally going with grain. When the meat is sliced when it's done is when you slice against the grain. Apply even layer to taste of Brazilian Salt to all sides of the Picanha. Season all sides of the pineapples squares with Habanero Sea Salt to taste Using a Trompo King or Skewers, stack the Picanha curving the meat into a C shaped form and also stack the pineapples.
3. Smoking/Searing Directions
4. Ignite lump charcoal and preheat grill to 300°. Add the Char-Griller Grills Smokin' Stone & Pizza Stone for the smoking portion of the cook. Add the Trompo King or Skewers with the Picanha to the grill/smoker. Smoke the Picanha until internal temperature 125° is met, takes about 40 minutes. Remove the Trompo King or Skewers with the Picanha from the grill/smoker and set aside. Remove the Char-Griller Grills Smokin' Stone & Pizza Stone using a Char-Griller Grills Grill Glove and place under the grill/smoker. Time to sear the Picanha to internal temperature: 135° Add a bit more lump charcoal to the grill/smoker, insert the grill grates, open up the top and bottom vents to allow the grill/smoker to get hot: 420° and over. Place the Picanha onto to the grill/smoker grates for two minutes each side or until internal temperature 135° is reached. Remove the Picanha from the grill/smoker, add additional Brazilian salt to taste. Allow the meat to rest for 10-25 minutes before slicing. Slice the Picanha against the grain and enjoy

Grilled Potatoes With Jalapeños

Cooking Time: 15 Min

Ingredients:
- 2-3 large Russet potatoes
- Original All-Purpose BBQ Rub
- Jalapeño olive oil, or preferred
- 1-2 jalapeño peppers, sliced
- Salt and pepper, to taste

Directions:
1. Rinse and scrub the potatoes and dry with paper towel. Cut potatoes into wedges, place in a Dutch oven on the stove and cover with water. Add salt if needed. Bring water to a rolling boil for 3 minutes.
2. Remove potatoes and rinse with cold water to stop the cooking process. Place potatoes in a gallon size storage bag with olive oil, sliced jalapeños, Original All-Purpose BBQ rub, or your favorite rub, and salt and pepper, to taste. Close bag and gently shake to evenly coat potato wedges with seasoning.
3. Place potato wedges on the grill at 350°F for 8-10 minutes, to desired crispness.
4. Recipes developed in partnership with our friends, Ken & Patti Fisher at Date Night Doin's. Visit their website at www.datenightdoins.com for BBQ and smoking recipes, videos, product reviews, and all things BBQ!

Smoked Bacon-brisket Bbq Beans

Cooking Time: 4 Hrs

Ingredients:
- Brown Sugar Baked Beans- 85 Ounces
- White Beans- 15 Ounces
- Pinto Beans- 15 Ounces
- Kidney Beans- 15 Ounces
- Canned Diced Tomatoes- 28 Ounces
- Cooked Brisket- 2 Hefty Handfuls
- Large Sweet Onion- 1
- Minced Garlic- 1 Clove
- Vegetable Oil- 1 Tablespoon
- Beer- 1/2 Cup
- Garlic Powder- 1 Tablespoon
- Brown or Stone Ground Mustard- 2 Tablespoons
- White Vinegar- 1/4 Cup
- Louisiana Hot Sauce- 2 Tablespoons
- Bacon- 1 Pound

Directions:

1. Start by preparing your AKORN or favorite Char-Griller smoker for indirect heat at 275°f. I prefer using applewood for this recipe but use your favorite wood. I've done these beans with mesquite, cherry, and also hickory and they have always turned out great.
2. Set burner to med-high heat and pour vegetable oil into skillet. Saute chopped onion and minced garlic to slightly soften and brown. Set aside.
3. Slice uncooked bacon into 2" bite sized squares (Pull out entire pound of bacon slices and cut all at once) Set aside.
4. Pour assorted beans into large mixing bowl. Add your diced tomatoes. Combine remaining ingredients (minus the bacon) into the bowl and stir until all ingredients are evenly mixed with beans.
5. Pour contents into large baking pan. Lay bacon over top of beans piece by piece, rooftop style. Once the beans are covered, if you end up with extra bacon pieces, build a second layer around the outside and work your way inward toward the middle.
6. I like to sprinkle a little extra Char-Griller Rib Rub or Pepper on the rooftop bacon but this is optional.
7. Once smoker is running steady around 275°f place beans inside and let the magic happen!
8. Check every hour. Cook Time for these beans averages about 3 ½ hours- 4 hours. You are looking for the top to have a dark rich mahogany color, a caramelized look, and rooftop bacon should be fairly firm.
9. Let beans rest 10-15 min to slightly cool before eating!

Grilled Flank Steak With Vegetables

Cooking Time: 20 Min

Ingredients:
- 1.5 Pound Flank Steak
- Smoked Paprika - 1.5 tsp
- 2 Garlic Cloves, Minced
- Salt and Pepper to Taste
- 4 Ears of Corn
- Two Large Zucchini, Cut in Half Lengthwise
- 1 Pint Cherry Tomatoes
- Olive Oil - 3 Tbs
- 1.5 Tbs Fresh Rosemary, Chopped
- Red Wine Vinegar - 1 Tbs
- 2 Garlic Cloves, Minced (Oil Dressing)
- Canola Oil - 2 Tbs

Directions:
1. Season flank steak with paprika and garlic. Rub on all sides and season with salt and pepper. Brush with canola oil.
2. Brush corn, zucchini, and tomatoes with canola oil and season with salt and pepper.
3. Preheat grill to medium high heat.
4. Add flank steak to grill, flip once and cook to desired doneness. About 4 to 6 minutes per side, let rest 5 minutes.
5. Add vegetables to grill and turn occasionally until lightly charred all over.
6. Whisk olive oil, rosemary, red wine vinegar, garlic and salt and pepper to taste in a small bowl.
7. Brush steak and drizzle vegetables with olive oil mixture and serve with steak immediately.

Flavor Pro™ Smoked French Onion Dip

Cooking Time: 2 (plus Overnight In The Fridge) Hrs

Ingredients:
- 2 Tbsp Salted Butter
- 2 Yellow Onions, Sliced into 1/4 inch Rings
- 3 Cloves of Garlic, Minced
- 2 Cups Sour Cream
- 1 Cup Mayonnaise
- 1 tsp Fresh Thyme
- 1 tsp Worcestershire Sauce
- 1 tsp Kosher Salt
- 1 tsp Freshly Ground Black Pepper
- Chives, Chopped for Garnish
- Kettle Chips for Serving

Directions:
1. Prepare Flavor Pro™ for 225°F. Add coals and smoking wood to the far left slot in the Flavor Drawer. Close the left smoke stack and leave the right stack fully open. Light coals using the two gas burners on the left.
2. Add onions to foil pan and place foil pan on the right side of the grill (opposite the heat source)

3. Smoke onions for 90 minutes adding coals and wood as needed to control temperature and smoke flow.
4. Heat the butter in a cast iron skillet over medium-high heat using two of the Flavor Pro™ gas burners.
5. Add the smoked onion rings to the skillet and saute for 20-25 minutes or until dark brown and caramelized. Add garlic and thyme leaves and saute for another 2 minutes then remove from heat.
6. Let cool then finely chop onion mixture to your desired consistency for the dip.
7. In a bowl, mix sour cream, mayo, Worcestershire sauce, salt, and pepper. Fold in the onion mixture.
8. Refrigerate overnight to allow flavors to intensify.
9. Garnish with chives and serve with kettle chips. Enjoy!

Bbq Glazed Bacon Wrapped Brussels Sprouts

Cooking Time: 30 Min

Ingredients:
- 1 lb. medium Brussels sprouts, stems removed
- 10-12 slices bacon, halved
- 1/3 C. BBQ sauce
- Salt and pepper, to taste

Directions:
1. Pre-heat grill to 400°F. Rinse Brussels sprouts, and pat dry with a paper towel, removing any loose outer leaves if needed. 2. Cut each bacon strip in half. Wrap 1 bacon strip snuggly around each sprout ensuring the ends overlap by ½″. 3. Lay the bacon wrapped sprout seam side down in a baking pan. 4. Place the pan on the grill and roast for 15 minutes at 400°F. 5. Remove the pan from the grill and brush each sprout with a layer of BBQ sauce. 6. Place the pan back on the grill and roast for another 15 minutes or until the bacon is crispy and the sprouts pierce easily with a knife.
2. Place a toothpick in the center of each sprout for easier handling before serving.

Loaded Grilled Radish Bites

Cooking Time: 25 Min

Ingredients:
- 6 Large Radishes, Washed and Halved
- 2 Tbsp Butter
- 1 Tbsp Herb & Sea Salt Blend
- 1/4 Cup Shredded Cheddar Cheese
- 1/4 Cup Sour Cream
- 2 Slices Bacon, Crumbled
- 1 Tbsp Finely Chopped Fresh Chives

Directions:
1. Melt butter and combine with herbed sea salt. Pour over radishes in a bowl and toss to coat.
2. Lay the radish halves over a wire rack and grill at 425 for 20 to 25 minutes, or until tender.
3. Top with cheese, dollops of sour cream, crumbled bacon, and chives.

Buffalo Baby Back Ribs: Grilled N' Smoked

Cooking Time: 3 Hrs

Ingredients:
- Full Slabs of Baby Back Ribs.
- Sharp Knife
- Olive Oil
- Goya Sazón
- Loot n' Booty Everything Rub
- Frank's Red Hot Buffalo Wing Sauce
- Spritzer Water Mixed with Goya Sazón Seasoning
- Ranch Sauce

Directions:
1. Trimming
2. Using a sharp knife slice and remove any meat loose on the ends of the ribs. Also remove any excess fat from the top/meat side of the ribs.
3. Tip: If you can pull any fat, you should trim it.
4. Flip the ribs over so the bones are facing up. Remove the membrane and discard. Remove any excess fat.
5. Seasoning
6. Begin by leaving the ribs bone side up. Apply coating of olive oil for the binder.
7. Tip: don't apply olive oil or rubs on the sides of the ribs. This helps the

8. Flip ribs to the top/meat side of the ribs. Apply coating of olive oil for the binder.
9. Tip: seasoning the bottom of the ribs first will help prevent the top/meat side seasonings from being messy.
10. Using Gaoya Sazón & Loot N' Booty Everything Rub, apply even coating of the rubs on the ribs.
11. Ribs are ready to be grilled.
12. Grilling & Smoking
13. Using the Char-griller Grills Flavor Pro, fire it using Fogo Charcoal Premium Lump Charcoal Blends to high heat.
14. Grill the ribs for 2-4 minutes total on the meat side down on the grill grates then reverse sear them for an additional 2-4 minutes.
15. Flip the ribs so the meat side is facing up and grill for an additional 1-2 minutes.
16. Remove ribs from the direct heat from the lump charcoal and offset them opposite side of the lump charcoal.
17. Close the top smoke stacks to a lower setting. This will allow you to quickly lower your fire to grill for smoking temperature . Lock in the temperature when it hits temperature 325°-350° by adjusting the smoke stacks.
18. Add favorite smoking wood: used hickory wood log for the cook.
19. Spritz with water & Goya Seasoning every 30 minutes and rotate ribs.
20. , After smoking for 2 hours 40 mins, warm and apply Frank's Red Hot Buffalo
21. Remove Ribs and drizzle ranch atop the ribs.
22. Allow ribs to rest for 15 minutes.
23. Slice and enjoy with carrots and celery.

Skillet Corn Bread

Cooking Time: 25 Min

Ingredients:
- 1¼ C. coarsely ground yellow cornmeal
- ¾ C. all-purpose flour
- ¼ C. granulated sugar
- 1 stick unsalted butter, melted (reserve 1 Tbsp.)
- 2 Tsp. baking powder
- ½ Tsp. baking soda
- 1/3 C. whole milk
- 1 C. buttermilk
- 2 eggs, lightly beaten
- 1 Tsp. salt

Directions:
1. Pre-heat grill to 375° F and place a cast iron skillet inside to heat while making the batter. 2. In a large bowl, whisk together the cornmeal, flour, sugar, salt, baking powder, and baking soda. Add in the milk, buttermilk, 7 Tbsp. melted butter and eggs. 3. Carefully remove the hot skillet from the grill. Coat the bottom and sides of the hot skillet with remaining butter. 4. Pour the batter into the skillet and bake for 20-25 minutes, or until a toothpick inserted into the center comes out clean.
2. Allow to cool for 10 to 15 minutes and serve. Top with honey or melted butter, if desired.

Grilled Chicken Sandwiches

Cooking Time: 15 Min

Ingredients:
- 4 Boneless Skinless Chicken Breasts
- Choose a chicken Marinade here
- 4 Buns of your choice
- Optional Toppings: Condiments, Cole Slaw, Lettuce, Pickles, Bacon, etc.

Directions:
1. In a bowl, whisk together the ingredients to your marinade. Add the chicken breasts, combining thoroughly until all pieces are coated. Let marinate in the fridge for 30 minutes through overnight. Prepare your grill for direct heat and preheat to medium-high heat, adding chicken to the grill and brushing on any remaining marinade. Grill the chicken for 5-6 minutes per side or until internal temperature reaches 165°F. Serve grilled chicken breasts on buns with desired toppings. Enjoy!

Jalapeño Bacon Blanket Poppers

Cooking Time: 30 Min

Ingredients:
- 4 Jalapenos
- Char-Griller Steak Rub to Taste
- 1/3 Cup Cream Cheese
- 3 Slices of Bacon
- Shredded Cheese to Taste

Directions:
1. They came out perfect and he can't wait to make them again. It was quick, easy and delicious. He used the AKORN Jr to make these as it is the perfect size grill/smoker for these type of appetizer cooks and the grill will burn all day making it easy to make more during the game if you run out!
2. Mix cream cheese, shredded cheese, Char-Griller Steak Rub in a bowl and set aside.
3. Slice jalapeños through the middle to make it boat shaped.
4. Using a spoon remove the pith and seeds to create room for the filling.
5. Tip: If you like heat then leave some seeds behind. Seeds provide the heat.
6. Fill jalapenos with filling.
7. Slice bacon into small strips then lay it over the filling on the jalapenos.
8. Sprinkle a small portion of the Char-Griller Steak Rub on top of the bacon.
9. Fire up your Char-Griller Grill to 400°.
10. James used his AKORN Jr & Smokin' Stone with Fogo Charcoal Premium Lump Charcoal and FOGO Starters to ignite it.
11. Place Jalapeño Bacon Blanket Poppers in the grill/smoker and smoke for 30 minutes or when the bacon is golden brown.
12. Remove and enjoy!

Pretzel Ring Cheese Dip Recipe

Cooking Time: 45 Min

Ingredients:
- 2.5 Cups Shredded Cheddar
- 1 Cup Shredded Monetary Jack
- 1 Cup Shredded Pepper Jack
- 1 (8oz) Block Cream Cheese
- 1.5 Tbsp Dijon Mustard
- 2 Tbsp Fresh Chives, Chopped
- 2 Tsp Garlic Powder
- 2 tsp Paprika
- 1 Tbsp Flour
- 3 Tbsp Butter, Melted
- Salt and Pepper to Taste
- 2 (16.3 oz) Cans Refrigerated Biscuits
- 3 Tbsp Baking Soda
- 1 Large Egg Mixed with 1 Tbsp Water
- Coarse Salt

Directions:
1. Preheat Grill to 350 degrees.
2. Melt butter and whisk in one Tbsp flour.
3. In a large bowl, mix together 2.25 Cups of cheddar cheese, Monterey jack, Pepper Jack, Cream Cheese, Dijon, Chives, Garlic Powder, flour and butter mixture, paprika, salt and pepper.
4. Roll biscuits into a ball, slice the top with an X.
5. Using the side burner, bring 8 cups of water and baking soda to a boil. Whisk to fully dissolve baking soda. Reduce water to simmer.
6. Add biscuits in batches and cook until puffy (about 1 minute). Remove from water with slotted spoon and transfer to skillet to form a ring around outside of pan.
7. Brush biscuits with egg wash and sprinkle with kosher salt.
8. Transfer mixed dip to center of skillet and sprinkle with remaining ¼ cup of cheddar cheese.
9. Bake until biscuits are golden and dip is bubbly (about 33 to 35 minutes).
10. Garnish with chives before serving.

Grilled Breakfast Sandwiches With Blueberry Chicken Sausage

Cooking Time: 20 Min

Ingredients:
- Ground Chicken - 1 Lb
- Fresh Blueberries - 1/3 Cup
- Fresh Sage - 1 Tbsp, finely chopped

- Pure Maple Syrup - 2 Tbsp
- Butter - 1 Tbsp
- 6 Whole Wheat English Muffins
- 6 Eggs
- Shredded Cheddar Cheese - 1/2 Cup

Directions:
1. While the grill heats, combine ground chicken, fresh blueberries, sage, and half of the maple syrup. Form into 6 even patties and set aside. Mix remaining maple syrup with butter for maple butter.
2. Next, cut English muffins in half, and transfer eggs to a grill safe cooking pan. Top with salt, pepper, and cheese.
3. Once grill is hot, add sausage, English muffins, and eggs. Keep an eye on the English muffins- they only need about 1-2 minutes, just until they're toasted.
4. The sausage patties need 4 minutes per side, and the eggs will be done around the same time if you close the lid to help them steam.
5. Assemble the sandwiches- apply a layer of maple butter, and egg, and a sausage patty to each English muffin! Serve as is, or wrap in plastic wrap for breakfast prep during the week. You can microwave them for 60 seconds and you have a hot breakfast ready to grab as you head out the door! Enjoy!

Flat Iron™ Smash Burgers

Cooking Time: 10 Min

Ingredients:
- 1 1/2 Lbs Ground Beef
- 8 Slices Of Cheese
- 4 Burger Buns
- Salt & Pepper
- Lettuce
- Tomato
- Onion
- Pickle
- 1/2 Cup Mayo
- 1/4 Cup Dijon
- 1 Tbsp Honey
- 2 Tbsp Sweet Pickles (Diced Finely)
- 1 Tsp Garlic Salt

Directions:
1. Wash your hands!
2. Form ground meat into one ball, then with your hand, mark it in half, then in quarters, and then in 8ths. Think pie slices with your hand- this will let you divide the meat into 8 even portions. Roll each into a ball, and set aside.
3. Preheat your Flat Iron Gas Griddle to medium high heat on the three burners closest to the right. The very first burner, heat to low- this is the section you'll use to toast your buns.
4. Season Flat Iron Griddle, and evenly lay beef portions on the griddle, you'll know it's the perfect temperature when you hear a sizzle when the meat touches the heat.
5. Let beef sit for 2-3 minutes. Next, take a spatula and something with a flat base- like a jar, and lay the spatula onto of the meat, and press down with the jar, until the burger patties are smashed flat onto the griddle. NOW is when you season the top side with salt and pepper.
6. Once the edges are crispy and golden brown, flip the burgers, add a slice of cheese, and kill the heat. Let them cook for 2 more minutes on the other side. While they finish cooking, lay burger buns on the first section of the griddle to toast.
7. Combine sauce ingredients, mayo, Dijon, honey, sweet pickles, garlic salt in a bowl and stir.
8. Stack burger buns with two smashed patties, special sauce, and your choice of toppings. Enjoy & dig in, keep the napkins close, because these burgers are juicy and messy! My favorite!

Keto Cheesy Meatballs

Cooking Time: 45 Min

Ingredients:
- 1 Lb Sausage
- 1 Lb Ground Beef
- 1 Cup Bacon's Heir Pork Panko (Bread Crumb Alternative)
- 3-4 Tbsp All Purpose Rub (Garlic or your preferred choice)

- Pepper Jack Cheese Cubes (Or Your Preferred Choice)

Directions:
1. Preheat grill to 325F for indirect cooking.
2. Combine Sausage, Beef, Pork Panko, Rub and mix well.
3. Form 2" balls and press cheese cube into meatball and form around the cheese cube.
4. Place on grill indirect until an internal temp of 170F
5. Serve and enjoy!

Flat Iron Pineapple Coconut Pancakes

Cooking Time: 15 Min

Ingredients:
- 1 1/2 Cup of All-Purpose Flour
- 2 Tsp of Baking Powder
- 1 Tsp of Baking Soda
- 1/4 Cup of Sugar
- 1/2 Tsp of Salt
- 2 Large Eggs
- 1/4 Cup of Butter (Melted)
- 1 Tsp of Butter or Cooking Spray for Griddle
- 1 Cup of Crushed Pineapple
- 1 Cup of Shredded Coconut (Ground Finely)
- 1/4 Cup of Coconut Milk

Directions:
1. In a large mixing bowl, prepare the batter by stirring together baking powder, baking soda, sugar, salt, eggs, butter, crushed pineapple, coconut, and coconut milk. Slowly add flour until you achieve a nice batter, not too runny and not too thick. Mix until it is smooth with no lumps.
2. Heat the Flat Iron over Medium-High Heat and spray with cooking spray or melt butter. Pour pancake batter onto griddle with amount depending on desired size of pancakes.
3. When lots of bubbles form on top, flip over and cook the other side until lightly browned.
4. Serve warm and drizzle with honey or maple syrup.

Cheesy Stuffed Mushrooms N' Veggies Recipe

Cooking Time: 25 Min

Ingredients:
- 14 Mushrooms
- Feta Cheese
- Chihuahua Cheese
- Olive Oil
- Dry Parsley Flakes
- 1/2 Red Pepper
- 1/2 Yellow Pepper
- 1/2 Onion
- Char-Griller Grills Wok
- Ceramic Akorn Kamado Charcoal Grill and Smokin' Stone.
- Fogo Premium Lump Charcoal

Directions:
1. Remove Mushroom Stems Lightly coat each mushroom with olive oil. Mix the Feta and Chihuahua cheeses and stuff the middle of the mushrooms. Sprinkle dry parsley to taste on top. Largely dice the onion, red & yellow peppers. Add the onions, red & yellow peppers to the bottom of the Wok. Then add the stuffed mushrooms on top of the onions, red & yellow peppers. Ignite charcoal and preheat grill/smoker to 240° with the Smokin' Stone inserted. Place the Wok with the cheesy stuffed mushrooms n' veggies in the grill/smoker and smoke for 25 minutes. Rotate the Wok in the smoker/grill one time after 15 minutes. Remove from the smoker/grill and enjoy. No need to rest these! Right off the grill eating.

Oktoberfest Chili

Ingredients:
- 2 1/2 Pounds Fresh Bratwurst Links, Cut Into 1-inch Slices
- 1 Large Onion, Diced
- 1 Green Bell Pepper, Diced
- 3 Jalapeno Peppers, Diced
- 4 Cloves of Garlic, Minced
- 2 Cups Sauerkraut, Drained

- 2 (15 oz) Cans of Red Beans, Drained and Rinsed
- 2 (15 oz) Cans Petite Diced Tomatoes
- 1 (28 oz) Can Crushed Tomatoes
- 2 (15 oz) Cans Tomato Sauce
- 2 (12 oz) Cans Tomato Juice
- 1 (12 oz) Bottle of German Beer
- 1 Tbsp of Salt and Pepper
- 1 Tbsp Cumin
- 1/4 Cup Chili Powder
- 3 Tbsp White Sugar
- 2 tsp Garlic Powder
- 2 tsp Paprika
- 1 tsp Oregano

Directions:

1. Place the bratwurst into a large skillet with 1 tablespoon of bacon drippings over medium heat; cook and stir the bratwurst until the pieces are browned and no longer pink inside, about 15 minutes. Drain excess grease.
2. Place remaining 1 tablespoon of bacon drippings in a large, deep pot over medium heat, and cook and stir the onion, green and jalapeno peppers, and garlic until the onion is translucent, about 8 minutes.
3. Place the bratwurst into the pot with the vegetables, and stir in the sauerkraut, red beans, petite diced tomatoes, crushed tomatoes, tomato sauce, tomato juice, beer, salt, black pepper, cumin, chili powder, sugar, garlic powder, paprika, allspice, and oregano.
4. Bring the chili to a boil by getting your grill up to 275 degrees.
5. Place the pot on the grill and let it simmer for 5 hours, stirring occasionally.
6. Use a mixture of cherry and hickory chunks to get a good smoke profile for your chili.

Mrs. Ccbbq Mac N' Cheese

Cooking Time: 1.5 Hrs

Ingredients:

- 16 oz Elbow Macaroni
- 16 oz Cheddar Jack
- 16 oz Extra Sharp Cheddar
- 1/2 tsp Salt
- 1/2 tsp Black Pepper
- 1/4 tsp Ground Cayenne Pepper
- 1/2 tsp Cajun/Creole Seasoning
- 1 tsp Paprika
- 1 tsp Ground Mustard
- 2.5 Cups Milk
- 8 Fl. Oz. Heavy Whipping Cream
- 1 Egg
- 1/2 Stick Butter
- 1/4 Cup All Purpose Flour
- 8 Double Slices of Bacon

Directions:

1. Char-Griller Ambassador James Llorens of @certified.creole.bbq doesn't do all the grilling at home. His wife isn't shy about firing up the smoker and experimenting with new recipes like this delicious Mac n' Cheese recipe that is perfect for feeding a crowd.
2. Heat smoker/grill to 350°
3. Tip: For a lingering and not overwhelming smoke, add the pecan chunk on top the grill grate over the fire/charcoal.
4. Add the 8 double bacon slices to a baking sheet. Lightly season one side of the bacon with Cajun/Creole seasoning. Only one side so its not to salty.
5. Tip: Using a baking sheet allows for easy handling and less grill grate mess.
6. Place bacon in the smoker/grill: offset it opposite side of the fire/charcoal & wood chunk. Rotate once to allow for even cooking.
7. Remove when golden brown or after 25 minutes.
8. Chop up into small bits and set aside.
9. Boil water, add pasta & cook until al dente. Set aside.
10. To make the Roux: turn heat on side burner to medium and melt the butter.
11. Add small amounts of flour while whisking. Continue to whisk for 3-5 minutes until a darker color.
12. In this order, add milk, add heavy whipping cream, add milk, add ground mustard and continue to stir for 5 minutes or until thick.
13. Turn heat to medium-low.
14. Remove ¼ cup of roux. Using a separate bowl add the roux to the battered egg and whisk vigorously for 30 seconds then add and whisk it back into to the roux.

15. Add cheeses to the roux and melt down until it turns into a liquid. Leave a small amount on the side to top prior to baking.
16. Add Salt: ½ tsp, Black Pepper: ½ tsp, Ground Cayenne Pepper: ¼ tsp, Cajun/Creole Seasoning: ½ tbs, Paprika: 1 tsp to the liquid cheese and stir into the cheese.
17. Add pasta to the cheese and mix thoroughly.
18. Butter coat a high temperature dish and add the mac n' cheese. Top with cheese and pecan smoked bacon. Cover with a lid.
19. Heat gas grill to 350° and bake for 40 minutes.
20. Remove and enjoy.

Smoked Chicken Thighs And Veggies

Cooking Time: 30 Min

Ingredients:
- 4 Chicken Thighs (Skinless)
- 1 Crown Broccoli (Chopped)
- 1 Crown Cauliflower (Chopped)
- Smoked Cherrywood Sea Salt (To Taste)
- Rosy Cheeks Maple Bourbon Rub (To Taste)
- Bold Bayou Cajun (To Taste)

Directions:
1. Remove the skin from the chicken thighs; I start with the loose skin by the knuckle, grab the skin from underneath and pull up.
2. Season both sides of the thighs with sea salt. We use the smoked cherrywood sea salt to begin our layers.
3. Season both sides of the thighs with Rosy Cheeks (we did one in Bold Bayou ~ it's a little more cajun style and spicy). This is called layering your seasonings.
4. As the chicken sweats, chop up your veggies. Add them to a bowl and toss with oil and salt.
5. Heat your grill up to 250° - 275° for a low and slow cook.
6. Add chicken and veggies to the grill; add your smoking chips.
7. After about 10 minutes flip the chicken and veggies; feel free to add more chips if need be.
8. After about another 10 minutes begin to probe your chicken. You're looking for clear juices and a temp of no less than 165°. When you reach that Internal Temp (IT) pull the chicken and let it rest. Pull the veggies when crisp

Chimichurri Sauce

Cooking Time: 5 Min

Ingredients:
- 1 bunch parsley
- 1/2 bunch cilantro
- 3 garlic cloves
- 1/2 Tsp. oregano
- 1/4 Tsp cumin
- Salt and pepper to taste
- 3 Tbsp. fresh lemon juice
- Olive oil

Directions:
1. Add ingredients to blender
2. While blending, add in olive oil slowly to thicken sauce
3. Once blended, remove and add to your favorite meat

Grilled Mexican Street Corn

Cooking Time: 15 Min

Ingredients:
- 4-6 Ears of Sweet Corn (Husks Removed)
- 1/2 Cup of Mayonnaise
- 3 Tbsp Cilantro (Chopped)
- 1 Clove of Garlic
- 1 Cup Cotija Cheese (Crumbled)
- 6 Lime Wedges
- 1/2 Tsp Cayenne Pepper
- 1 Tsp of Ancho Chili Powder
- Sea Salt and Black Pepper to taste

Directions:
1. Heat grill to medium-high heat. Be sure grates are oiled. In a bowl, combine mayonnaise, cilantro, garlic, salt, and pepper. Mix thoroughly. Place cotija cheese on a plate or shallow bowl that can fit the length of corn. Place corn on grill in a single layer until charred on all sides. Remove from the grill. Brush each cob with the mayonnaise mixture then roll in cotija cheese so it is sparsely coated as not to be too overwhelming. Transfer

each completed cob to a baking sheet or serving plate and continue until all cobs are coated. Sprinkle corn with chili powder and cayenne pepper as desired. Sprinkle cilantro over the finished product. Serve warm with lime wedges.

Flat Iron Bacon Egg & Cheese

Cooking Time: 12 Min

Ingredients:
- 3-4 Bacon Slices (Per Sandwich)
- 1-2 Slices Of Your Cheese Of Choice Per Sandwich
- 1 Egg Per Sandwich
- 2 Slices Of Sourdough Or Bread Of Choice Per Sandwich
- 1/2 Stick Of Butter

Directions:
1. Set a heat zone on the Flat Iron to medium heat. Cook the bacon slices until crispy, 8-12 minutes. In a bowl, whisk together eggs with 2 Tbsp of water or 1 Tbsp sour cream. Remove the bacon from heat and drain with a paper towel. Heat another zone of the griddle to medium heat. Add about a tsp of butter and allow to melt. Once heated, add egg mixture. Once the egg begins to set, flip and/or stir until cooked. Add a Tbsp of butter to the same zone you cooked bacon on over medium-high heat. Assemble sandwiches with a bread slice, egg, bacon, cheese and another slice of bread on top. Add sandwiches to the heated zone with bacon grease and butter. Ensure both sides of the sandwich are toasted and the cheese is melted. Serve hot, enjoy.

Gravity 980 Smoked Mac & Cheese

Cooking Time: 1-2 Min

Ingredients:
- 6 Tbsp of Butter
- 3 Tbsp of Flour
- 3 Cups of Milk
- 6 Cups of Shredded Cheese of your choice
- Kosher Salt
- Black Pepper
- 2 Tsp of Paprika
- 4 Cups of Elbows, Macaroni, cooked
- 1 tsp of Cayenne Pepper

Directions:
1. Remove the fire shutter from your Gravity 980 before loading the hopper and lighting it. Set the temperature to 400°F. Place an aluminum or cast-iron pan on the grates. Melt your butter in the pan before whisking in flour and whisking until smooth. Add the milk and continue whisking until the mixture thickens. Add 4 cups of shredded cheese and continue stirring the mixture. Reduce the heat to 225-250°F and once the temperature begins to drop, stir in the macaroni and mix together with cheese mixture. Top with the remaining shredded cheese before closing the lid and smoking for 1-2 hours, depending on desired smokey flavor. Serve immediately. Enjoy!

Grilled Sausage

Cooking Time: 12 Min

Ingredients:
- 10-12 Fresh Sausage Links or Bratwursts
- Optional Servings components: Buns, Peppers, Onions, Dijon Mustard, Ketchup, Cheese, etc.

Directions:
1. Heat grill to medium-high heat. Cook them for 8-12 minutes turning occasionally to ensure they cook evenly and to prevent them from bursting. Allow the sausages to rest for 5-10 minutes. Serve in the desired manner. Enjoy!

Sweet And Tangy Apple Coleslaw

Cooking Time: 10 Min

Ingredients:
- 3 Cups Chopped Cabbage
- 1 Cup Grated Carrots
- 1/4 Cup Of Thinly Sliced Red Bell Peppers
- 1/4 Cup Of Thinly Sliced Green Bell Peppers
- 1 Cup Of Green Onions (Finely Chopped)
- 1/2 Cup Of Mayonnaise
- 1 Tbsp Fresh Lemon Juice
- 1/4 Cup Brown Sugar
- 1 Unpeeled Red Apple (Cored & Chopped)

Directions:

1. In a large bowl, combine cabbage, red and green apples, carrots, and green onions. In a small bowl, combine mayonnaise, lemon juice, and brown sugar. Pour the dressing over the salad. And mix thoroughly. For best results, chill for at least one hour before serving.

Pancake Burgers On The Char-griller Flat Iron

Cooking Time: 20 Min

Ingredients:
- 2 Lbs Ground Beef
- Instant Pancake Mix
- Pack of Bacon
- 2-4 Fresh Eggs
- Your Choice Of Cheese
- Salt & Pepper To Taste
- Optional: Maple Syrup

Directions:

1. Start with the bacon because it will take the longest crisp it up to your liking. Place off to side when done Roll up the ground beef in little balls and proceed to make smashburgers Once those are ready, place your cheese on top, then move to the side or take off the heat Give your batter another mix and make 4" circles enough for the burgers that you made Flip once they bubble up nicely While the pancakes are cooking, crack some eggs directly on the griddle Remove the pancakes and eggs from heat Build that monster sandwich! Top with maple syrup for an extra breakfast taste!

Grilled Lemon Parmesan Asparagus

Cooking Time: 10 Min

Ingredients:
- Asparagus - 2 lbs
- Lemons - 2
- Fresh Parmesan Cheese, Grated - 1/4 Cup
- Mixed Greens - 2 to 3 Cups

Directions:

1. Preheat grill on high for several minutes with lid closed. While it's heating, trim ends of asparagus.
2. Pro Tip// The goal with trimming asparagus is to remove the woody stem, but not waste any of the tender stalk.
3. To find out where the woody part ends, hold the asparagus and apply pressure at the edge, pulling up until 1-2 inches "snaps" off. Use that as a guide to trim the rest of the bunch.
4. Halve lemons. Once grill is hot, place lemon halves, cut side down on the grates.
5. Add asparagus to the grill, and turn every 2-3 minutes until asparagus is softened and charred to your liking.
6. Remove both asparagus and lemons from the grill.
7. Transfer to a serving plate, sprinkling with fresh parmesan, and squeeze the lemon juice, and season with salt and pepper.
8. Transform the leftovers into a quick salad- topping mixed greens with leftover grilled asparagus, cut into bite sized pieces, adding extra parmesan cheese, and more grilled lemon juice as a dressing. Enjoy!

Maple-dijon Grilled Chicken Sandwich

Cooking Time: 15 Min

Ingredients:
- 1 Lb chicken breast (Cut In Half Lengthwise and Then In Half Again)
- 1/2 Lb Sharp Cheddar Slices
- 1/2 Lb Sharp Cheddar Slices
- 1 Medium Apple (Sliced Thin)
- 1/4 Cup Red Onion (Sliced Thin)
- 1/4 Cup Fresh Cilantro (Leaves Only)
- 1/4 Cup Olive Oil
- 1/4 Cup Red Wine Vinegar
- 2 T Maple Syrup
- 1 T Dijon Mustard
- 1 Tsp Salt
- 1/2 Tsp Pepper
- 4 Burger Buns (Brioche or Any Choice)

Directions:

1. Preheat your Char-Griller to high heat. Scrape grates clean and spray with a high-heat non-stick spray.
2. Combine oil, vinegar, maple syrup, mustard, and salt in a jar, and shake till combined. Pour half of the dressing over the chicken and let it marinate while your grill heats up!
3. Next, add greens, cilantro, onion, and apple slices to a large bowl
4. Take marinated chicken to the grill. Grill on each side for 3 mins. Since the chicken is a thin cutlet, cook time is quicker! Once the chicken is cooked through on both sides, turn off the heat, and add slices of cheese to each piece. Close the grill and let cheese melt for 1-2 mins. Toast your buns at this time, too.
5. Pull chicken and buns from the grill, toss your salad with the remaining dressing, and pile your toasted buns with 2 pieces of the chicken, and a handful of salad. These sandwiches go perfectly with sweet potato fries for the Ultimate Fall dinner! Enjoy!

Grilled Red Onion And Brussel Sprouts Skewers

Cooking Time: 15 Min

Ingredients:
- 1 Lb of Brussel Sprouts
- 1 Large Red Onion
- 1/4 Cup of Extra Virgin Olive Oil
- 1/4 Cup of Balsamic Vinegar
- 1 Tbsp of Garlic (Minced)
- 1 Tsp of Paprika
- 1 Tsp of Garlic Powder
- 1 Tsp of Onion Powder
- 1 Tsp of Celery Salt
- Sea Salt and Pepper to Taste
- Pack of Skewers
- 1/4 Cup of Chopped Bacon (Optional)
- 1/4 Cup of Goat Cheese Crumbled (Optional)

Directions:
1. Preheat the grill to high setting or fire up coals. Cut brussel sprouts into halves and combine in a bowl with olive oil, minced garlic, and all seasonings. Cut onion into thick slices and mix in with brussel sprouts. Add brussel sprouts to skewers in a sequence of brussel sprout half, 2-3 onion slices, brussel sprout half, etc. Place skewers on the grill and turn often until sprouts and onions are fully cooked and tender. This will take between 10-15 minutes. Serve warm. Optionally, remove from skewers and combine in a bowl with bacon and crumbled goat cheese. Serve warm or refrigerate and serve cold.

Grilled Blue Cheese Wings

Ingredients:
- Fresh Chicken Wing Portions
- 1 Bottle Blue Cheese Dressing
- Salt & Pepper to taste
- 1 Cup Hot Sauce
- 2 Tbsp Butter

Directions:
1. Marinate the chicken wings overnight in the blue cheese dressing.
2. Grill until charred and crispy, and temperature reads at least 165 degrees Fahrenheit.
3. Season with salt and pepper to taste.
4. Melt the butter into the hot sauce, and serve along with the chicken as dip on the side.

Butternut Squash Soup

Cooking Time: 45-50 Min

Ingredients:
- 1 large butternut squash, halved and seeded
- ½ C. chopped shallot
- 1 Tsp. salt
- 4 garlic cloves, minced
- 1 Tsp. maple syrup
- ⅛ Tsp. ground nutmeg
- Freshly ground black pepper, to taste
- 3-4 C. vegetable broth
- 1-2 Tbsp. butter
- 1-2 Tbsp. heavy whipping cream
- Olive oil

Directions:
1. Pre-heat the grill to 425°F. Rub 1 Tsp. of olive oil over the inside of both halves of the squash and sprinkle

with salt and pepper. Wrap each half in foil, adding a ½ C. water to each. 2. Place on the grill and bake for 45-50 minutes, until squash is tender and completely cooked through. Remove from grill and allow to cool for 10 minutes. Unwrap, and use a large spoon to scoop the flesh into a bowl, discarding the skin. 3. In a large soup pot over medium heat, add olive oil and chopped shallot and sauté until the shallot has softened, 3-4 minutes. Add garlic and cook until fragrant, about 1 minute, stirring frequently. 4. Transfer the cooked shallot and garlic to a blender. Add the squash, maple syrup, nutmeg and freshly ground black pepper, to taste. Slowly add vegetable broth and blend until creamy. 5. Add 1- 2 Tbsp. heavy whipping cream to taste, and blend well. Taste and blend in more salt and pepper, if needed.

2. Serve immediately. Let leftover soup cool completely and refrigerate for up to 4 days or freeze for up to 3 months.

Flat Iron 3-step Breakfast Sandwiches

Cooking Time: 10 Min

Ingredients:
- 4 English Muffins
- 4 Eggs
- 4 Sausage Patties (optionally combine ground pork with herbs and spices of your choice and salt and pepper to prepare homemade patties)
- 4 Slices Of Cheese Or 1 Cup Of Shredded Cheese
- Any Condiments Of Your Choice

Directions:
1. Heat Flat Iron to medium-high heat. Cook sausages (or ham) for 2-3 minutes per side in one section and fry eggs in another section. Once you have space, toast each english muffin split in half and face down on the flat top. Assemble each sandwich with english muffin to start, spreading any condiments then stacking one sausage, one fried egg and cheese in between. Serve warm, enjoy.

Blueberry Bbq Sauce

Cooking Time: 20 Min

Ingredients:
- Olive Oil - 1 Tablespoon
- Diced Small Onion - 1/2
- Jalapeno, diced, (seeds and stems can be removed for milder sauce) - ½
- Cloves of Garlic - 2
- Fresh Blueberries - 1 Pound
- Ketchup - 1 Cup
- Bay Leaf- 1
- Pepper - 1/2 Teaspoon
- Kosher Salt - 1 Teaspoon
- Brown Sugar - 1/2 Cup
- Crushed Red Pepper - 1/2 Teaspoon
- Bourbon - 1/2 Cup
- Maple Syrup - 1/4 Cup

Directions:
1. Light charcoal and level out to one layer when ashed over
2. Place oil in cast iron pan with onion and jalapeno
3. When onion is translucent, add garlic and sauté until fragrant
4. Add remaining ingredients and stir to combine
5. Allow sauce to simmer until thickened, approximately 20 min. stirring frequently
6. Remove from heat and allow to cool
7. Remove bay leaf and blend the sauce
8. Glaze or serve with chicken or pork or store in an airtight container in the refrigerator

Cheesy, Bacon Bbq Meatloaf

Ingredients:
- 2 Lbs 80/20 Ground Beef
- 1 Lb Ground Pork
- 1/2 Yellow Onion (Diced)
- 1/2 Cup Bacon (Cut Up)
- 2 Cups Break Crumbs
- 3 Fresh Eggs
- Choice of BBQ Rub
- Choice of BBQ Sauce
- Package Of Mozzarella Cheese
- 1/2 Cup Brown Sugar

Directions:
1. Cook up the bacon and onions on your griddle or in a frying pan Let cool 30 mins Mix the ingredients in a

large bowl Pack the mixture into two regular sized loaf pans Sit in fridge for at least 1hr to harden up Cook on your smoker at 275-200 degrees (F) until 140(F) internal temp Glaze with your favorite BBQ sauce Continue to cook until internal temp is 160(F) Let rest 10-15 minutes Slice and enjoy!

Bacon Buffalo Chicken Dip

Cooking Time: 15 Min

Ingredients:
- 1Lb Chicken Breast
- Char-Griller Chicken Rub
- 1 Cup Mozzarella Cheese
- 1 Cup Cheddar Cheese
- 8 Oz Of Softened Cream Cheese
- 1 Cup Of Sour Cream
- 1/2 Cup Of Franks Red Hot Sauce
- 2 Tbsp Of Ranch Dip Mix
- 2 Slices Of Bacon(Chopped)

Directions:

1. Coat chicken generously with Char-Grillers Chicken Rub Smoke chicken at 375° indirect heat until chicken reaches an internal temp of 165° Once internal temp is reached pull chicken from the grill, my Akorn Kamado got the call for this recipe. Shred chicken with Char-Griller Meat Claws, a kitchen aid mixer is awesome for this it shreds the chicken really well. Mix all ingredients into shredded chicken Add to your favorite bake-ware, I used a stargazer cast iron skillet. Put back on the grill at 375° until cheese is melted and has a golden color. Garnish with scallions and blue cheese crumbles that's optional.

Butternut Squash Risotto

Cooking Time: 30-40 Min

Ingredients:
- 3 Tbsp. butter
- 1 small yellow onion, chopped
- 2 cloves garlic, pressed or minced
- 2 C. (32 oz.) chicken stock
- 1 C. water
- 1 C. heavy cream
- 1 ½ C. Arborio rice
- 1 small butternut squash (about 2 lbs), cubed for roasting
- ½ C. freshly grated Asiago cheese
- ½ C. dry white wine, optional
- 1 Tsp. salt, more to taste
- Freshly ground black pepper, to taste

Directions:

1. Preheat grill to 425°F, coat butternut squash with olive oil and season to taste with salt and pepper. Roast for 30-40 minutes.

2. Melt the butter in a skillet, add chopped onion and sweat for 3-5 minutes. Then add Arborio rice and sauté for 1-2 minutes. Add white wine to deglaze and stir.

3. Add stock, reduce liquid and add water as needed and stir occasionally. The rice will absorb the liquid as it cooks. Stir in heavy cream and bring to a boil. Add roasted butternut squash and cheese and season to taste.

4. Mix well and heat to be served with your favorite meat.

5. Suggestion: Serve risotto with carrot ribbons sautéed in olive oil and pair with a medium filet.

Smoked Mac And Cheese

Cooking Time: 1-2 Hrs

Ingredients:
- 6 Tbsp of Butter
- 1/3 Cup of Flour
- 3 Cups of Milk
- 6 Cups of Shredded Cheese of your choice
- Kosher Salt
- Black Pepper
- 2 Tsp of Paprika
- 4 Cups of Elbows, Macaroni, cooked
- 1 tsp of Cayenne Pepper

Directions:

1. Preheat the smoker to 225-250°F. Heat a large cast iron skillet to medium heat on your stove. Add butter and allow it to thoroughly melt. Whisk in the flour until bubbly and thoroughly combined. After 2-3 min, pour in the milk stirring constantly until the sauce thickens. Add 4 of the 6 cups of cheese, stirring until

thoroughly combined and melted. Mix in the seasonings then add elbows to the cheese sauce. Once thoroughly combined, sprinkle the remaining 2 cups of cheese over the top. Place the skillet into your smoker and allow it to cook uninterrupted for 1-2 hours depending on how intense you'd like the smoky flavor. Allow to rest for 5-10 minutes then serve immediately. Enjoy!

Gravity 980 Quick N' Fast Grilled Vegetables

Cooking Time: 5 Min

Ingredients:
- 1 Large Zucchini (Sliced)
- 1 Large Summer Squash (Sliced)
- 1 Red Bed Pepper (Sliced)
- 3 Large Portobello Mushrooms (Sliced)
- 1 Red Onion (Sliced)
- Kosher Salt
- Black Pepper
- 1 Tbsp of Garlic Powder
- 1 Tsp of Paprika
- 1 Tbsp of Italian Seasoning (or your choice of herbs)
- 1/2 Cup of Extra Virgin Olive Oil

Directions:
1. Remove the fire shutter from the Gravity 980. Load the hopper and set the temperature to 400°F. In a large bowl, combine all veggies with olive oil and seasonings. Place a grill wok on the grates and close the grill, allowing it to preheat for 2-3 minutes before adding vegetable mixture. Using a silicone spatula, open the grill and stir vegetables around in the wok, repeating the process until vegetables reach desired doneness. Serve hot or warm. Enjoy!

Hickory Smoked Deviled Eggs

Cooking Time: 45 Min

Ingredients:
- Eggs - 6
- Soaked Hickory Wood Chips
- Mayonnaise - 1/4 Cup
- Yellow Mustard - 1 Tablespoon
- Hot Sauce - 2 Teaspoons
- Apple Cider Vinegar - 2 Teaspoons
- Sea Salt and Pepper to Taste

Directions:
1. Hard boil six eggs. My fool proof method: put the eggs in a pot of water over high heat, bring to a boil, turn off and cover, let sit for exactly ten minutes, then drop eggs in an ice water bath.
2. Peel the eggs and smoke using water soaked hickory wood chips for 30 minutes, rotating half way through, or until you reach the desired amount of color.
3. Slice the eggs in half, remove the yolks, and thoroughly mix them with the ingredients
4. Pipe the yolk mixture into the egg whites and top with paprika, crumbled bacon, and chopped green onions.

Grilled Cilantro Garlic Parmesan Chicken Wings

Cooking Time: 30 Min

Ingredients:
- Room Temperature Water - 8 Cups
- Course Kosher Salt - 1/3 Cup
- Sugar - 1 Tablespoon
- Chicken Wings with Tips Removed, Drumettes and Flats Separated - 3 to 4 Pounds
- Oil for Grilling - 1 Tablespoon
- Unsalted Butter - 1/2 Cup
- Minced Garlic Cloves - 4
- Smoked Paprika - 1 Teaspoon
- Course Kosher Salt - 1 Teaspoon
- Black Pepper - 1/4 Teaspoon
- Grated Parmesan Cheese - 1/4 Cup
- Parmesan Cheese for Garnish - 2 Tablespoons

Directions:
1. These wings are quick-brined for 30 minutes in a simple solution of water, salt and sugar to achieve that juicy tender inside and crispy crunchy outside. They're tossed in a generous mixture of melted butter infused with garlic, parmesan, smoked paprika and salt.
2. Top the wings with some freshly chopped cilantro to add some bright Mexican-inspired flavors and enjoy!

3. Make a quick brine: In a large bowl, add water, coarse kosher salt and sugar. Stir together until the sugar and salt have completely dissolved. Add the chicken wings, cover the bowl with plastic wrap and refrigerate for 30 minutes.
4. Prepare wings: Remove the chicken wings from the brine and pat completely dry with paper towels. Place in a large mixing bowl, add in 1 tablespoon oil for grilling and toss together to coat.
5. Prepare the grill: Preheat grill to medium-high heat (about 400°F-450°F). Brush the preheated grill grate with cooking oil to prevent sticking by wiping it down with a folded paper towel that has been soaked in vegetable oil.
6. Grill the wings: Grill the chicken wings with the lid closed for about 8 minutes per side, rearranging them on the grill accordingly if you notice that some wings are cooking faster than others. Grilled wings are ready when the meat is no longer pink at the bone and the temperature in the thickest part registers at least 165°F. Remove from the grill and transfer to a large bowl.
7. Make the wing sauce: Heat a small pot or saucepan over medium heat. Add the butter and melt. Add the garlic and saute until fragrant, about 30 seconds. Add the smoked paprika, 2 tablespoons grated Parmesan cheese, black pepper and salt. Stir together to combine and remove from heat. 6. Coat the wings: Pour half of the garlic Parmesan wing sauce onto the grilled wings. Add the remaining 2 tablespoons grated Parmesan cheese and toss with the wings to combine. Pour the other half of the sauce in a small bowl or ramekin to serve as a dipping sauce if desired.
8. Serve: Top the wings with chopped cilantro and shredded Parmesan cheese. Serve with the reserved garlic Parmesan sauce and enjoy.

Fabulous Buttermilk Pancakes

Cooking Time: 4 Min

Ingredients:
- 2 Cups All Purpose Flour
- 1 Tsp Baking Soda
- 1 Tsp Salt
- 1 Tablespoon Sugar
- 1 Egg
- 3 Cups Buttermilk

Directions:
1. Preheat part of your griddle to 375°-400° Mix well all the dry and ingredients Mix the buttermilk into the dry ingredients, it's ok if lumpy. In a separate bowl, crack the egg and whisk it incorporating air into the egg until it is light and bubbly. Eggs that are not straight out of the refrigerator will whip up easier. Add the egg to the other ingredients and mix, JUST to incorporate. DO NOT OVERMIX Grease the area of the griddle for pancakes with vegetable oil Drop approximately 1/2 cup plus a little bit more of the batter onto the hot griddle and let it spread out. Cook until the bottom side is golden brown. Flip pancake and lightly brown. Serve with butter and warm maple syrup. Enjoy these light fluffy pancakes

Barbecue Chicken Foil Packets

Ingredients:
- Barbecue Sauce of Choice - 3/4 Cup
- Honey - 2 Tbs
- Apple Cider Vinegar - 3 Tbs
- Smoked Paprika - 1 tsp
- Chili Powder - 1/2 tsp
- Olive Oil - 1 to 2 Tbs
- 4 Boneless, Skinless Chicken Breasts
- 1 Zucchini
- 1 Red Bell Pepper
- 1 Red Onion
- Salt and Pepper to Taste
- Fresh Parsley

Directions:
1. Preheat grill to medium-high heat
2. Tear off or cut four large squares of foil
3. Chop the veggies into chunks
4. Place a chicken breast in the middle of each piece of foil
5. Divide vegetables evenly among packets
6. Drizzle chicken and vegetables with oil and season with salt and pepper to taste

7. In a bowl, mix barbecue sauce, honey, vinegar, chili power and paprika
8. Brush sauce on chicken and reserve some for later
9. Place foil packets on the grill for 7 to 8 minutes, then flip and grill for 6 to 8 minutes.
10. Remove from grill, carefully open packets, brush chicken with reserve sauce, top with parsley and serve.

Fried Kielbasa & Cabbage

Cooking Time: 30 Min

Ingredients:
- 6 Tbsp Butter, Divided
- 1 Tbsp Red Wine Vinegar
- 3 Cloves Garlic, Chopped
- 1/2 Onion, Chopped
- 14 oz. Kielbasa, Sliced
- 1 Head of Cabbage, Chopped
- 1 Tbsp Paprika
- 1 tsp Salt
- 1 tsp Pepper
- Parsley & Crushed Red Pepper to Garnish

Directions:
1. Pre-heat grill to 300°. Place cast iron skillet over direct heat.
2. Once skillet is heated up add 3 tbsp butter, garlic & onion. Cook down for a few minutes then add red wine vinegar. Mix together.
3. Then add kielbasa. Cook until browned. Add cabbage, rest of butter, paprika, salt & pepper. Mix.
4. Cook until cabbage is tender & slightly browned. Garnish with parsley & crushed red peppers.

Flavor Pro™ Smoked Chicken Breast

Cooking Time: 1 Hrs

Ingredients:
- 4 Boneless Skinless Chicken Breast
- 2 Tablespoons Salt-Free Chicken Seasoning
- 1 Tbsp Olive Oil
- 1 Lemon Juiced (Can Substitute 2 Tbsp Bottled Lemon Juice)
- 3 Cloves Garlic (Minced)
- 1/4 Cup Yellow Onion (Finely Chopped)
- 1/2 Tsp Oregano
- 1/2 Tsp Basil
- Pinch of Salt & Pepper
- 2 Tbsp Onion Powder
- 2 Tbsp Garlic Powder
- 1 Tbsp Chili Powder
- 1 Tbsp Paprika

Directions:
1. Rinse off your chicken breasts and pat dry with a paper towel. Trim off any excess fat or areas where meat is very thin. In a gallon sized ziplock bag, add chicken breasts and 1 Tbsp olive oil, 1 lemon, juiced, 3 cloves garlic, ¼ cup yellow onion, ½ tsp oregano, ½ tsp basil, pinch of salt & pepper. Let marinate for 1-2 hours or overnight if you so choose. Once marinated, rinse off the chicken and pat dry. Add your salt-free or 2 Tbsp onion powder, 2 Tbsp garlic powder, 1 Tbsp chili powder, 1 Tbsp paprika, 1 Tbsp parsley, 1 ½ tsp black pepper seasoning to all sides of the chicken breast. Place the seasoned chicken in the refrigerator for 10-15 minutes while your grill heats up. Prepare your Flavor Pro for indirect heat at 225° F by filling the far left slot of the Flavor Drawer with charcoal. Add a few chunks of smoking wood to the coals as well. I used hickory for this recipe but feel free to use whatever smoking wood you like. Use both burners on the left to light the charcoal. Once charcoal is lit, you may turn your burners off. Keep both smoke stacks open. Once your Flavor Pro is up to temperature, add your chicken breasts to the far right side of the grill grate, away from the heat source. Add coals and wood as needed to maintain your temperature. Smoke for approximately 1 hour or until your chicken breasts reach an internal temperature of 165° F. Be sure to keep a close eye on the internal temperature, going over 165° F may cause your chicken breasts to dry out. Let rest 10 minutes before slicing. Enjoy!

2-burner Flat Iron Grilled "bmp"

Cooking Time: 10 Min

Ingredients:
- 4 Slices of Baguette, Sourdough or Bread of Choice
- 6 Slices of Thick-sliced Bacon (Cooked)
- 4 Thick Slices of Fresh Mozzarella
- 1/3 Cup of Pesto
- 1/4 Cup of Extra Virgin Olive Oil
- Optional Toppings: Roma Tomato, Fresh Spinach

Directions:
1. This simple, yet savory sandwich elevates both grilled cheese and BLT all in one. Easily prepared on the Flat Iron, serve these Grilled "BMP"s for lunch, dinner or even brunch adding a fried egg.
2. Assemble each sandwich, starting by spreading a generous amount of pesto on one slice (or both) per sandwich. Add three slices of bacon then top with two slices of mozzarella. Optionally add tomato or spinach before stacking the second piece on top. With Flat Iron preheated to medium-high heat, add ½ the olive oil to flat top then add the sandwich. Allow to cook for 3-4 minutes before drizzling more olive oil on the top bread sliced then flipping over. Cook for an additional 3-4 minutes or until desired doneness. Serve immediately. Enjoy!

Fire Roasted Salsa Con Certi

Cooking Time: 30 Min

Ingredients:
- 3 tomatillos: remove flaky shell and rinse thoroughly using water
- ½ knob of Garlic, sliced in half: for fire roasting
- 1 clove of Garlic: fresh/raw for the Molcajete
- 1 Jalapeño
- 1 Serrano pepper
- 1 Guajillo Chili
- 1 Lime for juice
- 1 tbsp. salt
- Cilantro: small bunch
- 1/2 white onion (Tip: Yellow onion will make it sweet)
- Olive Oil: drizzle

Directions:
1. Preheat grill/ smoker to 300°.
2. Place the tomatillos, jalapeño, serrano pepper, sliced knob of garlic, onion and lime in the grill.
3. Tip: Try not to let the tomatillos burst, the goal is to keep juices inside.
4. Fire Roast for 25 minutes or until the veggies are tender. The tomatillos will turn a light brown color.
5. Remove the veggies from the grill.
6. Tip: After they cool off remove any burnt pieces from the veggies best as possible.
7. Using a Molcajete, first mix 1 tbsp. salt and one fresh/raw garlic and mix. Then add grilled garlic to the mixture with the jalapeño, serrano peppers (remember to remove the stems) and the Guajillo Chili (remove all the seeds/stem and soak in warm water for 10 minutes prior to using).
8. Mix in the Molcajete until it turn into a chunky paste.
9. Using a food processor, drizzle olive oil, add onion, add ingredients from the Molcajete, tomatillos (remember to remove the stems), lime juice and small cilantro bunch.
10. Mix for a few minutes until it's loose and a bit chunky.
11. Serve with tortilla chips or use on your tacos!

Herb And Garlic Lamb Rack

Ingredients:
- 8 Lamb Loin or Rib Chops
- 1/4 C. Olive Oil
- 1 Tbsp. Chopped Fresh Thyme
- 1 Tbsp. Chopped Fresh Basil
- 2 Tsp. Chopped Fresh Rosemary
- 2 cloves Garlic, minced
- Zest of 1 Lemon
- 1 Tsp. Salt
- 1/2 Tsp. Black Pepper

Directions:
1. Combine olive oil, thyme, basil, rosemary, garlic, lemon zest, salt and pepper in a bowl.
2. Rub lamb chops with the mixture to coat evenly.

3. Cover chops and refrigerate for 4 hours.
4. Bring your grill up to 500°F over direct heat.
5. Place chops on grill and cook for about 5 to 7 minutes per side or until temperature reaches between 145°-155°F.
6. Once cooked to desired doneness, remove chops from grill. Tent with foil and let meat rest for 10 minutes.

Char Grilled Wings

Cooking Time: 20 Min

Ingredients:
- Chicken Wings - 2 to 4 Pounds
- Hot Sauce - 1/2 Cup
- Melted Butter - 1/4 Cup
- Salt - 1 Tablespoon
- Hot Sauce (for Sauce) - 1/2 Cup
- Minced Garlic (for Sauce) - 2 Cloves
- Cayenne - 1 Teaspoon

Directions:
1. If you're like my family, you're counting down the days to football season. That means tailgates at the stadium, or in your own backyard, and if you've got the cute transportable AKORN Jr, Grilled Wings are absolutely in your tailgating future.
2. I do my wings a little differently, I like to soak them in plain old cayenne vinegar hot sauce for 48 hours before I grill them. This is 100% optional, but I'm telling you- the flavor profile is unreal. Add a few hunks of Applewood to your charcoal while grilling these for a flavor explosion. Pro Tip: Baste your wings in the sauce at the very end to keep them from burning. Since they marinated in the hot sauce for hours, the flavor is packed in. Let's dig in.
3. After rinsing and drying your wings, toss in hot sauce, avocado oil, and salt. Marinate for 24- 48 hours.
4. When you're ready to grill, add a few chunks of Applewood to your charcoal, and get the grill nice and hot. Oil your grates and spread the wings out evenly. Grill on each side for 8 minutes, until crispy and golden brown.

5. While the wings finish cooking, brush the buffalo sauce over each side, and turn 1-2 more times to allow the sauce to caramelize. Dip them in your favorite ranch or blue cheese, and enjoy!

Fresh Summer Corn Avocado Tomato Salad

Cooking Time: 10 Min

Ingredients:
- 2 Cups Cooked Corn (Grilled Is Preferred)
- 2 Avocados Cut Into Small Cubes
- 2 Cherry Tomatoes
- 1/3 Cup Of Chopped Red Onion
- 2 Tbsp Of Extra Virgin Olive Oil
- 1/2 Tsp Of Sea Salt
- 1/2 Tsp Of Black Pepper
- 1 Tbsp Of Lime Juice
- 1/4 Cup Of Cilantro

Directions:
1. Combine the primary salad ingredients: corn, avocado, tomatoes, and red onion in a large bowl. In a small bowl, combine the dressing ingredients: olive oil, sea salt, black pepper, lime juice, and cilantro until they are thoroughly mixed. Pour the dressing over the salad and mix thoroughly. Chill the salad for at least an hour before serving.

5-minute Avocado Dip

Ingredients:
- 1 avocado, pitted
- Juice of 1 lime
- Sea salt, to taste
- Cilantro, to taste

Directions:
1. Combine all the ingredients into a bowl and mash together with a fork, or pulse in a food processor until combined to desired consistency. Place aside in refrigerator until needed. Use for tortilla dipping or taco topping.

Competition Ribs Recipe

Ingredients:
- 2 Racks of St. Louis Spare Ribs
- 3 Tablespoons of Char-Griller Rib Rub
- Spray Bottle
- 1 Cup of Sugar In The Raw
- 2 Tablespoons of Real Butter
- 1/2 Cup of White Grape Juice
- 1 Cup of your Favorite BBQ Sauce

Directions:
1. Fire up the Char-Griller Akorn to 275 degrees, add two chunks of cherry wood, and place your Smokin Stone in so we are cooking indirectly. Trim any heavy fat, the skirt, and remove the membrane from your ribs. Season 1 and ½ Tablespoons of rub per side of each rack of ribs Place the ribs on to the cooker and spritz with spray butter after 45 minutes and continue to spritz every 30 minutes after that. At the 2 hour mark wrap your ribs in aluminum foil with ½ cup of sugar in the raw, 1 Tablespoon of butter, and !/4 cup of white grape juice, wrap meat side down and put them back on the akorn. After an hour check the ribs for tenderness, this will be an internal temperature around 203 and probe tender. Take the ribs out of the wrap and put them back on the cooker for 2 minutes to dry the rub. Remove from the cooker sauce your ribs with as little or as much sauce as you want, slice, and serve.

Mediterranean Veggie Burgers With Vegan Feta Dip

Ingredients:
- 1 1/2 Cups Brown Rice (Cooked)
- 1 1/2 Cups Sweet Potato (Steamed Or Roasted)
- 1 Egg
- 2 Cloves Garlic
- 3-4 Pepperoncini Peppers (Drained)
- 1/4 Cup Parsley (Fresh)
- 6 Buns
- 2 Tbsp Olive Oil
- Salt & Pepper To Taste
- Lettuce, Tomato, And Onion For Toppings
- 1/2 Cup Vegan Mayo, Or Vegan Yogurt
- 2 Tbsp Parsley (Chopped)
- 2 Pepperoncini Peppers (Chopped)
- 1 Clove Garlic (Minced)
- 1 Tbsp Lemon Zest
- 1 Tbsp Olive Oil
- Salt & Pepper To Taste

Directions:
1. In a food processor, combine brown rice, sweet potato, egg, garlic, pepperoncini peppers, parsley, salt and pepper, and pulse until well combined. You can also mash these ingredients with a fork if you prefer a chunkier texture, just dice the garlic, parsley, and peppers first.
2. Wet hands slightly, and form mixture into six evenly shaped patties. Let chill in the fridge or freezer for 10 minutes, until burgers have a chance to firm up a bit.
3. Combine ingredients(12-19) for Feta Dip and set aside. Pro Tip: dip is even better the next day after the flavors marry, if you have time to make it the day before!
4. Preheat Flat-Iron Gas Griddle to medium heat, and drizzle olive oil over the surface, using a towel and tongs to spread it across the griddle. Once it's been heating up for a few minutes, add burgers and buns to the grill. Let buns toast for 1 minute, then remove. Let burgers cook for 5 minutes on the first side, flip, then finish cooking for 5 more minutes.
5. Remove burgers from grill and begin assembling, piling L,T,O, and a burger on the toasted buns, finishing with a dollop of feta dip! Enjoy while warm! These burgers can keep in the fridge for 5 days, or frozen for up to three months.

Certified Competition Smoked Ribs Tips

Cooking Time: 3 Hrs

Ingredients:
- Breast of Spare Rib and Any Rib Trimmings
- Yellow Mustard
- Char-Griller Grills Rib Rub
- Apple Juice (Non Concentrate)

Directions:
1. Prep

2. Slice the breast into cubes and use any trimming with pieces of meat, discard any all fat pieces.
3. Apply even coating of yellow mustard for a binder.
4. Using Char-Griller Grills Rib Rub apply even coat of the rub on the meat.
5. Rib tips are ready to be smoked with the ribs.
6. Smoking
7. Using the Char-Griller Grills Smokin' Champ 1624, add the rib tips to the warming rack of the grill.
8. Spritz every 30-45 minutes with Apple juice.
9. Smoke for 3 hours.
10. Remove from the pit and enjoy.
11. Serving idea: serve with bbq sauce on the side with fries and white bread.

Reverse Seared Pesto Lamb Racks

Ingredients:
- 2 Cups Fresh Basil Leaves, Packed
- 1/2 Cup Freshly Grated Pecorino Romano or Parmesan Cheese
- 1/2 Cup Extra Virgin Olive Oil
- 1/4 Cup Pine Nuts, Toasted
- 2 Garlic Cloves, Minced
- 1/4 Teaspoon Salt, More to Taste
- Pepper To Taste
- 3 Lamb Racks
- Coarse Salt

Directions:
1. What is the reverse sear method and why do we do it? Reverse searing means to smoke the meat to just short of the desired doneness and then sear it off at the end to get that lovely (and tasty) flavor crust. If we sear first then smoke, the smoke will not penetrate the meat because of that flavor crust. This is the best of both worlds. It infuses the meat with wonderful smoke flavor and then has that lovely browning from the sears that caramelizes the proteins. Reverse searing is great for roasts like tri tip, standing rib roasts (prime rib), pork loin (and tenderloin), and thick steaks. Be careful. This method is addictive.
2. Combine all but the lamb racks and coarse salt in a food processor and blend until all those flavors create a thick, gooey, magnificent green paste.
3. Place the lamb racks into a large re-sealable plastic bag and pour the basil pesto over the top. Seal the bag and make sure the pesto coats all the meat. Place the bag in the fridge for 2-24 hours
4. Remove the lamb from the plastic bags and salt both sides before preparing the grill for about 250 degrees and place the smokin' stone in the bottom along with a chunk of pecan wood. Once the smoke starts rolling, we are ready to cook.
5. Place the pesto lamb racks over the Smokin' Stone and close the lid.
6. Smoke the lamb until it hits 120 degrees Fahrenheit.
7. Remove the lamb from the grill, take off the grill grates and, with heat proof gloves, take out the Smokin' Stone and stoke up the fire by stirring up the coals, opening the bottom vent wide open and adding more coal if necessary.
8. Once the fire kicks up to above 400 degrees, place the grill grates back on the AKORN and sear the lamb racks on both sides.
9. Once both sides are seared, the temp should be close to 140F and ready to serve. I'd say we nailed a rare to medium rare with these meat lollipops.

Smoked Bacon

Cooking Time: 3-4 Hrs

Ingredients:
- 1 6-8 Lb. Pork Belly
- 1/3 Cup of Kosher Salt
- 2 Tsp of Pink Curing Salt
- 1/4 Cup of Brown Sugar
- 1/4 Cup of Honey
- 2 1/2 Tbsp of Paprika
- 2 Tsp of Ground Black Pepper
- 1 Tsp of Cumin

Directions:
1. Rinse your pork belly and pat it as dry as possible with paper towels. Place in a plastic bag, thoroughly combining with all seasonings. Seal the bag and

refrigerate for 7-10 day, flipping once per day until the belly grows firm. The amount of days depends on how thick the pork belly is. Remove the pork belly from the bag, rinse and thoroughly pat it dry. To ensure it's completely dry, you may place it on a rack uncovered in the fridge for 24-48 hours. Preheat your smoker to 200°F. Smoke the belly for 3-4 hours or until the internal temperature reaches 150°F. Optionally remove the rind then allow it to chill in the fridge for 4-5 hours before slicing and cooking as desired. Enjoy!

Gravity 980 Reverse Seared Steak

Cooking Time: 30-45 Min

Ingredients:
- 4 Beef Steaks (Ribeyes, Strips, etc.)
- 4 Tbsp of Butter
- Kosher Salt
- Black Pepper
- Steak Rub/Seasoning (Optional)

Directions:
1. In a small bowl, thoroughly combine the seasonings. Coat your steaks with the seasoning mixture and allow them to sit at room temperature for 20-30 minutes. Remove the fire shutter from your Gravity 980, load then light it and set the temperature to 225-250°F. Smoke for about 35-45 minutes until the internal temperature has reached 110° for rare and 150° for well done. Increase your grill temperature to 550-700°F. Add 1 Tbsp of butter to each steak before searing. Sear the steaks for 1-2 minutes per side or until they reach your desired doneness. Allow the steaks to rest for 10 minutes before serving. Enjoy!

Grilled Tomato Salsa

Cooking Time: 15 Min

Ingredients:
- 4 Ripe Tomatoes
- 1 Small White Onion
- 1 Jalapeno
- 1/2 Cup Water
- 1/2 Cup Fresh Cilantro
- 1-2 Tbs Salt
- 2 Tbs Oil

Directions:
1. From Aubrey: End of summer means end of tomato season, and trust me, this is my least favorite statement, ever. I love tomatoes. I'll take any lengths to hold onto those delicious flavor bombs for as long as possible, and that's why I make big batches of grilled salsa as often as I can. It's so simple. Grill a few veggies, blend with cilantro, salt, and serve over tacos, chips, really anything. Let's do it.
2. Preheat your grill to high. Scrape the grates, and make sure they're clean and hot.
3. While the grill preheats, cut tomatoes and jalapeño in half, onion into quarters, and toss with 1 T of salt and the oil. Add to grill, and char on all sides for 3-4 minutes each turn, until nice color and marks appear on the outsides of the veggies.
4. Transfer grilled veggies to blender, add water, remaining salt, and the fresh cilantro. Pulse until salsa is the texture you like. If you like it chunky, 3-6 times should do it. If you prefer a restaurant style salsa, blend on high for 30-60 seconds.
5. Store in fridge for up to 10 days. Enjoy!

Flat Iron Artisan Garlic Bread Grilled Cheese

Cooking Time: 10 Min

Ingredients:
- 2 slices (per sandwich) of Pullman, Multigrain, or Sourdough bread (or your preferred Bread type)
- 1/3 Cup of Mozzarella Cheese, shredded (or your preferred Cheese type)
- 2 Tbsp of Extra Virgin Olive Oil
- 1 Tbsp of Butter (Melted)
- 1 Tsp of Garlic (Minced)
- 1 Tsp of Garlic Powder
- 1/2 Tsp of Parsley
- 1 Dash of Salt & Pepper

Directions:
1. Preheat Flat Iron to Medium Heat.

2. In a small bowl, combine olive oil, butter, garlic, and all spices and seasonings. Stir until all ingredients are mixed together.
3. Spread a spoonful of the oil mixture on the griddle and lay one slice of bread directly on top, allowing it to soak up the mixture.
4. Immediately add the desired amount of cheese on bread and place the other slice on top slightly smashing down.
5. Allow the bottom slice of bread to lightly fry and get crispy before flipping over using a spatula.
6. Gently lift the bottom of the sandwich and add another spoonful of the oil mixture underneath.
7. Cook both sides to desired crispiness and ensure cheese melts.
8. Serve hot.

Red Pepper Eggs

Cooking Time: 15 Min

Ingredients:

- Red Pepper Sliced as Rings (3/4in. Thick) - 2
- Eggs - 2
- Precooked Bacon, Crumbled - 5-7 Slices
- Shredded Pepper Jack Cheese - 1/4 Cup
- Butter
- Salt and Pepper - To Taste

Directions:

1. Preheat grill to 350 degrees and place skillet on heat
2. Melt butter (1-2 Tbsp) and cook red pepper slices for 4-5 mins per side to soften
3. Crack eggs directly into pepper rings, season with salt and pepper and close lid for another few minutes (longer for a more well-done egg)
4. After egg has cooked, sprinkle with pepper jack cheese and bacon crumbles. Serve for a yummy breakfast of champions!

Smoked Sausage Stuffing

Cooking Time: 60 Min

Ingredients:

- 1 16-Oz Bag Stuffing Cubes
- 4 Tablespoons Unsalted Butter (Melted)
- 1 Pound Fresh Sage Sausage (Casing Removed)
- 1 Medium Onion (Chopped)
- 2 Ribs Celery With Leaves (Chopped)
- 1/2 Teaspoon Kosher Salt
- 2 Diced Apples
- 1/2 Cup Dried Cranberries
- 1/4 Cup Fresh Flat-Leaf Parsley
- 3 Cups Chicken Broth
- 2 Eggs

Directions:

1. Preheat your smoker to 225 degrees F. Melt 2 Tablespoons of butter in a 12" cast iron skillet over medium-high heat. Add the sausage and break up with a wooden spoon. Cook for about 5 minutes. Add the onion, celery, and salt. Cook until the vegetables get soft, about 5 minutes. Turn off the heat and stir in the bread, apples, dried cranberries, and parsley, stirring gently to evenly distribute. In a large bowl, combine the broth and eggs, and pour it over the bread cube mixture in the skillet. Top with 2 Tablespoons of melted butter. Place the skillet full of stuffing on the smoker and cook for 60 minutes until the top is crisp and golden. Remove the cast iron skillet from the smoker and serve immediately or keep warm until ready to serve

Smoked Butternut Squash Soup

Cooking Time: 1 Hrs

Ingredients:

- 1 Butternut Squash
- Sea Salt
- Coconut Oil
- Fresh Rosemary
- 1 Onion
- Vegetable Broth

Directions:

1. Split a butternut squash down the middle and scoop out the seeds. Give it a little layer of coconut oil and top with sea salt. Add a stem of fresh rosemary to each side and put it on the grill. You're going to want to get your grill at about 300°. Place the squash on there to smoke until the flesh is easily manipulated with a fork (about an hour). Remove from grill. Slice up an onion and sautee

it in a pan over medium. Add half the pan to a blender, 5 cups of vegetable broth and 1 side of the squash (with rosemary pulled from the stem). Blend on high until everything looks blended. Salt and pepper to taste. Repeat with the other squash and onions. Serve and enjoy!

Flat Iron Hot Cakes

Cooking Time: 10 Min

Ingredients:
- 2 Cups Self Rising Flour
- 1 1/2 Cups Milk
- 1/2 Cup Greek Yogurt
- 2 Eggs
- 1 Tbsp Vanilla
- Fillings of Choice (We Did Chocolate Chips & Blueberries)

Directions:
1. In a large bowl, combine ingredients and whisk until smooth and creamy. I then pour my batter into a bottle that is pourable, this step is optional! Next, turn your Flat Iron Gas Griddle on medium heat, and let warm up for several minutes. Spray with cooking spray, or add some butter to the cooking surface. Pour even sized circles onto the Griddle, and let them sit for about 2 mins, until bubbles form around the edges. 4.Sprinkle with your filling of choice, and flip- giving the pancakes another 2 minutes on the final side. Serve with warm syrup and butter! Enjoy

Fresh Chili Lime Watermelon Fries

Cooking Time: 5 Min

Ingredients:
- 1 Seedless Watermelon
- 2 Tsp of Tajin Chili Lime Seasoning
- 1 Tsp of Sea Salt
- 1 Cup Greek Yogurt
- 1/2 Fresh Squeezed Lime
- 1/2 Tsp of Chili Powder
- 1 Tbsp Honey

Directions:

1. Slice the watermelon into long, "french fry" formation. Combine the sea salt, and chili lime seasoning in a large bowl. In a separate bowl, combine yogurt, lime juice, chili powder, and honey. Mix thoroughly. Serve the yogurt mixture alongside the watermelon for easy dipping.

Queso Fundido Stuffed Grilled Jalapeños

Cooking Time: 10 Min

Ingredients:
- 4-6 Large Jalapeños
- 1/2 Tbsp Minced Garlic
- 1/4 Cup Diced Onion
- 4 Ounces Chorizo
- 4 Ounces Shredded Mozzarella
- 1/4 Cup Heavy Whipping Cream

Directions:
1. Slice the jalapeños in half lengthwise. Crumble and cook the chorizo over medium heat along with the garlic and onion. Melt together mozzarella and heavy whipping cream until creamy, and combine with the chorizo. Spoon the mixture into the jalapeño halves, gently rest in a cast iron pan, and grill until browned and bubbly.

Grilled Pumpkin And Chayote Soup

Cooking Time: 45 Min

Ingredients:
- 2 Tbsp Olive Oil
- 1 Red Onion, Roughly Chopped
- 2 Garlic Cloves
- 1 Chayote, Remove Core and Cube
- 1 Carrot, Peeled and Rough Chopped
- 1 Celery Stalk, Rough Chopped
- 1 Red Bell Pepper, Rough Chopped
- 1 Pound Grilled Pumpkin Flesh
- 1 - 14 oz Can Diced Tomatoes
- 1 Bay Leaf
- 1 tsp Chili Powder
- 1 tsp Cumin
- 1 tsp Oregano
- 1/2 tsp Red Pepper Flakes

- 1/4 tsp Cinnamon
- 4 Cups Chicken Broth
- 2 Tbsp Apple Cider Vinegar
- 1 tsp Dried Thyme
- 1/2 tsp Oregano
- 1/2 tsp Marjoram
- Salt & Pepper

Directions:
1. Grill the pumpkin over indirect heat on a 375 degree grill for 20 minutes. Scoop out the flesh and cube.
2. Saute onions, garlic, carrot, celery, bell pepper, pumpkin and chayote in olive oil for 5 minutes.
3. Add chile powder, cumin, oregano, pepper flakes, cinnamon, thyme, oregano and marjoram to vegetables and stir to coat.
4. Add broth, canned tomatoes and vinegar and stir to mix well. Add bay leaf.
5. Heat to boil, lower to simmer. Simmer until vegetables are soft and tender. Season to taste with salt and pepper.
6. Serve with a garnish of crema and toasted pepitas.
7. Blend until smooth.

Gravity 980 Smoked Baked Potatoes

Cooking Time: 2 Hrs

Ingredients:
- 4 Large Russet Potatoes
- 4 Tbsp of Butter
- Kosher Salt
- Freshly Ground Black Pepper
- Optional Toppings: Chives, Bacon Bits, Shredded Cheese, Sour Cream etc.

Directions:
1. Get ready for an epic loaded baked potato bar for dinner with the Gravity 980. Easily smoke all your potatoes at once for tender, buttery bliss.
2. Remove the fire shutter from your Gravity 980 before loading your hopper and lighting it. Set the temperature to 225-250°F. Thoroughly wash your potatoes before poking with a fork all over. Coat each potato with olive oil, salt and pepper. Place the potatoes into the smoker and allow to smoke for 2 hours or until tender. Cut them open and serve with butter and desired toppings. Enjoy!

Smoked Garlic Herb Chili Flake Grilled Cheese Sandwich

Cooking Time: 5 Min

Ingredients:
- 2 Slices of bread (Buttered)
- 2 Slices Of Cheese (Your Preference)
- Garlic Herb Seasoning (To Taste)
- Smoked Chili Flakes (To Taste)

Directions:
1. Butter bread and sprinkle seasonings on, to taste Slice cheese, 2 per sandwich Heat up grill to 350° - 400° Place whole sandwich on grates, gently pressing to ensure a good grill mark contact; cooking for about 1 minute per turn Turn sandwich 45° to create a criss cross pattern Flip sandwich and repeat steps 4 and 5, pull when done and cheese is melted Cut in half and serve with a cup of warm tomato soup.

Grilled Mango Salsa

Cooking Time: 30 Min

Ingredients:
- Mangoes- 2
- Mini Bell Peppers- 1 Cup
- Jalapeno- 1
- Mini Tomatoes- 1 Cup
- Spring Onion/Scallions- 3
- Cilantro- 1/3 Cup
- Salt- 1 Tablespoon

Directions:
1. Not only do I shop at local stores and farmers markets to find seasonal produce, I support an Ohio based company called Perfectly Imperfect Produce. PIP is a subscription box that rescues "imperfect" produce, things maybe misshapen or bruised that don't make it to the grocery store, and packs it up in a box to deliver to your door weekly. I've been getting a box for over a year now and the element of surprise never fails! It's like a set of "Chopped" in my kitchen each week, figuring out how

to use up the leftover produce. This week we got a ton of salsa ingredients, and with what little sunshine Cleveland has seen this week, I knew I had to get in front of the grill. I used all organic mangoes, cherry tomatoes, jalapeno, mini bell pepper, local spring onions, -all from my PIP box, and added salt and cilantro from the pantry and fridge. Let's dig in!

2. Preheat your Char-Griller Grill to high. I used propane and love the quick heat up for veggies. Spray all your veggies with a little non stick spray- avocado oil is my choice, and lay out on the grill. Turn every 2-3 minutes, until color starts to mark the outer skin of the fruit and veggies.

3. After about 10-15 minutes, you can pull everything and turn the grill off.

4. After the goods come to room temperature, you can scoop the mango out of the skin, and roughly chop it with all of the other ingredients or add everything to a food processor and pulse on low until you reach the thickness you like.

5. Pro Tip: if you don't like much heat- only use ¼ of the jalapeno, and try to avoid the seeds. More seeds mean more heat- so proceed with caution.

6. Serve this delicious grilled salsa over grilled fish, chicken, or a combo of both on tacos! You can store it in the refrigerator for up to 10 days. Enjoy!

Chicken Breast Potatoes And Green Beans On The Char-griller Akorn

Ingredients:
- Your Favorite Boneless Chicken Breasts
- Package of Medium Red Potatoes
- Package Of Your Favorite Green Beans
- Salt
- Pepper
- Garlic
- Stick Of Butter
- Your Favorite Seasoning For The Chicken

Directions:

1. Cut up your potatoes to about 1" cubes Package up your potatoes in tin foil with some salt/pepper and 4-5 tabs of butter Package up your green beans in tin foil with salt/pepper/garlic and 4-5 tabs of butter Fire up the grill to about 400 degrees F Throw the green beans and potatoes wrapped in tin foil About 10-15 minutes later, flip the potatoes/green beans and add the chicken 10 minutes after the chicken has been cooking, flip it Continue cooking until the chicken has reached 167F internal temp - Let everything rest about 10 minutes Cut into and enjoy!

Chicken Fajita Quesadillas

Cooking Time: 20 Min

Ingredients:
- 3 Chicken Breast (Cut in Half)
- 1 Yellow Onion (Thinly Sliced)
- 1-2 Bell Peppers (Thinly Sliced)
- 2 Cups Cheddar Cheese (Freshly Grated)
- 6 Medium Tortillas
- 1 Tsp Ground Cumin
- 1 Tsp Ground Chili Powder
- 1 Tsp Garlic Powder
- 1 Tsp Salt
- 1 Tsp Pepper
- 2 Tbl Olive Oil or Avocado oil

Directions:

1. Heat your Char-Griller Flat Iron Gas griddle to medium heat, and spread avocado oil across the surface with tongs and a towel.

2. Turn the first section to high heat. Toss chicken breast in cumin, chili powder, garlic, salt, & pepper. Lay chicken on first section, over high heat, and cook 4 minutes per side.

3. Add onions and peppers to Flat Iron, and cook over medium until softened and cooked through.

4. After flipping the chicken breast, finally add the tortillas to the Flat Iron Griddle, and sprinkle evenly with cheese. Add a cooked chicken breast to each tortilla and a serving of the peppers & onions, folding each tortilla over the filling in half to make a moon shaped quesadilla.

5. Serve as is, or with a side salad. Enjoy!

Bbq Wang Thangs

Cooking Time: 75 Min

Ingredients:
- Whole Chicken Wings: 12-14
- Olive Oil
- Favorite Creole Seasoning: to taste
- 2 Jalapenos: Sliced
- Favorite Spicy BBQ Sauce: Used a Homemade Sauce
- Char-Griller Grills Smoking Champ 1733
- Fogo Premium Lump Charcoal
- Favorite Smoking Wood: Used Apple

Directions:
1. Rinse Chicken Wings with cold water and pat dry.
2. Trim/remove access fat, skin and hair.
3. Remove the Chicken Wing tip and separate the drum from the flat.
4. Apply coating of olive oil to all sides of the chicken wings.
5. Add Favorite Creole seasoning to the Chicken Wings.
6. Add Jalapenos.
7. Heat up the grill/smoker with lump charcoal to 340°
8. Place the chicken wings in the grill.
9. Flip Wings after 30 minutes.
10. Cook the chicken wings for 60 minutes and warm up the Spicy BBQ Sauce.
11. Sauce Wings and place them back in the grill/smoker for an additional 15 minutes.
12. Remove and enjoy!

Ratatouille

Cooking Time: 55-60 Min

Ingredients:
- 1-2 C. tomato-basil sauce
- 2 garlic cloves, minced
- 3-4 thyme sprigs
- 2 Tbsp. olive oil
- ½ Tsp. chili flakes
- 1 eggplant, thinly sliced
- 1 yellow squash, thinly sliced
- 1 zucchini, thinly sliced
- 1 red bell pepper, stemmed, cored and thinly sliced
- Salt and pepper, to taste
- 1 Tbsp. unsalted butter
- 1 Tbsp. all-purpose flour
- 1 C. milk
- 1/8 Tsp. nutmeg

Directions:
1. Pre-heat grill to 375°F. 2. Heat butter in a small saucepan, add flour and cook for 1-2 minutes. Gradually add milk, stirring continuously to avoid lumps. Continue cooking until béchamel sauce thickens and coats the back of a spoon. 3. Season with nutmeg, salt and pepper and stir. Set aside. 4. Spray an oval baking dish with cooking spray. In a medium bowl, mix together tomato sauce, minced garlic, thyme, red chili flakes, salt and olive oil. Spread a layer in bottom of baking dish. 5. Drizzle béchamel sauce on top and swirl into the tomato sauce. 6. Layer sliced vegetables on top in a spiral pattern. Drizzle with olive oil and sprinkle salt, thyme, and black pepper on top. Cover with parchment paper. 7. Transfer baking dish to grill and bake at 375°F for 55-60 minutes or until all vegetables are tender and tomato sauce is bubbling on the sides. Remove from grill and allow to cool for 5 minutes.
2. Serve ratatouille with crusty bread to scoop up the sauce, if desired. Enjoy!
3. Note: To same time in making spiral layers, pick slices of each vegetable and make a small stack, then place into the baking dish.

Lemon Pepper Wings

Cooking Time: 45 Min

Ingredients:
- 2-3Lb Chicken Wings & Drums
- 1.5 Tsp Dried Lemon Zest (Approx. 5 Lemons)
- 1 Tsp Kosher Salt
- 1 Tsp Coarse Black Pepper
- 1.5 Tsp Garlic Powder
- 1.5 Tsp Onion Powder
- 1 Tbsp Olive Oil
- 6 Tbs Butter
- 1.5 Tsp Coarse Black Pepper
- 1 Tsp Fresh Lemon Zest (Approx. 1 Lemon)
- 1 Lemon (Juiced)

Directions:
1. Collect lemon zest from approximately 5 lemons. Bake lemon zest in an oven on lowest setting until it has completely dried out (20-30 minutes). In a small shaker combine dried lemon zest, 1 Tsp black pepper, ½ garlic powder, ½ onion powder.
2. Apply a 1 Tbsp of Olive oil onto the wings to help act as a binder for the rub. Generously coat the wings on all sides with the lemon pepper rub.
3. Heat grill to 375 F. Place chicken wings on the grill once the grill has reached desired temperature.
4. In a heat safe bowl combine butter,1 ½ black pepper, 1 Tsp fresh lemon zest, and the juice of 1 lemon. Bring the mixture to a boil and reduce heat to let simmer.
5. Once the chicken has reached an internal temp of at least 165 F you can remove from the grill and place in a large bowl. Toss the wings in the lemon pepper sauce mixture. Serve and enjoy!

Ale Chicken Drumsticks

Ingredients:
- Drumsticks- 14
- Ale of Choice- 3 ounces
- Char-Griller Chicken Seasoning- 2.5 Teaspoons

Directions:
1. Soak for an hour in 3 oz of ale of choice
2. Rub down with 5 teaspoons of Char-Griller chicken seasoning
3. Smoke uncovered for and hour on an aluminum foil sheet at 250°F, wrapped in foil until done

Ribeye Roast On The Char-griller Akorn Kamado

Ingredients:
- Full Boneless Ribeye Roast
- Olive Oil
- - Salt & Pepper Or Your Favorite Spices

Directions:
1. Remove roast from fridge, pat dry with paper towels, apply some olive oil and season with your favorite seasonings. Leave on counter while you work on the next step Set your Kamado to 250-275 degrees F and set up for indirect cooking with a deflector. Place roast directly on grates Monitor internal meat temperature until at least 125 degrees F for rare / medium rare. Remove from heat and let rest for 30 minutes Slice your roast - 3/4" slices Enjoy!

Flat Iron Homestyle Hash Brown Patties

Cooking Time: 10 Min

Ingredients:
- 1 1/2 Lbs of Russet Potatoes
- 1 Tbsp of Fresh Chives (Minced)
- 1 Tbsp of Fresh Parsley (Minced)
- 1/2 Tsp of Salt
- 1/2 Tsp of Black Pepper
- 1/2 Tsp of Garlic Powder
- 1 Tbsp of Olive Oil or Canola Oil

Directions:
1. Wash, peel, and dry potatoes. Grate them into shreds then press with a paper towel to eliminate moisture.
2. Preheat Flat Iron to medium-high heat.
3. In a medium bowl, mix together grated potatoes, parsley, chives, salt, pepper and garlic powder in a bowl.
4. Drizzle oil on griddle.
5. Form potato mixture into patties and place on the griddle.
6. Cook each side for about 5 minutes or until crispy and golden brown.

Marinated Flat Iron Steak On The Flat Iron Portable Griddle

Cooking Time: 20 Min

Ingredients:
- 16 Oz Flat Iron Steak
- ¼ Cup Worcestershire Sauce
- 1 Tbsp Balsamic Vinegar
- 1 Tbsp Dijon Mustard
- 1 Tbsp Char-Griller Steak Seasoning

Directions:

1. In a bowl, combine Worcestershire, vinegar, mustard, and Char-Griller Steak seasoning. In a gallon-sized plastic bag, pour marinade over flat iron steaks. Be sure to coat entirely. Marinate in the refrigerator for 30-60 minutes. Remove steaks and discard the marinade. Preheat your Char-Griller Flat Iron Griddle to high heat. Season steaks with salt and pepper to taste. Cook to medium rare (130°f) for best results. About 12-14 minutes, turning once at the halfway point. Use a meat thermometer to ensure proper doneness. Remove steaks and let rest for 5 minutes. Slice thinly across the grain and enjoy!

Mexican Street Corn

Cooking Time: 15 Min

Ingredients:
- 4 ears fresh corn, in the husk
- ¼ C. mayonnaise
- ¼ C. sour cream or Mexican crema
- ½ C. finely crumbled Cotija or feta cheese, plus more for serving
- ½ Tsp. ancho or guajillo chili powder, plus more for serving
- 1 medium clove garlic, minced
- ¼ C. cilantro, finely chopped
- 1 lime, cut into wedges

Directions:
1. Pre-heat grill to 350°F. Trim the stalk slightly to avoid burning the tips of the corn. 2. Place directly on the grill for 15 minutes, rotating occasionally until the husks are slightly charred. Set aside to cool for 5 minutes. 3. While corn is on the grill, combine mayonnaise, sour cream or crema, cheese, chili powder, garlic, and cilantro in a large bowl. Mix well and set aside. 4. Pull back the husks on the corn, remove any remaining silk and cut off the stem. 5. Transfer to a large baking dish and pour in the mayonnaise mixture from Step 2. Roll the corn in the mixture until evenly coated. Slice corn cobs if desired or leave whole.
2. Transfer to a plate, sprinkle with extra cheese and chili powder and serve immediately with lime wedges. Enjoy!

Supreme Grilled Portobello Pizza

Ingredients:
- 1-4 Portobello Mushroom Caps
- 2 Tbsp Olive Oil
- 2 tsp Garlic Powder
- 1/2 Cup Pizza Sauce
- 1 Cup Shredded Mozzarella Cheese
- 1/2 Cup Cooked Sausage Crumbles
- 1/4 Cup Green Pepper, Chopped
- 1/4 Cup Onion, Chopped

Directions:
1. Scoop out the gills and cut out the stem of the portobello mushroom cap and brush with a mixture of olive oil and garlic powder.
2. Grill for 10 minutes at 425 degrees.
3. Top each with sauce, cheese, sausage, peppers and onions, return to grill for another 10 minutes. Serve!

Foil Packet Loaded Grilled Potatoes

Cooking Time: 15 Min

Ingredients:
- 4 Large Potatoes, Cubed Or Sliced (1 Potato Per Packet) Feel free to substitute a Sweet Potato If You'd Like
- Aluminum Foil
- 1 Stick Of Butter
- Salt and Pepper To Taste
- 1 Onion (Diced)
- 1 Cup Of Mushrooms (Sliced)
- 1 Cup Of Cheese (Shredded)

Directions:
1. Arrange each foil packet by lightly spraying or oiling the bottom before adding 1 potato, butter, salt and pepper to taste, onions, mushrooms, and cheese. Fold each packet closed before placing it on the grill for 30-35 minutes or until contents are soft to your liking. Add any additional toppings like bacon bits, sour cream or chives. Serve warm, enjoy!

Hasselback Potatoes

Cooking Time: 15 Min

Ingredients:
- 1 lb. extra-large baking potatoes
- ½ lb. Applewood smoked bacon
- 2-3 slices of cheddar cheese, or preferred, cut into 1" squares
- 1 stick butter, melted
- 1 Tsp. dried minced onion
- ½ Tsp. garlic powder
- 1 Tsp. chili powder
- ½ Tsp. smoked paprika
- ¼ Tsp. Kosher salt
- ¼ Tsp. black pepper
- 1-2 green onions, thinly sliced (optional)
- Sour cream (optional)

Directions:
1. Scrub potatoes, rinse and pat dry with paper towel.
2. Fry bacon in a pan to desired crispness according to package directions, drain grease and crumble when cool. Set aside in a small bowl.
3. Combine dried minced onion, garlic powder, chili powder, smoked paprika, Kosher salt and black pepper into a small bowl and mix well. Poke each potato several times with a fork, brush with olive oil and season with rub ingredients, to taste.
4. Wrap each potato in 2 layers of aluminum foil and place on the grill at 400°F for 1 hour to bake.
5. After potatoes are done, remove from grill and slice each potato equally into ½-1" sections, leaving a ½ inch at the bottom.
6. In between each slice, place a small slice of cheese and some bacon. Brush with melted butter and sprinkle your seasoning of choice.
7. Place potatoes in a large cast iron skillet to bake on the grill at 400°F for 15 minutes, or until cheese is melted.
8. To serve, top with sour cream, more crumbled bacon and sliced green onions if desired

Smoked Irish-style Lamb And Potatoes

Cooking Time: 3 Hrs

Ingredients:
- 4-5 lb. boneless leg of lamb
- 3 Tbsp. fresh rosemary
- 6 cloves garlic, minced and divided into 3rds
- 2 Tbsp. black pepper
- 3 Tbsp. Kosher salt
- 3 Tbsp. olive oil
- 15 medium potatoes, quartered
- 1 C. diced onion
- 1 bell pepper, seeded and diced
- Kitchen twine for tying
- Aluminum baking pan

Directions:
1. Rinse lamb and pat dry with paper towel.
2. Combine rosemary, 2/3 of minced garlic (4 cloves), 2 Tbsp. salt, pepper and olive oil into a small bowl and mix well.
3. Rub mixture all over lamb and tie securely in multiple spots with kitchen twine. Snip off any excess twine.
4. Combine potatoes, onion, pepper, remaining 1/3 of minced garlic (2 cloves), and 1 Tbsp. salt into sturdy pan. Mix well and set aside.
5. Add smokin' stone/heat deflector, place lamb on warming rack, and smoke at 250°F for 1 hour.
6. Place pan with potato mixture on grate under lamb (to catch drippings) and smoke for another 2 hours. Lamb is done when internal temperature reaches 140°F, for medium-rare.
7. Remove lamb from the grill, allow to rest for 20 minutes before slicing in 1"-1½" increments.
8. Cut and remove kitchen twine before serving.

Flat Iron Portobello Bun Burgers

Cooking Time: 10 Min

Ingredients:
- 1 Lb Ground Beef
- 1 Tbsp Onion Powder
- 1 Tbsp Garlic Powder
- 1 Tbsp Worcestershire Sauce
- 1/4 Cup Minced Garlic
- Salt and Pepper
- 6-8 Portobello Mushroom Caps
- 2 Tbsp Of Olive Oil

- Cheese Slices Of Your Choice
- Your Favorite Burger Toppings

Directions:
1. In a bowl, mix ground beef, onion powder, garlic powder, minced garlic, salt and pepper, and Worcestershire sauce. Shape into burger patties. Heat a zone to your Flat Iron to medium heat. Add olive oil and mushroom caps. Cook for about 3-4 minutes on each side. Remove from heat and set to the side. Add burger patties and cook for about 5 minutes per side to desired doneness. Add cheese to burgers and allow them to melt. Assemble burgers with one mushroom cap, the burger and any additional toppings, then top with another mushroom cap. Serve hot. Enjoy!

Easter Brunch French Toast

Cooking Time: 8-10 Min

Ingredients:
- 2 thick slices of Challah bread
- 5 strips of bacon
- 6 eggs (3 for frying)
- 1 C. heavy cream
- ¼ C. milk
- 1 Tsp. cinnamon
- Juice of ½ lemon
- Butter as desired for skillets
- Pinch of salt, optional
- Maple syrup, for serving
- Fresh berries, optional, for garnish

Directions:
1. Fry bacon in a cast iron skillet to desired crispness according to package directions, drain grease and wipe pan. Set aside on a plate and keep warm. 2. While bacon is frying, add 3 eggs to another skillet and prepare as desired, scrambled, sunny side up, etc. Cover and keep warm. 3. Beat remaining eggs in a medium bowl and add heavy cream, milk, cinnamon, lemon juice and a pinch of salt, if desired. Whisk until well blended. 4. Dip Challah bread in mixture, making sure to evenly coat both sides and add to hot cast iron skillet. 5. Cook for 2-3 minutes on each side until golden brown.

2. To serve, top French toast with maple syrup and fresh berries.

Flat Iron Lime Chicken And Mango Salsa Quesadillas

Cooking Time: 20 Min

Ingredients:
- 1 Lb of Chicken Breast, Shredded or Sliced into thin Strips or Bite sized pieces
- 1 Tsp of Salt
- 1 Tsp of Pepper
- 1 Tsp of Garlic Powder
- 1 Tsp of Cumin
- 1 Tsp of Parsley
- 1/2 Tsp of Paprika
- 1/2 Tsp of Cayenne Pepper
- 1 1/2 Tbsp of Fresh Lime Juice
- 1 1/2 Tbsp of Extra Virgin Olive Oil
- 2 Mangoes, Diced (If not ripe/sweet enough, may add small drizzle of Honey)
- 1 Red Pepper (Diced)
- 1/4 Cup of Cilantro (Chopped)
- 1 Tsp of Fresh Lime Juice
- 3 Cups of Pepper Jack, Monterrey Jack, Colby Jack or Mexican Blend Cheese(Your Choice)
- 4 Large Flour Tortillas
- 2 Tbsp of Butter for Pan

Directions:
1. Preheat Flat Iron to Medium Heat.
2. In a large bowl, mix together chicken pieces, desired oil and all seasonings until every piece is coated.
3. Add chicken to griddle and saute 5-7 minutes until cooked through and lightly browned. Add lime juice and cook for another 2-3 minutes. Remove from griddle.
4. In a small bowl, combine ingredients 10-15 for the mango salsa.
5. On a plate or tray, begin to assemble the quesadillas. Sprinkle cheese to fully cover half of a flour tortilla, add seasoned chicken and salsa, top with more cheese and fold.
6. Reheating the griddle to Medium Heat, add 2 Tbsp of butter and allow it to melt down. Place tortillas on top

of butter and flip every 2 minutes until cheese is melted and both sides reach desired crispiness.
7. Serve warm.

Grilled Stuffed Peppers

Cooking Time: 50 Min

Ingredients:
- 1/2 Pound Ground Beef
- 1 Cup No Sugar Added Tomato Sauce
- 1/2 Onion, Diced
- 3 Assorted Bell Peppers
- 1 Cup Cauliflower Rice
- 2 Cloves Garlic, Minced
- 1 tsp Oregano
- 1 Tbsp Salt
- 1 Tbsp Pepper
- Shredded Cheese of Choice

Directions:
1. Preheat grill to 350 degrees with a hot and cold zone.
2. Preheat a cast iron skillet over the hot zone. Add a tablespoon of olive oil and saute onions until translucent, add ground beef, garlic, oregano, salt and pepper.
3. Mix and cook ground beef until no longer pink, add cauliflower rice and tomato sauce.
4. Stir and cook 4-5 mins until heated through. Set aside to cool slightly.
5. While cooling, cut the tops off of each pepper and scoop out the ribs and seeds of the peppers.
6. Spoon the filling into each pepper and top with shredded cheese of your choice.
7. Place peppers in cast iron pan and bake in preheated grill with lid closed for 30-40mins, over the cold zone, until peppers are soft and cheese is melted.

Smoked Mac 'n Cheese

Cooking Time: 25-30 Min

Ingredients:
- 1 lb. elbow macaroni
- 3 C. milk
- 6 Tbsp. unsalted butter
- ½ C. all-purpose flour
- 2 C. smoked Gouda cheese, grated
- 1 C. shredded Cheddar, grated
- 1½ C. panko breadcrumbs
- ½ Tsp. black pepper
- 1 Tsp. garlic powder
- ½ Tsp. onion powder
- ½ Tsp. mustard powder
- Kosher salt, to taste

Directions:
1. Add pasta to a large pot of boiling salted water and cook according to package directions, 6-8 minutes. Drain well.
2. Meanwhile, heat the milk in a small saucepan until hot, being careful not to boil it. Whisk together 6 Tbsp. butter and flour in a large pot. Gradually add hot milk and cook for 1-2 minutes, stirring continuously, until thickened and smooth.
3. Remove from heat and add cheese, salt, to taste, and pepper, garlic powder, onion powder and mustard powder. Add cooked macaroni and stir well. Spoon mixture into cast iron pan.
4. Stir in breadcrumbs and sprinkle on top. Place pan on the grill at 350°F with a Smokin' Stone under the grates and bake for 25-30 minutes, or until the sauce is bubbly and the macaroni is lightly browned on top.

Grilled Apple Strudel

Cooking Time: 30 To 45 Min

Ingredients:
- 4 Granny Smith Apples
- 1 Cup Brown Sugar
- 1 Cup Golden Raisins
- 1 Sheet Frozen Puff Pastry, Thawed
- 1 Egg
- 1/4 Cup Milk

Directions:
1. Preheat grill to 400 degrees F (200 degrees C).
2. Line a baking sheet with parchment paper.
3. Peel, core and slice 3 apples. Peel, core and shred 1 apple. Place all prepared apples in a large bowl.
4. Stir in brown sugar and golden raisins; set aside.
5. Place puff pastry on baking sheet and roll lightly with a rolling pin.

6. Arrange apple filling down the middle of the pastry lengthwise. Fold the pastry lengthwise around the mixture.
7. Seal edges of pastry by using a bit of water on your fingers, and rubbing the pastry edges together.
8. Whisk egg and milk together, and brush onto top of pastry.
9. Bake on the grill for 35 to 40 minutes, or until golden brown.

2-burner Flat Iron Hot Dogs

Cooking Time: 7-10 Min

Ingredients:
- 1 Tbsp of Extra Virgin Olive Oil or Canola Oil
- 6 Hot Dogs, brand of your choosing
- 6 Hot Dog Buns
- 3 Tbsp of Butter
- Optional Toppings: Chili, Diced Onions, Jalapeno, Shredded Cheese, Condiments, etc.

Directions:
1. Preheat the Flat Iron to medium heat before adding oil. Arrange hot dogs on the flat top facing the same direction after ensuring they are all coated in the oil. Once the first side browns after 7-10 minutes, flip all the hot dogs over. Once the other side browns to your liking and the hot dogs are plump and brown, remove from the griddle. Spread butter on the interior of each hot dog bun and place them face down on the griddle tip until they are toasted to your liking. Assemble the hot dogs by placing one into each bun and adding desired toppings. Serve immediately. Enjoy!

Smoke Roasted Coffee

Cooking Time: 15 Min

Ingredients:
- 1/2 Pound Green Coffee Beans

Directions:
1. Light a single chimney of charcoal and get it entirely lit.
2. Drop that down into our AKORN and start adding some smoking chips to the fire. You can use whichever smoke wood you like, today we are going to go with white oak.
3. Get yourself a cast iron skillet, today I'm using an 8 inch model, a whisk, a colander, and some green coffee beans. Now that you're all set put the skillet on the grill grate and let it get hot. Once it is warmed up go ahead and add as many coffee beans to it that you feel you can stir and continuously agitate, for us that's gonna be about half a pound.
4. From here on out just focus on stirring the beans and about every minute close your lid for 10 or so seconds to let those beans soak in that smoke. After about 15ish minutes you should start hearing the first crack, it'll sound like popcorn. If you want a lighter roasted coffee you can take your beans off now but for a more medium roasted coffee let it keep going until you hear a second round of cracking.
5. At this point you want to cool your beans down immediately. We're going to do this by tossing them in a colander.
6. Tossing them does two things, one is it helps the beans cool more quickly and the other is as the beans are tossed in the air the husks will float off and not remain in our coffee beans.
7. From this point you just need to set your beans aside loosely covered for a day so they can off-gas and finish the process.
8. After that grind them up , make coffee your favorite way and prepare to have some of the best coffee you've ever had, and you made it all yourself on the grill.
9. Let me know how it works out for you and till next time, y'all take it easy.

Grilled Summer Corn Salsa

Ingredients:
- Shucked Sweet Corn - 4 ears
- Lime - 1
- Oil - 1 Tablespoon
- Cherry Tomatoes, Halved - 1 Cup
- Large Red Onion, Finley Diced - 1/4 of Onion
- Chopped Fresh Cilantro - 1/4 Cup
- Jalapeno Pepper, Finely Diced - 1

- Garlic Clove, Minced - 1
- Olive Oil - 2 Tablespoons
- White Wine Vinegar - 1 Tablespoon

Directions:

1. Growing up in a Mexican household, corn made an appearance on my kitchen table every day in some form or another - tortillas, street corn, cornbread and so many others! This Grilled Summer Corn Salsa is a new and delicious way of preparing fresh corn that's easy to make and perfect for BBQs. Serve it on top of your favorite grilled meats or as an appetizer with chips!
2. Prepare: Preheat grill to medium-high heat (between 400°F-450°F). Brush shucked corn and lime halves with 1 tablespoon oil.
3. Grill the corn: Grill the ears of corn with the lid closed for 10-15 minutes, turning occasionally, until corn is caramelized and dark brown spots appear on the kernels.
4. Grill the lime: While the corn is cooking, grill the lime halves cut side down on the cooking grates and remove them after grill marks appear, about 2-4 minutes.
5. Cool: Transfer the grilled ears of corn and lime halves to a large plate and let cool for 5 minutes, or until cool enough to handle.
6. Combine: Cut the grilled corn off the cob and transfer to a large mixing bowl. Squeeze the juice out of the grilled lime halves and add in all of the remaining ingredients. Toss together to combine, cover and refrigerate for 1 hour, up to 8 hours.
7. Serve with tortilla chips, on carne asada, or in a burrito bowl. Store leftovers in an airtight container in the refrigerator for up to 1 week.

Asian-inspired Sesame Soy Sauce

Cooking Time: 8 Min

Ingredients:
- 1/4 Cup Honey
- 1/4 Cup Soy Sauce
- 2 Tbsp Sesame Oil
- 1 Tbsp Sesame Seeds (Optional)

Directions:

1. In a small saucepan, add sesame seeds and lightly toast on medium heat for about 2 minutes before whisking in soy sauce, honey, and sesame oil. Bring the mixture to a brisk simmer over medium heat for about 2-3 minutes, stirring occasionally. Reduce heat to low heat and allow it to continue simmering for about 5-7 minutes. Allow sauce to thicken. Serve over a meat or dish of your choice or as a dipping sauce.

Flat Iron Fast Garlic & Balsamic Greens And Onions

Cooking Time: 10 Min

Ingredients:
- 3 Cups of fresh Spinach
- 3 Cups of fresh Kale
- 1 Tbsp of Garlic (Minced)
- 1 Cup of Red Onion (Sliced)
- 1 Cup of fresh White Mushrooms (Sliced)
- 2 Tbsp of Extra Virgin Olive Oil
- 1 1/2 Tbsp of Balsamic Vinegar
- Salt and Pepper to Taste

Directions:

1. Rinse off all vegetables thoroughly and strain.
2. Slice the onion and mushrooms.
3. Heat the Flat Iron to Medium Heat with 1 Tbsp of olive oil, then add minced garlic, onion, and mushroom. Stir until both are softened and water has cooked out
4. Add Balsamic Vinegar and continue to stir until it is absorbed. Remove from heat and set aside.
5. Heat another Tbsp of Olive Oil over Medium Heat. Add Spinach and Kale and stir until they begin to soften. Add the Onion and Mushroom mixture, then season with salt and pepper to taste. Cook until desired softness.
6. Serve warm.

Pork Tenderloin With Apple Chutney

Cooking Time: 25 Min

Ingredients:
- Pork Tenderloin - 1 to 1.5 Pounds
- Char-Griller Rib Rub
- Yellow Mustard - 1Tbs

- 5 Cups Cubed Apples
- 1 Cup Apple Juice
- 3 Tbs Apple Cider Vinegar
- 1 Tbs Butter
- 1 Tbs Olive Oil
- 1 tsp Honey
- 1 tsp Cinnamon Sugar
- 1/2 tsp Salt
- 1/2 tsp Dry Mustard
- 1/2 tsp Ground Ginger
- Pinch of Cayenne Pepper (Optional for Added Heat)

Directions:
1. Preheat grill to 325 F. Trim excess fat off pork tenderloin and apply yellow mustard as a binder. Season liberally with Char-Griller Rib Rub.
2. Put the pork tenderloin onto the grill once the temperature of the grill has reached 325 F.
3. Once the pork tenderloin has reached an internal temp of 145 F remove from the grill and let rest for 10 minutes. Serve with apple chutney and enjoy!
4. In a medium pot combine all the apple chutney ingredients and bring to a boil. Reduce heat to a simmer and cook until the apples are tender.
5. Serve and enjoy!

Honey Mustard Chicken

Cooking Time: 35 Min

Ingredients:
- 2-3 Lbs Split Chicken Breast
- 1/4 Cup Honey
- 1/4 Cup Mustard
- 1 Tsp Kosher Salt
- 1/2 Tsp Coarse Black Pepper
- 1/4 cup Honey
- 1/4 Cup Mustard
- 2 Tsp Apple Cider Vinegar
- 1 Tsp Worcestershire Sauce
- 1/2 Tsp Hot Sauce

Directions:
1. Trim any excess fat off the chicken and place in a container with the marinade mixture consisting of honey, mustard, salt, and pepper. Let chicken marinate for 3 or more hours.
2. When ready to cook prepare the grill to a temperature of 375 F. Remove excess marinade from the chicken and place indirectly on the grill.
3. Create your honey mustard sauce in a heat resistant bowl by adding honey, mustard, apple cider vinegar, Worcestershire sauce, and hot sauce. Bring to a boil and let simmer.
4. Once chicken has reached an internal temp of 160-162 F brush on the honey mustard sauce and let the chicken continue to cook till internal temperature is 165 F
5. Pull the chicken off the grill at internal temperature of 165 F. Serve and enjoy!

Egg Roll Burgers

Cooking Time: 15 Min

Ingredients:
- Ground Chicken - 1 lb
- Ginger Paste - 1 Tbs
- Sesame Oil - 1 Tbs
- Soy Sauce - 2 Tbs
- Coleslaw Mix - 2 cups
- Chopped Scallion - 1/4 Cup
- Chopped Cilantro - 1/4 Cup
- (Sesame Aioli) Mayonnaise - 1 Cup
- (Sesame Aioli) Sesame Oil - 1/4 Cup
- (Sesame Aioli) Soy Sauce - 2 Tbs
- (Sesame Aioli) Sriracha - 2 Tbs
- (Sesame Aioli) Honey - 2 Tbs

Directions:
1. Suggested Toppings: Coleslaw Cabbage, Fresh Cilantro, Avocado, Sliced Cucumber
2. In a large bowl, combine ground chicken, ginger paste, coleslaw mix, soy sauce, scallion, sesame oil, and cilantro. Form into 4 patties, and set aside.
3. Mix ingredients for crack sauce, set aside.
4. Preheat your Char-Griller. I used propane today, and cranked the heat to high. I love to sear my burgers on high, and then turn the heat to medium low to let them cook a little slowly. So- make sure your grill is nice

and hot, scraped clean, and spray your burgers with some non-stick spray for insurance.

5. Sear on each side for 3 minutes, then turn the heat to low, and close the lid- letting them cook through for 8 minutes.
6. Now we assemble! Grill your buns for extra points, then slather each side with the sauce. Add coleslaw mix, sliced avocado, cilantro, cucumbers, and the burger! Dig in and enjoy!

Dr. Pepper Bbq Chicken Wings

Cooking Time: 45 Minutes To 1 Hrs

Ingredients:
- Chicken Wings - 3 lbs
- 1 Tbsp Char-Griller Original Rub
- 12 oz. Dr. Pepper
- 1/4 Cup Water
- 1.5 tsp Brown Sugar
- 1 Tbsp Worcestershire Sauce
- 1.75 Cups Ketchup
- 1 Tbsp Chili Powder
- 1.5 tsp Kosher Salt
- 1.5 tsp Coarse Black Pepper

Directions:
1. Dry off chicken wings with a paper towel. Season wings with Char-Griller Original Rub lightly on both sides. Start fire and get grill up to 350 F.
2. Once grill is up to 350 F place the wings on the grill.
3. Pour Dr. Pepper into a small saucepan over medium heat and reduce until a syrupy consistency, approximately ½ cup reduced.
4. Add water, brown sugar, Worcestershire sauce, ketchup, chili powder, salt, and pepper to the saucepan and stir until the sauce has melded.
5. Set aside till wings are ready.
6. When the wings hit an internal temp of 165 F – 170 F it is time to remove them from the grill and put in a heat-safe bowl to sauce.
7. Pour sauce mixture onto the wings and toss until all sides of the wings are covered evenly.
8. Place on a serving platter and enjoy!

Bbq Bacon Cheeseburger Roll

Cooking Time: 50 Min

Ingredients:
- 6 Slices of Bacon
- 1/2 Pound of Ground Beef
- 2 Tbsp BBQ Spice Rub of Choice
- 1-2 Jalapenos, Diced
- 2 Sticks Cheddar Cheese (or Cheese of Choice)
- 1/4 Cup Sugar Free BBQ Sauce

Directions:
1. Setup grill for dual zones and preheat to 350 degrees.
2. Place bacon side by side on a sushi mat facing lengthwise.
3. Mix together ground beef, spice rub and jalapeños in a bowl.
4. Place beef mixture on the bacon leaving an inch farthest away from you uncovered.
5. On the end closest to you, place the cheese sticks in the meat mixture, opposite direction of the bacon.
6. Roll away from you using the sushi mat.
7. Grill on the cold side of the grill for 45mins on a grate or cast iron skillet.
8. Baste with bbq sauce, grill for 5 minutes, baste again, then grill for another 5 minutes.
9. Remove and let rest.
10. Slice into rolls and serve.

Hassleback Potatoes

Cooking Time: 25 Min

Ingredients:
- 6 Russet Potatoes
- 1 Pack of Cheddar Cheese Slices
- 1 Pack of Pepper Jack Slices
- Chipotle Powder
- Oregano
- Salt and Pepper to Taste
- Cooked Bacon (Diced)
- Chives (Sliced)
- Sour Cream

Directions:

1. Set up the Flavor Pro for indirect cooking. Ignite burners and turn to medium high. Cut thin slices in the width of the potatoes, but be careful to not slice all the way through. Wrap the potatoes in foil and place on the side of the grill away from the burners. Allow to cook until tender. About 45 minutes to an hour. Remove potatoes from grill and unwrap. Place alternating slices of cheddar and pepperjack in the potato. Season potatoes with chipotle powder, salt, pepper, and oregano. Place potatoes back on the grill unwrapped for 10 to 12 minutes or until cheese is melted. Garnish with bacon, chives, sour cream and serve.

Satay Chicken Wings

Cooking Time: 40 Min

Ingredients:
- 1 Dozen Party Wing Sections
- 1 Tbsp Cayenne Pepper
- 1 Tbsp Ground Coriander
- 1 Tbsp Turmeric Powder
- 1 Tbsp Salt
- Olive Oil
- 3/4 Cup Coconut Milk
- 3/4 Cup Peanut Butter
- 2 Tbsp Sriracha
- 1 Clove Garlic Minced Fine
- 1 Tbsp Ginger Paste
- 1 Tbsp Soy Sauce
- 1 Tbsp Lime Juice

Directions:
1. Preheat grill dual zoned to 350 degrees. In a large bowl toss the wings with the oil and coat evenly with the cayenne, turmeric, coriander and salt. Grill over the cold zone with the lid closed for 40 minutes.
2. While the chicken is grilling, combine the coconut milk, peanut butter, sriracha, garlic, ginger, soy sauce and lime juice in a bowl. Whisk until well incorporated.
3. After 40 minutes, remove the chicken and toss in the sauce. Place wings on the hot side of the grill and grill until sauce chars slightly. Around 3-5 minutes per side.

Chicken Lollipops

Cooking Time: 1.25 Hrs

Ingredients:
- Chicken Legs - 10
- Char-griller Grills Chicken Rub & Loot n' Booty Everything Rub
- Olive Oil
- Favorite BBQ Sauce
- Charcoal & Favorite Wood for Smoking

Directions:
1. Using the pairing knife and kitchen scissors, slice above the chicken ankle and slice around bone.
2. Using a paper towel pull back the tendons from the knob of the chicken leg and remove all the stringy tendons.
3. Wrap small piece of foil around the chicken leg.
4. Apply olive oil with brush to all sides of the chicken leg.
5. Season with favorite rubs.
6. Stand up the chicken legs on the baking rack: legs up.
7. Tip: to avoid issues with the chicken leg standing properly. Place two of them next to each other for support on the knobs of the chicken legs. During and after the cook they will be able stand on their own.
8. Preheat your Char-griller Grill/Smoker: ignite your charcoal using the Char-griller Grills Chimney. Maintain your fire temperature at 350°-400° through out the cook. Add favorite smoking wood atop the grill grate for a lingering smoke.
9. Tip: offset the fire/charcoal: place you fire opposite side of where your food will be placed.
10. Simply place the baking rack with the chicken leg lollipops on the opposite side of the fire
11. Tip: Every so often easily move the baking rack in a circular setting for even cooking. Use your Char-grill Grills heat resistant gloves for easy handling.
12. Cook chicken leg lollipops until they reach internal temperature 185° and not the normal 165° temperature for chicken.
13. Tip: Use the Char-Griller folding probe to take the guesswork out your cook.

14. Warm up your favorite BBQ sauce.
15. When internal temperature has been reached and BBQ sauce is warm, dip and coat the chicken leg lollipops into the sauce until they are nice and saucy.
16. Place the chicken leg lollipops back on the baking rack and in the Smoker/grill for an additional 15 minutes.
17. When done remove the foil from the chicken leg lollipops and dip and coat the chicken leg lollipops in the BBQ sauce one last time.
18. Place on a serving tray and enjoy.
19. Tip: Allow to rest for five minutes before eating.

Smoked Mashed Potatoes

Cooking Time: 1.5 Hrs

Ingredients:
- 3 Lb Bag Yukon Gold Potatoes
- 1 stick unsalted butter
- 1 Cup Heavy Whipping Cream

Directions:
1. Mashed Potato Process
2. Peel and cut potatoes so all so they are about the same size. This will ensure proper doneness throughout Bring 6 quarts of water to a rolling boil and add ¼ cup of Kosher Salt Cook potatoes until fork tender Drain Potatoes and return to same pot Add stick of butter (sliced evenly into 8 pcs) Add heavy whipping cream Add salt and pepper mix With a hand mashed (not electric mixer), mash potatoes and mix thoroughly Electric hand blender can cause the potatoes to get very gummy Allow potatoes to cool Scoop all potatoes into a 10" cast iron skillet Add 3 to 4 more thin slices of cold butter on top of potatoes
3. Smoking Process
4. Start smoker and heat to ambient temperature of about 250 degrees Add smoking wood I used post oak but I think either hickory or pecan would also be good Place skillet with potatoes on smoker for about 90 minutes or until potatoes are starting to turn golden brown on top Remove and serve immediately!

Grilled Carrots

Cooking Time: 25 Min

Ingredients:
- 2 Lbs. of Carrots, peeled with both ends trimmed
- 2 Tbsp of Olive Oil
- 2 Tsp of Kosher Salt
- Ground Black Pepper
- 1/2 Tsp of Cayenne Pepper
- 1 Lemon

Directions:
1. Combine the carrots with olive oil, salt, pepper and cayenne pepper. Heat one side of your grill to medium-high heat, turning often for 5-6 minutes until they begin to develop a char. Move the carrots to the indirect side of your grill and allow them to continue cooking for 15-20 minutes or until they are tender. Season to taste with any additional spices and serve immediately. Enjoy!

Smoked Buffalo Chicken Wing Dip

Cooking Time: 3.5 Hrs

Ingredients:
- 1 Small Chicken (4 to 6 lbs)
- 1/2 Cup Char-Griller Chicken Rub
- 1 Can of Beer
- 1/3 Cup Veggie Cream Cheese
- 1/3 Cup Blue Cheese Dressing
- 1/3 Cup Buffalo Sauce
- 1 tsp Garlic Powder
- 1/2 tsp Salt
- 1/2 tsp Pepper
- Celery, Carrots, Baguette, Crackers For Dipping

Directions:
1. From Aubrey: I don't know who needs to hear this, but SMOKED CHICKEN BELONGS IN BUFFALO CHICKEN DIP! It's football season, and if you're a fan of the games, or a fan of the snacks (hello, it's me), this smoky twist will truly take your tailgating to the next level. Let's dig in.
2. Fill a chimney with charcoal, and 3-4 small pieces of mesquite. Light, and let coals get hot. Add to smoke box, and adjust the air-flow to a small flow to ensure temperatures sit right around 275.
3. Rub chicken with Char-Griller Chicken Rub, and "stand up" on beer can. Place in smoker, close lid, and let

smoke for 3 hours, until chicken is done and has reached 165 internal degrees. Let cool, then shred.

4. Preheat oven to 375, and mix 1.5 cups shredded chicken with cream cheese, blue cheese dressing, buffalo sauce, garlic powder, and salt & pepper.

5. Transfer to an oven safe dish, and bake for 20 minutes, until golden brown and bubbly.

6. Serve with your favorite items for dipping. Enjoy!

Smoked Sweet Potatoes With Cinnamon Maple Butter

Ingredients:
- 5 Sweet Potatoes or Yams
- Olive Oil
- Himalayan Pink Salt
- Thai Spice
- Sugar Free Maple Syrup
- Maple Cinnamon Seasoning
- Butter

Directions:
1. Start by venting the potatoes with a fork Brush EVOO on the potatoes, fully covering them Sprinkle with Himalayan pink salt Heat your grill to 300° (We used our Akorn with B&B lump charcoal) Put the smoking stone in place Place your potatoes around the grill so they get indirect heat (This allows them to cook and absorb the smoke flavor without burning) Add a flavor chunk (We used Cherry) Flip the potatoes at the 1 hour mark Pull the potatoes when they are soft and have some give when you press in on them (Be careful as these will be extremely hot) Open the potatoes down the middle (Again, use caution as they will be hot) Use a fork to mix in Thai spice seasoning with the potato Add a dallop of butter and let it melt for an amazing side to Thanksgiving
2. Sugar Free Maple Cinnamon Butter
3. stick of butter, salted and soft SF Maple Syrup, 1/4 cup Maple Cinnamon Spice, 2 TBSP

Southwest Potato Skins

Cooking Time: 15 Min

Ingredients:
- 4 Potatoes, Cleaned
- 2 Tbsp Olive Oil
- Salt and Pepper to Taste
- 2 Tbsp Chopped Green Onions
- 2 Cups Chopped Spinach
- 1/2 Cup Corn
- 1/2 Cup Canned Black Beans, Drained and Rinsed
- Juice of Half a Lime
- 1/4 tsp Salt
- 1/2 tsp Cumin
- 1 Cup Monterey Jack Cheese, Shredded

Directions:
1. Light grill for indirect heat and heat grill to 350
2. Poke holes all around each potato with a fork. Brush potato with olive oil and season with salt and pepper
3. Place on grill for approximately 40 minutes, turning halfway through
4. In a skillet over medium heat, add corn, spinach, onions, beans, lime juice, and seasoning
5. Cook for 10 minutes until ingredients are heated through
6. Remove skillet from heat and allow to cool slightly
7. While filling is cooling, split potatoes in half lengthwise
8. Scoop out center of potato halves, leaving ¼" of the potato along the skin
9. Add a big pinch of cheese to each half, then fill cavity with a spoonful of filling
10. Sprinkle a generous amount of cheese on top of each half
11. Place potato halves directly on grill grates and grill until cheese is melted

Bbq Fiends Chicken Lollipop Recipe

Cooking Time: 45 To 60 Min

Ingredients:
- Chicken Drumsticks - 2 lbs
- Char-Griller Chicken Rub 1/4 Cup
- BBQ Sauce of Choice - 3/4 Cup
- Apple Juice - 1/4 Cup
- Honey - 1 tsp

- Tiger Sauce - 1 tsp
- Coarse Black Pepper - 1 tsp

Directions:

1. With your boning knife cut where the chicken starts to thin out going towards the joint. Cut all around the bone and use a paper towel to help with the removal of the skin and joint. Push the meat down towards the thick end of the drumstick to form the lollipop presentation.
2. Tip: You will notice tendons and a little bone that runs parallel to the leg after you have cut it. Make sure to remove these with your boning knife or kitchen shears.
3. Once all your drumsticks have been trimmed and free of tendons it is time to wrap the exposed bones in foil (this will help with presentation so you don't end up with burnt bones).
4. Tip: During this step I usually start my fire prep by lighting my charcoal chimney.
5. Next, use your seasoning and apply liberally to your lollipops. Make sure to get as even as a coat as possible.
6. For chicken lollipops, grill with indirect heat because you are looking to keep them moist and without char marks. Pour your charcoal chimney into one half of the grill and adjust air ducts.
7. Get your grill up to 325 F.
8. Add oak chunks as well just to give the meat an extra layer of flavor.
9. Once grill is up to temp arrange your chicken lollipops so they are standing up on the half of the grate that is not above the flame.
10. Tip: While your grill is coming up to temp you can refrigerate your chicken to help the seasoning process and to firm up the chicken a bit more. I find this helps with them standing up in lollipop form.
11. Let the grill do its work.
12. Start preparing the glaze by combining BBQ sauce, apple juice, honey, tiger sauce, and black pepper in a microwavable safe cup. Set aside till it is time to glaze.
13. Tip: I always warm my sauce right before it is time to glaze so that it is smooth and doesn't tack on to the meat too heavily. Microwave for 1 to 1 1/2 minutes right before you glaze.
14. Once your chicken has reached internal temp around 165 F, it is time to glaze.
15. Dip each chicken lollipop into the cup with your glaze mixture until you have obtained a nice shine.
16. Quickly put the chicken back on the grill and let the internal temp reach 170 F.
17. At this point you will pull the chicken off the grill and dip in the glaze again if needed.
18. Put on a platter and cover loosely with foil. Let rest.
19. Once the chicken has rested for about 10 minutes it is time to impress your family and friends.
20. Take that foil off and let the crowd be in awe of your creation! I promise they will be even more impressed once they get a taste!

2-burner Flat Iron Seasoned Mushrooms

Cooking Time: 5 Min

Ingredients:

- 1 Lb. of Portobello or Button Mushrooms Sliced
- 2 Tbsp of Butter
- 1 1/2 Tbsp of Extra Virgin Olive Oil
- 1 Tbsp of Soy Sauce
- 2 Tbsp of Minced Garlic
- Salt and Pepper to taste

Directions:

1. Perfect for serving alone, in a salad or even atop a burger, these seasoned and sautéed mushrooms are a must in your cooking arsenal. Once you make 'em once, we know you'll make 'em again. Give this easy and delicious dish a try tonight!
2. After preheating Flat Iron to medium-high heat, add oil and butter to the cooktop. Once the cooktop is heated, quickly toss the mushrooms with the soy sauce and garlic. Add the mushroom mixture to the cooktop ensuring the olive oil and butter are evenly distributed. Allow the mushrooms to brown for at least 5 minutes before flipping or stirring. Continue stirring mushrooms around the cooktop until they are done to your liking. Sprinkle desired amount of salt and pepper. Serve alone or as an addition to a meal of your choice. Enjoy!

Flavor Pro Bacon Wrapped Jalapeño Poppers

Cooking Time: 20 To 25 Min

Ingredients:
- 10 Jalapeno Peppers
- 1 (8 oz) Package of Cream Cheese, Softened
- 1 Package of Shredded Cheddar Cheese
- 20 Slices of Thin Cut Bacon
- 1/2 tsp Chipotle Powder
- 1/2 tsp Garlic Powder
- Salt and Pepper to Taste

Directions:
1. Halve the jalapeños and clean out all the seeds.
2. Mix together the cream cheese, 1 cup of cheddar cheese, chipotle powder, garlic powder, salt and pepper.
3. Fill the pepper halves with cream cheese mixture.
4. Wrap the peppers in strips of bacon.
5. Set up the Flavor Pro for direct cooking
6. Add 20 to 30 charcoal briquettes to the flavor drawer
7. Ignite charcoal with gas burners set to medium high
8. Once charcoal is lit, turn off gas burners and allow to fully ash over.
9. At this point, you can add a handful of soaked wood chips if desired.
10. Place wrapped jalapeños on grill for 20 to 25 minutes or until bacon is crispy.
11. Remove from grill and serve.

Pumpkin Pie Burnt Ends

Cooking Time: 2 Hrs

Ingredients:
- 4 to 5 Sweet Potatoes
- 5 Tbsp Pumpkin Pie Spice
- 2 Tbsp Brown Sugar
- 2 Sticks of Butter
- 1 Cup Packed Brown Sugar
- 2 Tbsp Light Corn Syrup
- 1/2 tsp Cinnamon
- 1/2 tsp Nutmeg
- 1 Cup Chopped Pecans

Directions:
1. "With Thanksgiving right around the corner and pumpkin spice season in full effect I thought it would be a great time to unveil my latest creation and show you how to make pumpkin pie burnt ends on the Char Griller AKORN Kamado.
2. This recipe can be served as appetizers, dessert, or just a decadent snack on these crisp fall days. There's not much to it but it is 100 percent worth the time to do it and do it right."
3. Start half a charcoal of chimney, drop into AKORN after fully ashed over and add two pieces of apple wood.
4. Insert Smokin' Stone, close AKORN and adjust dampers until it reaches 325 degrees.
5. Clean, peel, and cut 4 to 5 sweet potatoes into burnt end chunks roughly an inch and a half by an inch and a half.
6. Once your sweet potato burnt end chunks are cut, get them into some water for about half an hour to soak and get rid of some starch.
7. After they soak, pat them dry and begin to apply your pumpkin spice seasoning.
8. Once all the sides are coated in seasoning go ahead and load the sweet potato burnt ends onto a cooling rack and apply a little bit of brown sugar to the top of them.
9. Place the cooling rack on the AKORN grate and let it cook for about 2 hours.
10. Tip: I'd recommend coming out and checking them every half an hour by squeezing the biggest chunk and once it feels soft enough that you could squish it they're done.
11. In true burnt end fashion we need to sauce them up, so we'll throw together a praline sauce by combining the butter, 1 cup brown sugar, corn syrup, cinnamon, nutmeg, and chopped pecans.
12. Coat the sweet potatoes in the sauce and roast in the AKORN for about 3 minutes.
13. At this point they're ready to eat, just add some whipped cream and enjoy.
14. This recipe exceeded all of my expectations so definitely give it a try and if you do, let me know how it turned out for you.

Caribbean Jerk Pork Pineapple Salsa

Cooking Time: 20 Min

Ingredients:
- Pork Tenderloin - 1 to 2 Pounds
- Jerk Seasoning - 2 Tablespoons
- Whole Pineapple - 1
- Olive Oil - 1 Teaspoon
- Charcoal
- Additional Pineapple, Chopped - 1 Cup
- Large Tomatoes, Chopped - 2
- White Onion, Finely Chopped - 1/2 Cup
- Jalapeno (seeds removed to preference), Finely Chopped - 1/2 Jalapeno
- Pineapple Juice - 2 Tablespoons

Directions:
1. Jerk Pork Directions:
2. Remove all excess fat and silver skin from the pork tenderloin. Use the olive oil as a slather on both sides of the pork tenderloin to help get the rub to stick. Carefully season both sides of the pork tenderloin with the jerk seasoning making sure it has a nice even coat.
3. Let the pork tenderloin rest and absorb the seasoning while you prep the pineapple. Split the pineapple vertically and use a knife and spoon to hollow one side of the pineapple out (this will be the presentation side.) Be sure to save the pineapple as it will be used later for the salsa.
4. Start prepping your fire and working on getting your grill up to 325 F. Once your grill has reached 325 F put the pork tenderloin on indirect heat. Once the pork tenderloin has reached around 150 F internal move it to direct heat and sear it until internal is 160 F. Pull the pork tenderloin and let rest for 10 minutes. Cut up into 1 ½ inch cubes and serve with pineapple salsa. Enjoy! *Tip* While your grill is hot put some pineapple on it to add an extra layer of flavor to your salsa.
5. Pineapple Salsa Directions:
6. In a bowl combine the pineapple, onion, jalapeno and pineapple juice. Let marinate for 3-5 minutes.
7. Add chopped tomatoes into the bowl with the other ingredients. Stir well.
8. Let the mixture marinate so the flavors can meld. Serve and enjoy! *Tip* If you let the pineapple salsa marinate for 1-3 hours the flavors will have time to meld together.

Dirty Bird Chicken Wings

Cooking Time: 30 Min

Ingredients:
- 12 to 14 Whole Chicken Wings
- Olive Oil
- Char-Griller Creole Seasoning to Taste
- Sazon to Taste
- Adobo to Taste
- Char-Griller Lemon Pepper Rub
- Garlic Powder to Taste

Directions:
1. Rinse Chicken Wings with cold water and pat dry.
2. Trim/remove access fat, skin and hair.
3. Apply coating of olive oil to both sides of the chicken.
4. Add Sazon, Char-Griller Grills Creole, Char-Griller Grills Lemon Pepper and adobo seasonings.
5. Heat up the AKORN Kamado with lump charcoal to 375°
6. Place the chicken wings in the grill.
7. Flip the wings in 15 minutes.
8. Grill the chicken wings until internal 175° and remove.
9. Eat them right off the grill and enjoy!

Blueberry Jalbanero Smoked Wings

Cooking Time: 2.5 To 3 Hrs

Ingredients:
- Blueberries - 1 Cup
- 1/2 Jalapeno - seeds removed/chopped
- 1/2 Habanero - seeds removed/chopped
- 2 Garlic Cloves - Minced
- Ketchup - 1/4 Cup
- Molasses - 1/8 Cup
- White Vinegar - 1 and 1/3 Tbsp
- Ground Mustard - 1/2 Tbsp
- Spicy BBQ Sauce - 2 Tbsp

- Salt and Pepper to Taste
- Chicken Wings (Frozen or Fresh) - 3 Lbs
- Char-Griller Chicken Rub

Directions:
1. Add all ingredients, expect the wings and Char-Griller Chicken Rub, to sauce pan on medium high heat until it simmers stirring often.
2. Drop to medium-low heat and cook for 30 minutes. Should continue to slightly simmer. Berries will burst.
3. After the 30 minutes, take off heat and let cool for 15 minutes. Add contents to food processor and pulse until you get a smooth consistency similar to a thicker buffalo wing sauce. Continue to let cool then refrigerate until it's ready to add to wings.
4. Set up Char-Griller for indirect heat at 325°f and use cherry wood or your favorite smoking wood
5. Thaw wings and pat dry. Coat wings with Char-Griller chicken rub and let sit for 10-15 min in refrigerator while your grill comes to temp.
6. Tip: You can use Fresh Chicken Wings here if you prefer
7. Once the grill is reaches 300-325°f, place wings on baking pan with cooling rack or directly on the grates.
8. Rotate and flip wings once every 30-45 minutes to ensure an even cook. Wings are done when you have a nice rich mahogany color. Looking for internal temp of 170-180°f. Usually 2 ½ - 3 hours in the smoker should do the trick.
9. Brush on Blueberry Jalbanero wing sauce and enjoy!

Smoked Classic Apple Pie

Cooking Time: 45 Min

Ingredients:
- 8 oz Cream Cheese, Softened
- 1/2 Cup Butter, Softened
- 1.5 Cups of Flour
- 1/4 Cup of Sugar
- 6 Cups of Apples
- 1/4 Cup Flour (Filling)
- 3/4 Cup of Sugar (Filling)
- 1 tsp Cinnamon (Filling)
- Dash Salt (Filling)
- 2 Tbsp Butter (Filling)

Directions:
1. There's just something different about anything you make outside on a grill. With just the right amount of smoke we're gonna push this American classic over the edge and make it a next level crowd pleaser. Here's Cookout Coach's Smoked Apple Pie Recipe.
2. Load Char-Griller AKORN with charcoal and light ¾ chimney full of charcoal. Once the chimney is completely lit add it to the AKORN along with one chunk of apple wood.
3. Place the Cooking Stone in place along with the grate and allow the AKORN to come up to 375 degrees with no visible smoke.
4. Core, peel, and quarter 6 cups worth of apples and set aside.
5. Combine crust ingredients together until the dough is formed
6. Add pie filling ingredients to the cut apples and workin in gently. Once there are no more visible dry ingredients place mixture to the side.
7. Either roll out or use your hands to form the crust into a pie pan and cover the bottom and sidewalls.
8. Add apple mixture into the pie pan keeping the apples as even as possible.
9. Add 2 Tbsp of butter and 2 Tbsp of caramel to the top of the apples.
10. Roll out the remaining dough to make a cover for the pie, place cover over the pie and pinch together where the top meets the sides.
11. Cut 4 slits in the top of the pie.
12. Place pie pan on grate at 375 degrees. And let cook for 45 min or until the top of the crust is golden brown.
13. Remove from grill and let cool. Slice and enjoy.

Grilled Juicy Skirt Steak With Cilantro Pesto

Ingredients:
- Orange Juice - 1/2 Cup
- Lime Juice - 1/4 and 3 Tablespoons (Save 3 Tablespoons for Sauce)
- Olive Oil - 1/4 Cup

- Soy Sauce - 2 Tablespoons
- Worcestershire Sauce - 2 Tablespoons
- Apple Cider Vinegar - 1 Tablespoon
- Minced Garlic - 1 Tablespoon
- Red Pepper Flakes - 1/2 Teaspoon
- Ground Cumin - 1/4 Teaspoon
- Skirt Steak - 1 to 2 Pounds
- Kosher Salt and Pepper to Coat
- Loosely Packed Cilantro - 3 Cups
- Cotija Cheese - 1/3 Cup
- Chopped Red Onions - 1/4 Cup
- Garlic - 1 Clove
- Coarse Kosher Salt for Sauce - 1 Teaspoon
- Ground Pepper for Sauce - 1/4 Teaspoon
- Olive Oil for Sauce - 1/2 Cup
- Lime Juice - 3 Tablespoons
- Slivered Almonds - 1/2 Cup

Directions:
1. For the skirt steak:
2. Make the marinade: In a medium bowl, whisk together all of the ingredients except for the skirt steak.
3. Marinate in the fridge: Place the skirt steak in a large baking dish or gallon size zip lock bag and pour the marinade on top. Turn the steak a few times until it's completely coated with marinade and refrigerate for 2 to 6 hours. Do not marinate for longer than 8 hours because the meat will start to break down.
4. Preheat grill to medium-high heat (about 400°F-450°F) for direct-heat grilling.
5. For Gas Grilling: Simply light all the burners on high, close the lid and let the grill heat up for 5-10 minutes.
6. For Charcoal Grilling: Open the lid and the bottom/side vents, remove the grill grates and set aside. Fill a chimney starter with charcoal briquettes. Place one or two fire starter cubes or wadded-up newspaper onto the charcoal grates and place the chimney starter on top. Light the cubes or newspaper underneath the chimney and let the briquettes heat up for 15 minutes. When the briquettes are lightly covered with ash, use a pair of heat-resistant insulated gloves and carefully spread out the hot coals in an even layer. Carefully place the cooking grates back on, close the lid, open the top vent and let the grill heat up for about 5-10 minutes.
7. Prepare the steak: Remove steak from marinade and discard any excess marinade. Pat steak dry with paper towels and season lightly with coarse salt and black pepper on both sides.
8. Grill the steak: Grill the skirt steak with the lid closed for about 3-4 minutes per side for medium rare, or longer depending on the thickness and your desired doneness.
9. Rest and Slice: Transfer the grilled steak to a cutting board and let it rest for 5 minutes. Slice thinly across the grain and serve with cilantro pesto.
10. For the pesto:
11. 1. Combine cilantro, cojita, red onion, almonds, garlic clove, coarse kosher salt, ground black pepper, olive oil, and 3 Tbs lime juice to food processor or blender and pulse until mostly smooth.

Smoked Mac & Cheese

Cooking Time: 1-2 Hrs

Ingredients:
- 1 Package of Elbow Macaroni
- 1/2 Stick of Butter
- 1/4 Cup of All Purpose Flour
- 1 Cup of Heavy Cream
- 1 Cup of Milk
- 2 Cups of Cheddar Cheese (Shredded)
- 1 Cup of Gouda Cheese (Shredded)
- 1 Cup of Colby Jack Cheese (Shredded)
- 1/2 Cup of Cream Cheese
- 2 Tbsp of Black Pepper
- 1 Tsp of Cayenne Pepper
- 1 Large Cast Iron Skillet

Directions:
1. Boil elbow macaroni according to package instructions for al dente. Preheat the smoker to 225 degrees using a fruity hardwood like apple or cherry in the smokebox. If your grill does not have the smokebox attachment, easily turn it into a smoker by arranging coals/wood opposite of where you place the mac and cheese pan. If you place the pan on the right side of the

grates, simply place wood on the right side for an indirect cooking experience. Heat the cast iron skillet over medium heat, then melt butter and whisk in flour. While continuing to whisk, add milk and heavy cream bringing to a boil. Reduce to low-medium heat and whisk in cream cheese until smooth. Whisk in the rest of the cheeses continuing to stir until melted and smooth Turn off the heat then stir in macaroni noodles until thoroughly mixed with cheese sauce Place the entire skillet in the smoker and cook for 1-2 hours until desired doneness. Keep in longer for more smoky flavor. Serve hot.

Maple Bourbon Rubbed Stuffed Chicken Breasts

Cooking Time: 20 Min

Ingredients:
- 6 Chicken Breasts
- Sea Salt To taste
- Maple Bourbon Rub, To Taste (Or Your Favorite Chicken Seasoning)
- 3 Sweet Peppers (Diced)
- 1 Jalapeno (Diced)
- 1/2 White onion (Diced)
- 1/2 Cup Mozzarella Cheese (Shredded)

Directions:
1. Step 1 - Dice peppers and onions and brown in skillet, set aside
2. Step 2 - Shred cheese, set aside
3. Step 3 - Tenderize each chicken breast with a fork, pay dry
4. Step 4 - Season with salt and let the chicken sweat for a few minutes, stuff with peppers and cheese and season chicken breasts
5. Step 5 - Heat grill up to about 450° ~ place chicken on grill and cook to an IT of 165°. Make sure to toss in a chunk of cherry for that nice smokey flavor
6. Step 6 - Pull, let rest and serve with some pan sheet veggies or a salad

Caprese Grilled Chicken

Cooking Time: 20 Min

Ingredients:
- 4 Boneless Skinless Whole Chicken Breasts
- 4 Slices of Fresh Mozzarella Cheese
- 6 Slices of Roma Tomato
- 6 Large Basil Leaves
- 2 Tbsp of Unsalted Butter
- 1/4 Cup of Balsamic Vinegar
- 2 Tsp of Salt
- 2 Tsp of Black Pepper
- 1 Tsp of Dried Oregano
- 1 Tsp of Dried Basil
- 1/2 Tsp of Cayenne Pepper
- 1 Tsp of Garlic Powder
- 1 Tsp of Onion Powder

Directions:
1. Spice up your regular backyard BBQ with an inviting rendition of an Italian classic. Check out this Caprese Grilled Chicken recipe for flavor that won't disappoint.
2. Preheat the grill to medium-high heat. Be sure grates are lightly oiled. Season the chicken breast with salt, pepper, oregano, dried basil, cayenne pepper, garlic powder and onion powder. Place chicken on the grill. On the stove, combine balsamic vinegar and butter. Place on high heat until boiling then reduce to low heat and simmer until reduced by half. Reduction should be thickened. Once chicken is nearly finished, top each breast with a slice of mozzarella. Cook for a few additional minutes until melted. Remove the chicken from the grill and top each breast with a tomato slice and basil. Drizzle to your liking with reduction. Serve immediately, enjoy!

Smoked Roasted Vegetables

Cooking Time: 15 Min

Ingredients:
- 1 medium onion
- 1 zucchini
- 1 small green bell pepper
- 1 small red bell pepper
- 1 small yellow bell pepper
- Vegetable oil, for brushing

- Salt and pepper, to taste

Directions:
1. Pre-heat grill to 400°F. Rinse all produce and pat dry with paper towel. 2. Slice bell peppers in half and remove stem, core and seeds. Remove outer layers of onion and slice in half. Slice zucchini in half and remove ends. 3. Place vegetables on grill, equally spaced apart and grill for 10-12 minutes, turning occasionally, until vegetables are tender and grill marks develop. Skins of bell peppers should be lightly charred. 4. Lightly brush vegetables with olive oil. Sprinkle with salt and pepper or your favorite seasoning.
2. Slice vegetables into 1" strips when cooled enough to handle and serve. Enjoy!

Smoked Rack Of Lamb With Orange Marmalade Glaze

Ingredients:
- 3-4 lb Rack of Lamb (Untrimmed)
- Dried Rosemary - 2 Tbsp
- Coarse Ground Pepper - 2 Tbsp
- Kosher Salt - 2 Tbsp & 1 tsp
- Olive Oil 3/4 Cup
- White Pepper - 1 tsp
- Orange Marmalade - 6 oz Jar
- Orange Juice - 6 oz
- Butter - 2 Tbsp

Directions:
1. Take lamb rack and trim any excess fat.
2. You want the fat cap to be about ½ inch thick on the cap side of the rack.
3. Mix rosemary, black pepper, salt and olive oil together in a bowl to make marinade.
4. Place lamb rack in ziptop bag and pour marinade mixture inside.
5. Ensure that the marinade is covering the rack and remove as much air from the bag as possible (if you have a FoodSaver even better).
6. Allow the lamb rack to marinate for a minimum of 8hrs.
7. Once you remove the lamb from the bag, let the olive oil drain in a pain.
8. For added crust, sprinkle a 50/50 mix of coarse ground pepper and Kosher salt on the fat cap before cooking
9. Combine orange marmalade, orange juice, salt and pepper and olive oil in a sauce pan and mix together to make glaze.
10. Bring to a low boil and simmer for 15 minutes stirring periodically.
11. This will allow the glaze to reduce and thicken.
12. Once ready to serve, add the melted butter and stir.
13. Prepare your grill for indirect heat.
14. Using lump charcoal and post oak (or your favorite type of smoking wood), heat the grill to a consistent 260°F.
15. Place the rack of lamb bone side down.
16. Insert an internal meat thermometer in the thicket part of the rack, being careful not to have the thermometer touching bone
17. This will cause a false temperature reading and a raw rack of lamb.
18. Once the rack has reached an internal temperature of 130-135°F (for medium rare) remove the lamb.
19. OPTIONAL – increase your grill temperature to 500°F and sear the lamb, fat side down for 2-3 minutes maximum for a nice charred outer texture
20. Remove rack from grill and let rest for 10 minutes.
21. With a large carving knife, slice between the bones to create the lamb chops.
22. Drizzle with glaze or serve glaze on the side

Grilled Romaine Salad With Creamy Jalapeno Ranch Dressing

Cooking Time: 20 Min

Ingredients:
- Bacon - 6 Strips
- Cherry Tomatoes - 10.5 Ounces
- Sweet Corn - 2 Ears
- Romaine Lettuce (halved lengthwise) - 3 Heads
- Olive Oil - For Greasing
- Crumbled Cotija Cheese - 1 Cup
- Hard Boiled Eggs (Halved) - 4
- Flaky Sea Salt and Ground Pepper

- Mayonnaise - 6 Tablespoons
- Milk - 6 Tablespoons
- Sour Cream - 1/4 Cup
- Dried Parsley - 1/4 Teaspoon
- Onion Powder - 1/4 Teaspoon
- Chopped Chives - 1 Tablespoon
- Garlic - 1 Clove
- Coarse Kosher Salt - 1/4 Teaspoon
- Ground Pepper - 1/4 Teaspoon
- Lime Juice - 2 Tablespoons
- Cilantro - 1/4 Cup
- Pickled Jalapeno - 4 Slices

Directions:
1. For the salad:
2. Cook the bacon: Place bacon strips in a cold large nonstick skillet. Turn the heat to medium and cook for 8-12 minutes, turning occasionally, until brown and crispy. Transfer to a large plate covered in paper towels and set aside to cool.
3. Preheat grill to medium-high heat (about 400°F-450°F) for direct-heat grilling.
4. For Gas Grilling: Simply light all the burners on low, close the lid and let the grill heat up for 5-10 minutes.
5. For Charcoal Grilling: Open the lid and the bottom/side vents, remove the grill grates and set aside. Fill a chimney starter with charcoal briquettes. Place one or two fire starter cubes or wadded-up newspaper onto the charcoal grates and place the chimney starter on top. Light the cubes or newspaper underneath the chimney and let the briquettes heat up for 15 minutes. When the briquettes are lightly covered with ash, use a pair of heat-resistant insulated gloves and carefully spread out the hot coals in an even layer. Carefully place the cooking grates back on, close the lid, open the top vent and let the grill heat up for about 5-10 minutes.
6. Skewer the tomatoes: While the grill is heating up, thread the cherry tomatoes onto 4 large metal skewers. (If using wooden skewers, be sure to soak the skewers in water for 20 minutes beforehand so they don't burn on the grill.)
7. Prepare the remaining ingredients: Brush or spray the ears of corn, cherry tomatoes and the inside of the romaine lettuce halves with olive oil or cooking spray.
8. Grill the corn: Grill the ears of corn with the lid closed for 10-15 minutes, turning occasionally, until corn is caramelized and dark brown spots appear on the kernels. Transfer to a large plate or baking sheet and set aside.
9. Grill the tomatoes and lettuce: Grill the tomatoes and lettuce cut-side down with the lid open for about 3 minutes. Turn the tomatoes occasionally and remove when charred and blistered. Remove the lettuce when the cut-side is slightly charred. Be careful not to grill too much or the lettuce will wilt. Transfer to a large plate or baking sheet and set aside.
10. Cut the corn and crumble bacon: Cut the grilled corn off the cob and crumble the cooled bacon.
11. Serve: Place grilled lettuce cut-side up on a large serving platter and season with salt and pepper. Drizzle with creamy jalapeno ranch dressing and top with grilled corn kernels, grilled cherry tomatoes, crumbled bacon, cotija cheese and hard boiled eggs.
12. For the dressing:
13. Add all ingredients to a blender of food processor and blend until smooth.
14. (mayonnaise, milk, cup sour cream, dried parsley, onion powder, chopped chives, plus more for garnish, garlic, coarse kosher salt, ground black pepper, lime juice, cilantro, pickled jalapeños)

Cheddar Jalapeño Chicken Burgers

Cooking Time: 20 Min

Ingredients:
- 1 Package Of Ground Chicken
- 1/2 Cup Of Yellow Onion
- 1 Tbsp Of Cilantro
- 1 Tbsp of Parsley
- 2 Tbsp Of Minced Garlic
- 2 Tbsp Of Finely Chopped Jalapeno
- 1 Tsp Of Cumin
- 1 Tsp Of Black Pepper
- 1 Tsp Of Paprika
- 1/2 Cup Of Cheddar Cheese (Tiny Cubes or Shredded)
- 1 Tbsp Of Sea Salt

- Lettuce
- Mayonnaise As Needed
- Sliced Red Onions
- 4-6 Burger Buns

Directions:

1. In a medium bowl, combine the ground chicken, garlic, onion, jalapeño, cheese, and all seasonings and spices. Mix thoroughly using your hands, but be sure not to over ground the meat. Form patties of your desired thickness and size. Cook the burgers on your preferred grill over medium-heat, ensuring they are thoroughly cooked before serving, given it is a poultry product. Serve patties on a burger bun, topped with mayo, lettuce, onions, and any other desired condiments.

Easy Grilled S'mores

Cooking Time: 5 Min

Ingredients:

- 4 Whole Graham Crackers Split Into Halves (8 Total)
- 4 Jumbo Marshmallows
- 2 Chocolate Bars
- Aluminum Foil

Directions:

1. If not already fired up, preheat the grill to medium heat. Arrange 4 aluminum foil packets, with one fully assembled s'more per packet (one chocolate square and one marshmallow per 2 graham cracker squares.) Grill each packet for about 5 minutes or until the marshmallows are melted. Additionally, you can only put the chocolate and graham crackers in the foil alone and individually roast marshmallows on a skewer for that delicious charred taste prior to layering on your s'more. Serve immediately, enjoy!

Louisiana Hot Link Sausage & Smoked Cornbread Dressing

Cooking Time: 60 Min

Ingredients:

- Cornbread: 2 1/2 Cups, Crumbled
- Salt: to taste
- Creole Seasoning: to taste
- Garlic Powder: to taste.
- Celery: 2 Ribs (Diced)
- White Onion: 1/2 cup (Diced)
- Olive Oil: 2 Tablespoons
- Cranberries: 1/3 Cup
- Chicken Stock: 2 Cups
- Char-Griller Grills Competition Pro 8125
- Fogo Eucalyptus Lump Charcoal with Mesquite & Apple Smoking Wood.
- Disposable Gloves: Golden Protective Services Black Diesel Gloves

Directions:

1. Heat up a skillet with olive to medium heat and sauté the Evergood Louisiana Hot Link Sausage, cranberries, onions, celery and also add garlic powder. Cook until the veggies are soft and sausage starts to brown, takes roughly 15 minutes. Then set aside to cool down for a few minutes. Using a large bowl, combine the crumbled cornbread, Creole Seasoning, salt, sausage/veggie mix and chicken stock. Combine thoroughly with your hands with disposable gloves. Mixture will be moist. Add mixture to a pan. Fire up your smoker/grill to 250° and smoke uncovered for 60 minutes. It will become golden brown. Serving Tip: taste excellent with brown gravy. Serve and enjoy!

Bourbon Maple Grilled Wings

Cooking Time: 1 Hrs

Ingredients:

- 3 Lbs Chicken Wing Sections
- Char-Griller Chicken Rub - 3 Tbsp
- Butter - 1 Tbsp
- Finely Diced Onion - 2 Tbsp
- 1/2 Cup Bourbon Whiskey
- 3/4 Cup Grade-A Maple Syrup
- Tomato Paste - 2 Tbsp
- 1 Sprig Fresh Rosemary
- A Drop of Hot Sauce
- Char-Griller Chicken Rub - 1.5 Tbsp (For Sauce)

Directions:

1. Make Sauce: Melt butter in a medium saucepan over low-medium heat. Add onion. Allow to cook for 4 minutes, stirring once.
2. Add whiskey, maple syrup, tomato paste, rosemary, Char-Griller Chicken Rub, and hot sauce. Use whisk to combine. Bring heat to low and simmer for 6 minutes, stirring occasionally. Set aside to let cool.
3. Rinse wings and pat dry with paper towel. Coat all sides of wings with Char-Griller Chicken Rub. (Tip: Use binder like a light coating of vegetable oil or mustard to help rub stick.
4. Prepare gas side of Char-Griller Texas Trio for indirect heat. Ignite the center burner and turn to high. Leave left and right burners in the off position.
5. Place wings on left and right side of the center burner. Keep smaller wings further away from the flame.
6. Close lid and allow to cook for 20 minutes.
7. Flip wings over and cook for another 20 minutes.

Flat Iron Lemon Pesto Vegetable Medley

Ingredients:
- 1/2 Cup Of Pesto (Homemade or Store-bought)
- 1 Fresh Lemon
- 1 Lb Zucchini Cut Into Small Chunks
- 1 Lb Yellow Squash (Cut Into Small Chunks)
- 1 Orange Bell Pepper (Cut Into Medium Chunks)
- Salt and Pepper To Taste

Directions:
1. In a bowl, combine pesto, butter and juice from half the lemon (optionally grate lemon zest in as well). Add salt and pepper as needed. Whisk thoroughly. Toss vegetables into pesto mixture and mix until all pieces are coated. Cover the bowl and place in the refrigerator. Marinate for 2 hours - overnight. Preheat Flat Iron to medium heat and add vegetables. Cook for 20 minutes or until desired tenderness. Serve hot. Enjoy!

Grilled Cauliflower

Cooking Time: 20 Min

Ingredients:
- 2 large heads cauliflower
- ¼ C. extra-virgin olive oil
- ½ Tsp. garlic powder
- ½ Tsp. paprika
- Kosher salt
- Freshly ground black pepper
- 2 C. shredded Cheddar
- Sriracha sauce for drizzling
- 8 slices cooked bacon
- 2 Tbsp. finely chopped chives

Directions:
1. Remove and discard the leaves from each cauliflower head, then trim the stem so that the cauliflower can lay flat on cutting board. (Leave the core intact!)
2. Cut each cauliflower into thick slices about 3/4" thick. Reserve any loose florets to cook with the steaks. In a small bowl, whisk together olive oil, garlic powder, and paprika. Season mixture with salt and pepper.
3. Heat a grill or a grill pan to medium. Brush one side of each steak with the olive oil mixture and place the brushed side down on a grill. Brush the top sides with the olive oil mixture and cook until tender and charred in spots, about 8 minutes per side. Top each cauliflower with cheese and cook until melted.
4. Toss extra florets in the olive oil mixture and grill, turning often, until charred and tender, about 6 minutes.
5. Drizzle cauliflower with sriracha sauce then sprinkle cooked bacon and chives on top.

Irish Nachos

Cooking Time: 15 Min

Ingredients:
- 3 Medium Size Russet Potatoes (Sliced 1/4 Thick)
- 1 Cup Shredded Cheese
- 4 Slices of Bacon
- 1 Green Onion (Sliced Thinly)
- Sour Cream
- Char-Griller Original Seasoning
- Sea Salt
- Oil

Directions:
1. Heat 2 middle burners on the flat iron to medium Add bacon slices and cook until crispy, flipping once during cooking. Slide bacon over to the side to stay

warm while cooking the potatoes Increase heat to high and add a tablespoon or two of oil to griddle, over any remaining bacon grease and allow to heat up Add potato slices on top of oil and season with Char-Griller's seasoning and sprinkle evenly with salt Allow potatoes to crisp up, about 7-8 minutes and flip each slice over. Season again with Char-Griller's seasoning and salt and allow to get brown and crispy on the other side Remove bacon from griddle, crumble, and set aside Remove potatoes from griddle and add to an over safe plate. Add cheese and bacon and place plate directly back on the griddle. Cover with a melting dome or large metal bowl and allow cheese to melt Carefully remove plate with a pot holder when cheese is melted. Garnish with green onions and a spoonful of sour cream

Smoked Sweet Potatoes

Cooking Time: 20 Min

Ingredients:
- (5) Sweet Potatoes or Yams
- Olive Oil
- Himalayan Pink Salt
- Thai Spice
- Sugar Free Maple Syrup
- Maple Cinnamon Seasoning
- Butter

Directions:
1. Start by venting the potatoes with a fork Brush EVOO on the potatoes, fully covering them Sprinkle with Himalayan pink salt Heat your grill to 300° Put the smoking stone in place Place your potatoes around the grill so they get indirect heat (This allows them to cook and absorb the smoke flavor without burning) Add a flavor chunk Flip the potatoes at the 1 hour mark Pull the potatoes when they are soft and have some give when you press in on them (Be careful as these will be extremely hot) Open the potatoes down the middle (Again, use caution as they will be hot) Use a fork to mix in Thai spice seasoning with the potato Add a dollop of butter and let it melt
2. Sugar Free Maple Cinnamon Butter

3. stick of butter, salted and soft SF Maple Syrup, 1/4 cup Maple Cinnamon Spice, 2 TBSP

Classic Bbq Sauce

Cooking Time: 3 Min

Ingredients:
- 2 Cups Of Ketchup
- 2 1/2 Tbsp Honey
- 1/4 Cup Apple Cider Vinegar
- 2 Tsp Liquid Smoke
- 4 Tbsp Brown Sugar
- 2 Tsp Paprika
- 1 Tsp Garlic Powder
- 1 Tsp Onion Powder
- 1 Tsp Yellow Or Dijon Mustard
- 1/2 Tsp Black Pepper
- 1/2 Tsp of Sea Salt

Directions:
1. Whisk together all the ingredients in a saucepan over medium heat. Bring the mixture to a simmer before reducing to low heat. Simmer for about 10 more minutes until the sauce thickens. Transfer to an airtight container and store in the refrigerator.

Gravity 980 Smoked Ribs

Cooking Time: 2 Hrs

Ingredients:
- 1 Rack of Baby Back Ribs
- 1 Cup of Apple Cider Vinegar or Apple Juice
- 1/4 Cup of Water
- Olive oil
- 2 Tbsp of Brown Sugar
- 1 Tbsp of Chili Powder
- 1 Tbsp of Paprika
- 1 Tsp of Cumin
- Kosher Salt
- Black Pepper

Directions:
1. Accomplish mouthwatering ribs in half the effort with the Gravity 980. Go low n' slow for the perfect

baby backs and turn all of your attention to the taste and flavor of your food.

2. Combine all seasonings in a small bowl. Combine water and apple cider/juice in a spray bottle. After removing the membrane from your ribs and patting dry, rub your seasoning into the meat with your hands. Remove the fire shutter from your Gravity 980, load the hopper then light it and set the temperature to 225-250°F. Place the ribs on the rack with the meat facing up. Smoke for 3 hours without opening the lid. Spritz the ribs generously with the apple/water mixture every hour until ribs reach desired doneness. Optionally, for the 3-2-1 method, after the first 3 hours, wrap the ribs then return to the smoker for 2 hours before unwrapping and smoking for 1 additional hour. Glaze the ribs with your favorite BBQ sauce and return to the Gravity for 20 minutes. Glaze one more time and smoked for 10 more minutes. Allow the ribs to rest for 10 minutes before cutting. Enjoy!

2-burner Flat Iron Eggplant Parmesan

Cooking Time: 10 Min

Ingredients:
- 1 Large Eggplant, 1/2 inch slices
- 2 Large Tomatoes, 1/2 inch slices
- 1/2 Cup of Extra Virgin Olive Oil
- 2 Tbsp of Minced Garlic
- 1 Tbsp of Italian Seasoning or Choice of Herbs
- 1/2 Cup of Grated Parmesan
- 1 Cup of Shredded Mozzarella
- Salt & Pepper
- Optional Toppings/Garnishes: Balsamic Vinegar, Basil Leaves

Directions:
1. Preheat your Flat Iron to medium heat. In a small bowl, combine olive oil and minced garlic. Align eggplant and tomato slices on a baking sheet and brush each side with the olive oil mixture. Sprinkle each side with salt and pepper as well. Allow 3-4 minutes for the oil to set in. In a small bowl, combine Italian Seasoning with Mozzarella and Parmesan cheeses. Place the eggplant and tomato slices on the preheated griddle.

Cook for about 4-5 minutes per side once they begin to brown. Flip and cook for 2-3 more minutes. Place one tomato slice on each eggplant slice. Top with the cheese and herb mixture. Allow to cook for 4-5 more minutes or until the cheese has melted. To quickly melt cheese, cover with the Char-Griller Basting Dome. Remove each eggplant tomato stack from the griddle and top with balsamic vinegar, basil leaves or any other desired additions. Serve with crostini or as your main dish. Enjoy!

Flavor Pro Smokey Grilled Chicken Wings

Cooking Time: 20 To 25 Min

Ingredients:
- 4 Pounds of Chicken Wings
- Char-Griller Chicken Rub
- Olive Oil
- BBQ Sauce of Your Choice (If Desired)
- Wood Chips of Choice

Directions:
1. Prepare the Flavor Pro for direct grilling – Light the gas burners and reduce to medium heat and allow to preheat.
2. Rub chicken wings with olive oil and season liberally with Char-Griller Chicken Rub.
3. Add one handful of soaked wood chips to the Flavor Drawer.
4. Place chicken wings on grill and allow to cook for 20 to 25 minutes or until internal temperature is 170 degrees.
5. Remove wings from grill and toss with favorite BBQ sauce if desired.

2-burner Flat Iron Omelet Rounds

Cooking Time: 15 Min

Ingredients:
- 4 Large Eggs
- 4 Tbsp of Milk or Water
- 1/3 Cup of Shredded Cheese
- Salt and Pepper to taste

- Optional Toppings: Diced Onion, Diced Peppers, Diced Mushroom, Chopped Bacon or Sausage

Directions:

1. In a small bowl, whisk together your eggs, milk/water, salt, pepper, and any desired ingredients. Preheat your Flat Iron to medium heat. Gently grease the inside of your egg rings (Optionally, you can use a large outer slice of an onion). Place them on the cooktop and allow them to warm up for 2-3 minutes. Carefully pour your egg mixture into each ring, filling nearly to the top. To thoroughly cook the egg all around, cover with the Char-Griller Basting Dome. Cook for about 10 minutes until eggs are cooked to your liking. Add cheese to the top of each round and cover once more with the Basting Dome. Remove from the Flat Iron. Serve immediately. Enjoy!

Creole Smothered Chicken

Cooking Time: 40 Min

Ingredients:
- Chicken Legs
- Shortening
- File (Pounded or powdered sassafras leaves)
- Paprika
- Cajun/Creole Seasoning
- Chicken Bouillon Powder
- 4 oz Water
- 1.5 Tbsp Garlic-fresh or jarred
- 1/2 Onion, Chopped
- 3 Tbsp Self-Rising Flour
- 1 Cup White Rice

Directions:

1. This was a weekly staple in my house growing up. My Mom & both Grandmothers all made it and they all made it all amazing. It's a very popular and easy dish to make with big time Louisiana flavor and lot's of history behind it.
2. It's also simple & low cost to make & you can use any cut of chicken you have available, it doesn't have to be chicken legs. I began to make this dish long before I started to BBQ. It's one that is close the heart and will always be served at my house."
3. Generously season chicken on all sides with: paprika, Cajun/Creole seasoning & Chicken Bouillon powder.
4. Add Shortening to Cast Iron skillet: enough to coat the bottom of the cast iron skillet.
5. Heat cast iron skillet to medium/high heat on your Char-griller Grills side burner.
6. Add chicken to the cast iron skillet once the oil is hot.
7. Brown one side of the chicken, turn the chicken then add the chopped onions & chopped garlic to the chicken & cook for five minutes.
8. Add flour & mix thoroughly for a few minutes.
9. Add bottled water & mix thoroughly.
10. Lower the side burner to low heat.
11. Add Filé & mix thoroughly.
12. Allow the chicken & gravy to cook on low heat for roughly 25-30 mins. No need to use a lid/cover.
13. Tip: turn chicken roughly every 5-10 minutes for even cooking.
14. Cook chicken to internal temperature 165°.
15. Cook 1 cup of white rice in 2 cups of water and salt to taste.
16. Boil water to high with the rice & all the ingredients & stir. Wait until you see the water boiling, once it begins to boil turn the the dial on the side burner to low.
17. Cover the pot with a lid and let the rice slowly cook for about 30 minutes.
18. Serve over white rice & favorite vegetable.
19. Enjoy.

Mushroom Bacon Swiss Blended Bison Burger

Cooking Time: 15 Min

Ingredients:
- Baby Bella Finely Chopped Mushrooms - 12 Ounces
- Ground Bison - 2 Pounds
- Chopped Bacon - 6 Strips
- Steak Seasoning - 2 Tablespoons
- Ranch Seasoning - 1 Tablespoon
- Crushed Pork Rinds - 1 Cup
- Swiss Cheese

- Caramelized Onions

Directions:
1. Mix mushrooms, bison, bacon, seasoning & crushed pork rinds.
2. Form into burger patties.
3. Grill in cast iron skillet.
4. Top with swiss cheese & caramelized onions

Raptor Claws

Cooking Time: 2 Hrs

Ingredients:
- 4 jalapeño peppers
- 1 lb. ground sausage, divided into 4 equal parts
- Jalapeño cream cheese
- Original All-Purpose BBQ rub, to taste
- Favorite BBQ sauce

Directions:
1. Pre-heat grill to 250°F. Rinse jalapeños and pat dry with paper towel. 2. Cut the top off each jalapeño and remove the core and seeds. 3. Stuff with cream cheese. 4. Wrap ¼ lb. of sausage around each jalapeño, starting from the open end and leaving the tip of the jalapeño uncovered. 5. Season sausage with your favorite rub, or use Original All-Purpose BBQ rub, to taste. 6. Place on the grill at 250°F to smoke for 1 hour before turning. 7. Smoke for another 30-45 minutes. 8. Baste with your favorite BBQ sauce and smoke for an additional 15 minutes.
2. Remove from grill, allow to cool and serve.

Smoked Bone-in Pork Shoulder Steak

Cooking Time: 2 Hrs

Ingredients:
- Bone-in Pork Shoulder Steaks (1 1/2 to 2 in. thick) - 2
- Char-Griller Rib Rub- To Your Tasting
- Cranberry Juice - 1/2 Cup
- BBQ Sauce - 1/2 Bottle
- Apple Wood/Charcoal

Directions:

1. Season both sides of the pork steaks liberally with Char-Griller Rib Rub. Set aside and to allow the steaks to marinate. Begin prepping the fire to 275 F. *Tip* Put a water pan inside your smoker to allow for extra moisture.
2. Once the smoker has reached 275 F put the pork steaks onto the grill and let the smoker do the work.
3. Around the 45-minute mark pull the steaks and wrap individually with foil and add ¼ of the cranberry juice to each foil packet. Put back on the smoker at 275 F.
4. Once the steaks reach around 198 F take them out of the foil packet and sauce with your favorite BBQ sauce. Put back in smoker for another 10 minutes to let the sauce settle.
5. Pull the steaks from the grill and let rest for 10 minutes. Serve and enjoy!

Brown Sugar Maple Bacon

Ingredients:
- 1 3.5 pound Pork Belly (Skin Removed)
- 1 Cup of packed Brown Sugar
- 1 Cup of your favorite Maple Syrup
- 2.5 Tablespoons of Kosher Salt
- 1.5 Tablespoons of ground Black Pepper
- 0.5 teaspoons of Cinnamon
- 1.25 teaspoons Of Curing Salt

Directions:

1. Get your pork belly completely thawed in the refrigerator. Remove from packaging and remove the skin (if the butcher has not previously done this for you). Completely pat dry on all surfaces. Set aside. In a one (1) gallon sealable freezer bag, combine your Brown Sugar, Maple Syrup, Kosher Salt, Black Pepper, Cinnamon and Curing Salt. Mix well. Place your pork belly inside the sealable bag with all of the curing ingredients. Seal the bag and move belly and ingredients around to cover all sides of the belly completely in the solution. Squeeze all of the air out of the bag (or as much as you can) and place the bag with the belly on a cooking rack or in a shallow pan. This will catch any liquid seepage from the bag over the 7 days.

2. Pro Tip: Using 2 bags, the outer bag will catch seepage and this will not affect the curing process.
3. Pro Tip: Use a vacuum sealed bag for this step if you have the means, otherwise the sealable bags work fine.
4. Place inside the refrigerator where it will remain for 7 days. FLIP the bag ONCE per day (preferably every 24 hours exactly). After 7 days, removed the bag from the fridge, remove the belly from the bag and RINSE thoroughly. The idea is to get all of the excess curing solution off of the exterior of the belly. You should notice your belly has taken on a darker color form the brown sugar and maple syrup. This means your cure has taken to the meat!! Once rinsed off, pat dry again with paper towels, removing as much excess moisture as possible. Set aside in your fridge for another 30 minutes to an hour, to further let it air dry in the cool temps. Get your grill/smoker/cooker up to a temperature of 180 degrees Fahrenheit (82.2 Celsius) for an indirect cooking method. Place the pork belly on the cooking grates away from the heat source. Cook belly until an internal temperature of 155 degrees Fahrenheit (68.3 Celsius) is achieved.
5. Pro Tip: Use probe thermometers to better keep track of the cookers temperature and the belly's internal temperature.
6. Once the internal temp is achieved, remove belly from the cooker and let rest on a cutting board, loosely covered in foil for approximately 20-25 minutes. All done! Slice it as thin or as thick as you prefer, fry it up and enjoy!! Store in vacuum sealed bags and keep it in your fridge or freezer

Jalapeño Poppers

Cooking Time: 30 Min

Ingredients:
- 12-14 Jalapeños
- 1 Lb Bacon
- 1 Block Cream Cheese
- 2 Tbsp Morton Salt Nature's Seasoning

Directions:
1. Preheat grill to 325F and set up for indirect cooking. Halve and core jalapeños. Mix cream cheese and nature's seasoning well. Fill jalapeños halves with cream cheese mixture and wrap in bacon. (Tip Grill Pinz are great for holding bacon in place.) Grill indirect until bacon crisps up (approx 30-40 minutes) Remove, let cool a few minutes and enjoy!

Perfect Ribeye Steaks On The Akorn

Cooking Time: 30 Min

Ingredients:
- Ribeye Steaks From Butcher Or Local Market
- 5-6 Medium Potatoes
- Couple Handfuls Of Green Beans
- Butter
- Olive Oil
- Salt/Pepper to Taste

Directions:
1. Set Akorn/Kamado to about 400 degrees F Take Steaks out of fridge, pat down with paper towels, drizzle and wipe down with small amount of olive oil and season with your favorite spices! Salt and Pepper are fine here. I like to leave the steaks out of fridge at this point on the counter, but you may put back in fridge if you like. Slice/chop up potatoes into 1" cubes, place in aluminum foil packet with butter and your favorite spices (again, salt/pepper will taste great!) Place green beans in aluminum foil packet with butter and favorite spices Once grill is up to temp, place potatoes and green beans directly on the grates. After 20 minutes, flip potatoes and green beans 15-20 minutes later remove potatoes and green beans Let grill raise temp until about 450-500 F Place steaks directly on grill and let cook for 2 minutes Twist steaks 90 degrees and let sit for 2 minutes (creates the crosshatch) Flip steaks and let cook for 2 minutes Twist steaks and let cook for 2 minutes You should now be at rare / medium rare - continue to cook until you reach the desired temperature your family likes. Enjoy!

Flat Iron Sundried Tomato Omelet

Cooking Time: 10 To 15 Min

Ingredients:
- 2 to 3 Eggs
- 2 Tbsp Milk

- 1 Tbsp Sundried Tomatos
- 1 to 2 Slices Diced Ham
- 1/8 Cup Mozzarella Cheese, Shredded
- Fresh Basil, Chopped
- Salt and Pepper to Taste

Directions:
1. Whisk together eggs, milk, and salt and pepper
2. Preheat griddle to medium high and add desired oil
3. Pour egg mixture on griddle using the spatulas to make sure it doesn't spread too much.
4. Allow to cook for 2 to 3 minutes and add in tomatoes, cheese, ham and basil to one side of the omelet and use the spatula to fold over the other side to make the omelet.
5. Turn down the burner to medium low and allow to cook until cheese is melted, flipping once.

Smoked Jerk Chicken

Ingredients:
- 1/2 Onion, Chopped
- 4 Green Onions, Chopped
- Fresh Thyme - 2 Tbsp
- Ginger - 1.5 Tbsp
- 8 Garlic Cloves
- Cinnamon - 1 Tbsp
- Allspice - 1 Tbsp
- White Pepper - 1 Tbsp
- Sea Salt - 2 Tbsp
- Nutmeg - 1/2 Tbsp
- Brown Erythritol (or Brown Sugar) - 2 Tbsp
- Sugar Free Honey - 2 Tbsp
- Soy Sauce - 2 Tbsp
- Chicken Boullion Powder - 1 Tbsp
- 2 Scotch Bonnet or Habanero Peppers
- 3 Pounds of Bone-In Chicken Pieces

Directions:
1. Blend all of the ingredients until well incorporated. The mixture will be thick and paste-like, not completely smooth.
2. Put the marinade in a large plastic bag with 3 pounds of bone in chicken pieces, and marinate for at least 24 hours.
3. Smoke chicken for 3 hours at 275 with wood of choice.
4. Serving suggestion: Pair with braised cabbage.

Bacon Cinnamon Rolls

Cooking Time: 8 To 10 Min

Ingredients:
- Can of Cinnamon Rolls
- 8 Slices of Bacon

Directions:
1. Heat AKORN with Smokin' Stone and drip pan to 350 degrees.
2. Grease an 8 or 9 inch round pan.
3. Open the can of cinnamon rolls and separate the rolls.
4. Unroll the Rolls.
5. Cook bacon on grill until crisp but still flexible.
6. While bacon is still warm, places two slices of bacon on top of 1 unrolled cinnamon bun and roll bun back up.
7. Repeat steps for other rolls.
8. Place cinnamon rolls in pan and cook until golden brown.
9. Top with icing and serve warm.

Sweet Potato Medallions

Cooking Time: 30 Min

Ingredients:
- 1 Large Sweet Potato, 1/2 inch slices
- Olive Oil
- 4 oz. Goat Cheese
- 1 Tbsp Heavy Cream
- 1 Tbsp Honey
- 1 Tbsp Dried Cranberries, Chopped
- 1 Tbsp Walnuts, Chopped
- 1 tsp Fresh Thyme, Chopped

Directions:
1. Light grill for indirect heat and heat grill to 375 degrees
2. Brush both sides of the sweet potato slices with olive oil
3. Sprinkle them with cinnamon and sugar on both sides

4. Place slices directly on grill or on a mesh cooking tray
5. Allow the slices to cook for 15 minutes then turn over and cook for an additional 15 minutes
6. Mix together goat cheese, cream, and honey in a small bowl
7. Spoon a teaspoon of the cheese mixture on the warm sweet potato slices
8. Sprinkle each slice with cranberries, thyme, and walnuts
9. Drizzle with honey before serving

Grilled Lemon Pepper Potatoes

Cooking Time: 20-25 Min

Ingredients:
- 1 Lb Of Russet Or Red Potatoes (Sliced Or In Cubes)
- 1/2 Tbsp Of Garlic Powder
- Extra Virgin Olive Oil
- Salt
- Char-Griller "Lemon Pepper" Rub

Directions:
1. Preheat your grill to high heat. In a bowl, toss potatoes with a generous amount of olive oil, garlic powder, salt and desired amount of salt and the Char-Griller "Lemon Pepper" Rub. Place potatoes in a foil packet. Fold it to cover the food and twist the edges to seal it close. Place on your grill and cook for 20-25 minutes or until desired tenderness or crispiness., ensuring to mix/flip potatoes midway through.

2-burner Flat Iron Asparagus

Cooking Time: 5 Min

Ingredients:
- 1 Lb of Asparagus, woody ends cut off (for more tender results, lightly boil them for 2-3 minutes first)
- 2 Tbsp of Extra Virgin Olive Oil
- 2 Tsp of Garlic Powder
- 1/2 Tsp of Salt
- 1/2 Tsp of Pepper

Directions:

1. Pat your asparagus spears completely dry. In a small bowl, combine olive oil, garlic powder, salt and pepper. Toss the asparagus with the oil mixture, ensuring each spear is thoroughly coated. Heat your Flat Iron to medium-high heat. Arrange asparagus on the cooktop in a single layer. Cook for 4-5 minutes before turning them with tongs, allowing the other side to cook. Continue turning until they are tender to your liking. Remove from the griddle and serve hot or warm. Enjoy!

Grilled Garlic Bread

Cooking Time: 3-5 Min

Ingredients:
- 1 Loaf of French bread
- 1 Cup Of Salted Butter(Soft)
- 5 Tbsp Of Extra Virgin Olive Oil
- 1 1/2 Tbsp Of Minced Garlic
- 2 Tsp Of Parsley
- 2- 3 Tbsp Char-Griller "Garlic & Herb" Rub

Directions:
1. Preheat your grill to medium heat. Combine all ingredients aside from bread into a bowl and whip together. You should have a whipped, buttery consistency. Split the bread in half lengthwise before cutting in half or simply cut it into slices. Spread the mixture onto the face of the bread. Lightly brush some of the mixture onto the sides and bottom as well. Place your bread on the grill and cook for 3-5 minutes or until desired crispness or brownness before flipping over. Remove from the grill and if there are burnt minced garlic pieces, feel free to brush them off. Sprinkle with parsley and cut to desired serving sizes. Serve warm, enjoy!

Bacon Egg And Cheesesteaks

Cooking Time: 20 Min

Ingredients:
- 2 (12 Oz) Packs Of Shaved Steak
- 1 Lb Provolone Cheese
- 4-5 Fresh Eggs
- 4-5 Hoagie Rolls

Directions:

1. Cook the bacon to your liking – move to the side (non-heated) Cook up the shaved steak until the pink is about gone – move to the side Crack your eggs and fry them to your liking Make piles of the meat, top with cheese, then bacon, then the fried eggs Use the rolls like a tent to melt the cheese Scoop them up on to a platter / plates

Griddle Cheesesteaks

Cooking Time: 15 Min

Ingredients:
- 2 Lbs of Shaved Beef Steak
- 2 Tbsp of Extra Virgin Olive Oil
- 2 Cups of Thinly Sliced White Onions
- 1 Cup of Chopped Green Peppers
- 4 Sub Rolls
- 4 Tbsp of Unsalted Butter
- 12 Slices of Provolone Cheese
- Sea Salt and Black Pepper to taste

Directions:
1. Heat the olive oil on medium heat in one zone of Flat Iron. Add onion and green peppers, seasoning with desired amount of sea salt and black pepper. Stir until softened. Remove from heat. Add raw steak to the same zone of the Flat Iron on medium heat. Lightly season with salt and pepper to taste. Using spatulas, shred and stir steak, ensuring all of the steak browns. Add onion and peppers to steak and thoroughly mix together, allowing them to continue to cook together for 2 minutes. At the same time, melt butter in a separate zone on medium heat. Place rolls open and faced down and allow the inside to brown and lightly toast. Set aside. Separate steak into 4 equal piles then add 3 slices of cheese to melt along each pile. Place one toasted sub roll face down on top of each steak pile and use spatula to scoop steak, onion and pepper mixture into the roll. Serve hot, enjoy.

Grilled Arrachera Pita

Cooking Time: 15 Min

Ingredients:
- 1-2 Pounds of Arrachera Steak
- Favorite Marinade
- Pita
- Pita Toppings: Tomatoes, Cheese, Onions, Ranch Etc.

Directions:
1. Make your favorite marinade. James used a combination of Char-Griller Steak Rub, Pompeian Olive Oil, Blues Hog Raspberry Chipotle, McCormick Parsley Flakes & fresh garlic.
2. Place the marinade in a bowl with the arrachera. Set in the fridge for roughly three hours.
3. Fire up your Char-griller Grill and preheat to high heat.
4. Tip: Arrachera/skirt steak is thin and is best when cooked quickly.
5. Remove the arrachera from the the marinade and allow to get to room temperature.
6. Place the arrachera on the grill over the hot coals for roughly 5-6 mins per side.
7. Remove the arrachera from grill and allow to rest for five minutes. Then chop it up into small pieces.
8. Warm the Pitas on the grill for a few seconds on each side and remove.
9. Create the pita by adding the arrachera and then top it off with tomatoes, onions and then drizzle it with ranch.
10. Enjoy!

Garlic And Herb Grilled Zucchini

Cooking Time: 10 Min

Ingredients:
- 2-3 Zucchini (Cut Into 1/2 Inch Slices)
- 1/4 Cup of Extra Virgin Olive Oil
- 2 Cloves of Garlic(Minced)
- 1 Tbsp of Italian Style Seasoning
- 2 Tbsp of Shallot(Minced)
- 1 Tbsp of Fresh Rosemary(Finely Chopped)
- 1 Tbsp of Fresh Parsley(Chopped)
- Sea Salt and Black Pepper to Taste

Directions:
1. Preheat the grill to medium/high heat. In a bowl, combine ¾ of the olive oil, garlic, Italian seasoning,

shallot, rosemary, parsley and a dash of salt and pepper. Toss zucchini slices in the remainder of olive oil and lightly season with salt and pepper. Grill in a single layer and cooked until both sides have a light char and desired softness. Remove from the grill and drizzle with olive oil and herb mixture. Serve hot.

Grilled Fire Veggies

Cooking Time: 10 Min

Ingredients:
- Large Carrot Sliced in 1/4in. Bias Slices - 1
- Thinly Sliced Radish - 2 to 3
- Green and Red Pepper Rings - 1 Each
- Large Tomatoes Sliced in Wedges - 1 to 2
- Leek Sliced Along the Stem - 1
- Yellow Squash Sliced in 1/4in. Bias Slices - 1
- Cloves of Fresh Garlic Minced Finely - 2
- Salt and Pepper
- Olive Oil - 2 to 3 Tablespoons

Directions:
1. Toss all ingredients in a bowl and throw it on the grill
2. Cook at 350 degrees for 7 to 10 mins for a nice charred and still crunchy taste!

Saucin' Bacon Wrapped Cheesy Meatballs

Cooking Time: 1 Hrs

Ingredients:
- 1 Lb of Ground Beef
- Block of Cheddar Cheese
- Half Slab of Bacon
- Grill Pinz or Toothpicks

Directions:
1. pound Ground Beef: shape into meatball after meat is seasoned. Season meat with Loot N' Booty What's Your Beef Rub & Everything Rub to taste. ½ block cheddar cheese cut into small cubes: add cheese to the middle of the meatball. Half Slab of Bacon cut into half slices: Wrap meatball with the bacon. Seal bacon using Grill Pinz or toothpicks Prep grill/smoker: Used Char Griller Grills King Griller Smokin' Ace. Preheat grill/smoker & Smoke meatball at 300°: Used Fogo Lump Charcoal & Fogo Starters. Place meatballs in the Smokin' ACE and smoke for 40 minutes. Add sauce to the meatballs and smoke for an additional 20 minutes or until internal temperature 165°: Used Flo's Flavor Savory Sweet BBQ Sauce. Remove meatballs from the smoker & enjoy!

Good Morning Chili

Cooking Time: 2 Hrs

Ingredients:
- 16 Oz Original Pork Sausage, Cooked
- 8 Slices Bacon, Cooked
- 2/3 Cup Green Pepper, Chopped
- 2/3 Cup Yellow Pepper, Chopped
- 2/3 Cup Yellow Onion, Chopped
- 15 oz Can Black Beans, Drained
- 15 oz Can White Navy Beans, Drained
- 15 Oz can Stewed Tomatoes
- 10 oz Can Rotel
- 2 Tbsp Chili Powder
- 1 Tbsp Ground Mustard
- 1 tsp Onion Powder
- 1 tsp Coarse Ground Black Pepper

Directions:
1. Prepare AKORN for indirect heat at 250°F
2. Add all ingredients, undrained, to a large grill safe pot.
3. Cover and cook for approximately 2 hours, stirring occasionally. Once green peppers are tender to your liking, chili should be ready to pull off the grill.
4. Serve immediately and enjoy!
5. Optional - Serve chili over shredded hashbrowns and top with egg sunny side up, cheese, avocado, and hot sauce!

Certified Competition Smoked Ribs

Cooking Time: 3 1/2 Hrs

Ingredients:
- Full Slabs of Spare Ribs
- Sharp Knife

- Yellow Mustard
- Blues Hog Original Dry Rub Seasoning and Sauce.
- Blues Hog Original BBQ Sauce
- Sweet Baby Rays Barbecue Sauce
- Char-Griller Grills Rib Rub.
- Foil
- Butter
- Honey
- Apple Juice (Non Concentrate)
- Light Brown Sugar
- Golden Protective Services Nitrile Powder Free Gloves

Directions:
1. Trimming
2. Using a sharp knife slice and remove the breast piece which is the rib tip from the rack of ribs and set the breast aside for rib tip prep later. Then square out the ribs by removing the ends only if the they are
3. not straight. Also remove any access fat from top/meat side of the ribs.
4. Tip: If you can pull any fat, you should remove it. Tip: to remove the breast, lineup your knife with the fat line that is between the breast and rack of ribs. Some of the bones when slicing may be tough and thick but apply some pressure for a clean snap/break
5. Flip the ribs over so the bones are facing up. Remove the flap meat and set aside for rib tip prep later. Remove the membrane and discard. Remove any access fat.
6. Seasoning
7. Begin by leaving the the ribs bone side up. Apply coating of yellow mustard for a binder.
8. Tip: don't apply yellow mustard or rubs on the sides of the ribs. This helps the exposed bones from getting burnt during the smoking process.
9. Using Char-Griller Rib Rub & Loot N' Booty Everything Rub, apply even coating of the rubs on the ribs.
10. Tip: using two rubs versus all three Rubs on the bottom of the ribs helps prevent the bottom of the ribs from burning during the Smoking process.
11. Flip rubs to the top/meat side of the ribs. Apply coating of yellow mustard for a binder.
12. Tip: seasoning the bottom of the ribs first will help prevent the top/meat side seasonings from being messy.
13. Using Blues Hog Original Dry Rub Seasoning, Char-Griller Rib Rub & Loot N' Booty Everything Rub, apply even coating of the rubs on the ribs.
14. Ribs are now ready to be smoked.
15. Smoking
16. Using the Char-Griller Grills Smokin' Champ 1624, using the side firebox with fire up Fogo Premium & Eucalyptus Lump Charcoal blends. Use mesquite mini logs. Lock in the temperature to 220°-240°.
17. Tip: face the bone side of the ribs towards the side firebox.
18. Spritz every 30-45 minutes with Apple juice and rotate ribs.
19. Maintain Fire: add Fogo Charcoal and mesquite mini logs or chunks as needed.
20. Smoke for 3 1/2 hours.
21. Rib Wrapping
22. Using two pieces of foil, add butter, honey, blues hog original bbq/Sweet Baby Rays Barbecue sauces, rubs used, light brown sugar and apple juice to the foil. Then place ribs on top of the ingredients meat side facing down, then add additional butter, bbq sauce and rubs used to the bottom of the ribs. Fold the foil and they are ready for the pit again.
23. Place back in the smoker with meat side down and the bones facing the side firebox.
24. Allow to cook for 1 hour 30 minutes.
25. Remove ribs from the foil, sauce and leave on the smoker for 20 minutes.
26. Tip: discard the rib juices I using the Char-Griller drip pan that is under the grill grates and toss the foil away.
27. Remove Ribs and allow to rest for 15 minutes. Slice and enjoy.

Creole Italiano Spaghetti And Smoked Meatballs

Cooking Time: 1.2 Hrs

Ingredients:
- Ground Beef - 1 Pound

- Ground Sausage - 1 Pound
- Grated Cheese - 1/4 Cup
- Italian Bread Crumbs - 1/2 Cup
- Egg - 1
- Milk - 1/3 Cup
- Onion Diced - 1/2 an Onion
- Chopped Garlic - 3 Cloves
- Chopped Parsley - 2 Ounces
- Basil - to taste
- Spaghetti Noodles

Directions:
1. Prepping Directions:
2. Gather, combine & mix the listed ingredients in a large bowl for mixing:
3. Ground beef, ground sausage, grated cheese, Italian bread crumbs, egg, milk, onion, garlic, parsley, salt, black pepper, Italian seasoning, baking rack, rubber gloves.
4. Tip: Don't over mix the ingredients. Stop mixing once all the the ingredients are combined.
5. Shape meatballs into a ball to desired size. Most of the ones I made were Medium-Large in size.
6. Place meatballs on a baking rack. Using the baking rack allows easy for easy handling during the cooking process.
7. Cooking Directions:
8. Preheat your Char-Griller grill/smoker to 350°: ignite your charcoal using the Char-Griller Grills Chimney.
9. I used Fogo Charcoal Eucalyptus blend with two mesquite wood chunks atop the grill grate. Placing the wood chunks atop grill grate provides a slow lingering smoke to prevent the meatballs from being over smoked.
10. Maintain your fire temperature at 350°- 400°.
11. Offset your fire/charcoal: place your fire/charcoal opposite side of where your food will be placed. I placed my charcoal on the right side of the grill and the meatballs on the left.
12. Simply place the baking rack with the meatballs on the opposite side of the fire.
13. Tip: Every so often easily move the baking rack in a circular motion for even cooking. Use your Char-grill Grills heat resistant gloves for easy handling.
14. Cook the meatballs until they reach internal temperature 165°.
15. Tip: use the Char-Griller folding probe to take the guesswork out your cook.
16. Warm up your favorite spaghetti sauce in your large cast iron skillet on the gas side of the grill at 260°—300°. Add basil and olive oil ingredients to your favorite sauce to kick up the flavor.
17. Add meatballs to the sauce on the gas side of the grill and cook for 30 minutes at 260°-300°. Stir occasionally and then remove from the grill.
18. Using the side burner add water to your large pot.
19. Bring water to a boil with a pinch of salt then add the spaghetti noodles.
20. Strain noodles when done.
21. Plate and enjoy your wonderful meal.

Simple Seasoned Dressed Greens

Cooking Time: 5 Min

Ingredients:
- 2 Cups Of Freshly Washed Spinach
- 2 Cups of Freshly Washed Kale
- 2 Tbsp Of Extra Virgin Olive Oil
- 2 Tbsp Of Lemon Juice
- 2 Tbsp of Romano Or Parmesan Cheese
- 1 Tsp Of Paprika
- 1/2 Tsp Of Celery Seed
- 1/2 Tsp of Garlic Powder
- 1/2 Tsp of Sea Salt
- 1 Tsp Of Black Pepper

Directions:
1. Retire your boring old salad recipe and spice it up with this Simple Seasoned, Dressed Greens recipe.
2. In a large bowl, toss spinach and kale together. In a small bowl, combine seasoning mixture. Lightly toss greens with olive oil, lemon juice, and choice of cheese. Once the salad is fully dressed, pour over Paprika,Celery Seed, Garlic Powder,Sea Salt,Black Pepper and mix thoroughly until the entire salad is coated in both the dressing and seasoning mixture. Serve immediately or chill before serving.

Smoked Beer Can Chicken Recipe

Cooking Time: 2.5 Min

Ingredients:
- 1 Whole Chicken (4-5 Lbs)
- 3 Tbsp of Extra Virgin Olive Oil
- 2 Tbsp of Salt
- 2 Tsp of Black Pepper
- 2 Tbsp of Dry Rub of Choice
- 1 Can of Beer of Choice

Directions:
1. Combine seasonings and spices in a bowl to prepare the ultimate rub for chicken. Coat the entire chicken with olive oil then season(including the cavity) with the rub and store the remainder in an airtight container for a future cook. Preheat the smoker to 225-275 degrees by adding desired coals to your Side Fire Box If you do not own a Side Fire Box, you can still enjoy the smoking experience. Simply arrange coals opposite of where you plan to place the chicken. If you will sit the chicken in the middle of the grill, arrange coals on the perimeter, and so on. Pour out (or drink!) ¼ to ½ of the can of beer. Place the chicken at the center of the grill on top of the beer can with the chicken legs and beer can holding it up. Close the smoker and allow chicken to cook until internal temperature reaches 165 degrees (around 2 hours). Remove chicken and wrap in aluminum foil or butcher paper, allowing to rest for at least 20 minutes before carving. Serve warm, enjoy!

Flat Iron Southern Salmon Cakes

Cooking Time: 20 Min

Ingredients:
- 1 can Salmon drained and flaked (You can alternatively use freshly baked Salmon after letting it rest)
- 1 cup of Onion (Finely diced)
- 1 Tsp of Old Bay Seasoning
- 1/2 Tsp of Salt
- 1/2 Tsp of Black Pepper
- 1/2 Tsp of Garlic Powder
- 2 Tbsp of Olive Oil or Canola Oil
- 2 Eggs (Beaten)
- 1/4 Cup of Parsley (Minced)

Directions:
1. Thoroughly pick through flaked salmon and remove all bones.
2. In a large bowl, add the salmon, eggs, onion, Old Bay, salt, pepper, and garlic powder. Mix together.
3. Shape mixture in small 2-3 inch wide patties.
4. Heat Flat Iron to Medium Heat, adding desired oil amount.
5. Fry each patty for about 5-6 minutes on each side until golden brown or desired crispiness.
6. Remove from heat and sprinkle finished product with parsley (For an extra layer of flavor: serve with a dollop of sour cream)
7. Serve warm.

Smokin' Whole Bone-in Ham

Cooking Time: 7 Hrs

Ingredients:
- Fresh Whole Bone-In Ham: 18 pounds
- Olive Oil: Small Coat, Used for a Binder
- Char-Griller Grills Creole and Sweet & Spicy Seasonings: to taste
- Sazon Seasoning: to taste
- Char-Griller Grills Smokin' Champ 1733
- Lump Charcoal & Mesquite Smoking Wood
- Char-Griller Grills Drip Pan
- Char-Griller Grills Charcoal Chimney
- Char-Griller Grills Remote Thermometer
- Favorite Glaze: I used a homemade Spicy Strawberry & Raspberry glaze

Directions:
1. Prepping Directions
2. Using a sharp knife, score the fat on top of the ham on a diagonal into squares. This helps the seasonings penetrate the meat and allows extra smoke into the meat. Coat all sides with olive oil. Season all sides with Char-Griller Grills Creole, Sweet & Spicy and Sazon Seasonings to taste It's now ready for the smoker!
3. Smoking Directions
4. Clean out the Char-Griller Smokin' Champ 1733 smoker and insert the Char-Griller Grills Drip Pan filled with water to the top into the main cooking area under

the grill grates in the ash pan area. Using the Char-Griller Grills Charcoal Chimney fire up a full chimney of lump charcoal to 250°-300°. Release the lump charcoal on top a mesquite smoking log. Allow the smoker to thoroughly warm up, about 20 minutes. Place the ham in the smoker over the drip pan. Check in on the ham and side firebox every 60 minutes. Rotate the ham for an even smoke and also add lump charcoal/Smoking wood as needed. Insert the Char-Griller Grills Remote Thermometer to monitor the internal temperature. Smoke ham to internal temperature 135° then glaze all sides of the ham with your favorite glaze. Smoke the glazed ham to internal temperature 140°. Remove the ham from the smoker and allow it to rest for 30 minutes. Slice and enjoy!

Smoked Baked Beans

Cooking Time: 1.5-2 Hrs

Ingredients:
- 2 lbs. ground beef or sausage
- 15 oz. can of black beans
- 15 oz. can of kidney beans
- 15 oz. cans of baked beans
- 3 peppers (sweet, red bell, and green bell), seeded and diced
- 1 large sweet onion, finely chopped
- 4 cloves garlic, minced
- 3 to 6 jalapeños, seeded and diced
- 2 C. sweet BBQ sauce
- ¾ C. brown sugar
- ½ C. Dijon mustard
- ½ C. chopped cilantro
- Salt and pepper to taste

Directions:
1. Brown ground beef or sausage in large cast iron skillet, seasoning with garlic, salt and pepper 2. Combine black beans, kidney beans, baked beans, onion, peppers, jalapeños, BBQ sauce, brown sugar, Dijon mustard, and chopped cilantro 3. Season to taste with salt and pepper and mix well 4. Cook uncovered for 1½ - 2 hours at 325°F, stirring every 15-20 minutes

Spicy Thai Grilled Chicken Quarters

Ingredients:
- 4 Tbsp Red Curry Paste
- 2 Tbsp Yellow Curry Powder
- 1 Cup Coconut Milk
- 1/4 Cup Coconut Aminos
- 2 Tbsp Minced Garlic
- 1 Tbsp Granular Sweetener
- 1 Tbsp Ground White Pepper

Directions:
1. Whisk or blend all ingredients together until combined. Slather onto chicken quarters and refrigerate for 4 hours or overnight. Preheat dual zone grill to 350 degrees. Shake off excess marinade and place chicken in cool side of the grill. Grill covered for approximately 1 hour or until the chicken has reached 165 degrees in the center. Garnish with fresh lime wedges, chopped cilantro and/or chopped roasted peanuts.

Smoked Potato Salad

Cooking Time: 90 Min

Ingredients:
- 2 lbs. of Russet Or Red Potatoes
- 2 Cups of Mayonnaise
- 1 Tbsp of Yellow or Dijon Mustard
- 1 Celery Stalk (Finely Diced)
- 2 Hard-Boiled Eggs (Peeled And Diced)
- 1 Tsp of Chopped Dill
- 1 Tbsp of Sweet Relish
- 1/2 Red Or Yellow Onion (Diced)
- 1 Tbsp of Apple Cider Vinegar
- Salt and Black Pepper to Taste

Directions:
1. Preheat your smoker to 200-225°F. Smoke for about 90 minutes or until desired tenderness. Allow the potatoes to cool before slicing into small cubes. Toss with the apple cider vinegar then thoroughly mixing in the remainder of the ingredients. Serve immediately or serve chilled. Enjoy!

Alabama White Sauce

Cooking Time: 3 Min

Ingredients:
- 2 Cups Mayonnaise
- 1/3 Cup Horseradish
- 2 Tsp Dijon Mustard
- 1/3 Cup Apple Cider Vinegar
- 2 Tbsp Lemon Juice
- 1/4 Tsp Minced Garlic
- 1 Tsp Sea Salt
- 1 Tsp Black Pepper
- 1/2 Tsp Cayenne Pepper
- 1/2 Tsp Oregano Flakes
- 1/2 Tsp Garlic Powder

Directions:
1. Alabama White Sauce is a creamy, tangy, with just a pinch of heat.
2. Combine all the ingredients together in a medium bowl. Whisk until the mixture is creamy. Store in an airtight container and refrigerate until ready to use.

Grilled Bacon And Blue Cheese Wedge Salad

Cooking Time: 10 Min

Ingredients:
- Iceberg Lettuce- 1 Head
- Chopped Tomato
- Chopped Bacon
- Chopped Red Onion
- Mayonnaise - 1/2 Cup
- Heavy Whipping Cream - 1/4 Cup
- Sour Cream - 1/4 Cup
- Blue Cheese Crumbles - 1/2 Cup
- Worcestershire Sauce - 1 Teaspoon
- Chopped Fresh Parsley to Taste
- Sea Salt and Pepper to Taste

Directions:
1. Cut a head of iceberg lettuce into 4 wedges. Place cut side down on a very hot Char-Griller grill grate until marks appear, then flip to the other cut side of the slice and repeat.
2. Mix ingredients for the dressing together.
3. Drizzle the grilled wedge with the dressing, top with more blue cheese crumbles, chopped tomato and red onion, and bacon

Basic Thanksgiving Turkey Brine

Cooking Time: Varies Min

Ingredients:
- 2 Gallons Water
- Peels of 3 Oranges
- Peels of 3 Lemons
- 1 Cup Kosher Salt
- 1/3 Cup Brown Sugar
- 1/2 Fresh Sage Leaves
- 2 Bay Leaves
- 1 Tbs Whole Peppercorns
- 6 Cloves Garlic Peeled and Smashed

Directions:
1. Fill bucket with 2 gallons water
2. Add salt, stir until dissolved
3. Add other brine ingredients
4. Add turkey, making sure it is fully submerged if possible. If not, try to turn turkey every 6-8 hours.
5. Brine for 24-48 hours (aiming for 48 hours is best)
6. Tip: Either store your turkey in the fridge while brining or place in a large cooler and cover with ice.
7. Then rinse the brine off and use a salt free seasoning before putting turkey on smoker.

Bacon Bourbon Compound Butter

Cooking Time: 10 Min

Ingredients:
- Softened Butter - 1 Stick
- Crumbled Crispy Bacon - 1 to 2 slices
- Bacon Grease - 1 Tablespoon
- Bourbon - 1 Tablespoon

Directions:
1. Crisp bacon and crumble.
2. Thoroughly mix bacon into softened butter with the bourbon and scoop onto a square of parchment paper, rolling up into a log, and twisting the ends closed.
3. Wrap in plastic wrap and refrigerate until firm.

4. *Serve on top of steaks to add more flavor*

Smoked Chex Mix

Cooking Time: 1-1½ Hrs

Ingredients:
- 3 C. corn Chex cereal
- 3 C. rice Chex cereal
- 3 C. wheat Chex cereal
- 1 C. mixed nuts
- 1 C. mini pretzels
- 6 Tbsp. unsalted butter
- 2 Tbsp. Worcestershire sauce
- 1½ Tsp. seasoned salt
- ¾ Tsp. garlic powder
- ½ Tsp. onion powder
- 1 Tsp. cayenne pepper, optional

Directions:
1. Pre-heat grill to 250°F. Melt butter in a small pan and mix in Worcestershire sauce, seasoned salt, onion powder, garlic powder, and cayenne pepper, if using. 2. Place Chex cereal, mini pretzels and mixed nuts in a large roasting pan. Add melted butter mixture and stir to evenly coat. 3. Place pan on the grill and smoke at 250°F for 1-1 ½ hours, and stir every 15-20 minutes. 4. Remove pan from grill and spread smoked Chex mix on paper towel-lined plate to cool.
2. Store in an airtight container or storage bag. Enjoy!

Super Pro Rotisserie Prime Rib

Cooking Time: 180 Min

Ingredients:
- Prime Rib: Two Bones (6 Pounds)
- Olive Oil
- Char-Griller Grills Chili Lime: to taste.
- Sazon: to taste.
- Brazilian Salt: to taste
- Fresh Parsley Flakes or Fresh Cilantro Flakes: to taste. Used Cilantro. You can also use dry flakes if fresh is not available.
- Kitchen Twine
- Char-Griller Grills Super Pro & Rotisserie Kit
- Fogo Eucalyptus Lump Charcoal

Directions:
1. Rinse and pat dry the prime rib. Trim access fat and skin. French cut the bones with a knife. Apply coating of olive oil to all sides. Season all sides with Sazon, Chili Lime seasonings and Brazilian Salt. Add kitchen twine in the middle of the bones on the meat and knot. Add to rotisserie rod and lock in using the rotisserie forks. Then Sprinkle fresh parsley or cilantro flakes. Heat grill with lump charcoal: When coking over an open fire I don't cook at specific temperature. I begin with an equivalent of a ½ chimney full of lump charcoal and monitor the fire by feel. I place the charcoal in the middle of the grill in the back. As the charcoal burns I add pieces as the cook goes along. Place rotisserie in the grill. Roast until internal 115°. Remove from the grill. Allow to rest for 15 minutes. Slice and enjoy!

Aubrey's Og Grilled Chicken

Cooking Time: 15 Min

Ingredients:
- 3-4 Large Chicken Breasts
- 2 Tsp. Garlic Powder
- 2 Tsp. Dried Oregano
- 1 Tsp. Salt
- 1 Tsp. Pepper
- 1 Tsp. Chili Flakes
- 1/3 C. Red Wine Vinegar
- 1/4 C. High Heat Oil (like Avocado)
- Fresh Parsley and Lemon to Garnish

Directions:
1. If you haven't already, split your chicken breasts in half. This ensures uniform size chicken that will grill all at the same time, allowing even heat distribution, quick cooking, and preventing thicker parts of the chicken from cooking too quickly, causing the rest to dry out.
2. In a jar, mix garlic powder, oregano, salt, pepper, chili flake, vinegar, and oil together to make your dressing. Huge congrats! You just made homemade Italian dressing, Mega Yum! Pour half of the dressing marinade over your chicken and save the remaining amount to drizzle over the finished product.

3. Preheat your grill, I crank the heat to high, close the lid, and let the grates get screaming hot- this creates a non stick surface, allowing us to use minimal oil, but grabbing maximum flavor. Once the grill is hot, 500+ degrees, lay your chicken out, and reduce the heat to medium, leaving the grill lid open.

4. After 4 minutes, rotate your chicken 180°F, and let it cook for an additional 3 minutes on that side- this creates diamond marks, fancy! Also, the diamonds are totally optional. You can also just let it remain in one spot for the first 7 minutes.

5. After 7 minutes passes, flip your chicken, and close the lid. Set your timer for 7 more minutes, and then your chicken should be good to go! If you're not sure if your meat is done, stick a meat thermometer in the thickest part of the protein, and with poultry, 165°F means it's fully cooked!

6. Pro Tip: Let your meat rest for 15 minutes before cutting, this allows the juices to redistribute, aka they won't run out as soon as you cut into the chicken, leaving you with a dry piece of meat.

7. Drizzle finished chicken with remaining Italian dressing, and garnish with sliced lemon and fresh parsley! Enjoy.

Buttery Cinnamon Apples

Cooking Time: 30 Min

Ingredients:
- 8 Apples
- Cinnamon (To Taste)
- Sugar (To Taste)
- 2 Sticks Of Butter
- 1/4 Cup Of Brown Sugar

Directions:

1. First, you're going to want to peel your apples, at least I'm going to want to. You can leave the skins on if you want, I prefer them almost applesauce level of soft.

2. Whether you leave the skins on or off, you definitely want to remove the core. Only a complete lunatic would leave the core in the apple and try to eat it.

3. I used about 8 apples in my cook, and added two full sticks of quartered butter to them. No need to premelt, your smoker is going to do that work.

4. Now you'll want to hit it with a generous helping of cinnamon and sugar. You really can do this to your taste, I'm going to go heavy, because, I mean, I'm not doing this for health and prosperity over here.

5. We are going to toss them in the smoker at 300 degrees for about a half an hour, and then we are going to pull them, and add about ¼ cup of brown sugar.

6. Toss it back in the smoker, mine took about another 30 minutes, and that's it. It's probably the easiest thing you'll ever cook.

Grilled Corn

Cooking Time: 10 Min

Ingredients:
- 6 ears of corn, shucked
- 1/2 Cup of Butter
- Kosher Salt
- Optional: Char-Griller Garlic & Herb Rub

Directions:

1. Heat grill to high heat. Add corn to the grates, turning often until they develop a char, 10-15 minutes. Remove corn from the grill and spread butter all over, then season to taste with salt. Serve hot or warm. Enjoy!

Oktoberfest Skillet

Ingredients:
- 2 White Potatoes
- Olive Oil - 2 Tbsp
- Caraway Seeds - 1/2 Tbsp
- 4 Thick Cut Bacon Slices
- 4 Brats
- Medium Yellow Onion - Diced
- Red Apple - Diced
- 1/3 Red Cabbage - Diced
- Dijon Mustard - 1 Tbsp
- Sauerkraut - 1/2 Cup
- 12 oz German Style Beer
- Fresh Pepper - 1/2 tsp
- Ground Nutmeg - 1/2 tsp

- Fresh Sage - For Garnish, If Desired

Directions:
1. Preheat grill for medium-high indirect cooking.
2. Combine diced potatoes, olive oil, and caraway seeds in a cast iron skillet. Cook over indirect heat for 30 to 45 minutes.
3. Grill bacon and brats over direct heat. 3 minutes per side.
4. Slice bacon and brats and combine with onions, sauerkraut, apple, cabbage, pepper, nutmeg, beer, and potatoes in skillet.
5. Cook over indirect heat for 20 minutes.
6. Serve with pretzels and beer.

Donut Monte Cristo

Cooking Time: 5 Min

Ingredients:
- Glazed Donuts - 2
- Ham - 4 Slices
- Turkey - 4 Slices
- Swiss Cheese - 2 Slices
- Raspberry Jam - 2 Tablespoons

Directions:
1. Light charcoal and level out to one layer when ashed over
2. Cut donuts in half lengthwise
3. Add 2 slices of ham, 2 slices of turkey, and a slice of cheese to each donut
4. Spread jam on top halves of each donut assemble sandwiches
5. Place each sandwich on the grill. Close the lid for approximately 1-2 minutes. Check after 1 minute. The sandwich is ready to flip when the donut easily releases from the grates
6. Flip the sandwiches and close the lid again for another 1-2 minutes
7. Remove from grill carefully. The sugar from the glaze will be very hot
8. Allow to cool for a few minutes

Cajun Sausage & Pepper Egg Muffins

Cooking Time: 25 Min

Ingredients:
- Zesty Sausage - 10 Ounces
- Diced Green Pepper - 1/3 Cup
- Diced Sweet Red Pepper - 1/3 Cup
- Diced Yellow/Sweet Onion - 1/3 Cup
- Diced Shredded Potatoes (Hash Browns from Bag) - 1/3 Cup
- Eggs - 1 Dozen
- Shredded Pepper Jack Cheese - 1 1/2 Cup

Directions:
1. Prepare Char-Griller Akorn for indirect heat at 350° Optional: Add your favorite smoking wood for a kiss of smoke flavor. Apple wood works great with this recipe.
2. Using stove, cook sausage, peppers, and onions in skillet over medium-high heat until sausage starts to brown and vegetables tenderize. About 8-10 minutes. Set aside on paper towel to drain and cool down.
3. Add eggs to large mixing bowl along with cajun seasoning. Beat well. Mix in about 1 cup of the pepper jack cheese. Stir in sausage, peppers, and onions.
4. In a jumbo 6 cup muffin pan, add about ⅔ cup mixture to each muffin cup. Sprinkle remaining ½ cup pepper jack cheese on top of each.
5. When Akorn is up to temperature (350°f grate level) Smoke/Bake in Akorn for 20-25 minutes. Look for a golden brown color to form. Pull when internal temperature is around 160°f and knife inserted into center comes out clean.
6. Add your optional toppings and serve immediately. Enjoy!
7. Optional Toppings: Sour cream, Parsley, Cherry tomatoes, and Hot Sauce

Flat Iron Pancakes

Cooking Time: 20 Min

Ingredients:
- 3 Cups of Flour
- 2.5 tsp of Baking Powder
- 2 tsp Salt
- 2 Tbsp Sugar
- 2.5 Cups of Milk
- 2 Eggs
- 6 Tbsp Melted Butter

Directions:
1. Combine all ingredients and mix until smooth
2. Heat a lightly oiled griddle to medium high heat
3. Pour scoops of batter onto griddle using approximately ¼ cup for each pancake
4. Brown on both sides and serve hot.

Vinegar Based Sauce

Cooking Time: 3 Min

Ingredients:
- 1 Cup Apple Cider Vinegar
- 1 Tbsp Ketchup
- 1 1/2 Tbsp Brown Sugar
- 1 Tbsp Salt
- 1 Tsp Black Pepper
- 1 Tsp Crushed Red Pepper
- 1/2 Tsp Cayenne Pepper

Directions:
1. In a small bowl combine all the ingredients. Whisk together thoroughly. Store in an airtight container and allow ingredients to remain mixed overnight before use.

Smoked Bacon Wrapped Water Chestnuts

Ingredients:
- 1 Lb Bacon
- 2 (8 oz) cans of Water Chestnuts
- 1 Cup Packed Brown Sugar
- 2 Cups Ketchup
- 2 Tbsp Worcestershire Sauce
- 2 Tbsp Dijon Mustard
- Toothpicks

Directions:
1. Prepare AKORN or charcoal grill for 375°F
2. Add mild smoking wood like maple or apple for smoke flavor
3. Cut bacon slices in half. Wrap one slice of bacon around each chestnut. (For sliced water chestnuts, stack them three high, then wrap) Secure the wrap with a toothpick. Arrange the wraps in a foil pan or baking dish
4. In a medium-sized mixing bowl, combine ketchup, brown sugar, Worcestershire sauce, and mustard and stir well. Set aside.
5. Bake the wraps with no sauce for 10 to 15 minutes
6. Remove from wraps and drain out 75% of the grease. Keep the rest in pan.
7. Pour the sauce over the wraps. Be sure all wraps are coated well.
8. Bake/Smoke for 30-35 minutes.
9. Serve immediately and enjoy!

Flat Iron Cereal French Toast

Cooking Time: 15 Min

Ingredients:
- 2 Cup of Crushed Cereal (Your Favorite Kind)
- 12 Slices of Thick Sliced Bread
- 4 Eggs
- 1/2 Cup Brown Sugar
- 1/2 Cup Heavy Cream
- 1 Cup Whole Milk
- 1 Tbsp Cinnamon
- 1 Tbsp Vanilla
- Pinch of Salt
- 1/4 Butter

Directions:
1. Heat flat iron with one side burner on low and others right between low and medium
2. Toast bread on griddle for a few minutes on each side to dry out slightly and remove promptly
3. Whisk together sugar, cinnamon, and eggs until creamy and mixed thoroughly (this is the secret to not having an eggy ring on your French toast)

4. Add cream, milk, vanilla, and salt to egg mixture and whisk thoroughly
5. Dip a slice of bread into the mixture and flip to coat
6. Dip the slice of bread into the crushed cereal and turn to coat
7. Place butter on griddle and allow to melt, spread evenly across griddle
8. Place each slice of French toast on griddle and allow to toast for 4-5 minutes per side
9. When toasted and cooked through, place slices of bread on the low heat side of the griddle until the remainder is finished

Spicy Vindaloo Chicken Thigh Skewers

Ingredients:
- 2 Lbs Chicken Thighs
- 2 Medium Onions(Rough Chopped)
- 1 Tomato (Quartered)
- 1 Tbsp Avocado Oil
- 2 Jalapenos (Chopped)
- 1 Tsp Tamarind Concentrate
- 8 Cloves Garlic
- 1/2 Inch Fresh Ginger Or 1 Tbsp Minced Ginger
- 2-4 Tbsp Kashmiri Red Chili Powder
- 1/2 Tbsp Mustard Seeds
- 1/2 Tbsp Black Pepper Corns
- 1 Tsp Cumin Seeds
- 1 Tbsp Coriander Seeds
- 1/2 Tsp Fenugreek Seeds
- 1 Inch Cinnamon Stick
- 4 Tbsp White Vinegar
- 1/2 Tsp Ground Turmeric
- 1 Teaspoon Brown Sweetener
- 1 Tbsp Salt

Directions:
1. Place mustard seeds, black peppercorns, cumin seeds, coriander seeds, cinnamon stick and fenugreek seeds in a small bowl. Add white vinegar to soak the seeds until softened. Place chicken in a large bowl or ziploc bag. Add seed mixture and the remaining ingredients into a blender and blend until smooth. Add mixture to chicken and coat thoroughly, refrigerate over night. Preheat grill to medium high heat. Skewer chicken thighs and place on grill. Grill for 15-20 mins or until chicken is 165 degrees, flipping half way through.

Keto Burger Bites

Cooking Time: 25 Min

Ingredients:
- Pound Of Ground Beef
- Pickles (Sliced)
- Grape Tomatoes (Halved)
- Mini Cheese Squares
- Butter Lettuce Leaves
- Salt, Pepper, Garlic Powder To Taste Or Your Favorite Burger Seasoning

Directions:
1. Mix burger and seasoning together in bowl, shape into mini patties
2. Heat grill to 400° ~ you're going to cook these hot and fast
3. Slice up pickles, cheese (into squares) and tomatoes
4. Place burgers on grill until IT hits a minimum of 140°; add cheese and remove when melted
5. Lay burger on plate, add pickle slice and halved tomato; slide a toothpick through the top to keep everything together
6. Serve as an appetizer, tailgate snack or full meal

Grilled Watermelon Salad

Cooking Time: 10 Min

Ingredients:
- Watermelon - Small
- Feta - 4 oz
- Mint - 1 Bunch
- Basil - 1 Bunch
- Limes - 2
- Balsamic - 2 Tbs
- Red Onion - 1 Sliced
- Olive Oil - 3 Tbs
- Salt - 1 tsp

Directions:
1. Slice red onion and place in a bowl of ice water. Leave submerged for 10 minutes. 2. Slice the end off

each side of the watermelon. Stand watermelon on its end. Slice the rind off. 3. Cut watermelon into slices. 4. Brush Watermelon with olive oil and set aside. 5. Preheat charcoal grill to medium and oil the grates. 6. Grill the watermelon slices until they are just marked. About 2 minutes on each side. 7. Set aside to cool. 8. In a bowl, whisk together olive oil, balsamic, lime juice, and salt. 9. Roughly chop the mint leaves and basil. 10. Cut watermelon into chunks, add to a bowl. 1 Add feta, herbs, and dressing. Toss gently. 12. Serve right away and enjoy.

Smoked Pimento Cheese Spread

Cooking Time: 2 To 4 Hrs

Ingredients:
- 1 Pound Extra-Sharp Cheddar Cheese (Block of Cheese)
- 8 Ounces Cream Cheese, Softened
- 1 Cup Sour Cream (Extra if making Spider Web Garnish)
- 1 Cup Mayonnaise
- 1/2 tsp Garlic Powder
- 1/2 tsp Ground Cayenne Pepper
- 1/2 tsp Onion Powder
- 1 Jalapeno Pepper, Diced
- 8 oz Jar Diced Pimentos, Drained
- Salt and Pepper to Taste

Directions:
1. Prepare grill for indirect smoking. Light between 4 to 6 briquettes or about a quarter chimney starter of lump charcoal.
2. Add fully ashed over charcoal to one side of the grill and place a handful of soaked wood chips on the coals.
3. Close the lid and close all the dampers almost all the way.
4. You want the temperature to be as low as possible,
5. Place the blocks of cheese on a wire rack.
6. Fill a drop pan with ice and place the rack on top of the pan filled with ice.
7. Place the pan and the rack with the cheese on the grill on the opposite side of the charcoal.
8. Add more wood chips when needed to maintain smoke.
9. Remove cheese from grill after 2 to 4 hours depending on desired level of smoke.
10. Grate cheese and add to large bowl.
11. Combine cheese with cream cheese, sour cream, mayonnaise, jalapeños, pimentos, and all spices. Mix well.
12. Transfer to serving bowl.
13. To make it spooky, place some sour cream in a plastic bag and cut off the tip of the bag. Use the bag and sour cream to create a spider web design on top of cheese spread.
14. Serve with chips, crackers, or veggies.

Perfect Smoked Crispy Chicken Wings On The Akorn

Cooking Time: 45 Min

Ingredients:
- 1 Pack Of 6 Whole Chicken Wings
- 1 Tbsp Of Kosher Salt
- 1/4 Cup Of Your Favorite Wing Sauce Or Glaze

Directions:
1. Light a full chimney of charcoal. Fill the akorn with unlint coal with enough room to put the smoking stone in place. Dump the fully lit chimney on the unlit coals and add one piece of hickory wood at the edge of the lit coals. Place the smoking stone and oiled grate in place. Open the top and bottom vent on the Akorn to the number 3. Season the bottom side of the chicken wings evenly with the kosher salt then place them on the akorn around where the edge of the smoking stone is below them. After ten minutes flip the wings over and inward to protect them from the direct heat. Also give the grate ¼ turn. Open the top vent up to the number 4. After ten minutes flip the wings back over and give the grate another ¼ turn. After ten minutes flip the wings back over and give a final ¼ turn. After ten minutes check the wings internal temperatures, they should be around 200 degrees. Place the wings in a bowl and pour the sauce or glaze over the top and toss until they are evenly covered. Enjoy!

2-burner Flat Iron Spiced Sweet Potato Home Fries

Cooking Time: 10 Min

Ingredients:
- 4 Large Sweet Potatoes (Cubed)
- 1/4 Cup of Water
- 1/4 cup of Extra Virgin Olive Oil
- 2 Tbsp of Garlic Powder
- 1/2 Tbsp of Salt
- 1/2 Tbsp of Black Pepper
- 2 Tsp of Cumin
- 1 Tsp of Cayenne Pepper
- 1 Tsp of Cinnamon
- 1 Tsp of Paprika
- 1 Tsp of Curry Powder

Directions:

1. Perfect for any meal of the day, these tender, Spiced Sweet Potato Home Fries are the perfect addition to your plate, delivering on a perfect balance between sweet and spicy, sure to leave both your taste buds and stomach satisfied.
2. With Flat Iron preheated to high heat, add water and sweet potato cubes to the cooktop before covering with Char-Griller Basting Dome. Cook for 7-8 minutes or until potatoes are tender. Remove the basting dome, allowing the rest of water to evaporate if it isn't already. Remove potatoes from the cooktop and add to a large bowl, combining with olive oil, and all seasonings and spices. Reduce Flat Iron heat to medium and add the sweet potatoes to the cooktop. Allow them to cook, untouched for at least 4-5 minutes before flipping and stirring occasionally. Cook for 7-8 minutes or until desired doneness. Serve immediately. Enjoy!

Grilled Bruschetta Brie

Cooking Time: 10 Min

Ingredients:
- 1-2 Wheels of Brie
- 2 Cups Tomatoes on the Vine
- 1 Baguette, Sliced Thinly
- 1 Clove Garlic, Smashed
- 1/3 Cup Parsley, Chopped
- 1/3 Cup Olive Oil
- Salt & Pepper to Taste

Directions:

1. It's nice to have the grill on when the kitchen is slam packed full of baked dishes and people waiting to make their mark on thanksgiving dinner, so a grilled app is a must do, this year! Let's dig in!
2. Preheat Char-Griller to medium high, I prefer charcoal at this time for that extra Smokey flavor!
3. Brush Brie and tomatoes with 2T olive oil, and season with salt and pepper. Slice baguette into thin slices and brush with an additional 1 T olive oil.
4. Grill bread for 2 mins per side, Brie 3-4 mins per side, and tomatoes on the vine, until charred and softened. Pull everything from the grill.
5. Toss grilled tomatoes with remaining olive oil, crushed garlic, chopped parsley, and a sprinkle of salt and pepper.
6. Spread melted Brie over grilled baguette and top with the grilled tomato bruschetta! Have a wonderful holiday, and enjoy!

Candied Bacon Recipe

Cooking Time: 35 Min

Ingredients:
- 9 Slices of Bacon
- Brown Sugar - 1/3 Cup
- Cinnamon - 1/4 tsp
- Black Pepper - 1/4 tsp

Directions:

1. Heat grill to 350 indirect heat. Combine brown sugar, cinnamon, and pepper in a small bowl. Dip each piece of bacon, front and back, in sugar mixture. Place bacon strips on a greased wire rack. Sprinkle remaining sugar over bacon. Place rack on the grill grates and cook bacon for 30-35 minutes until crispy. Remove from grill and allow to cool. Chop the bacon into small pieces. Place a small handful of bacon aside for topping. Make the bourbon glaze.

Flat Iron Banana Pancakes

Cooking Time: 10 Min

Ingredients:
- 1 Cup Of All-Purpose Flour
- 2 Ripe Bananas Mashed (The More Ripe /Brown The Better)
- 1 Tsp Of Baking Powder
- 2 Tsp Of Granulated Sugar
- 1/2 Tsp Of Salt
- 1 Egg (Beaten)
- 1 Cup Of Milk
- 1 Tbsp Of Vegetable Oil
- 1 Dash Of Cinnamon (Optional)

Directions:

1. Combine all the dry ingredients in one bowl and all the wet ingredients in another. Add the flour mixture into the batter and continue stirring until as smooth as possible. Some lumps are normal because of the bananas. Heat the Flat Iron to medium-high heat and add oil or butter of your choice. Pour the batter onto the griddle in desired shape and size. Each pancake will be ready to flip once the top side becomes filled with holes/bubbles. Cook until each side is golden brown. Serve hot with freshly sliced bananas, whipped cream, syrup, honey or any topping of your choice. Enjoy!

Flat Iron Spinach & Feta Omelette

Cooking Time: 10 Min

Ingredients:
- 2 Large Eggs
- 2 Tsp of Butter
- 1 Cup Spinach (Chopped)
- 1 Tsp of Water or Milk
- 2 Tbsp of Feta Cheese (Crumbled)
- 1/2 Tsp of Salt
- 1/2 Tsp of Pepper
- 1/2 Tsp of Cayenne Pepper
- 1/2 Tsp of Garlic Powder

Directions:
1. Heat the Flat Iron to medium heat. Melt the butter.
2. Add spinach to the griddle and stir until slightly softened.
3. While spinach cooks, in a small bowl, whisk together the eggs, water or milk, and seasonings for 1 minute.
4. Pour the egg mixture over the spinach.
5. Sprinkle feta cheese crumbles evenly over egg.
6. Once the egg begins to set at the bottom, use a spatula to occasionally raise the edges of the omelette so that uncooked egg will run off from the top.
7. Once it is cooked completely through, fold it in half or into thirds.
8. Serve hot.

Smoked And Stuffed Meatballs

Cooking Time: 80 Min

Ingredients:
- 1.5 Lbs Ground Beef
- 1/4 Cup Pork Panko (Ground Pork Rinds)
- 1 Tbsp Favorite BBQ Spice Rub
- 1/2 Tbsp Dried Thyme
- 1/2 White Onion (Finely Diced)
- 3 Cloves Garlic (Finely Minced)
- 2 Tbsp Worcestershire Sauce
- 1 Large Egg
- 1 Tbsp Parmesan Cheese (Shredded)
- 4 Mozzarella Cheese Sticks, Cut Roughly 1/2 Square Pieces
- 1 Cup Sugar Free Barbecue Sauce

Directions:
1. While preheating, mix together the Panko, spice rub, thyme, onion, garlic, Worcestershire, egg and Parmesan cheese in a large bowl Add in the ground beef and mix until incorporated.
2. Place a ball of the ground beef mixture in the palm of your hand, flatten, and place a piece of the cheese in the center. Fold up the sides of the meat mixture to completely cover the cheese and roll into a ball.
3. Place in a large cast iron skillet. Repeat until finished. Smoke at 225 for 45-50 min until they reach a temp of 155. Remove skillet and cover the meatballs in the BBQ sauce. Put back in your smoker and continue to cook for 15-20 mins or until an internal temperature of 165 degrees.
4. Serve immediately.

Cheesy Potatoes

Cooking Time: 50 Min

Ingredients:
- 10.5 oz. can condensed cream of mushroom soup
- 1 ½ C. sour cream
- 32 oz. pkg. frozen potatoes, thawed
- 12 oz. sharp cheddar cheese, shredded
- 3 C. cheese crackers, crushed
- 1 C. Parmesan cheese, grated
- 3 Tbsp. butter, melted

Directions:
1. Combine cream of mushroom soup and sour cream in a large bowl and mix well.
2. Stir in potatoes and cheddar cheese until well blended.
3. Pour mixture into a cast iron skillet
4. Combine cracker crumbs, Parmesan cheese and melted butter together to make topping and evenly spread over the potatoes and cheese mixture.
5. Place on the indirect side of the grill and bake at 350°F for 50 minutes.
6. Recipes developed in partnership with our friends, Ken & Patti Fisher at Date Night Doin's. Visit their website at www.datenightdoins.com for BBQ and smoking recipes, videos, product reviews, and all things BBQ!

Fried Chicken On The Grill

Cooking Time: 20 Min

Ingredients:
- 4 Boneless Skinless Chicken Breasts
- 4 Tbsp Sucklebusters Clucker Dust
- 1/2 Cup Pork Panko

Directions:
1. Preheat grill to 325F. Cut chicken breast in half, place in bowl, add seasoning and mix well. Add pork panko and mix well. Place on grill over direct heat, flipping occasionally until chicken probes at least 165F internal. (I tend to take my chicken to 175F) Remove from grill, serve and enjoy!

Flat Iron Tomato Soup Grilled Cheese

Cooking Time: 8 Min

Ingredients:
- 8 Slices of Bread (Your Favorite Kind)
- 4 Slices of Cheese (Your Favorite Kind)
- 2 Tomatoes (Cut Into 8 Slices)
- 8 Leaves of Fresh Basil
- 1 Tbsp of Garlic Salt
- 1 Tbsp of Olive Oil

Directions:
1. Drizzle bread with olive oil, and sprinkle slices with garlic salt. Arrange on Flat Iron Griddle, and let the bread begin to toast for 2 minutes.
2. Next, layer your Slice of bread with cheese, slices of tomato, and basil. Arrange the rest of the ingredients on the bread and the cheese to melt, about 5 more minutes.
3. Fold opposite half onto it's match, and pull sandwiches from Griddle. Cut in half, and enjoy!

Sweet N' Spicy Bbq Sauce

Cooking Time: 2 Min

Ingredients:
- 1 Cup Of Ketchup
- 3/4 Cup Brown Sugar
- 1/4 Cup Honey
- 1/8 Cup Apple Juice
- 1/4 Cup Apple Cider Vinegar
- 1/4 Cup Water
- 1 Tbsp Worcestershire Sauce
- 2 Tsp Of Yellow Mustard
- 1 Tsp Of Paprika
- 1/2 Tsp Of Crushed Red Pepper
- 1/2 Tsp Of Cayenne Pepper
- 1/2 Tsp Of Garlic Powder
- 1 Tsp of Sea Salt
- 1 Tsp Of Black Pepper

Directions:
1. Combine all the ingredients into a saucepan. Whisk them together until it's smooth and add to medium-high heat. Bring to a boil. Reduce the heat and allow to simmer for 2 minutes, continuing to stir occasionally. Let cool for about 10 minutes before storing in the refrigerator in an airtight container.

2-burner Flat Iron Simple Lo Mein

Cooking Time: 10 Min

Ingredients:
- 1 package of Lo Mein Noodles
- 1 Tbsp of Extra Virgin Olive Oil
- 1 Cup of White or Button Mushrooms (Sliced)
- 2 Tbsp of Minced Garlic
- 4 Cups of Spinach (or another vegetable of your choice)
- 1 Red Pepper (Thinly Sliced)
- 1 Carrot (Shredded)
- 1/2 Cop of Snow Peas
- 2 Tbsp of Soy Sauce
- 2 Tsp of Honey
- 1/2 Tsp of Ground Ginger
- 1 Tsp of Sesame Oil
- 1/2 Tsp of Sriracha or Chili Sauce

Directions:
1. Bring the flavors of your favorite takeout home to your backyard. This simple Lo Mein recipe makes it easy to incorporate your favorite veggies, tailoring it to your liking, while still delivering on explosive flavors. Serve it as a main dinner dish or with a side of your favorite chicken or beef.
2. Cook Lo Mein noodles according to package instructions. Drain and set aside. In a small bowl, combine soy sauce, honey, ginger, sesame oil and sriracha/chili sauce. Mix thoroughly and set to the side. Heat the Flat Iron to medium-high heat. Add oil to the cooktop then add garlic, mushrooms, red pepper, carrot and snow peas. Cook for 3-4 minutes until tender then add spinach and cook until wilted. Pour the soy sauce mixture over vegetables and mix thoroughly. Add Lo Mein noodles then mix thoroughly, ensuring all the noodles become coated and browned. Cook for 2-3 minutes before removing from the cooktop. Serve immediately. Enjoy!

Rack Of Lamb With A Bourbon Glaze

Cooking Time: 35 Min

Ingredients:
- Rack of Lamb
- 2 Tbsp. Char-Griller Steak BBQ Rub
- 3 Tbsp. Dijon Mustard
- 1 Tbsp. Crushed Rosemary
- 1 Tbsp. Thyme
- 1 Tbsp. Bourbon
- 1 Tbsp. Agave Nectar
- 1 Tbsp. Olive Oil

Directions:
1. Rub Rack of Lamb with 1 Tbsp. of your favorite red meat rub like the Char-Griller Steak BBQ Rub.
2. While the rub soaks into the meat, prepare your glaze by adding Dijon Mustard, Crushed Rosemary, Thyme, remaining 1 Tbsp. Char-Griller Steak BBQ Rub, Bourbon, Agave Nectar and Olive Oil together in a bowl. Place in refrigerator.
3. Heat Char-Griller AKORN Kamado Grill to 450°F. Sear Rack of Lamb on all sides, about 2 minutes per side.
4. Set lamb aside and adjust AKORN vents so the temperature falls to 350°F. Add Smokin' Stone to AKORN.
5. Paint wet glaze all over the lamb, making sure it is generously coated.
6. Put the lamb back on the grill and insert a thermometer. Cook lamb until internal temperature reaches 125°F.
7. Rest lamb for 10 minutes before serving. Cut into two-bone sections and serve.

Grilled Pumpkin Chili

Cooking Time:

Ingredients:
- 1 Pound Ground Pork
- 1 Medium Onion, Diced
- 1 Red Bell Pepper, Diced
- 2 tsp Minced Garlic
- 1 Chipotle Pepper with Adobe Sauce, Finely Chopped
- 1 Pound Grilled Pumpkin Flesh
- 2.5 Cups Chicken Broth
- 2 Tbsp Apple Cider Vinegar
- 1.5 Tbsp Chili Powder
- 1 Tbsp Ground Cumin

- 1 Tbsp Sea Salt
- 1 tsp Ground Pepper
- 1/4 tsp Cayenne Pepper
- 1 tsp Cinnamon
- 1 Bay Leaf

Directions:
1. Place ground pork in large saucepan over medium heat. Add onion, pepper, garlic, chipotle and pumpkin and cook until pork is browned and vegetables become tender.
2. Add chili powder, cumin, salt and pepper, cayenne and cinnamon. Mix. Add chicken broth and vinegar, mix well, add bay leaf. Bring to boil and reduce to simmer for at least 30 minutes.
3. Slice pumpkins in half to form "bowls," scoop out the strings and seeds, brush with olive oil, and grill until tender with grill marks. Serve!

Grilled Cheese With Apples

Cooking Time: 10 Min

Ingredients:
- Eight Slices of Bread
- Honey Mustard
- Two Apples (Pink Lady or Granny Smith)
- 16 Slices of Cheddar Cheese

Directions:
1. Preheat grill to medium heat.
2. Cut apples into thin slices.
3. Tip: Use a Mandolin to get the slices really thin. Don't forget to use the hand guard!
4. Spread 1 tsp of mustard on one side of each of the slices of bread.
5. Place one slice of cheese on each bread slice and top with apples. Top with an additional slice of cheese.
6. Coat both sides of each of the sandwiches with butter or cooking spray.
7. Place sandwiches on grill and flip after 5 minutes.
8. Remove sandwiches from grill after an additional 5 minutes or when the cheese is melted.
9. Remove from grill and serve.
10. Yield: 4 Sandwiches

Smoked Jalapeño Mac & Cheese

Cooking Time: 45 Min

Ingredients:
- 6 oz macaroni cooked and drained
- 1/2 C. diced bacon
- 1 onion, diced
- 1 jalapeño stemmed, seeded, and minced
- 2 garlic cloves minced
- 2 Tbsp. flour
- 2 Tbsp. butter
- Salt and pepper to taste
- 8 oz IPA beer
- 2 C. shredded cheddar cheese
- 6 oz shredded sharp cheddar cheese
- 4 oz Velveeta cheese cut in 1/2" cubes
- 1/3 C. Panko
- 1/2 Tsp. smoked paprika

Directions:
1. In a large cast iron skillet, heated on a grill over low heat, cook the bacon until the fat has started to render. Add the onion and cook, stirring, until soft, about 5 minutes. The bacon should be nice and crispy. Stir in the jalapeño and garlic and cook for 30 seconds. 2. Add the flour and stir to coat. Add the butter. Whisk in the beer a little at a time, to form the roux. Season with salt and pepper. 3. Melt in the cheddar cheese and 3 ounces of the Sharp cheddar. Stir until melted and creamy. Fold in the cooked noodles. 4. Press the cubes of Velveeta into the mac and cheese randomly. 5. Toss the panko, paprika and remaining 3 ounces of cheese in a bowl to combine. Sprinkle over the top of the pan. Cook for another 20-25 minuets directly over low heat, until bubbly with grill lid closed if using. 6. Allow to cool for 5 minutes before serving.

RECIPE INDEX

2-burner Flat Iron Asparagus 185
2-burner Flat Iron Easy Shrimp Tacos 44
2-burner Flat Iron Eggplant Parmesan 180
2-burner Flat Iron Grilled "bmp" 147
2-burner Flat Iron Hot Dogs 162
2-burner Flat Iron Omelet Rounds 180
2-burner Flat Iron Seasoned Chicken Breasts 27
2-burner Flat Iron Seasoned Mushrooms 169
2-burner Flat Iron Simple Lo Mein 202
2-burner Flat Iron Spiced Sweet Potato Home Fries 199
5-minute Avocado Dip 148

A

Akorn Cinnamon Streusel Coffee Cake 93
Akorn Dino Beef Plate Ribs 80
Alabama White Sauce 192
Ale Chicken Drumsticks 157
All American Blended Burger 79
Apple Chipotle Glazed Smoked Ham 104
Arrachera Skirt Steak Tacos 63
Asian Chicken Salad 30
Asian Pork Belly Skewers 107
Asian-inspired Sesame Soy Sauce 163
Aubrey's Og Grilled Chicken 193

B

Baby Back Ribs 100
Bacon And Pineapple Wrapped Meatballs 55
Bacon Bourbon Compound Butter 192
Bacon Bourbon Compound Butter Recipe 114
Bacon Buffalo Chicken Dip 143
Bacon Burger With Shallots 75
Bacon Buster Burger 78
Bacon Cheeseburger Pizza-dough Balls 63
Bacon Cinnamon Rolls 184
Bacon Egg And Cheesesteaks 185
Bacon Garlic Burger With Chipotle Mayonnaise 48
Bacon Ring Burger With Mushrooms 70
Bacon Wrapped Chicken Thighs 29
Bacon Wrapped Kabob 110
Bacon Wrapped Kielbasa 110
Bacon Wrapped Kielbasa Bites 105
Bacon Wrapped Pork Tenderloin Stuffed With Jalapeño Cream Cheese 114
Bacon Wrapped Seafood Stuffed Shrimp 34
Barbecue Chicken Foil Packets 145
Barbecued Turkey 32
Basic Thanksgiving Turkey Brine 192
Bbq Bacon Cheeseburger Roll 165
Bbq Burnt Ends 116
Bbq Crunch Wrap 85
Bbq Fiends Barbacoa Tacos 74
Bbq Fiends Beef Fajitas 48
Bbq Fiends Chicken Lollipop Recipe 168
Bbq Fiends Oktoberfest Beer Brats 117
Bbq Glazed Bacon Wrapped Brussels Sprouts 132
Bbq Pork Spare Ribs 104
Bbq Wang Thangs 155
Beef Brisket 56
Beef Ribs 76
Beef Tenderloin 52
Beer Brat Bites 53
Beer Brats With Marzen Beer Kraut 129
Beer Brined Grilled Costillas Beef Short Ribs 75
Beer Can Roasted Turkey Breast 24
Beer Cheese Sauce 121
Beer Soda Can Chicken 32
Biscuits, Briskets, And Gravy 47

Blackened Catfish 39
Blueberry Bbq Sauce 142
Blueberry Jalbanero Smoked Wings 171
Blueberry Pork Belly Burnt Ends 108
Bone-in Pulled Ham 111
Boneless Chicken Thighs Broccolini & Cheesy Potatoes 28
Boneless Wings Made From Chicken Thighs On The Char-griller Akorn Kamado Grill! 117
Bourbon Glaze For Candied Bacon Scones 88
Bourbon Maple Grilled Wings 177
Brazilian Smoked N' Seared Picanha 129
Breakfast Bomb - Homemade Stuffed Breakfast Sausage 112
Breakfast Burritos On The Flat Iron 50
Breakfast Pizza 15
Brisket Hash On The Flat Iron Portable 52
Brown Sugar Glazed Smoked Ham 106
Brown Sugar Maple Bacon 182
Buffalo Baby Back Ribs: Grilled N' Smoked 132
Buffalo Lemon Shrimp 34
Buffalo Ranch Chicken 28
Burnt Ends And Tips 65
Butternut Squash Risotto 143
Butternut Squash Soup 141
Buttery Cinnamon Apples 194

C
Cajun Sausage & Pepper Egg Muffins 195
Candied Bacon Recipe 199
Candied Bacon Scones With Bourbon Glaze 90
Candy Jar Brownies 91
Caprese Burger 61
Caprese Grilled Chicken 174
Caribbean Jerk Pork Pineapple Salsa 171
Cedar Plank Salmon 40
Cedar Plank Smoked Salmon 36
Certified Competition Smoked Ribs 187
Certified Competition Smoked Ribs Tips 149
Certified Creole Ynot Beef N' Bacon Jerky 56
Certified Grilled And Smoked Baby Back Ribs 101
Certified Grilled Chicago Style Hot Dogs 47
Certified Pork Butt 108
Char Grilled Wings 148
Cheddar Jalapeño Chicken Burgers 176
Cheeseburger Chili With Burger Bun Croutons 128
Cheesecake Stuffed Apples 94
Cheesy Beef Burritos 61
Cheesy Chipotle Chili 77
Cheesy Potatoes 201
Cheesy Stuffed Mushrooms N' Veggies Recipe 136
Cheesy, Bacon Bbq Meatloaf 142
Cherry Chipotle Buffalo Wings 26
Chicken Breast Potatoes And Green Beans On The Char-griller Akorn 155
Chicken Cordon Bleu 25
Chicken Fajita Quesadillas 155
Chicken Fajitas 27
Chicken Lollipops 166
Chicken Lollipops By Jeremy Souza 33
Chicken Teriyaki 21
Chi-lanta Pork Belly Burnt Ends 61
Chili In A Bread Bowl 50
Chili Jalapeño Burger 76
Chili Mesquite Lime Shredded Chicken Street Tacos 19
Chimichurri Sauce 138
Chipotle Orange Glazed Bacon Wrapped And Stuffed Pork Loin 106
Chocolate Chip Skillet Cookie 89
Chocolate Lava Cake 96
Chorizo Taquitos 78

Classic Bbq Sauce 179
Classic Smoked Spatchcocked Turkey 20
Coffee & Cocoa Tri-tip 82
Cold Weather Chili 71
Competition Ribs Recipe 149
Corned Beef Brisket And Potatoes 62
Cowboy Steak With Asparagus And Onion 122
Crab-stuffed Grilled Flank Steak With Asparagus 55
Crème Brûlée 92
Creole Blackened Salmon 37
Creole Hush Puppy Fried Chicken Legs & Thighs 23
Creole Italiano Spaghetti And Smoked Meatballs 188
Creole Latin Spatchcock Turkey 24
Creole Latin Spiced Rotisserie Chicken 20
Creole Smokin' Fried Wings 33
Creole Smothered Chicken 181
Curried Chicken Skewers 26

D
Dark Roast 72
Deep Dish Apple Pie 96
Dirty Bird Chicken Wings 171
Donut Monte Cristo 195
Double Cheeseburger Kabobs 54
Double Stack Cheeseburger 72
Dr. Pepper Bbq Chicken Wings 165
Dry Aged Rib Roast 87

E
Easter Brunch French Toast 160
Easter Sunday Coleslaw For Pulled Pork Sandwiches 117
Easter Sunday Texas-style Pulled Pork 113
Easy Chicken And Cheese Quesadillas 19
Easy Grilled S'mores 177
Egg Roll Burgers 164

F
Fabulous Buttermilk Pancakes 145
Father's Day Baby Back Ribs 107
Faux Apple Pie 98
Filet Mignon, Risotto, And Asparagus 67
Fire Roasted Salsa And Homemade Tortilla Chips 127
Fire Roasted Salsa Con Certi 147
Fire-grilled Pizza 15
Fish And Chips 45
Fish Tacos 43
Flat Iron 3-step Breakfast Sandwiches 142
Flat Iron Artisan Garlic Bread Grilled Cheese 151
Flat Iron Bacon Egg & Cheese 139
Flat Iron Banana Pancakes 200
Flat Iron Candied Sweet Potatoes 120
Flat Iron Cereal French Toast 196
Flat Iron Cheesy Pizza Bagels 17
Flat Iron East Meets West Chicken Fajitas 22
Flat Iron Fast Garlic & Balsamic Greens And Onions 163
Flat Iron French Toast 128
Flat Iron Griddle Beef Shank Quesadilla Tacos With Consumé 49
Flat Iron Griddle Breakfast Sandwich 114
Flat Iron Griddle Classic Steak Street Tacos 85
Flat Iron Griddle Sizzler N' Veggies Sammies 83
Flat Iron Homestyle Hash Brown Patties 157
Flat Iron Hot Cakes 153
Flat Iron Lemon Pesto Vegetable Medley 178
Flat Iron Lime Chicken And Mango Salsa Quesadillas 160
Flat Iron Pancakes 196
Flat Iron Philly Cheesesteak 80
Flat Iron Pineapple Coconut Pancakes 136
Flat Iron Portobello Bun Burgers 159

Flat Iron Sausage And Peppers Hash 77
Flat Iron Southern Salmon Cakes 190
Flat Iron Spinach & Feta Omelette 200
Flat Iron Steak Fajitas 81
Flat Iron Sundried Tomato Omelet 183
Flat Iron Tomato Soup Grilled Cheese 201
Flat Iron™ Smash Burgers 135
Flat-iron Pizza Quesadillas 14
Flavor Pro Bacon Wrapped Jalapeño Poppers 170
Flavor Pro Cedar Plank Salmon 40
Flavor Pro Hot And Fast Ribs 129
Flavor Pro Italian Sausage Burgers 68
Flavor Pro Pork Steaks 101
Flavor Pro Quick And Easy Grilled Pork Tenderloin 115
Flavor Pro Smoked Eggs 119
Flavor Pro Smoked Pork Shoulder 111
Flavor Pro Smokey Grilled Chicken Wings 180
Flavor Pro™ Flank Steak Tacos 73
Flavor Pro™ Reverse Seared Steak 52
Flavor Pro™ Smoked Chicken Breast 146
Flavor Pro™ Smoked French Onion Dip 131
Flavor Pro™ Smoked Turkey Breast 126
Foil Packet Loaded Grilled Potatoes 158
Foil Packet Short Ribs 86
Fresh Chili Lime Watermelon Fries 153
Fresh Garlic Parsley Butter Salmon 41
Fresh Summer Corn Avocado Tomato Salad 148
Fried Bacon And Cabbage 122
Fried Chicken And Corn 21
Fried Chicken On The Grill 201
Fried Kielbasa & Cabbage 146

G

Garlic & Herb Seasoned Potatoes 123
Garlic And Herb Grilled Zucchini 186
Garlic Butter 123
Garlic Lover's Chicken 28
Garlic Parmesan Chicken Wings 27
Glazed Oatmeal Raisin Cookies 90
Good Morning Chili 187
Gravity 980 Brisket 58
Gravity 980 Grilled Lobster Tails 35
Gravity 980 Grilled Pizza 14
Gravity 980 Quick N' Fast Grilled Vegetables 144
Gravity 980 Reverse Seared Steak 151
Gravity 980 Smoked Baked Potatoes 154
Gravity 980 Smoked Chicken Wings 31
Gravity 980 Smoked Mac & Cheese 139
Gravity 980 Smoked Pork Shoulder 100
Gravity 980 Smoked Ribs 179
Griddle Cheesesteaks 186
Grilled Adobo Wings 125
Grilled Apple Strudel 161
Grilled Arrachera Pita 186
Grilled Bacon And Blue Cheese Wedge Salad 192
Grilled Blue Cheese Wings 141
Grilled Breakfast Sandwiches With Blueberry Chicken Sausage 134
Grilled Bruschetta Brie 199
Grilled Caesar Salad 84
Grilled Caprese Pizza 15
Grilled Carrots 167
Grilled Cauliflower 178
Grilled Cheese With Apples 203
Grilled Chicken And Broccoli Stir-fry 29
Grilled Chicken And Vegetable Kebabs 21
Grilled Chicken Sandwiches 133
Grilled Chilean Sea Bass 46
Grilled Cilantro Garlic Parmesan Chicken Wings 144
Grilled Coconut Lime Foil Packets 38
Grilled Corn 194

Grilled Duck Breast 25
Grilled Eggs Benedict With Grilled Lemon Hollandaise 121
Grilled Fathead Pizza 16
Grilled Fire Veggies 187
Grilled Flank Steak With Vegetables 131
Grilled Garlic Bread 185
Grilled Juicy Skirt Steak With Cilantro Pesto 172
Grilled Lemon Parmesan Asparagus 140
Grilled Lemon Pepper Potatoes 185
Grilled Lobster Tails 36
Grilled Mango Salsa 154
Grilled Mexican Street Corn 138
Grilled Nachos 29
Grilled Pineapple 127
Grilled Pizza Chicken Wings 32
Grilled Pork And Sweet Potato Verde Chili 102
Grilled Pork Chops 112
Grilled Potatoes With Jalapeños 130
Grilled Pumpkin And Chayote Soup 153
Grilled Pumpkin Chili 202
Grilled Pumpkin Pie With Smoked Gingersnap Crust 90
Grilled Red Onion And Brussel Sprouts Skewers 141
Grilled Ribeye Steak 80
Grilled Romaine Salad With Creamy Jalapeno Ranch Dressing 175
Grilled Salmon 36
Grilled Sausage 139
Grilled Seafood Boil 42
Grilled S'mores 4 Ways 88
Grilled Steak Caesar Salad 71
Grilled Stuffed Peaches 89
Grilled Stuffed Peppers 161
Grilled Stuffed Pork Chops 103
Grilled Summer Corn Salsa 162

Grilled Swordfish With Lemon-caper Sauce 35
Grilled Tilapia 36
Grilled Tomato Salsa 151
Grilled Watermelon Salad 197
Guinness Cupcakes With Whiskey Salted Caramel Buttercream 98

H

Hasselback Potatoes 158
Hassleback Potatoes 165
Herb And Garlic Lamb Rack 147
Hickory Smoked Deviled Eggs 144
Homemade Grilled Meatballs 64
Honey Chipotle Chicken Wings 22
Honey Mustard Chicken 164
Honey Sriracha Lime Salmon 40
Honey-bourbon Glazed Salmon 34
Hoppin' John 103
How To: Easy Dry Rub Grilled Pork Tenderloin 110

I

Inch-thick Onion Char-burgers 51
Irish Nachos 178
Italian Burgers 60
Italian-style Meatballs 65
Izzy's Cowboy Grillers 30

J

Jalapeño Bacon Blanket Poppers 134
Jalapeño Popper Pizza 126
Jalapeño Poppers 183

K

Ken's Famous Baked Beans 126
Keto Burger Bites 197
Keto Cheesy Meatballs 135
Keto Grilled Brie 118
Korean Style Beef Short Ribs 58

L

Left Over Cheesy Mac N' Smoked Brisket Meat Pies Recipe 72
Leftover Brisket Nachos 54
Lemon Pepper Shrimp 37
Lemon Pepper Wings 156
Loaded Grilled Radish Bites 132
Lobster Mac 'n Cheese 44
Lobster Roll 39
London Broil N' Veggie Skewers 66
Lou's Peach Cobbler 95
Louisiana Hot Link Sausage & Smoked Cornbread Dressing 177
Lou's Beef Brisket 67
Lou's Beef Plate Ribs 67
Low Carb Blueberry Cobbler 92

M
Mac & Cheese Stuffed Meatballs On The Char-griller Akorn 59
Maple Bourbon Rubbed Stuffed Chicken Breasts 174
Maple-dijon Grilled Chicken Sandwich 140
Marinated Flat Iron Steak On The Flat Iron Portable Griddle 157
Meat Loaf 81
Meat Lovers Pizza 14
Mediterranean Chicken & Mushroom Burger Bowls 124
Mediterranean Veggie Burgers With Vegan Feta Dip 149
Memphis-style Dry Ribs 115
Mexican Street Corn 158
Mini Smash Burgers 57
Mrs. Ccbbq Mac N' Cheese 137
Mushroom Bacon Swiss Blended Bison Burger 181

O
Oklahoma Onion Burgers 55
Oktoberfest Beef Short Ribs 74
Oktoberfest Chili 136
Oktoberfest Schweinebraten 116
Oktoberfest Schweinshaxe - Smoked Pork Shanks 107
Oktoberfest Skillet 194
Orange Pork Belly Burnt Ends 105
Over The Top Chili On The Grand Champ 82
Oysters "dougie-feller" 45

P
Pancake Burgers On The Char-griller Flat Iron 140
Pastrami Swiss Burger 66
Peppered Sirloin With Bacon-mushroom Sauce 64
Pepperoni Pizza 16
Perfect Ribeye Steaks On The Akorn 183
Perfect Smoked Crispy Chicken Wings On The Akorn 198
Pesto Burrata Grilled Pizza 17
Picanha Crostini 56
Picnic "fried" Chicken 33
Pineapple Upside-down Cake 93
Plum Galette 89
Pork Belly Burnt Ends On The Akorn 114
Pork Belly Street Tacos 106
Pork Brisket Burnt Ends 74
Pork Tenderloin Sliders 110
Pork Tenderloin With Apple Chutney 163
Pretzel Ring Cheese Dip Recipe 134
Puffy Pancake With Fruit Compote 95
Pulled Chicken Crunch Wrap Style Burritos 26
Pumpkin Pie Burnt Ends 170

Q
Queso Fundido Stuffed Grilled Jalapeños 153
Quick And Easy Grilled Pork Tenderloin 103

R

Rack Of Lamb With A Bourbon Glaze 202
Raptor Claws 182
Raspberry Chipotle Glazed Pork Tenderloin 115
Ratatouille 156
Red Pepper Eggs 152
Reverse Sear Ribeye 71
Reverse Seared Pesto Lamb Racks 150
Reverse Seared Tri-tip Pico De Gallo 58
Ribeye Roast On The Char-griller Akorn Kamado 157
Roasted Spatchcock Turkey 18
Rosemary Shrimp Skewers 37

S

Salmon Burger 37
Salted Caramel Chocolate Tart 88
Satay Chicken Wings 166
Saucin' Bacon Wrapped Cheesy Meatballs 187
Saucy Brisket Burnt Ends 83
Sausage Bbq Meat Balls 123
Seared Scallops With Pancetta 45
Seared Sesame Ahi Tuna 39
Serrano Beer Cheese 117
Shrimp & Sausage Skewers 69
Shrimp 'n Grits 62
Shrimp 'n Grits 43
Shrimp Po' Boy With Garlic Parsley Butter 42
Shrimp Tacos 38
Simple Seasoned Dressed Greens 189
Simple Smoked Bbq Pork Belly 112
Skillet Brownie On The Grill 96
Skillet Corn Bread 133
Skirt Steak Gyros 70
Skirt Steak Pinwheels 86
Smash Burgers 48
Smoke Roasted Coffee 162
Smoked & Spiced Pumpkin Seeds 123

Smoked And Spiced Nuts 118
Smoked And Stuffed Meatballs 200
Smoked Apple Crumb Pie 97
Smoked Bacon 150
Smoked Bacon Wrapped Cheese Stuffed Avocado 52
Smoked Bacon Wrapped Water Chestnuts 196
Smoked Bacon-brisket Bbq Beans 130
Smoked Baked Beans 191
Smoked Baked Spaghetti 79
Smoked Beef Chili 63
Smoked Beef Ribs 59
Smoked Beer Can Chicken Recipe 190
Smoked Blueberry Crisp 98
Smoked Bone-in Pork Shoulder Steak 182
Smoked Brisket 49
Smoked Buffalo Chicken Wing Dip 167
Smoked Butternut Squash Soup 152
Smoked Candied Pecans 92
Smoked Carolina Turkey 31
Smoked Cedar Plank Salmon 125
Smoked Chex Mix 193
Smoked Chicken Thighs 25
Smoked Chicken Thighs And Veggies 138
Smoked Chili 73
Smoked Chili Hotdogs 113
Smoked Chocolate Chip Cookies 94
Smoked Classic Apple Pie 172
Smoked Corned Beef 60
Smoked Garlic Herb Chili Flake Grilled Cheese Sandwich 154
Smoked Irish-style Lamb And Potatoes 159
Smoked Jalapeño Mac & Cheese 203
Smoked Jerk Chicken 184
Smoked Jerky 68
Smoked Lamb Shank 127
Smoked Mac & Cheese 173

Smoked Mac 'n Cheese 161
Smoked Mac And Cheese 143
Smoked Mashed Potatoes 167
Smoked Meatballs With Sweet And Sour Sauce 109
Smoked Meatloaf 73
Smoked Mexican Burgers 53
Smoked Pimento Cheese Spread 198
Smoked Pork Loin 102
Smoked Pork Shoulder 102
Smoked Potato Salad 191
Smoked Prime Rib 85
Smoked Queso Dip 121
Smoked Rack Of Lamb With Orange Marmalade Glaze 175
Smoked Rib Chili 118
Smoked Roasted Vegetables 174
Smoked Sausage Stuffing 152
Smoked Spatchcock Turkey 23
Smoked Sweet Garlic Chili And Teriyaki Wings 120
Smoked Sweet Potatoes 179
Smoked Sweet Potatoes With Cinnamon Maple Butter 168
Smoked Turkey Breast 31
Smoked Turkey Legs 18
Smoked White Chocolate Christmas Candy 97
Smokin' Champ Smoked Beef Back Ribs 84
Smokin' Whole Bone-in Ham 190
Southwest Potato Skins 168
Spaghetti Stuffed Meatloaf 65
Spicy Caribbean Shrimp 39
Spicy Crawfish Dip 41
Spicy Honey Glazed Wings 31
Spicy Thai Grilled Chicken Quarters 191
Spicy Vindaloo Chicken Thigh Skewers 197
Spooky Brain Cinnamon Buns 92
Spring Tomahawk Steak And Vegetables 77
St. Louis-style Ribs 104
Steak And Shrimp On The Flat Iron 54
Steak Night! Steak, Shrimp And Asparagus On The Akorn 50
Steamed Mussels With Pancetta 43
Strawberry And Rhubarb Crumble Pie 93
Super Pro Rotisserie Prime Rib 193
Supreme Grilled Portobello Pizza 158
Sweet And Tangy Apple Coleslaw 139
Sweet N' Spicy Bbq Sauce 201
Sweet Potato Medallions 184

T
Teriyaki Chicken And Mango Skewers 120
The All American Burger 59
The Flintstone Steak 69
Turkey Leg Lollipops 19
Turkey Tips 18
Turkey-mushroom Burger 30

U
Ultimate Pork Belly Sliders 100
Ultimate Stack Burger 47

V
Vegetarian Shepherd's Pie 124
Vinegar Based Sauce 196

W
Weeknight Smokehouse Ribs 69

www.ingramcontent.com/pod-product-compliance
Lightning Source LLC
Chambersburg PA
CBHW081409080526
44589CB00016B/2511